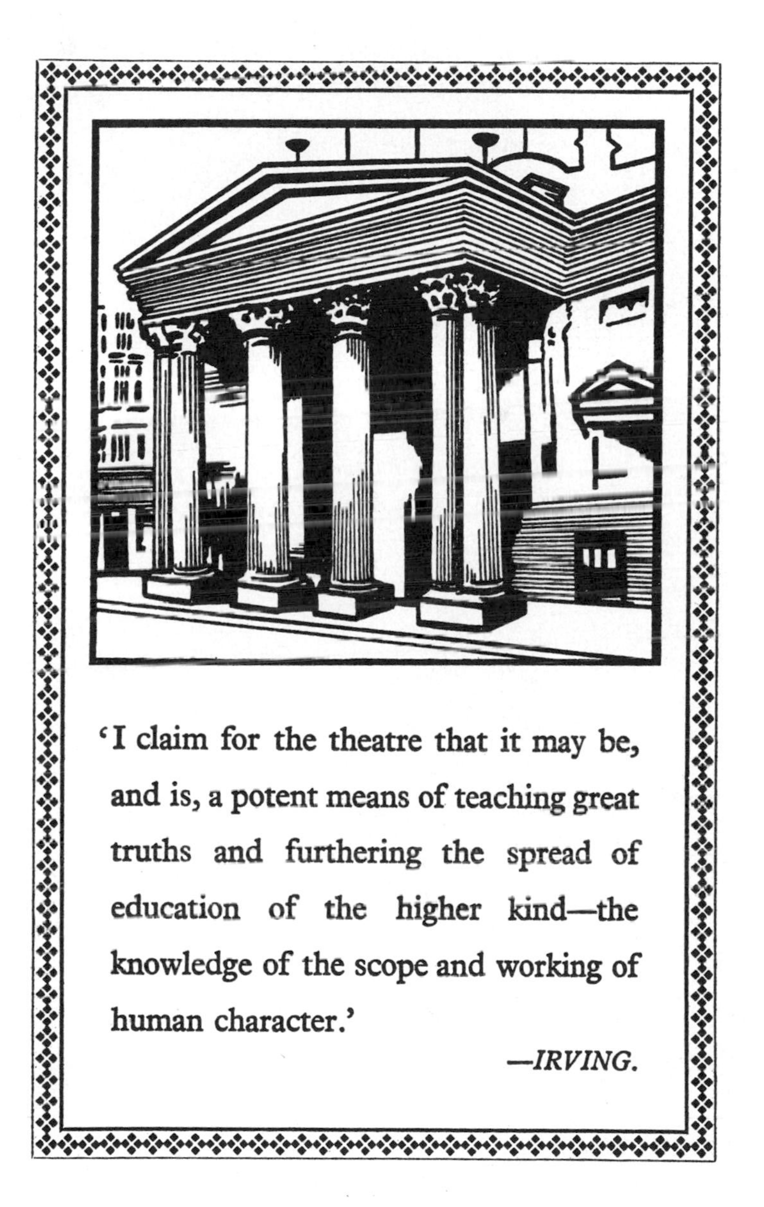

'I claim for the theatre that it may be, and is, a potent means of teaching great truths and furthering the spread of education of the higher kind—the knowledge of the scope and working of human character.'

—*IRVING.*

IRVING

A PENCIL SKETCH BY SIR BERNARD PARTRIDGE

WE SAW HIM ACT

A SYMPOSIUM ON THE ART OF

SIR HENRY IRVING

LITT.D. CAMBRIDGE AND DUBLIN; LL.D., GLASGOW

A SERIES OF ESSAYS, ARTICLES AND ANECDOTES, PERSONAL REMINISCENCES AND DRAMATIC CRITICISMS WRITTEN BY HIS CONTEMPORARIES, COLLECTED AND COLLATED BY

H. A. SAINTSBURY

EDITED BY

H. A. SAINTSBURY AND CECIL PALMER

BENJAMIN BLOM New York/London

First Published 1939
Reissued 1969 by
Benjamin Blom, Inc., Bronx, New York 10452
and 56 Doughty Street, London, W.C. 1

Library of Congress Catalog Card Number 70-81219

Printed in U.S.A. by
NOBLE OFFSET PRINTERS, INC.
NEW YORK 3, N. Y.

OBITUARY

THROUGHOUT the preparation of this book I have always been conscious of the fact that whereas, for me, it has been a lovely labour, it was for my distinguished colleague, the late H. A. Saintsbury, a labour of love. My own humble satisfaction in seeing the fruition of our united efforts is sensibly diminished by the knowledge that the man to whom is mainly due the credit for such praiseworthy qualities as the book may possess, has not survived to receive it from those infinitely more entitled than I am to bestow it.

The unavoidable postponement of the publication of this book, from last spring to the present autumn, tested Saintsbury's philosophy to breaking point. I am sure that those who have generously contributed to this symposium will not resent the statement that Saintsbury claimed this composite tribute to his belovèd Irving *as his very own.* His possessiveness was the measure of his enthusiasm for the task and of his courage in fulfilling it. It was obvious to me, as it must have been to others, that Saintsbury's days were numbered. His bodily sufferings were painful to witness. His mental tortures distressing to contemplate. Our numerous editorial conferences will always remain in my memory as occasions when one man's quiet courage epitomized the power of the spirit when the body is broken. I could wish that such rare spiritual tenacity of purpose had prevailed, but, alas, there is no soft beatitude in death, death is but death!

My greatest hope is that this literary memorial to Irving will be adjudged both honourable and worthy. I wish it because I know that Saintsbury will be listening for the verdict. If the proud, indomitable, incomparable figure of Irving emerges from these pages it will be because those who have written them have imperishable memories of his histrionic genius. Editorially, it was in this spirit of gratitude and admiration that Saintsbury sculptured the figure upon this monument, for only the humble pedestal is mine.

CECIL PALMER.

Lady Dickens wishes it to be stated that the sections on *Philip* written exclusively by her are the second last paragraph on page 78, and from "One day when Irving was driving down Piccadilly" on page 79, to the end.

CONTENTS

LIST OF ILLUSTRATIONS

BY WAY OF PROLOGUE

'THEY come like shadows, so depart'—'the abstract and brief chronicles of the time'—'and leave not a wrack behind!'

I emulate the vice, if it be, of the actors of a past generation, and my mind travels the years. It is a Sunday evening; I am in the bar-parlour of a well-known Midland hostelry. Five Legitimate Leading Men had graciously allowed me—all their gestures were gracious—the privilege of summoning the drawer and replenishing the cups, ale being then fourpence a quart and a whisky-and-soda the same price. Conversation flowed as smoothly as the liquor till closing time—and after. The local Inspector of those days was not averse from 'burning a cup of sack' with the players, and sack in plenty was burnt; but those Five never wilted, never halted, never boggled a cue—no matter who supplied it, landlord, barman, Inspector, local grocer, or we humbler 'hams'—always the apt quotation sprung unhesitatingly in rejoinder. I will engage that not one of the Five spoke an original phrase, nor failed to cap the point, throughout the session.

'And leave not a wrack behind!'

It is not inapposite to recall this memory, for in just such an atmosphere, some thirty years earlier, he to whom that phrase can never apply set out to master the elements of an art in which he was to prove supreme. And now that he has passed, that large and gracious spirit can still touch, through memory, those of his friends and lovers and faithful comrades as surely, as deftly, as deeply, as when he held communion with them in the flesh—or was it spirit *then?* That serenity, so rarely ruffled, seemed at times inhuman. A paradox he was, so human yet so remote, so little servile even to that public whose 'faithful servant' he proclaimed himself, yet so much the slave of his art; aloof and convivial, ribald on occasion; ascetic as any anchorite. None was better loved, none more revered, more execrated and traduced. Children and dogs adored him.

It has been my proud and happy task to assemble and collate these fragments, a task laid upon me by my friend R. N. Green-Armytage, who, with Sir John Martin-Harvey, set the tablet that marks a cottage at Keinton Mandeville, in the county of Somerset, as Irving's birthplace. For the form adopted I must accept responsibility; but it seemed to me that tribute paid to him, while it is still possible, by those who saw his work in each of the parts that made him famous, each weighed by a different hand, must by its diversity have a fuller, wider, and therefore perhaps more permanent value than any recording by a single hand however expert. Accordingly I invited those whose judgment of the man and his work is here set forth to unite in contributing each his quota, that a concrete and reliable verdict might emerge. Many are actors, some are critics and so qualified to expound the subtleties of that unique technical equipment. The playgoer judges solely by results; the expert probes more deeply and apprehends the means, the springs, and the causes of action. I wanted no chorus of eulogy; I have sought the co-operation simply of those who remembered, knowing well that in estimating a personality so marked, so vital, it was inevitable that some could not escape an antagonistic bias. Here, then, is the verdict of his contemporaries, save in a single instance. It seemed to me that there was one matter that would be better judged on the evidence alone, uninfluenced by any kind of personal prejudice, and that is the matter of a pamphlet, *The Fashionable Tragedian*, published when Irving had won to the height of fame as an actor, in the year before he became a manager—a man striving to establish himself rather than a man established. Therefore I invited Mr. Cecil Palmer, of the Savage Club Masonic Lodge (of which Irving was a founder member and the first Treasurer in that same year, 1877, in which the pamphlet appeared), to judge it on its face value as a piece of considered criticism. It was typical of so much with which Irving had to contend that it is essential to consider it if one would appreciate the splendour of his triumph.

Mr. Cecil Palmer has also given invaluable help in editing and preparing this volume for the press. To him and to all the Contributors, as well as to Sir Bernard Partridge and other owners of copyright in illustrations and photographs, I offer most cordial thanks for making this work a possibility, knowing well that if it falls short of what I had hoped to accomplish the blame is mine alone.

Finally, I have been so fortunate as to interest Her Majesty Queen Mary in this Symposium and She has graciously allowed me to publish a list of the plays in which She saw Irving act, and to indicate those which Her Majesty preferred.

H. A. SAINTSBURY.

GREEN ROOM CLUB,
6 February, 1939.

Her Majesty Queen Mary

graciously allows the publication, in facsimile, of a list of the plays produced at the Lyceum Theatre and the Theatre Royal, Drury Lane, in which Sir Henry Irving appeared and which Her Majesty has marked to indicate those which She witnessed. Her Majesty has further graciously allowed it to be stated that of the fourteen plays in which She saw Sir Henry Irving act the two which made the most impression on Her Majesty and in which She liked Sir Henry Irving best were *The Bells* and *The Lyons Mail.*

AT THE LYCEUM THEATRE:-

On			Irving played:-	In
11	September	1871	Landry Barbeau	Fanchette
23	October	1871	Jingle	Pickwick
25	November	1871	Mathias	The Bells
1	April	1872	Jeremy Diddler	Raising the Wind
28	September	1872	Charles I	Charles the First
19	April	1873	Eugene Aram	Eugene Aram
27	September	1873	Cardinal Richelieu	Richelieu
7	February	1874	Philip	Philip
31	October	1874	Hamlet	Hamlet
18	September	1875	Macbeth	Macbeth
14	February	1876	Othello	Othello
18	April	1876	Philip of Spain	Queen Mary
12	June	1876	Doricourt	The Belle's Stratagem
29	January	1877	Richard III	Richard the Third
19	May	1877	Lesurques and Dubosc	The Lyons Mail
9	March	1878	Louis XI	Louis the Eleventh
8	June	1878	Vanderdecken	Vanderdecken
17	April	1879	Claude Melnotte	The Lady of Lyons
27	September	1879	Sir Edward Mortimer	The Iron Chest
1	November	1879	Shylock	The Merchant of Venice
20	May	1880	Count Tristan	Iolanthe
18	September	1880	Fabien and Louis dei Franchi	The Corsican Brothers
3	January	1881	Synorix	The Cup
2	May	1881	Iago	Othello
23	July	1881	Modus (in a scene from)	The Hunchback
26	December	1881	Digby Grant	Two Roses
11	March	1882	Romeo	Romeo and Juliet
11	October	1882	Benedick	Much Ado about Nothing
14	June	1883	Robert Macaire	Robert Macaire
8	July	1884	Malvolio	Twelfth Night
27	May	1885	Doctor Primrose	Olivia
19	September	1885	Mephistopheles	Faust
1	June	1887	Werner	Werner
28	September	1889	Robert Landry	The Dead Heart
20	September	1890	Edgar of Ravenswood	Ravenswood
5	January	1892	Cardinal Wolsey	Henry the Eighth
6	November	1892	King Lear	King Lear
6	February	1893	Thomas Becket	Becket
11	January	1895	King Arthur	King Arthur
4	May	1895	Corporal Brewster	A Story of Waterloo
14	May	1895	Don Quixote	Don Quixote
22	September	1896	Iachimo	Cymbaline
10	April	1897	Napoleon	Madame Sans-Gene
1	January	1898	Peter the Great	Peter the Great
4	May	1898	Doctor Tregenna	The Medicine Man
11	April	1899	Maximilien Robespierre	Robespierre
15	April	1901	Coriolanus	Coriolanus

AT THE THEATRE ROYAL DRURY LANE:-

30	April	1903	Dante	Dante

The dates given above are in each case of the first performance of the play at the Lyceum Theatre.

I

IRVING as LANDRY BARBEAU

Lyceum Theatre, 11th of September, 1871:—

FANCHETTE

OR WILL O' THE WISP

(*Derived from La Petite Fadette by George Sand through a German adaptation, Die Grille*)

WRITTEN BY MRS. H. L. BATEMAN

Fanchette	MISS ISABEL BATEMAN
Mother Fadet	MISS G. PAUNCEFORT
Madame Barbeau	MRS. F. B. EGAN
Madelon	MISS MARION HILL
Rosalie	MISS MAUDE MIDDLETON
Julie	MISS ELLEN MAYNE
Marie	MISS JENNY HENRI
Annette	MISS ELLEN LEIGH
Leontine	MISS MAUDE MORICE
Suzanne	MISS MURRAY
Father Barbeau	MR. ADDISON
Landry Barbeau	MR. HENRY IRVING
Sylvinet Barbeau	MR. GEORGE BELMORE
Father Caillaud	MR. COLLETT
Martineau	MR. A. TAPPING
Etienne	MR. JOHN ROYSTON
Claude	MR. FOTHERINGHAM
Pierre	MR. W. L. BRANSCOMBE
Antoine	MR. F. RIVERS

SYNOPSIS OF SCENERY: ACT I, SCENE 1. *Homestead of the Wealthy Breton Peasant;* SCENE 2. *Landscape;* SCENE 3. *Rocky Glade near the Mill Stream. Hut of Fadet, the reputed Witch. Distant view of the Village of La Priche.* ACT II. *Public Square in the Village, decorated in honour of the Festival St. Andoche, Characteristic Dances by the Villagers.* SCENE 2. *A Street in the Village.* ACT III. *Breton Landscape, with the Village Fountain.* ACT IV. *The Breton Homestead.*

FOR this play, which had been tried out in the previous March at the Theatre Royal, Edinburgh, Bateman had now gathered together, to support his young daughter Isabel in the name-part, a company of actors of recognized merit, among them one Henry Irving, who had impressed him in the part of Digby Grant in Albery's *Two Roses* at the Vaudeville (June

1870). Under the title of *The Grasshopper*, another version of George Sand's story had been produced without much success at the Olympic Theatre in August 1867. It may, therefore, be thought that the omens were not propitious. And indeed, considered as theatre stuff, there is little to be said for the story as it stands—or sprawls. Revenge is the motive, uncertainly developed to a conclusion uncertainly dramatic.

The scene opens in the house of Father Barbeau, a well-to-do French farmer. Madame Barbeau is disturbed over the sudden disappearance of Sylvinet, a weak-minded younger son, morbidly jealous for his brother Landry, whom he has caught making love to a Mlle Madelon, and has gone off vaguely intending suicide. The family is proposing to consult Mother Fadette, a reputed witch, when Fanchette, the old woman's granddaughter, enters through the long window seeking a strayed chicken. Securing it, she departs, and shortly encounters Sylvinet, who airs his woes and announces his resolve to starve himself to death. Fanchette rates him, but presently directs him to a hiding-place. Landry Barbeau interviews Mother Fadette, who says that Sylvinet has drowned himself; but Fanchette, appearing, tells him that his brother is in hiding. When Landry promises to do anything she asks if only she will take him to Sylvinet, she complains that he has avoided her since she saved him, a year before, from her namesake, the real Will-o'-the-wisp. He renews his promise, however, and is directed to Sylvinet's retreat. Dancing to her own shadow in the moonlight, Fanchette vows to make Landry dance next day with her at the Feast of St. Andoche.

Fantastically attired in a dress which had been her mother's, Fanchette goes to the Feast and claims Landry for her partner. Greatly mortified, he yields, followed by the taunts of Madelon and the peasants. Declaring that Fanchette has bewitched him, they would have snatched from her neck, had not Landry intervened, a locket which she opens to reveal to him a written prayer to the Madonna, given to her by old Fadette, who had brought her up in the fear of Heaven even while she belaboured and clothed her in rags. Fanchette asks Landry to forgive her for making him dance with her, then hurries away to her grandmother's hut, where Landry afterwards finds her passionately weeping. She tells him the sad story of her life, tries to explain her recent conduct, and expresses regret for the humiliation she has put upon him. She offers to put matters right with Madelon, but Landry will not hear of it. He is anxious to kiss Fanchette, as he should have done at the end of the dance, but she says he must not now claim a privilege he had chosen to forgo in public.

When Fanchette begins to dress like other girls, Landry discovers that she is much more attractive than Madelon. On overhearing her tell Madelon that she felt sure Landry loved her, Madelon, dearly, and Madelon's bitter rejoinder that she cared not a straw for him, Landry makes known his presence, avows his love for Fanchette, and asks her to be his bride. Father Barbeau, and Caillaud, the father of Madelon, now inform him that his marriage with Madelon is arranged, and when Landry declares he will marry no one but Fanchette his father angrily refuses his consent and they separate. Fanchette meanwhile confides to her grandmother that she loves Landry, but vows never to wed him without his father's consent. Father Barbeau calls on Fadette and offers her money if she will send Fanchette away. Fadette scorns his offer and denounces him for having prevented her own marriage with his twin brother in their youth. He shall yet know sorrow in his son's unhappiness—her avenger unaware.

Dying, Fadette leaves a fortune to Fanchette, who consults old Barbeau on the management of her affairs. On his urging marriage, she answers that the father of the man she loves refuses his consent. Barbeau swears the father must be a fool to object to a daughter-in-law so rich, sensible and modest. Finally, captivated, he solicits her hand for his son Landry.

So runs the story of the play in which Irving was assigned the part of Landry Barbeau, the bucolic lover of wild Fanchette, and one may think *now* that no more unsatisfactory part, indeed that no more unsatisfactory play, could have been chosen for the exercise of the player's powers. What he made of it may be gathered from the papers of that distant day. 'The gloomy moods of Landry, in whom there is much of that sullen ferocity which George Sand is in the habit of ascribing to provincial lovers, are graphically depicted by Mr. Henry Irving'—and this verdict of John Oxenford's was supported by the critics of *The Telegraph*, *The Standard*, and *The Globe*. And now—who was this player, this Henry Irving, whose genius shone even through the absurdities of Landry Barbeau?

. . . . . .

Keinton Mandeville in Somerset. Grey village in the West, where the mists of land and sea mingle and wreathe about Quantocks and Mendips, and the mists of time give their weathering to Glastonbury, which is Avalon, the 'Isle of the Blest,' and to the 'Isle of Princes,' which is Athelney.

'I will not tell you that on the Quantock Hills my father fed his flock, though he was a Somerset man before me. Nor will I pretend that I mused deeply on Alfred, who made his stronghold among the Somerset Saxons. But I think it is possible that a child on the height of Avalon may have taken into his blood subconsciously the old legends of Arthur.' The words were spoken at a meeting of Somersetshire men in Liverpool, a few months before his death in 1905, by Sir Henry Irving—born on 6 February 1838, at Keinton Mandeville.

John Henry Brodribb was the only child of Samuel Brodribb and Mary his wife, a Cornishwoman *née* Behenna, humble folk whose chief assets in life were soundness of constitution and uprightness of character. They had kept a shop in the village, but failed to make it keep them, and at the time of their son's arrival they occupied two small rooms in a six-roomed cottage. And the youngster was scarcely more than four years old when they removed to Bristol. He had therefore not lived long enough in the God-forsaken little village, as he calls it, to muse on Alfred or deeply on any subject, his memories of the place having most to do with a ram that attacked him when he had toddled into a neighbour's meadow, and with guinea-fowls that perched on ghostly trees and made uncanny sounds. 'What part they have played in my career I do not know, unless they gave me a dramatic yearning for the society of Shakespeare's raven which doth bellow for revenge.'

The sojourn in Bristol was of equally short duration, and his memories of it were equally few. At the launching in 1845 of the *S.S. Great Britain*—the first iron screw steamer—the child was impressed by the Prince Consort's moustache, and would not be content until his own upper lip had been embellished with burnt cork by a friendly chemist. An occasion far more significant, in that it struck the first spark of his life's ambition, was the morning when he saw Van Amburgh, the lion-tamer, drive twenty-four horses down Park Street and give a performance afterwards in the lions' den.

Harder times befell, and the little family broke up, Mrs. Brodribb betaking herself to London after first travelling to Halsetown in Cornwall, there to commit her child to the care of her sister Sarah, wife of Captain Isaac Penberthy, a mining engineer well known in the county. His grief at first parting from his mother abode in the son's memory to the end of his days. The Penberthys were a splendid type, upright and deeply religious, and with them and their children, two boys and a girl, John Henry spent the next six years of his life. The local

Cornish scene impressed itself vividly on his mind, coloured his early thought, and subtly tempered through all his years the artist's soul of him. Long after leaving it he conjured up visions of Halsetown, 'a village nestling between sloping hills, bare and desolate, disfigured by great heaps of slack from the mines, and with the Knill monument standing prominent as a landmark to the east. It was a wild and weird place, fascinating in its own peculiar beauty, and taking a more definite shape in my youthful imagination by reason of the fancies and legends of the people.'

The wind of circumstance had seemed to be contrary, but the gods in their wisdom saw that it would be for the good of Henry Irving that John Henry Brodribb should live his most impressionable years in familiar contact with nature and human nature in their sterner yet not ungenerous moods. So it was that the prologue to all the acts of the Lyceum came to be written there and then in Halsetown. Its rocks and streams and desolate hill-sides, its mines and slag-heaps, its village folk austerely kind, were charactered in the mind of the great actor-to-be to remain there significant always. While he could not yet have been half aware, the very genius of the place had entered into and claimed him for its own—a genius in turn fiercely bright and darkling, with a wild, a brooding, at times a sinister quality that chimed with and served in some measure to intensify a quality natively belonging to the Celt that was in him. Some tincture his spirit caught from the good red earth, his shy but royal spirit a splash of the purple that bathed and transfigured the hill-sides about Halsetown in the haze that gathered at the going down of the sun. To these influences his youthful spirit responded more instantly than he knew and more fully perhaps than he ever knew, so hidden often from himself are a man's spiritual processes. As a child in Halsetown he may sometimes have stood at night upon a silent hill under the stars and heard:

> The song of kings of kingdoms when
> They rise above their fortune Men,
> And crown themselves anew.—
> The song of courage, heart and will
> And gladness in a fight,
> Of men who face a hopeless hill
> With sparking and delight. . . .
> The song of fighters great and small,
> The song of pretty fighters all
> And high heroic things.

And it may even be that long years after, remembering, he had been fain sometimes to own—this romantic who was never a sentimentalist—

> I stood upon that silent hill
> And stared into the sky until
> My eyes were blind with stars and still
> I stared into the sky.

Irving has now become a legend, and one of the conditions of legend is mystery. To those who knew him living, and not least to those who knew him best, Irving the man was an enigma. Many beside who hold dear his living memory have sought in vain to penetrate the secret. It is not enough to say that he triumphed by the sheer force of his genius. We would know by what influence more than another it was disposed and quickened, whence came the wind that warmed, the still small voice that wakened, the spark that touched it to flame. (And other mysteries there are—of hearts 'pregnant with celestial fire,' yet fated to go out in dumb forgetfulness, of glorious dreams that flicker and fade on grey horizons, of the Vision caught for a moment and for ever lost.) It is because I believe the secret of Irving to be held in great part *there*, that I have tarried thus by the way in Halsetown. There, too, he gained the bodily vigour that was to stead him well in the arduous years ahead. His power to endure he attributed 'to the free and open and healthy years I lived at Halsetown, and to the simple food and regular routine ordained by my aunt. . . . I was a wiry youth when the time came for me to join a London school.'

The time came in 1849, and the school was the City Commercial School, George Yard, Lombard Street. He lived with his parents on the top floor of No. 65 Old Broad Street, where his mother was caretaker. At home the boy kept white mice and play-acted with a wooden sword for his principal 'prop,' and at the school entertainments, held at Sussex Hall, he recited and took part in minor theatricals. Many years later, William Creswick, a well-known tragedian of the day, recalled having been present when the boy had played Adrastus in a scene from *Ion* and 'left his schoolfellows a long way behind.' On leaving school, in 1851, he was placed in the office of Paterson & Longman, Solicitors, of Milk Street, Cheapside, whence, after a year, he migrated to the counting-house of a firm of East India merchants, Thacker & Co., in Newgate Street, where he remained four years. Merchandising, however, no more than the law, had any attraction for him whose heart was now firmly set on the stage.

Often he would rise at four o'clock in the morning and walk to the river-side for a bathe, and for a long period lived chiefly on bread and butter in order to save money for books (one more example of the methods by which those ridiculous Victorians became Eminent). He took lessons in dancing, went twice a week for two years to Shury's school of arms in Chancery Lane for fencing lessons, and joined the City Elocution Class, which met in a room under a railway arch in Gould Square, Fenchurch Street, before it found a more permanent home in Sussex Hall. The class was conducted by Henry Thomas, a disciple of Charles Mathews and himself an able teacher, besides being a gay, mercurial spirit. From the beginning, young Brodribb was able to electrify the class with his dramatic representations. His appearance at this time has been described by one who knew him. He was tall for his age, and dressed invariably in a black cloth suit, with a deep white linen collar turned over the top of his jacket. His handsome face, with eyes bright and flashing with intelligence, was surmounted with a mass of wavy black hair.

The meetings of the class were devoted to recitations and theatricals by the members, with Thomas as chairman, and instruction came chiefly by way of mutual criticism in matters of enunciation and gesture. The pieces played were mostly of a light character. In December 1853, Brodribb played Captain Absolute in *The Rivals*, with Charles Dyall (a schoolfellow and lifelong friend, afterwards curator of the Liverpool Art Gallery) as Sir Anthony. In April 1854, he played in a farce, *Catching an Heiress*, and in the autumn in another farce, *My Wife's Dentist*. He was always word-perfect, and successful in every part he undertook. When, in July 1884, the Irving Amateur Dramatic Club entertained their President at supper at the Freemasons' Tavern, he recalled in the course of his speech an occasion when the old City Elocution Class had given a performance of a comedy, *The Honeymoon*, at the Soho Theatre (afterwards the Royalty), and his ambition had for the first time known the satisfaction of 'a real stage, real scenery, real footlights, real dresses, real everything. . . . It was rather a memorable occasion for me—and to those, I should think, who saw me! Rehearsals were out of the question altogether, and the supporters were principally a lot of superannuated actors.' But it was his first appearance on the stage of a regular theatre, and therefore, for us, important.

Sadler's Wells—what brave visions the name conjures up! The young Brodribb made his first acquaintance with the inside of a theatre when he was taken to Sadler's Wells to see Samuel Phelps play Hamlet. Thereafter he lost no opportunity of seeing Phelps act, and made it a practice always to study the play beforehand. Here, mention should be made of his first visit to a theatre *alone*, if only because the experience remained vivid in his memory. Weighed down with a sense of sin, he stole into the gallery of the Adelphi, half expecting it to collapse under him. He recovered his spirits when a neighbour engaged him in conversation, and presently became so interested in the show, which consisted of *The Haunted Man*, *The Enchanted Isle*, and a farce, *Slasher and Crasher*, that he left the theatre reluctantly at one o'clock in the morning, arriving home to find his mother nearly frantic with worry at his prolonged absence.

After awhile—at the age of sixteen—he introduced himself to William Hoskins, then a member of Phelps's company, who was so impressed by the boy's eager talent that he agreed to give him tuition, and, later, presented him to Phelps. The tragedian listened approvingly to a recital of Othello's Address to the Senate, but adjured the lad not to think of joining an ill-rewarded profession. "Well, sir, it seems strange that such advice should come from you, seeing that you enjoy so great a reputation as an actor. I think I shall take my chance and go upon the stage." "In that case, sir," rejoined Phelps, "you may come next season to Sadler's Wells, and I'll give you two pounds a week to begin with." The astonished youngster stammered his thanks, but did not close with the offer. He had already made up his mind that he would begin his acting career in the provinces. Hoskins, who was just about to sail for Australia, then told Mrs. Brodribb that if she would allow her son to accompany him he should have an engagement at five pounds a week. The good mother, however —remembered by Dyall as being rather tall, somewhat stately, and very gentle—had her own views on the theatre. 'On one occasion she came to me with tears in her eyes and implored me to dissuade John from thinking of the stage as a profession'; and now she firmly—and fortunately—vetoed the Australian idea. Whereupon Hoskins assured her that the time would come when Master John Henry would earn fifty pounds a night *as an actor*. To the boy, Hoskins said: 'You will go upon the stage. When you want an engagement present this letter, and you will find one.' The letter was addressed to E. D. Davis, a well-known actor-manager in the north.

So William Hoskins sailed away to Australia. And before the year was out—it was 1856—the letter he gave on parting to his young friend, John Henry Brodribb, had opened the door of fame to Henry Irving. Of whom it was to be written on a day long after: 'It can be said of him as of no other man of the day, whatever his country or position, that he stood absolutely foremost in his line, and that his place is conceded among the immortals.'

F. C. OWLETT.

Fanchette, The Will o' the Wisp, is avowedly derived from Mme Birch Pfeiffer's adaptation to the German stage of Mme George Sand's novelette, *La Petite Fadette*. A dramatic rendering of this work was presented some five years ago (1866) at the Olympic Theatre. Stage versions of *La Petite Fadette* have, however, won triumphs in America, and Mr. Bateman, the new impresario of the Lyceum Theatre, has thought it worth while to commence his campaign as a metropolitan manager with another attempt to convert to theatrical uses the prettiest of Breton stories. This proceeding says perhaps more for his courage than for his judgment.

No pains have been spared in the way of bettering the good chances of the new venture. 'Characteristic Breton music' has been expressly composed by Mr. Edward Silas; new Breton costumes have been supplied of quite unimpeachable picturesqueness; the scenery provided by Messrs. Craven and Cuthbert is of excellent quality; and a meritorious troop of actors has been engaged. The accessories, indeed, are all that could be wished; the deficiency is in the substance. As a play, *La Petite Fadette* could only be accepted by an audience predisposed to value the idyllic above the dramatic. And then it has to be considered that the literary art and grace of the original are lost in the process of translation; the present version being especially noticeable for its flat and poverty-stricken English.

The theme is of the slightest kind. Fanchette, a young girl who lives in a wretched hovel with her grandmother, La Mère Fadet, a reputed witch, is induced by her affection for Landry Barbeau, a handsome peasant, to reform the squalor of her life, to assume a comely aspect, and to become a respectable member of society. Landry, then, in his turn, loves Fanchette, jilting for her sake his former mistress, Madelon, 'the belle of La Priche.' Barbeau, a rich farmer, the father of Landry, objects to his son's marriage with one so poorly provided for as Fanchette. But Father Barbeau's scruples presently disappear upon the discovery that La Mère Fadet has died, leaving a handsome fortune to her grandchild. So the curtain is allowed ultimately to descend upon the union of the lovers, leaving unsolved a difficulty that has ensued from Landry's drawing an unlucky number, and being therefore bound to serve his country as a conscript. A comic character, whose claims to be entertaining, however, are ineffectual enough, is provided in the person of Sylvinet, the brother of Landry, who follows at a distance the example of that more prosperous suitor, and, like him, first plays court to Madelon, and then woos Fanchette. But Sylvinet is left in the end disconsolate, the victim of unstable and unrequited affection. The audience are permitted to assume that he joins the army in his brother's stead.

Fanchette is represented by Miss Isabel Bateman, the daughter of the manager, an actress possessed of all the confidence which should come of skill and practice, but whose art is at present in a very crude and undisciplined condition. The gaiety of Fanchette's earlier scenes lacked spontaneity and ease, while the graver passages of the part failed to impress from their deficiency in pathetic expression. Miss Bateman appears to be much more able to display force than to depict feelings. Her elocutionary method is faulty, and she adopts the monotonous delivery and the drawling pronunciation of particular words which would seem to be established mannerisms of the American theatre. Possibly in some less ambitious character the lady may by and by more successfully assert her claims to be accounted an actress of value. Of the other characters in the drama little was demanded beyond their promenading the stage in Breton costumes and taking part in the numerous prolonged and rather vapid conversations. Mr. Irving was a picturesque figure as Landry Barbeau, but the part is a thankless one, and far removed from the ordinary range of the actor's impersonations. Certain of the love scenes, however, in which Landry appears were skilfully and feelingly rendered. Mr. Addison did all that was possible with the character of Father Barbeau. Mr. Belmore toiled sedulously to invest the shadowy Sylvinet with some show of comic substance, but the task was not to be accomplished. The speeches he was required to deliver were no laughing matter. La Mère Fadet is only the conventional crone of the stage—bound to thump her crutch frequently upon the boards and shriek with painful vehemence imprecations and menaces at the other characters. Miss Pauncefort sufficiently met these physical requirements of the part.

The reception of the play was not much wanting in enthusiasm; but the enduring success of *Fanchette* is hardly to be looked for. A first night's applause is but as the firing of blank cartridges. Considerable noise ensues, but there is no other appreciable result. The drama's prospects depend almost altogether upon its completeness as a sort of pastoral spectacle.

DUTTON COOK.

From *Nights at the Play*. A View of the English Stage, by Dutton Cook. Reprinted by kind permission of Messrs. Chatto & Windus.

IRVING *As MATHIAS*

II

IRVING as JINGLE

Lyceum Theatre, 23rd of October, 1871 :—

PICKWICK

(*An adaptation from Pickwick Papers by Charles Dickens*)

WRITTEN BY JAMES ALBERY

Samuel Pickwick, Esq., G.C.M.P.C.	MR. ADDISON
Alfred Jingle	MR. HENRY IRVING
Sam Weller	MR. GEORGE BELMORE
Job Trotter	MR. ODELL
Old Weller	MR. FRANK HALL
Mr. Perker	MR. F. W. IRISH
— Nupkins, Esq.	MR. GASTON MURRAY
Fat Boy	MR. J. ROYSTON
Augustus Snodgrass, Esq.	MR. HERBERT CRELLIN
Tracy Tupman, Esq.	MR. EDWARD DYAS
Nathaniel Winkle, Esq.	MR. W. L. BRANSCOMBE
Mr. Wardle	MR. COLLET
Mr. Jinks	MR. FREDERICKS
Grummer	MR. A. TAPPING
Miss Arabella	MISS MINNIE SIDNEY
Miss Emily Nupkins	MISS MARION HILL
Miss Witherfield	MISS CAROLINE EWELL
Miss Rachel Wardle	MISS KATE MANOR
Miss Smithers (Maid at the White Hart) *afterwards* *Mary (Attendant on Mrs. Winkle)*	MISS ANNIE LAFONTAINE
Ellen	MISS MAUDE MIDDLETON

Schoolgirls, Maid-servants, Gamekeepers, Constables.

N.B. Emily Wardle of the Book is Emily Nupkins in the Play.

ACT I, SCENE. *Wardle's House.* ACT II, SCENE 1. *Yard of the White Hart Inn, Borough;* SCENE 2. *Sitting-room, No. 5;* SCENE 3. *The Angel, Bury St. Edmunds;* SCENE 4. *Miss Witherfield's Seminary.* ACT III, SCENE 1. *Great White Horse, Ipswich;* SCENE 2. *Corridor in the Great White Horse;* SCENE 3. *Bedroom in the Great White Horse.* ACT IV, SCENE 1. *Coffee-room in the Great White Horse;* SCENE 2. *Street in Ipswich;* SCENE 3. *Library of Mr. Nupkins.*

PICKWICK was a remarkably good dramatization by James Albery of Charles Dickens's immortal *Pickwick Papers*. There was an ideal cast. Irving was absolutely a perfect Jingle.

'Old Addison' as we always called him (I can't remember his Christian name—father of Carlotta and Fanny Addison) looking Pickwick perfectly and realizing him as well as anybody could —George Belmore, another perfect performance, as Sam Weller. Tracy Tapmann, Augustus Snodgrass, Nathaniel Winkle all remarkable. Odell, too, was magnificent as Job Trotter. The women did not amount to much. Rachel Wardle was, I think, played by Miss Pauncefort. Old Wardle was very good, but I cannot remember who played him. It was an exceedingly good night's entertainment, but like almost every Dickens dramatization, it proved a failure.

When my father, H. L. Bateman, opened The Lyceum Theatre he engaged Henry Irving, George Belmore and Charles Warner as his leading men. My mother wrote the play, *Fanchette*, a romance founded on George Sand's novel, *La Petite Fadette*. The leading lady was my sister Isabel, a girl of sixteen, whose whole previous stage experience was a three months' tour with our sister, Kate Bateman (Mrs. Crowe). She was lovely to look at, quite gifted, and her extreme youth gave an extra charm to her performance. Unfortunately for the play, my father, a great admirer of Irving's, allowed him to do as he greatly desired and play the part of the young lover, Landry. Irving had just made a great success in the part of an elderly man, Digby Grant—a very fine performance of a character part, but unfortunately he could not quite forget Digby Grant while he was impersonating the young lover, Landry Barbeau. The audience could not forget Digby Grant either, and the fate of the play was sealed.

While *Pickwick* was being acted Irving brought Leopold Lewis to talk about his translation of Erckmann-Chatrian's *Le Juif Polonais*—and long were the talks, and wonderful the result.

My father had engaged Irving as his leading man for three years. He had not only seen Irving as Digby Grant but had also heard him recite *The Dream of Eugene Aram*, and he at once knew that Irving would become a great tragic actor, probably the greatest tragic actor who had been seen for years.

My father saw what a great creation Irving could make of this part of Mathias, how much greater than that of the French actor who had already made a success of the play in France. His forecast, of course, was entirely realized.

VIRGINIA COMPTON.

When *Pickwick* was first produced it was not a success. Like almost every Dickens dramatization it proved an unsatisfactory play in spite of some excellent performances by the Company. For example, the critic of *The Daily Telegraph* wrote a devastating review; he called it a travesty. 'Lovers of Dickens,' he said, 'must have shuddered when they saw scene after scene from their beloved book torn to ribands by the greedy adapter.' But surely the art of dramatizing a novel is not to reproduce its scenes photographically—that is the art of the present-day cinema—but to make the characters live in settings that shall recreate the spirit of the story. It is for that reason, I think, that Dickens dramatizations have been so rarely successful; their authors have tried to crowd into three hours in the theatre a novel of hundreds of thousands of words. *David Copperfield*, for instance, has half a million words. How can we possibly have, in the theatre, in three hours, more than half a dozen of our favourite scenes? And then what happens if *my* favourite scenes are not *your* favourite scenes? I cannot help thinking that James Albery's plan of 'tearing the book to ribands' in order to preserve the characters and the spirit of the story rather than the exact sequence of events, gives us a better result than what used to be called the 'scissors and paste' method of dramatization. Which is what *The Daily Telegraph's* critic, at that time, seems to have wished for.

But to put *The Pickwick Papers* on the stage was an almost impossible task. The one character in the story that is essentially dramatic is Jingle, and when the play was remodelled with him as its central figure, it succeeded. It was then cut to three acts, other characters were added, and it was played with *The Bells*.

Nearly seven years later, on 8 July 1878, it was entirely re-written and again acted with *The Bells*. Irving was then an established favourite, and the public welcomed him in the two parts, so widely contrasted, of Mathias and Jingle in the same evening. The four acts had now been reduced to six scenes, and the whole play centred in Jingle; in fact the episodes were labelled: Jingle the Stroller; Jingle the Lover; Jingle the Financier; Jingle the Dandy; Jingle the Swindler and Jingle the Penitent. This was a very drastic revision, but it proved to be to the public's taste and served Irving well for many years. And well it might, for his performance was masterly. As Alfred Jingle, the voluble, tricky *Chevalier d'Industrie:* the strolling player masquerading as a gentleman, his humour and characterization were faultless, he acted not alone in speech, but with his hands; every gesture adding value to his words.

Henry Irving's lengthy experience as a Stock actor had taught him the tricks of suiting the word to the action, the action to the word. He was a perfect character comedian, his remarkable personality, his timing, his every movement were wonderful. I have always felt that, great as were his triumphs in drama, the highest spots were often in his touches of comedy. His Mephistopheles was terrific but what one remembers best was his sardonic humour; the grim humour of Louis XI, the frank humour of Benedick, the crafty humour of Richelieu and above all his wonderful creation of Digby Grant, that bombastic, pretentious, sly, ungrateful humbug who accepted favours when in embarrassed circumstances and who, during his temporary enjoyment of prosperity, evinced such gross ingratitude. It left an impression on my youthful mind never to be forgotten. In voice, deportment and action he made the character, so skilfully drawn, a living embodiment of a fascinating although contemptible personality.

But Jingle is my theme, and Jingle is an honest man compared with Digby Grant.

Mr. T. Edgar Pemberton, the author of *Dickens' London*, which was published in 1875, wrote very wisely on the subject in *Dickens and the Stage*. He records the first dramatization of *The Pickwick Papers* by Mr. Stirling, produced at the City of London Theatre by Mr. Beasley, its Manager, on 27 April 1837, and he adds: 'For obvious reasons *The Pickwick Papers* will never make a satisfactory acting play, and yet for the sake of one marvellous impersonation its stage representation will always be welcome and memorable to the playgoers of to-day. Of course we allude to the "Jingle" of Mr. Henry Irving. This splendid piece of character acting would no doubt have excited the admiration of Dickens himself. The impudent strolling player is personified to the life and the creation of Dickens stamped with the hall-mark of the acting genius of Irving is a thing once seen, to be ever remembered.' Indeed it seemed almost impossible to realize that this mercurial personality was the same actor we had seen half an hour earlier in the tragic death throes of Mathias.

Irving owed a great deal to Dickens. As an actor, Dickens and his friend Toole had given him some of his greatest opportunities. Toole rescued him from a series of villains when he induced F. B. Chatterton, the Manager of Drury Lane, to release him from the cast of *Formosa*, in which he was playing Compton

Kerr, 'the high-bred rascal of modern days.' He joined Toole at the Gaiety Theatre under John Hollingshead's management to play Mr. Reginald Chevenix in *Uncle Dick's Darling*, a play by H. J. Byron, written expressly for Toole. Now Mr. Chevenix was none other than Mr. Dombey under another name and Irving had made a great success as Dombey in Manchester nine years earlier. That success he repeated as Mr. Chevenix. Toole describes this in his Reminiscences:

> 'It was at Edinburgh that I first met Irving about the year 1857. I met him later at Manchester, where our friendship commenced. . . . He was always a very studious and careful actor, always made remarkable and complete studies of his characters. There was nothing conventional about what he did. He seemed, so to speak, always to have got inside the part he played, and to have learned something new about it; not new in the sense of being simply new, but something belonging to the part that other actors had not found out. . . . One often hears people talk about luck in a man's success, and I have heard it applied to Irving as a reason for his position, but people who speak of Irving in this way do not know how hard he worked for his success. It was as Chevenix in *Uncle Dick's Darling* that he impressed Dickens so strongly. He said of Irving: "That young man will be a great actor."
>
> 'What I admire about Irving is the calm, steady way in which he has marched to the front, and the gentle, unostentatious way in which he has kept there. He might have been excused, as the world goes, if he had put on side and even forgotten some of his friends, but he is just the same kind, generous fellow.
>
> 'At the Queen's our first production was Byron's admirable play, *Dearer than Life*. It followed up a line of character in which I had been fortunate enough to interest the public and the Press. Michael Garner has always been a favourite with my audiences, and the play is made memorable by Charles Dickens predicting that there was an actor playing "Bob Gassitt" at the Queen's who would be heard of again. That actor was our friend Irving. And what a support I had! You don't get such a cast nowadays. Fancy—Wyndham, Clayton, Brough, Nellie Moore, and Irving!'[1]

Irving also played Bill Sikes during this season, giving a very grim and powerful performance. 'It was,' wrote W. H. Pollock, 'an absolutely life-like and consistent character throughout. Years afterwards, I asked Irving where he had

[1] From *Reminiscences of J. L. Toole*. Related by himself, and chronicled by himself and Joseph Hatten. Illustrated by Alfred Bryan and W. H. Margetsen. 2 vols. Hurst & Blackett Ltd., 1889.

found a model for this striking rendition. He replied: "I got it by quietly observing certain street corners." As he spoke, he became for the moment one of those fellows, hang-dog, suspicious, truculent with an air that indicated a desperate daring if he were brought to bay.'

Irving also scored a striking success in the widely contrasted part of the bluff Yorkshireman, John Perrybingle, in Boucicault's version, then called *Caleb Plummer*, of *The Cricket on the Hearth*.

All this led up to his engagement at the Vaudeville for the part of Digby Grant in *Two Roses*. It was his great success in this that led to his acceptance as a leading London actor. It was a close circle in those days and none but those who had passed the test of technical apprenticeship could hope to retain a position on the London stage. Audiences were even more cruel in their outspokenness than the Press, who were then most searching in the detail of their criticism of an actor, and it was no uncommon thing for a new-comer to be told frankly and loudly by the gallery to 'go back to the provinces and learn your business!'

It was when 'Colonel' Bateman saw Irving as Digby Grant that by a curious intuition he divined in him a great Richelieu, so when he took a lease of the Lyceum Theatre he engaged Irving as his leading man.

The Lyceum had had many vicissitudes in its hundred years of existence, though the actual building that was to become so famous dated from 1834. Madame Vestris had triumphed there and Austin Brereton gives an account of old Walter Lacey's description of its decoration: 'The whole place,' he said, 'was hung with imitation lace; it was a fairy-like oriental ecstasy! The figure groups and raised ornaments were modelled by Bartolozzi."[1] But in 1869 it had fallen into sad decay and successive plasterings and re-paperings had overlaid this daintiness and even in Fechter's time it was by no means a 'fairy ecstasy.'

Manager Bateman opened the theatre in September 1871; in 1874 it passed to his widow, who relinquished it to Irving, who had been its mainstay from the first, at the end of 1878, and for twenty more years it flourished under his direction. I saw many productions under his *régime*. Two of the most striking to my mind were his creation of the hypnotic Doctor in a play that failed to attract called *The Medicine Man;* it was

[1] These Bartolozzi ornaments were discovered when the theatre was stripped for redecoration in 1878 and carefully preserved by Irving's instruction to be worked into the new scheme of decoration.

an impersonation that I believe might have turned a somewhat weak play into a success had it been possible to produce it to-day —but there is none to fill his place. The other part that lives vividly in my mind is his Iago, which he alternated with Othello, sharing the *rôles* with the American actor, Edwin Booth. As Iago, Irving was better suited than as the Moor and there is no question that on the night he played it he completely eclipsed the American star. Whether you agree with his reading of the Moor's Ancient or not, it was a great creation. The bluff soldier or the Italianate schemer? It is a subject for endless controversy.

> ' Locked in the countless chambers of the brain
> Our thoughts are linked by many a hidden chain;
> Awake but one, and lo, what memories rise—'

Do you remember? What a flood of recollections that simple phrase revives.

I have laboured in every branch of the theatrical business, hazardous, nowadays, owing to the vast competition of other forms of entertainment that claim the public's favour, but I feel that as long as the spoken word exists the beautiful art of the living theatre must prevail. It is 'not for an age but for all time' and no doubt some other genius will arise to carry on the tradition. But now, in the autumn of life, I say in all sincerity, I thank God I had the opportunity of seeing Henry Irving.

GEO. M. SLATER.

I recall two renderings of Jingle, one a great actor's, the other, a great poet's.

Swinburne had proposed to read *Pickwick* aloud to Watts-Dunton, Miss Theresa Watts-Dunton, and myself.

His reading from the printed page was sometimes monotonous, but the Jingle passages he had by heart, and so recited—practically acted.

He was not a playgoer as Watts-Dunton was, but he knew Irving, who had been his guest, and of whom he once remarked that he liked the great actor too much to wish to see him play Hamlet. In so saying, Swinburne's intention was not to belittle Irving but to imply of Hamlet, as drawn by Shakespeare, that no actor should come betwixt the wind and Shakespeare's conception of the character, as there could be only one conception of Hamlet, and for that, we must go to Shakespeare.

But though no playgoer, I suspect that his love of Dickens

had lured him to see Irving as Jingle, for Swinburne's rendering of the part—unlike as was his high-pitched falsetto to Irving's gruff and sometimes sepulchrous utterance—seemed to me an unconscious imitation of the actor's, even in the matter of mannerisms.

One of Irving's mannerisms as Jingle was, suddenly, to drop and to deepen his voice; and another was, when supposed to be thinking, as suddenly, to lift an eyebrow upward; and Swinburne (quite unconsciously, I am sure) thus let his voice fall, and thus elevated an eyebrow when representing Jingle for our entertainment.

I was little more than a lad when Irving played Jingle at the Lyceum toward the end of the 'seventies,' but, since then, I saw him in other *rôles*, and my opinion for what it is worth—or more likely for what it is not worth—is that it was one of his most successful.

This may, or may not have been due to the fact that, in the *rôle* of a strolling and needy player, Irving, who, if not needy, was scarcely likely at that stage of his career to be flush of money, had only to be *himself* and, as himself, was already Jingle. To act the part was unnecessary. It came naturally to him. Here, perhaps, an actor-reader will say:

> 'To be oneself on the stage is *not* acting. The task of an actor is, metaphorically speaking, as entirely to shed his own personality as a snake sheds or sloughs off its skin at certain seasons. The actor must so creep out of his own personality and into the personality of another person—most of all, must so creep into the very brain of that other person—that he IS that other person. The actor has called another person into being. In a very real sense that other person has been "created" by the actor. So, for you to attribute Irving's success as Jingle to the fact that, as Jingle, the great actor had only to be himself is all nonsense.'

Very likely, for, of actors and acting I write, from the actor's point of view, as one who is no more than a layman. None the less, I shall always think that, as Jingle, Sir Henry Irving was more natural, less saturnine, stagey, and melodramatic than in any other *rôle* in which I saw him. In those other *rôles* his diction seemed to me more self-conscious, more measured, and more orotund; and though Jingle's staccato and snappy way of interjecting himself into the conversation was the reverse of Irving's usual manner—so naturally was it all done that one would not have been surprised to learn that, in private life, the great actor thus interjected scraps of sentences (like thrown pebbles) into the pool of conversation. Moreover, Irving's high shoulders, his lanky and somewhat skimpy figure, clad in ill-fitting and shabby clothes, brought Jingle as vividly before us as if Dickens had drawn the picture with Irving as his model.

COULSON KERNAHAN.

III

IRVING as MATHIAS

Lyceum Theatre, 25th of November, 1871 :—

THE BELLS

(*An adaptation of Le Juif Polonais by M. M. Erckmann-Chatrian*)

WRITTEN BY LEOPOLD LEWIS

Mathias	MR. HENRY IRVING
Walter	MR. FRANK HALL
Hans	MR. F. W. IRISH
Christian	MR. H. CRELLIN
Mesmerist	MR. A. TAPPING
Doctor Zimmer	MR. DYAS
Notary	MR. COLLETT
Tony	MR. FREDERICKS
Fritz	MR. FOTHERINGHAM
Judge of the Court	MR. GASTON MURRAY
Clerk of the Court	MR. BRANSCOMBE
Catherine	MISS G. PAUNCEFORT
Annette	MISS FANNY HEYWOOD
Sozel	MISS HELEN MAYNE

ACT I. *The Burgomaster's Inn at Alsace.* ACT II. *Best Room in the Burgomaster's House.* ACT III. *Bedroom in the Burgomaster's House.* VISION. *The Court.* PERIOD. *Alsace*, 1833.

IN answer to the request that I should contribute some reminiscences of one of Sir Henry Irving's parts, I have thought it might perhaps be of interest if I put down some very early recollections of a performance by him as Mathias in *The Bells*. That performance was in the old Theatre Royal, Belfast, during one of Irving's provincial tours, either in 1873 or a little later. I cannot be certain as to the exact year.

And may I, in passing, pay a tribute to all that this Theatre Royal did for myself and others in the way of dramatic entertainment and education in the 'seventies and 'eighties of the last century ? It was there that I saw Barry Sullivan as Sir Giles Overreach in Massinger's *A New Way to Pay Old Debts*, that play which so curiously kept its place in the regular theatrical repertory at a time when nearly all Elizabethan dramas, except Shakespeare's, had fallen out of it. Shakespeare himself, somewhat later, was kept brightly burning by visits from Sir

Frank Benson and his company. J. L. Toole, whose friendship with Irving was to become almost legendary, showed his command over pathos as well as humour in a now apparently forgotten piece, *Dearer than Life*. It was at Belfast in the early 'eighties that I saw Pinero's *Money Spinner*, in which the future author of *The Second Mrs. Tanqueray* had begun to fulfil Irving's prophecy to him when he was a junior member of the Lyceum Company and had written some short pieces for it, that if he went on as he had begun he would be sure to reach a good position as a dramatist. And I remember, too, a performance in the Theatre Royal of *Two Roses*, that attractive play by James Albery, whose centenary has also fallen in 1938. Irving had made his first notable success as Digby Grant in this piece at the Vaudeville in 1870, and it is pleasant to know that it has been again acclaimed in a recent revival under the auspices of Mr. Bronson Albery.

It was not, however, till he appeared on the stage of the Lyceum as Mathias in *The Bells* on 25 November 1871 that Henry Irving took his place in the great theatrical succession that begins with Richard Burbage and Edward Alleyn and that comes down through Betterton and Garrick and Edmund Kean. Indeed, Irving's triumph as Mathias on that November night of 1871 has much in common with Kean's triumph as Shylock at Drury Lane on 26 January 1814. Both had to fight against the opposition and doubts of the management. With Kean it was hostility to his conception of the part; with Irving the distrust went even deeper. In *The Bells*, a version by an old Bohemian, Leopold Lewis, of *Le Juif Polonais* by MM. Erckmann-Chatrian, he had seen, with the intuition of genius, a piece that would repair the sagging fortunes of Colonel Bateman at the Lyceum. But Bateman had been unconvinced, and there is this to be said for him that *Le Juif Polonais* had been designed as 'une simple étude dramatique tenté sans aucune préoccupation du théâtre.' How could he foresee that this 'Etude dramatique,' turned into English, would become one of the most arresting melodramatic productions in the history of the European stage? Fortunately Bateman's hand was forced by the appearance of another version of *Le Juif Polonais* at the Alfred Theatre on 13 November. *The Bells* was put into rehearsal at the Lyceum, and in the words of Mr. Gordon Craig: 'on that night of 25 November, and not before, the greatest actor of the century sprang into existence —Brodribb became Henry Irving.' Mr. Craig, in his delightful book of reminiscences, makes his curtain rise on:

'. . . the excitement which lies in the words: "I am going to see Irving in *The Bells*. It is two o'clock, and the play does not begin until eight o'clock, nor will Irving, dressed as Mathias, be at the door which is so suddenly flung open, until fifteen minutes past eight. But we know what we are going to get, and when it comes it will beggar our expectation."'

Now this does *not* describe my own situation when as a boy I went to see *The Bells* at the Theatre Royal, Belfast, accompanied by a theatre-loving family retainer. We certainly did not know what we were going to get, though what came did indeed beggar anything that we could have expected. My impression is, though here my memory may be at fault, that I did not know beforehand what the subject of the play was to be, that I simply went to see Irving in one of his famous parts. But even had I been acquainted with the story of the Alsatian burgomaster and the murder of the Polish Jew, I could never have anticipated the overpowering effect of Irving's acting and the eerie background of the piece.

I have never seen *The Bells* again, but I have recently gone through the text of the play in French's acting edition to test how far any other features of the piece linger in my memory. I can recall broadly the opening scene, on Christmas Eve, 1833, in the village of the Burgomaster's residence before Mathias enters. But I had forgotten the talk about the approaching marriage of his daughter Annette to Christian, the Quartermaster of Gendarmes, and the good-humoured jealousy of his disappointed rival, Hans. And I had but the faintest memory of Father Walter's account of the arrival of the Polish Jew, with his girdle full of gold, at the inn that very day fifteen years ago, his mysterious murder, and the vain efforts to find the criminal. All this was virtually gone from me. Yet, Mr. Gordon Craig speaking of Lyceum performances at a later period, of this preliminary episode, records: 'I think that never was our Company seen to better advantage than during this brief quarter of an hour; and although they played the whole piece admirably it was before Irving's coming on to the stage that they were best.'

But the fact remains that, for myself, in my very young days, the interest really began with the entrance of Mathias in his long cloak covered with snow, and his cry to Annette who thinks that it is perhaps Christian returning: 'It is I—It is I.' It would be idle for me to attempt to rival Mr. Craig's masterly analysis of Irving's gestures and movements while he was taking off his coat and boots and listening to the talk in the inn-room. But what I recall vividly is the first mention of the mesmerist at whose performance Mathias had been present:

> Mathias: It was a Parisian who did extraordinary tricks. He sent people to sleep.
> Annette: Sent people to sleep!
> Mathias: Yes.
> Catherine: He gave them something to drink, no doubt.
> Mathias: No, he simply looked at them and made signs and they went fast asleep.
> Hans: This Parisian sends people to sleep, and when they are asleep they tell him everything that weighs upon their conscience.

The interest in the occult goes through successive phases, as we see it mirrored in drama. Shakespeare brings on his stage ghosts and witches. Ben Jonson exploits the contemporary belief in the magic of alchemy. To the nineteenth century the mesmerist was a figure steeped in fascination; to-day his place would be taken by the psycho-analyst, and the playwright would be making capital out of the complexes and the subliminal self.

But this is not all. There are more obvious changes from age to age in the external mechanism of daily social life. Will some dramatist in the future be able to thrill his generation with ghostly blasts of motor-horns or the 'chug-chug' of the engine? However this may be, it was fortunate both for playwright and actor that the Polish Jew on the night of his murder was driving in a sledge drawn by a horse carrying bells. Who can ever forget the astonishingly weird effect as the talk turns again to the Polish Jew's winter, and as Mathias stops in the act of raising a glass to his lips; of the first distant sounds of the bells rapidly growing louder—bells heard by none of the company in the inn except himself, as Banquo's ghost at the banquet is visible to Macbeth alone. Indeed, Macbeth's words, allowing for the distance between a king and a burgomaster, and between melodrama and tragedy, are strikingly apt:

> 'The times have been
> That, when the brains were out, the man would die
> And there an end: but now they rise again . . .
> And push us from our stools.'

For as Mathias, now left alone at the stroke of ten—the very hour when the Polish Jew arrived at the inn on the Christmas Eve of fifteen years ago—comforts himself with the thought 'The Jew is dead,' then, as the stage-direction runs, 'the back of the scene rises and sinks,' disclosing the episode of the murder while 'the Jew in the sledge suddenly turns his face, which is ashy pale, and fixes his eyes sternly upon him.' Had Mathias been Macbeth he would have cried:

> 'Avaunt! and quit my sight! let the earth hide thee. . . .
> Thou hast no speculation in those eyes
> Which thou dost glare with.'

But instead he utters a cry of terror and falls senseless—and with Irving's acting this had an equally overpowering effect.

I don't suppose I would have felt this any the less had I known then what Bram Stoker revealed in his *Personal Reminiscences of Henry Irving*, that the 'sink-and-rise' of the vision, taken over with other properties from Colonel Bateman, was a ramshackle affair. 'The whole stuff was simply rotten with age and wear. . . . The canvas had been almost held together by the overlay of paint; and as for the wood it was cut and hacked and pierced to death; full of old screw-holes and nail-holes.' Indeed, the whole scenery for *The Bells* had been manufactured out of odds and ends in the theatre. Such, at any rate, is Bram Stoker's description of it, after it had been unpacked for use in New York during Irving's American tour of 1883-4, though Austin Brereton, in his biography, it is fair to add, is more complimentary to Colonel Bateman's properties.

In my recent reading of the play I found that the Second Act, including Mathias's conversations with his doctor and with Christian, and the signing of the marriage contract between the latter and Annette, had faded from my memory, which was blank till the beginning of Act III, when after the ceremony Mathias retires to his lonely bedroom and lies down to sleep with the words: 'No more Bells! To-night I triumph; for conscience is at rest.' And how vividly do I recall the curtain rising at the back of the gauze (symbolizing that what takes place is in a dream) and disclosing the Court of Justice with Mathias seated on a stool in the centre. And I can recall as if it were yesterday the shattering impression of the scene in which Mathias, under the power of the mesmerist, re-enacts the murder of the Jew and hears the dread sentence that he is to be hanged by the neck until he is dead. And when the dream is over and the crowd outside come to wake him on the wedding morning, I can still shudderingly remember him staggering out from the alcove in the bedroom and crying: 'The rope! The rope! Cut the rope!' before, with the sound of the bells again in his ears, he falls dead in the midst of his friends. And the sound of those bells haunted me for months to come.

. . . .

During its first run at the Lyceum in 1871–2, *The Bells* was played for one hundred and fifty-one nights, and it has been calculated that Irving appeared in the piece over eight hundred times. These included some very notable occasions. It was the play with which he opened his first theatrical tour in the United States before an enthusiastic New York audience at the Star Theatre on 29 October 1883. At the Theatre Royal, Sandringham, by command of the Prince and Princess of Wales (afterwards King Edward VII and Queen Alexandra) it was played before them and Queen Victoria. It was followed by the Trial Scene from *The Merchant of Venice*, and thus Queen Victoria had the opportunity for the first time of seeing both Henry Irving and Ellen Terry act. On 25 November 1896, the twenty-fifth anniversary of the first performance of *The Bells*, a presentation was made to Irving by the whole Lyceum company and staff, of a silver bell some two feet high, modelled by Alfred Gilbert, with the inscription on the curve:

Honour to Irving.
Through the Love of His Comrades.
I ring through the Ages.

Of these and other memorable productions of the play accounts have been given by journalists and biographers. I can contribute only the reminiscences of a performance in a provincial theatre in my youthful days. Yet these may, perhaps, in their own modest way, have a distinctive interest. It was my good fortune later to live in London through the period when the fortunes and fame of the Lyceum Company were at their highest. I saw Irving then in many of his most notable parts, among them Shylock, Macbeth, Benedick, The Vicar of Wakefield, Mephistopheles, and they remain treasured memories. But none is so sharply outlined and unique as that of Mathias on the stage of the old Theatre Royal, Belfast.

It was with *The Bells* that Irving's career as an actor in its highest phase had begun. In a sense it was with *The Bells* that it ended. During his last provincial tour in the autumn of 1905 he announced a week's programme at Bradford which was to close with *The Bells* on 14 October. Owing to his increasing feebleness he yielded to the solicitations of his company and consented to substitute a less exacting part than that of Mathias on the Saturday. But he was not destined to see that day. On the previous evening, after performing Becket, he went back to his hotel to receive the summons of 'the fell sergeant' who was 'swift in his arrest,' or to use words older than those so often spoken by Henry Irving when Hamlet lay dying, and to close with the sound of bells other than those that tortured Mathias :

> 'For though the day be never so long,
> At last the bell ringeth to evensong.'

FREDERICK S. BOAS.

The Bells—apart from the first act which was heartbreaking —was a piffling melodrama. I would rather see the old man in it than any ten of to-day's young men playing Œdipus, Lear, and the entire classic repertory. In my considered view great acting in this country died with Irving, and I haven't seen smell or sight or hearing or feel or taste of it since.

If our young playgoers saw Irving they would burst like electric-light bulbs.

If you saw Irving you don't need to be told what he was like. If you did not, what's the good? The age has its Robert Taylors and Jessie Mathewses. Why tamper with fragrance? Why cloud the dewy present with immortal dust? It lives, we remember, and the young generation doesn't care.

JAMES AGATE.

IV

IRVING as JEREMY DIDDLER

Lyceum Theatre, 30th of March, 1872 :—

RAISING THE WIND

WRITTEN BY JAMES KENNEY

Jeremy Diddler	MR. HENRY IRVING
Fainwould	MR. ODELL
Plainway	MR. GASTON MURRAY
Sam	MR. F. W. IRISH
Richard	MR. BRANSCOMBE
Waiter	MR. TAPPING
John	MR. RIVERS
Miss Durable	MRS. F. B. EGAN
Peggy	MISS LAFONTAINE

SCENE I. *The Public Room in an Inn.* SCENE II: *The outside of Plainway's House.* SCENE III: *A Room in Plainway's House.*

WHY Irving should have given us this delightful old Farce[1] is at first sight not quite clear. He had recently scored a triumph as Jingle, to whom Jeremy is a very near relative, nearer certainly than a cousin; why essay another of the kin?

The truth is that though James Albery's version of *Pickwick* had been pruned and revised, its four acts reduced to three, its title changed to *Jingle*, and new characters added from the novel by the practised hand of E. L. Blanchard, it was still far from satisfactory and was now to be laid on the shelf till 1887, when it was revived in yet another new form. Jeremy, then, may be said to have deputised for Jingle.

But it is not to be supposed that Irving was content to reproduce as Jeremy his successful performance of Jingle; in his hands Jeremy Diddler was a new creation and a vastly amusing one. Nothing but his extraordinarily ingratiating manner would ever have reconciled you to the idea that the scamp could be tolerated in any decent society, yet such was his charm, his address, his smiling confidence, and that beneficent air of conferring a favour while he picked your pocket, that you welcomed his approach and regretted his departure. The

[1] First produced at Covent Garden in 1803 with 'Gentleman' Smith (the original Charles Surface) as Jeremy Diddler.

critical way in which he inspected your waistcoat—his own was buttoned to the throat to disguise the absence of a shirt—his bland manner in throwing open your coat and smoothing its lapels that he might survey that waistcoat of yours to better advantage and all this done with such a kindly and critical solicitude that you felt he was conferring a favour, was captivating, ingratiating, fascinating. It sounds ridiculous, and ridiculous in fact it was, though not so ridiculous as it sounds, for it was instinct with humour of a kind as inexplicable as irresistible. There are no jokes so funny as those that won't bear explanation.

Irving had had a long apprenticeship to farce acting and the invention of inconsequential humour on which so many farces depend. It was a significant stroke of fortune that his first professional instruction was by William Hoskins, the light comedian of Phelps' Sadler's Wells Company, famed for his Mercutio, Lucio, and kindred parts. Then, too, Irving's early association with Toole, his friendship with Charles Mathews, all no doubt helped to develop the genial and humorous aspects of his temperament.

His career was full of coincidences; his first professional appearance at Sunderland, in *Richelieu*, foreshadowed 'Colonel' Bateman's premonition, when he heard him recite Hood's poem of *Eugene Aram* and he saw him as Digby Grant, that here was a Richelieu. The next night he appeared as the Second Officer in *The Lady of Lyons* and Claude Melnotte became his earliest ambition. During that first week in Sunderland, Tom Mead played Shylock; Sam Johnson was the low comedian of the company. Thus an association that was to last many years was foreshadowed.

Irving remained at Sunderland five months. In February 1857 he went to Edinburgh, where for two and a half years he worked with an indefatigable ardour unequalled by any star that ever shone. It is significant that again his opening part was Gaston d'Orleans, with that ominous line, 'Here's to our enterprise.' The Richelieu was Barry Sullivan. In September 1859 he realized his ambition to play Claude Melnotte. It was for his benefit and final performance in Edinburgh. He had now played four hundred and twenty-eight parts, probably more than any other star actor has ever played in his whole career.

On 24 September he made his first appearance on the London stage at the Princess's Theatre in *Ivy Hall*, an adaptation by John Oxenford (critic of *The Daily Telegraph*) of Octave Feuillet's *Roman d'un Jeun Homme Pauvre*. The play did not succeed.

Irving was dissatisfied with his insignificant part and terminated his contract with Augustus Harris, the manager.

It was now, on 19 December, that he gave his reading of *The Lady of Lyons* at Crosby Hall which won him such flattering criticism—especially from *The Daily Telegraph.*

In March 1860 came an episode that probably did more to mould Irving's character than anything he had yet encountered. He was engaged by the Brothers Webb, joint managers of the Queen's Theatre, Dublin, well known for their performances as the two Dromios. To the Othello of T. C. King, on his opening night, he played Cassio and to not one word he spoke would the audience listen. They cat-called, they jeered, they hooted, and to this barrage of savagery he presented an impassive front. For three weeks this hostility continued, but the victim remained unmoved and immovable.

This was not criticism, but an expression of resentment against the management who had dismissed a favourite actor named George Vincent, engaging Irving in his place. At last the management took a hand and an extra force of police was drafted into the gallery, who soon succeeded in quelling the disturbance. Simultaneously, an appeal from the stage for fair play turned the tide and for the last week of his month's engagement the fickle Galleryites did their best to make amends. But there is no doubt that 'gruelling' added an element to Irving's character that was to serve him in the future, when attacks even more savage—because more intelligent—were to be made upon him. But such was the effect of that Dublin episode that, as Bram Stoker tells us, twenty-five years were to pass before he could bear to refer to the subject.

From Dublin he passed to Glasgow and Greenock, and thence to an engagement that was to prove momentous in his career at the Theatre Royal, Manchester. Irving joined the company in Manchester at the same time as Miss Henrietta Hodson, who became the wife of Henry Labouchere, subsequently his manager at the Queen's in Long Acre. John Knowles was the manager of the Theatre Royal, and Charles Calvert stage manager, and Irving owed much to Calvert and his wife, who became his very sincere friends. Irving's salary was three pounds a week, of which he scrupulously sent thirty shillings to his father. As he worked only for about thirty-five weeks in the year it is no exaggeration to say that he existed in a perpetual state of impecuniosity. He told a story that has been so often repeated that it may seem idle to set it down again, but it is so characteristic of the times and the state of the profession in those ardent 'sixties', ardent, I mean, in their devotion to the Drama, that I make no apology for telling it once more. A member of the company, one Joseph Robins, who had had a haberdashery business in London, sold it to go on the stage, but like a wise man he had taken the precaution to stock an ample chest with wares from his shop and had brought it with him to Manchester. On Christmas Day he invited Irving to dine at his lodging. Irving arrived in a pitiable condition; he was thinly clad, wearing the lightest summer underclothing, and shivering with the intense cold. Robins received him genially and looking at his watch, saying: "Nearly dinner-time; no doubt you'd like a wash," ushered him into a bedroom where a bright fire was burning, and on a chair before it a suit of stout woollen underclothing airing. Not without some hesitation, and having manœuvred strategically for the door, the host delivered his exit speech: "Those things on the chair, old man, I think you'd better put 'em on. It's deuced cold, even for the time of year, you know"—and vanished. Irving was not ashamed to tell us that he wept.

During his first season he was given few opportunities though he played some thirty parts. It was not until the next season, 1861, that he began to attract the attention of the local Press. His Dombey in a Dickens adaptation with the American comedians, Mr. and Mrs. W. T. Florence, appears to have been his first real hit, an achievement for a man of his years—he was only twenty-three. The similarity of Mr. Chevenix in *Uncle Dick's Darling*, which H. J. Byron wrote for Toole, to Dombey, accounts for the success he afterwards made in that part.

Other visiting stars whom he supported in the season were Gustavus Vaughan Brooke, whom G. H. Lewes called 'The Boanerges of the Stage,' and Edwin Booth to whom he played Laertes, Cassio, Banquo, and some others. Opportunity came, too, of repeating his favourite Claude Melnotte for the benefit of a fellow-actor.

At a banquet given in his honour in Manchester in 1881 he referred to the uphill task he had had at that time. 'I found it a difficult thing to make my way at all with the audience; and I believe the audience, to a certain extent, was right. I think I was too raw, too unacceptable.' But in the end he won not only their esteem, but their affection and, greatly daring, for his benefit on 20 June 1864 he attempted the part of Hamlet for the first time.

Meanwhile, in the beginning of the same year he had

attracted the attention of Dion Boucicault by his performance of Hardress Cregan in *The Colleen Bawn;* this was to have a fortunate result.

During a vacation, when some members of the company appeared at the Theatre Royal, Oxford, Irving played Henry Neville's celebrated part of Bob Brierley in Tom Taylor's *The Ticket of Leave Man,* Claude Melnotte and Hamlet again, also Macduff.

On returning to Manchester he played Jim Dalton, 'the Tiger,' in support of Henry Neville himself as Bob Brierley and another of Henry Neville's celebrated parts, Maurice Warner in *Camilla's Husband* by Watts Phillips, author of *The Dead Heart.* Jim Dalton no doubt foreshadowed his success later, at the Queen's, as Bill Sikes and even Dubosc. Maurice Warner might also be considered the forerunner of Romeo and Edgar of Ravenswood.

The next milestone in this amazing career of hard work was also a vacational adventure. About this time a pair of swindlers, calling themselves the Davenport Brothers, had created a considerable stir with their spiritualistic *séances;* and the ever gullible public, or a considerable portion of it, was completely taken in by their 'manifestations' and 'phenomena.' So successful were they, and so confident, that in an unfortunate hour (for them) some sane person having challenged their *bona fides,* they offered a hundred pounds to whomever could perform their feats. The reward was attractive, and three young actors of the Theatre Royal Company determined to compete for it. Accordingly, Philip Day, and that sprightly comedian, Fred Maccabe, afterwards celebrated for his single-handed entertainment, 'Begone Dull Care,' having carefully studied the Davenports' method and detected their trickery, took the Liberty Hall of the Manchester Athenæum and on 25 February 1865 proceeded to give their demonstration. They invited five hundred representative citizens and Henry Irving acted as spokesman and introducer. After a speech explaining exactly what they proposed to do, Irving made up, *coram populo,* with wig and beard, cravat and tightly buttoned surtout, and gave a burlesque impersonation of the Doctor Fergusson who had acted as introducer—or as we might say to-day, *compère,*—to the celebrated Brothers. Irving's success was instantaneous; he had the audience in fits of laughter by the mock seriousness of his address, and as his colleagues were equally successful in their imitation of the feats of the fraudulent mediums, which were nothing more than very neat conjuring tricks, the exposure was complete. It is not recorded that they got the hundred pounds.

The entertainment was repeated a week later in the Assembly Rooms of the Free Trade Hall and the place was besieged by the public. It had created a *furor*. So emphatic was this success that the management of the Theatre Royal endeavoured to persuade Irving to repeat it at their theatre. This Irving declined to do; it did not seem to him an entertainment fitting the dignity of the theatre, nor of his work there. This meant inevitably the termination of his engagement.

His last part at the Theatre Royal, Manchester, was Robert Macaire. He joined his old friend, Charles Calvert, now the prosperous manager of the New Prince's Theatre in the same City, where he was presenting his long and still remembered run of Shakespearean revivals. With him, Irving played Claudio in *Much Ado About Nothing*, Edmund in *King Lear*, and de Nemours in *Louis the Eleventh*.

This closed the season, and Irving bade a temporary farewell to Manchester after a benefit at the Free Trade Hall on 12 April 1865, at which the Davenport exposure was repeated. The performance concluded with *Raising the Wind*, in which he appeared as Jeremy Diddler, a part with which even at that early date his name had become associated. And that reminds me to look up what Walter Herries Pollock said: '. . . his Jingle from first to last was a most vivacious performance, but, to my thinking, not to be compared with his Jeremy Diddler in *Raising the Wind*. Possibly he felt a lesser freedom in dealing with a character created by Dickens than he did when dashing through the irresponsible humours of a part sketched with boisterous spirit by Kenney.'

From Manchester he passed to Edinburgh again, where he played Macaire once more; then to Bury, where he repeated Hamlet.

After playing Iago and Macduff in Oxford he travelled to Birmingham, where he played Laertes to Fechter's Hamlet.

His next engagement of any importance was in Liverpool, where he supported his old friends, Charles Mathews and E. A. Sothern. Then to Newcastle-upon-Tyne, where he again supported Toole as John Perrybingle and Brown in *The Spitalfields Weaver*.

It was now, and not until now, that Irving enjoyed his first stroke of good fortune, after ten years of incessant struggle, privation, and often starvation, for though he had been working almost continuously his salaries had been very small and his father had still to be supported.[1] On 30 July 1866 Dion Boucicault produced his drama, *The Two Lives of Mary Leigh*, at the Prince's Theatre, Manchester, and remembering Irving's success as Hardress Cregan, engaged him for the part of Rawdon Scudamore. Irving was wise enough—and by now confident enough—to stipulate that if the new play should succeed and be brought to London, he should play the part he was now to create, a part described by *The Manchester Guardian* as 'a thorough rogue.' Of this more anon. Suffice it to say that his success brought him offers from Charles Reade and Tom Taylor as well as confirmation by Boucicault of an engagement for London as Rawdon Scudamore.

Before leaving Manchester, once more he played the Ghost in *Hamlet*, his old part of Bob Brierley and the wily Fouché in Tom Taylor's *Plot and Passion*.

Irving had now played 588 parts, when he was engaged to support Miss Herbert, the manager of the St. James's Theatre, London, and also to stage manage. He was engaged specifically to play Rawdon Scudamore and expected that to be his first part, but there was still delay. However, there was compensation in his pronounced success as Doricourt on the first night of the season, 6 October 1866.

The title of Boucicault's play was changed to *Hunted Down*. It was produced on 5 November 1866, and ran for three months, at that time a very long run indeed. Irving's success was immediate and decisive.

Writing to Bram Stoker on 24 May 1906, Sir Henry Dickens told him that his father, Charles Dickens, seeing Irving's performance exclaimed: "Mark my words, that young man has a great future before him."

George Henry Lewes, the essayist and critic, visiting the theatre with George Eliot remarked: "In twenty years he'll be at the head of the English stage." To which George Eliot replied: "He is there, I think, already."

But there was much opposition yet to be faced and twelve more years of hard work before he was recognized in that position.

A VICTORIAN PLAYGOER.

[1] Samuel Brodribb died 20 June 1876. He lived to see his son become famous as an actor, but not long enough to know that he also won fame as a manager.

IRVING *as* *CHARLES I*

FROM A DRAWING BY SIR BERNARD PARTRIDGE

V

IRVING as CHARLES I

Lyceum Theatre, 28th of September, 1872 :—

CHARLES THE FIRST

WRITTEN BY W. G. WILLS

Charles I	MR. HENRY IRVING
Oliver Cromwell	MR. GEORGE BELMORE
Marquis of Huntley	MR. ADDISON
Lord Moray	MR. EDGAR
Ireton	MR. MARKBY
Pages	MISSES E. MAYNE AND J. HENRI
Princess Elizabeth	MISS WILLA BROWN
Prince James	MISS ALLCROFT
Prince Henry	MISS WELCH
Lady Eleanor Davys	MISS G. PAUNCEFORT
Queen Henrietta Maria	MISS ISABEL BATEMAN

ACT I. *Gardens at Hampton Court.* ACT II. *The King's Cabinet at Whitehall.* ACT III. *The Scottish Camp at Newark.* ACT IV. *Whitehall, at Daybreak.*

DIFFIDENCE must surely assail a normal person summoned to describe or analyse his reactions to abnormal genius. All art is *poiesis*, an experienced but not easily defined activity of the soul. For it implies articulate expression of feeling in terms of Beauty, itself an abstract quality which has largely eluded æsthetic philosophers from Aristotle to Professor Alexander. It is not primarily intellectual at all, though intellect will be implicit in its form and content. How, then, shall a man communicate his experience of any art who is not himself an artist? His poor attempt can only be an obvious *quantum valeat* postulating credentials, therefore, if his effort is to interest anyone but himself. Let me proffer these.

Irving, when I was born, was a man of forty and almost at the zenith of a prodigious fame, won after an apprenticeship of toil, trial, and error inconceivable in our softer days. He died, aged only sixty-seven years, when I was still on the pleasanter side of thirty. It is clear, therefore, that my experience of his amazing power was all too short. Fortunately, thanks to a remarkable mother, it was not delayed. To her the higher Drama seemed as important as 'the three R's,' so that, with her,

I had seen Herman Vezin as Macbeth before I was well out of the nursery. On my seventh birthday her gift was a copiously illustrated and still cherished *Shakespeare*, my birthday 'treat' being a week's orgy of Irving in a repertoire of plays, including *The Merchant of Venice*, at the provincial playhouse nearest to my childhood's home. It was then, as I now realize, that life began for me. Before my fifteenth year, I had seen most of the famed actors of that time and in more plays than my father had witnessed during the whole of his long, active, but more archæological life. If a fairly intelligent and imaginative child begins early enough it is surprising how percipient and critical he may become by the time he is the seasoned Londoner (and father himself) that I was before Irving's death in 1905.

By then I had seen this great actor scores of times and in most (though not quite all) of the plays produced by him since that far-away seventh birthday. Many of them I must have witnessed twenty times or more, and none of them on less than five or six occasions.

Thus my credentials consist simply in having made such use of my time and opportunities as to have had more visual experience of his powers than better men double my age could then usually claim. Needless to say, I had also read and studied all available literature concerned with the many plays in which he had appeared before my pupillage began, including, alas, his Hamlet, admittedly the greatest in all the splendid annals of our stage. Incidentally, it should be remembered that Irving had played no less than 428 parts before London had seen him at all—a record approached by no other English actor, the mighty Kean not excepted.

After this requisite preamble, let me say the little that I feel at all qualified to utter about a particular play—*Charles the First*—chosen not because it was my favourite in Irving's long repertoire, but because, while it aroused political controversies of an irrelevant kind, it exhibited Irving in one of the most beautiful and tender of his original 'creations,' using this word, of course, in its accepted theatrical sense. For, as Rodin reminded us, 'God alone creates; the artist reveals,' which no doubt is true, though I am also sure that God is Himself revealed more obviously by the artist than by the saint, if only for the reason that art communicates much that sanctity perforce conceals.

Naturally the play was Royalist. Indeed, its main weakness lay in a loading of the dice too heavily against England's first and (let us hope) last Dictator, so that an ideological conflict, which might have been intensely dramatic, was but little emphasized. The struggle was between anointed King and rugged fanatic, Stuart culture and dour, tyrannic Puritanism, rather than between contrasted political theories.

As Charles I the actor's *diablerie* and sardonic humour, his rascalities, venoms, vengeances, even his priestly and intellectual austerities were completely laid aside. Here, as with Dr. Primrose, Lesurques, and the final scenes of *Becket*, Irving was, as it were, irradiated. He seemed as one to whom some mystical experience of unearthly things had been vouchsafed.

How this effect was produced I cannot say. Mere technique, vitally important though it is, cannot work miracles. They are wrought from within. But the force of personality, which is a part of genius, can make them externally visible. Irving's smile, for instance, as all the world knows, was a most beautiful and revealing grace in itself. Nevertheless, a more practised pen than mine would be needed to describe the Stuart charm, pervading all that dynasty, with which Irving, by sheer concentration, so invested the grandson of Mary Queen of Scots that she seemed, even more than Henrietta Maria, to provide the clue to all that 'labyrinth of sorrow' of which her doomed descendant was so conscious at the end. Ellen Terry (as Henrietta) was so moved in certain scenes that, forgetting her art, she often wept unrestrainedly, without power even to control and *use* such weakness to good purpose, as Irving had done when similarly affected by her own Desdemona. The play abounded in great 'moments' greatly seized, yet seized with such simplicity and truth that the tears which they compelled were as unforced as they were inevitable. That this pale, 'Vandyck' King should be the same man whom we had seen but a few nights earlier as the bestial Dubosc, the decrepit Corporal Brewster, or the crafty spider-king, Louis XI, seemed quite incredible. The fact is that Irving's effects, as James Agate has observed, were 'magical,' and magic in artists, as in wizards, is hard to define.

Will anyone who was there forget the tensity of that scene outside the Queen's tent on Newark field when Charles reproaches the friend who had betrayed him? I cannot believe it. Yet how little the author's text conveys of what we saw and heard and felt at the time these words were spoken. Let me risk quotation, however, for the sake of those for whom the martyr king's last word 'REMEMBER,' was a whispered injunction which they have neither power nor inclination to ignore.

KING (*to Cromwell*). Sir, I can understand—one moment yet.
(*To Moray.*) Charles Moray ! I had meant to go in silence ;
But pain o'ermasters me and I must speak. Come nearer.
(*Moray approaches with downcast head, and gradually sinks on his knee during the speech.*)
I saw a picture once by a great master,
'Twas an old man's head.
Narrow and evil was its wrinkled front—
Eyes close and cunning ; a dull vulpine smile.
'Twas called a Judas ! Wide that painter erred.
Judas had eyes like thine, of candid blue ;
His skin was smooth, his hair of youthful gold ;
Upon his brow shone the white stamp of truth ;
And lips like thine did give the traitor kiss !
The King, my father, loved thine—and at his death
He gave me solemn charge to cherish thee,
And I have kept it to my injury.
It is a score of years since then, my lord,
Hast waited all this time to pay me thus ?
(*Charles turns to Cromwell.*)
Sir, you demand my sword, I yield it you.

Or again, in an earlier scene with Cromwell, when an (unfulfilled) promise of intellectual conflict seems imminent, we may recall the smouldering fires of lifelong conviction and a deadly incisiveness in Irving's delivery of the passage beginning :

' The people's rights, Sir, are indeed divine ;
Not so the wrong of rebels.

. . . . .

Hast thou no reverence for the marble pile
Of England's past ? O Sir, 'tis such as thou
Deface the fairest Monuments of history,
Inscribing with coarse sacrilege their names
On its most sacred tablets ; scarring beauty
That it took centuries to make, and but an hour to mar . . .'

For brevity's sake I have resisted a strong temptation to mark the significant pauses, gestures, and emphasis employed by Irving in these short excerpts which gave them a personal intensity quite independent of a mediocre author's text. Yet surely no actor, no audience, even in these days of celluloid, can fail to guess at the imaginative possibilities attaching to such moments when handled by the greatest actor within living memory.

It may be that ' fustian ' is the word which our more anæmic æsthetes would now apply to these dramas of Irving's day. Well, this is a personal commentary on his art as actor, not a defence of Bulwer Lytton, W. G. Wills, Sardou, and Conan Doyle; not even of Tennyson and Shakespeare, so conspicuously favoured by Irving who had little stomach for the sociologies of Ibsen and Shaw, whose works gave small scope for tragic power and those sweeps of passion for which his commanding personality was the perfect medium. Hence it is here enough to say of such plays as *The Bells*, *The Lyon's Mail*, and *Waterloo*, that this man of genius, whose god was Shakespeare, lifted them clean out of their hybrid forms into realms of symbolic, imaginative grandeur, and endowed them, for the time being, with those cathartic qualities of pity and terror which constitute the essence of the highest drama. That was the miracle wrought by Henry Irving. Edmund Kean wrought it too, perhaps, but had fewer chances than his successor and far less catholicity of experience. Small wonder, then, that Irving was at once the hero and unquestioned head of his calling. Small wonder that, thirty-three years after his death in harness, books are still written, exhibitions held, and tributes paid to his memory by members of the profession he loved, served, and adorned for half a century.

I had hoped to write intelligently concerning him in at least one play, but have failed, as all must fail who essay such a task. Perhaps it is not possible to describe the almost mystical effects of great art upon the soul. What are words until a poet uses them, and what are plays till set in motion by great acting? W. G. Wills is forgotten and his plays are all unread, but memories of Irving in *Olivia*, *Eugene Aram*, *Faust*, and *Charles I* remain and are a part of theatrical history. Happy indeed were we who, within the space of a few weeks, could see the Kendals, Hare, Wyndham, Tree, Bernard Beere, Compton, and the Tearles, each in a round of plays, and—HENRY IRVING.

R. N. GREEN-ARMYTAGE.

When words are inadequate to give expression to a deep feeling of reverence for one of the most hallowed remembrances of a lifetime, the picture must remain incomplete.

To try and describe the most perfect performance of Sir Henry Irving's life—so perfect that to those who loved the martyred Stuart it must have seemed a reincarnation of Charles himself—is an almost impossible task. Only those who were on the stage with him had the opportunity of realizing the incredible insight of the artistic beauty, gentleness, and resignation of this hapless monarch. This was not Henry Irving, it was the King himself. Sir Henry Irving had the extraordinary capacity, unequalled by any other actor, for bringing to this performance a spiritual beauty at the approach of death. This quality was in his Hamlet and his Becket, but most of all in Charles, a quality which I have only seen in Sarah Bernhardt as Joan of Arc when on her way to the stake. This was not a *woman*, it was a spirit, which one felt had passed beyond the agony of fire.

At the last revival of *Charles the First* during an American tour and for one performance at the Lyceum, I was the King's Page, and it was then that I realized the greatness of my master, and the poignant agony of the last days of martyrdom of Charles.

I remember that in the Tent Scene, when all was lost, and the King in the hands of Cromwell resigns his sword, I endured the awe and tearing sorrow that Christ's Disciples must have felt for their Master's agony at Calvary. *I was in the presence of a King!* As his Page my duty was to hand him a goblet of water, and in taking it from me he placed his hand upon my shoulder and our eyes met. For that second I looked into the eyes of one purged of all earthly feeling whom suffering could touch no more. The memory of that look is my most precious possession and the touch of his hand the greatest moment I have ever experienced on the stage. Even with his doom already sealed and with life ebbing hour by hour, this King could spare a thought for the Page who was serving him for the last time. As I have said, this scene was in a tent after his last betrayal, and was moving beyond words.

Miss Ellen Terry as the Queen was especially beautiful in this scene, and when she spoke the lines : 'I am not Queen but Wife, I go with him,' my grief was so overwhelming that I, too, could not follow ; I turned my back and broke into a very agony of sobs.

As the curtain came down, Miss Terry whispered, 'You had better run off,' but my master stretched out a restraining hand, and with a smile of incredible beauty said, 'No, let him stay on ! You see, he was my Page ! '

N. MARTIN-HARVEY.

VI

IRVING as EUGENE ARAM

Lyceum Theatre, 19th of April, 1873 :—

EUGENE ARAM

WRITTEN BY W. G. WILLS

Eugene Aram	MR. HENRY IRVING
Parson Meadows	MR. W. H. STEPHENS
Richard Houseman	MR. E. F. EDGAR
Jowell	MR. F. W. IRISH
Joey	MISS WILLA BROWN
Ruth Meadows	MISS ISABEL BATEMAN

ACT I. *The Vicar's Garden.* ACT II. *The Home Room of the Parsonage.* ACT III. *The Churchyard in the grey light of Dawn.*

MY playgoing started as early as 1865 at the old Theatre Royal, Gravesend (built in 1808 and still standing as Salvation Army Barracks). The Lupino Family were the annual stars, during the season, at the Bijou Theatre, Rosherville, close by, and I was constantly there also to see the Comic Ballets and Burlesques.

With the exception of being taken up to London to see the Pantomimes at Drury Lane and Covent Garden (where the Paynes were my great heroes), my next recollection of the drama is at the old Theatre Royal in Rochester where I was at school.

An interesting reminiscence of that time is constantly meeting Charles Dickens, he was a friend of the second master of the King's School, with whom I boarded, and he often came and talked to us boys, and on several occasions I went with school-fellows to two o'clock dinner with him at his house at Gad's Hill. That old theatre at Rochester is also still standing in use as a club, practically rebuilt except the outer walls. It was opened on 24 May 1791 and was built by Mrs. Baker, in my opinion the most interesting individual who ever existed in the world of the theatre (1740 to 1815). There is a splendid epitaph on her tomb in the graveyard of Rochester Cathedral. Charles Dickens refers to her in his *Life of Grimaldi.* And T. Dibden (the younger), who was with her as stock author, actor, and scene painter for several years, frequently refers to this truly remarkable woman in his books.

My family moved to London in 1870 and from that time, during my holidays, all my pocket-money was spent in the theatre. I went to the pits in the West End and also to all the outlying theatres—Pavilion, Britannia, Standard, Greenwich, Deptford, Surrey, Grecian,[1] Marylebone, and Albion. I certainly saw *every* pantomime in and around London for many consecutive years. My companion was usually a stage-struck groom in my father's employ.

I never had any personal knowledge of Henry Irving. I saw him in *Dearer than Life* at the Queen's Theatre in Long Acre, in *Two Roses* at the Vaudeville, and in every part he played at the Lyceum, failures as well as successes.

All my life I have been interested in the Theatre as an institution. My early manhood was spent in a prosaic family business. In October 1897 I came into theatrical affairs by building the Royal County Theatre, Kingston-on-Thames. Previously to that I knew no one connected with the theatre personally and I did not wish to do so. I was simply interested in the theatre as the theatre and not in any individuals. H. A. Saintsbury was the leading man on the first night of my professional management. I recollect that, as such, he kept up the dignity of the profession by coming down from London in a high hat and frock coat, and made me feel quite ashamed of the tweeds and caps in which I have habitually lived. Henry Irving was almost the only contemporary star who did not come to Kingston, the theatre was not large enough to attract him when he went to the Borough, Stratford, the Metropole, Camberwell, and other suburban theatres.

I went with Lewis Waller to the reception they gave him at Bath when he was playing at the Theatre Royal there, shortly before his death. It was a bitterly cold day and he stood with his hat off making a speech on the doorstep of a house where he had unveiled a plaque. I think he caught cold and probably hastened his end. I remember an episode.

As the big wigs took him into the Abbey on their way to the Town Hall a typical Bath spinster offered him a bunch of violets, curtsied, and said: " Sir Henry, will you please accept these flowers?" Irving took one blossom out of the bunch and put it in his button-hole and made the old lady quite happy

[1] Then known as the Alfred. *The Bells* was first produced here.

by saying: "Madam, I shall treasure *this flower* immensely." Gerald Lawrence (who was then Irving's leading man) can tell much more about that day than I can. I remember I sat opposite to him at lunch.

I distinctly remember being at the Lyceum on the first night of *Eugene Aram*. In those far-away days I don't think Henry Irving's name meant much to me, until I saw him in *Charles the First*. His performance in this play certainly left an impression on my mind and is most likely the reason why I went to see *Eugene Aram*, which I believe was his next character. I was anxious to see him act it as I had been taken (probably much against my will) to some hall, by a maiden aunt, to hear Irving recite Tom Hood's poem, and I had also seen *Eugene Aram* as a crude melodrama at one of the many country theatres that I had visited.

Did Irving's performance of the unfortunate schoolmaster leave any lasting impression on me? I tax my memory and I seem to recollect that it made me realize I was seeing an entirely new style of villain.

In the provincial theatres and the minor theatres of London the villain was invariably a very heavy person indeed with prominent black eyebrows, unshaven chin, a heavy moustache, and a deep, sepulchral voice. In Irving's performance of Eugene Aram I saw something of an entirely different type.

In Act I he was a mild, ascetic person making love to the parson's daughter in the most approved manner of the juvenile gent. In Act II—a parlour in the Vicarage—when his partner in crime came on the scene to blackmail him, he changed into a deranged, excitable man who lost his head. He had a long scene, played alone, in which he was harrowed by a guilty conscience. He looked into a mirror and exclaimed: 'Is this my face! My own face that I see before me!' or something of that sort, at which the pittites laughed heartily until the 'hushes' from the stalls and circle subdued their exuberance.

My recollection of Act III is that it was unduly long. The repentant sinner, in the arms of his lady love, was sitting on a grave in the churchyard until he departed this life, I suppose, of a broken heart. I do not remember him as appearing to be anything but in robust health in the previous act when he had a very rough-and-tumble row with his co-villain, who I recollect was an excellent actor named E. F. Edgar, who, I am told, was the grandfather of Edgar Wallace.

Eugene Aram certainly died peacefully in the arms of Ruth, the aforesaid parson's daughter (played, I think, by Miss

Bateman), murmuring something about her eyes being his 'final glimpse of Heaven.' This dying scene seemed to me to be inordinately long, but undoubtedly the author wrote it to give big emotional chances to the two leading players.

I seem to remember that my boyish impression of the play was endless talk devoid of interest and that my companion slept.

For *Eugene Aram* there must have been a boy's choir 'off,' because at the end of Act I the curtain came down with the singing of a hymn, with the lovers sitting hand in hand, and when the repentant villain died at the end of Act III the boys started singing 'off' again for the final curtain.

The play over, both Irving and Miss Bateman had tremendous receptions, and Irving made a speech of thanks and apologized for the absence of the author, W. G. Wills, who had also written the great success *Charles the First* which had preceded this play. A gentleman in dress clothes then came on and bowed. I suppose it was Mr. H. L. Bateman, the manager, as *Eugene Aram* was produced there previous to Henry Irving taking control of the theatre. Obviously *Eugene Aram* was not one of the great Lyceum successes, as I remember going there again, during my next holidays, to see *Charles the First* which had been revived.

Now I must confess that not only at the Lyceum but at the many other theatres I went to as a boy it was the production, the scenery, and the ensemble that concerned me very much more than the individual performers. I knew the names of all the scene painters and followed their work with greater interest than I did that of the actors. Hawes Craven had painted two magnificent sets for *Eugene Aram*. I remember the Vicarage Garden of Act I as one of the finest scenes I had ever seen, even at the Lyceum. The death scene of Act III was in a churchyard. In the centre a magnificent yew tree with the church seen through the branches on the left and with a distant view of the village on the right.

I do not think a schoolboy's criticism of an actor can be of much value, especially when he was very much more interested in the work of the scenic artist than he was in the performance of the leading man. I cannot do better than quote Dutton Cook's opinion in the defunct *Pall Mall Gazette*: 'The actor's self-abandonment to the passion of the situation and his powerful display of anguish are histrionic achievements of real note.'

I have referred to Hawes Craven. There were many other

admirable artists at that period. When one remembers their exquisite, scholarly, and artistic work, one deplores the fact that the beautiful art of the scene painter has been allowed to decay in favour of crude impressionist atrocities with flowers and foliage like starfish and octopi that constitute the 'decors' (what a horrible word!) of so many present-day productions.

PETER DAVEY.

It is nothing to say *Eugene Aram* is a success. This is a cold and cruel compliment to author and actor. It is wearisome and commonplace to start at once and talk of calls, and the delight of an audience, and showers of bouquets and fixed attention, and the shouts for the author, and the appearance of Mr. Bateman, the manager, and the usual signs of a successful first night. All these things have been done before. They may mean very much, or they may mean nothing at all. What we wish emphatically to point out, and at once, is this: *Eugene Aram* is no ordinary play. The acting of Mr. Irving is no ordinary acting. The verdict on this exceptionally artistic night will not be pronounced by those who consider the play very terrible, or by those who nod an assent to Mr. Irving's acting, and still say it is all very terrible, or by those who compliment Mr. Wills, and thrust in an aside as, 'Ah! yes, but it is all very terrible.' We believe fully and honestly the audience meant what it said last night. We believe all in the theatre were struck, amazed, and delighted.

But if they did not mean this, and went home saying exactly the contrary to what they expressed, *Eugene Aram* as a play, and as an artistic study, will still be judged and pronounced upon by the whole art-world of London. Whether it is liked or disliked, it will attract to the Lyceum all who have any sympathy with, or appreciation for, art. Whether it is hated or praised, it will do infinite good to the stage. Whether it is terrible or not, it will declare emphatically we have an artist among us who did last night a thing, whether it is pleasing or displeasing, which is a distinct honour to the English stage, and a crushing death blow to the assertion that we have no actors amongst us, that acting is a lost art, and that the stage is kept up only for the amusement of the idle, the frivolous, the uneducated, and the contemptible. Let those who will have every play made good in the end, and who would banish tragedy from the boards, avoid the Lyceum and *Eugene Aram*.

Let those who believe the theory of Mr. Boucicault, that an English audience must have a goody-goody termination to their amusement, steer clear of the new play. Let those who will not treat the drama as an intellectual study, and persist in viewing it as an after-dinner entertainment, take their stalls for another house. Let those who, in spite of contrary proof, bleat out the old platitudes about the degradation of the drama, the absence of life, heart, and soul in certain dramatic quarters, kindly stay away, for they are only impeding the progress of an onward, proud, and most praiseworthy movement.

But in all charity, let those who have some kindly feeling towards English dramatic art, in spite of innumerable difficulties, remain behind and see *Eugene Aram*. Let them linger awhile, and note carefully the performance of Mr. Irving. It is not, perhaps, a play that will please the multitude. It is no *ad captandum* succession of surprises, situations, and trial scenes. Eugene Aram is not tried for his life. We have no barristers and courts, and judges and docks. We have no 'forensic eloquence' with Mr. So-and-So in a wig and gown. We have no ghastly gibbet with Eugene Aram hanging in chains on Knaresborough Heath. There is little for the posters, but much, very much, for the imagination. We have here photographed the mind of Eugene Aram, the mind of a man who has murdered another fourteen years ago, the mind of a wretch who has hoped to live down conscience, and the mind of a poor devil who is flung once more amongst roses and love, and just as he is smelling the flower it falls to pieces in his hand.

The play contains three scenes in the after-life of an undetected murderer. In the first, haunted with dismal recollection, he still clings to life and hope. In the second, brought face to face with an accomplice, he still struggles to brave all with a desperate love of life, and the as desperate exercise of an iron will. In the last, cowed and stung with the sight of his victim's skull, he confesses his crime to his destined bride, and dies in her arms before justice seizes him for the scaffold. This is briefly and incompletely the study of Mr. Wills, perfected in so masterly a manner by Mr. Henry Irving. We suppose most of us are familiar with the story of Eugene Aram, the murderer, stripped altogether of its romance. Eugene Aram, in complicity with one Houseman, for the sake of vulgar plunder, brained a rascal called Daniel Clark, hid his body in a cave near Knaresborough, in Yorkshire, and fourteen years afterwards, when acting as an usher at a school in Lynn, Norfolk, was arrested for the deed. Houseman, like a base knave, turned King's evidence against his friend. Aram, after a masterly and scholarly defence, attempted to show that Clark had been intimate with his wife, but he was convicted, and, after attempting suicide, was hanged.

The first act is purely idyllic and contemplative. It shows us Aram's present life, and allows us a glance at his past career, and closes when an evening anthem is heard in the old village church, and Ruth, the Vicar's daughter, is folded in her loved Aram's arms. The story has commenced well, is replete with charm.

The second act is dramatic, for here Aram meets his old accomplice, Houseman, who has come to dig in the cave, and therefrom to extract some treasure which will frighten Aram into giving hush-money. All is peace at first in the old vicarage. The Vicar and Aram are playing at chess, and Ruth coquettishly offers to read the testimonial given to the schoolmaster by the villagers, when, at the mention of his past blameless life, Aram hurries out of the room. He is just in time, for, at that instant, enters Houseman, at the invitation of the Vicar. At the name of Aram, he starts, declares himself an old acquaintance, and foolishly attempts to poison Ruth against her lover, by a hint at some former mistress. The poor girl trembles at the blow, and the clouds darken more and more. The meeting of Aram and Houseman is, of course, the dramatic scene of the play, and the audience is prepared for it when Aram, closing the door behind his departing bride, says:

> 'Now nerve of iron and a brain of ice—
> Or in the closing of the door,
> I close the door of Heaven.'

It is a splendid battle between these desperate men, and the acting here is almost as good as any in the play. Houseman is a bully, and destitute of sentiment. Aram is in a white heat of passion. But Aram has his way. His arguments to Houseman are unanswerable, his threats are terrible. He is unabashed by the presence of the Vicar, and threatens his antagonist with vengeance before the magistrate. But suddenly there is a commotion without, and the whole situation changes. The villagers have been tracking the brutal stranger, and, digging in St. Robert's Cave, they have discovered the skeleton of Daniel Clark. They have found the knife of the murdered man, marked with his name. The old gardener recognizes in Houseman the companion of Clark, but Houseman, in fiendish desperation, in the full assembly, denounces Aram as the murderer:

> ''Tis false! I will not stand here as a guilty man—
> The murderer of Daniel Clark *stands there!*'

From this instant, the whole tone of Aram's demeanour changes, and from being a white-hot, passionate man, he is a hang-dog, beaten, defeated fellow. This is a splendid change on the part of the actor, and, if we mistake not, will be accepted as a triumph of Mr. Irving's acting in this most difficult scene. It was so sudden and complete, it electrified the audience, and the play was deservedly stopped for the applause. Left alone with his conscience, once more he gives himself up to a soliloquy, with which Mr. Irving brings down the curtain, after such acting, as surprised as much as it delighted. It made, deservedly, a deep impression on the audience.

The third act will provoke much controversy. It is, in reality, one tremendous soliloquy, and the excellence of Mr. Irving's acting is at once pronounced with the statement that it held the audience almost from the commencement. Aram is discovered by Ruth, half dying, and, having confessed, dies in her arms, as the sun rises upon the peaceful village.

That the actor could get such variety out of such an unrelieved scene is marvellous. It is all on his shoulders, but again and again the interest revives. The confession was listened to with the deepest attention, and the oncoming death, now at the tomb, now writhing against the tree, and now prostrate upon the turf, brings into play an amount of study which is little less than astonishing, and an amount of power for which credit would have been given to Mr. Irving by few who have seen his finest performances.

Such a performance will, of course, form the subject of many a future essay, analytical, detailed, critical, and, we trust, in some measure, worthy of so elaborate, sustained, and in most respects, masterly a study.

We have only, in conclusion, the welcome task of congratulating the coming season on a certain attraction. In many quarters we anticipate there will be adverse criticisms. It will be said the play is horrible beyond endurance, and many will, unfortunately, miss the pleasure of Mr. Irving's acting, for fear of shuddering more than ever over *The Bells*, or weeping more than ever over *Charles the First*. The three plays have literally nothing in common. *Eugene Aram* is no paraphrase of *The Bells*, and no hint of Mathias is given in Mr. Irving's performance.

EUGENE ARAM

Mr. Wills has executed a difficult task in our humble opinion remarkably well, and Mr. Irving's successful career has never shown such a stride as this in the right direction. The task of the play is herculean for any actor; and once more Mr. Irving has triumphed.

CLEMENT SCOTT.

VII

IRVING as CARDINAL RICHELIEU

Lyceum Theatre, 27th of September, 1873 :—

RICHELIEU

WRITTEN BY BULWER LYTTON

Cardinal Richelieu	MR. HENRY IRVING
Louis XIII	MR. JOHN CLAYTON
Gaston	MR. BEAUMONT
Baradas	MR. H. FORRESTER
De Mauprat	MR. J. B. Howard
De Beringhen	MR. F. CHARLES
Joseph	MR. JOHN CARTER
Huguet	MR. E. F. EDGAR
François	MR. H. B. CONWAY
De Claremont	MR. A. TAPPING
Captain of the Guard	MR. HARWOOD
First Secretary	MR. W. L. BRANSCOMBE
Second Secretary	MR. HENRY
Third Secretary	MR. COLLETT
Marion de Lorme	MISS LE THIÈRE
Julie de Mortemar	MISS ISABEL BATEMAN

ACT I, SCENE 1. *Salon in the House of Marion de Lorme ;* SCENE 2. *Richelieu's Cabinet in Palais Cardinal.* ACT II, SCENE 1. *Apartment in Mauprat's New House ;* SCENE 2. *Richelieu's Apartment, as before.* ACT III. *Richelieu's Apartment at Ruelle—a Gothic Chamber.* ACT IV. *Gardens in the Louvre.* ACT V. *The King's Closet at the Louvre.*

MORE than fifty years have come and gone since I first saw *Richelieu.* It was from a seat in the pit at the Adelphi Theatre, where I had gone with a fellow-student, who, like myself, was receiving instruction at the School of Dramatic Art in Argyle Street—where the Palladium now stands—from such able tutors as Mrs. Dallas Glyn, Mrs. Chippendale, and Horace Wigan, with a view to becoming actors.

The play of *Richelieu* was a favourite with us both and we were perfectly familiar with every scene, as it was constantly being rehearsed at the School, and Mrs. Dallas Glyn, who had supported Phelps in many of his productions at Sadler's Wells, did her utmost to reproduce that actor's mannerisms both of voice and gesture in whoever was fortunate enough to be allowed the part of the crafty Cardinal. But rehearsing it was one thing, seeing it acted was another. Why didn't Irving do it at the Lyceum? We knew enough of stage history to know that he *had* played it there in 1873. Why didn't he revive it? We were, of course, both ardent Irvingites. Sincere in our attachment to the stage, we liked drama that was clean and wholesome; plays in which the hero and heroine had at least some of the virtues and not *all* the vices, and we liked to see those plays well acted and mounted; that's why we went to the Lyceum. At that theatre a conscientious regard for correct detail was expected; even if you did not *know* you *felt* that the dresses, scenes, appointments, in fact everything there was *right*.

My friend had not been, as I had, a playgoer since about the age of eight years, so that he could not draw comparisons between Shakespearean productions seen at the Lyceum and some I had witnessed under F. B. Chatterton's management at Drury Lane. It seemed to me that at the Lane they needed only an excuse for a procession and they gave it to you. If the play had a martial atmosphere, like *Henry the Fifth* or *Macbeth*, you saw no show but shining armour. Charles Kean had, of course, done this before Chatterton but with a stricter regard for archæological accuracy, yet from a perusal of his programmes and the designs that were prepared for the plays he presented at the Princess's, he seems to have been addicted not only to processions but ballets whenever he could find an excuse for them.

Now Irving never overdid things; he knew exactly what *not* to do as well as *what* to do, and did them both judiciously. Of fourteen plays that were produced by Kean, nine were revived by Irving, and an old playgoer who had seen both was emphatic that they were done better at the Lyceum in every way. We were anxious to verify this, so applied to Horace Wigan, whose brother Alfred had been a member of Charles Kean's Company. Wigan was himself an excellent producer, a judge of acting, and had a long memory. He had seen Macready and did not care for him. Edmund Kean he could recall as Richard III in Cibber's adaptation, and particularly remembered a bit of business of Kean's at the murder of Henry VI by Gloster: at the line 'See how my sword weeps for the poor King's death,' Kean, as he stood sardonically contemplating the body of the dead monarch, suddenly raised his left arm and in doing so displayed the crimson lining of his cloak. This reflected the light from the floats back to his bright sword, which, being slightly twisted, gave the impression of blood running down the blade; letting the cloak fall, the blood vanished. It was a startling effect and sent a thrill through the house. Kean, Wigan told us, was full of such artifices and knew how and when and where to introduce them. Rather like Irving, we thought.

As Horace Wigan's brother Alfred—he would for ever talk of Alfred—had supported Charles Kean, we could not of course expect him to admit that Irving's productions were superior to those at the Princess's; 'as good, perhaps,' he said, 'but not better.' However, he had unstinted praise for the way crowds were handled at the Lyceum. 'Any fool,' he used to say, 'can get a crowd on to the stage. To get them off effectively is the problem. At the Lyceum they appear to have solved it.'

About this time it was announced that Edwin Booth, the American actor, was to appear at the Adelphi Theatre as Richelieu. We were there to give him a welcome. We saw him three times; we considered him great. Certainly the mounting of the play was tawdry and cheap, but Booth we voted fine. That was *acting* and no mistake; could Irving do better? We wondered why he didn't revive it. Unlike many of the critics, we thought this play a fine one. I think so still. It appeals strongly to the player who is a good actor and to the playgoer who can appreciate good acting. The Cardinal is a part that should only be attempted by an actor who has a thoroughly sound technique, for it will put to the test all the histrionic ability he may possess. It is indeed a Star's part. The supporting parts are also well characterised and the verse is fluent and effective in recital. Many passages, if not beautiful, suggest beauty.

I was to learn much from this play. Within twelve months of seeing Booth, I, as a member of the Torquay Stock Company, was cast for the part of Huguet in support of the tragedian T. C. King as the Cardinal. He was not good. He was far too robust and assertively masterful. He shone in such parts as Ingomar and William in *Black Eyed Susan*, but as Richelieu he was too heavy. Remembering Mrs. Dallas Glyn's instruction, it was obvious that his performance was modelled on that of Phelps, who, as Wigan had told me, copied Macready, who had created it. T. C. King and Barry Sullivan were possibly the last exponents of the old school of tragedy to which Phelps and Macready belonged. It was a school that practised a grandiloquent style, a school, as Vandenhoff says in his *Actor's Note Book*, that 'excelled in executive power and certainty of effect rather than in imagination, individualization of character or poetic feeling.' Now it was these qualities that made Irving different from the other actors of his day. I realized that when I saw him play Richelieu in 1892.

Naturally, the performances of Booth and King occupied my thoughts while I was waiting for the curtain to rise. I remembered the shabby stock scenery and crude accessories, so different from that perfection of detail to which we had grown used at the Lyceum. I had studied the period, so that when the curtain rose on the conspirators carousing in the house of Marion de Lorne it was with a critical eye that I surveyed the picture. It reflected the careless extravagance of the period; there was nothing assertive, nothing to distract attention from the business of the scene and the characters of Baradas and de Mauprat. The scene changes to a room in the Palais Cardinal—and it *was* a room in the Palais Cardinal! The entrance of Richelieu was the cue for much clapping of hands and shouts of encouragement for a favourite actor; my applause was for the player who realized so vividly the full-length portrait by Champaigne of Cardinal Richelieu which hangs in our National Gallery. It was an engraving of this picture that Irving gave to Booth and from which the American actor no doubt amended his make-up. But he never realized the original as Irving did. The Lyceum Chief might himself have sat for the portrait. The clean-cut and delicate features; the white hair, contrasting sharply with the dark moustache and pointed beard; the suggestion at once of power and irritability in the thin and compressed lips; that was said of Richelieu, it could also have been said of Irving as Richelieu.

I can see him now, warming his hands—hands with long supple fingers—over a fire, the flickering flames of which would at times give a momentary glow to his pale ascetic features. I call to mind the way he spoke of his enemies; he seemed to show no spite towards them, but sarcastic, pitying contempt. His ward, Julie, entered and the scene he had with her—as in all their scenes together—was played with such gentleness that we were convinced he spoke the truth. When he told Joseph he had promised her dying father that he himself would be a father to her, it was so sincere, so full of protective tenderness; all of which Julie seemed to take with her when she left him, for it was a very different Richelieu that turned to interview de Mauprat, who, as the girl went from the room, was brought into the Cardinal's presence.

Irving, who had a most expressive face, seemed to adopt a

different one for every character he met in this play. His bearing towards them also was different. I have never seen an actor who could be so effectively *still* as Irving could, and he assumed the most picturesque attitudes without the least affectation; they were at all times easy, natural, and appropriate. A scene from the play will exemplify this and illustrate how thoroughly he had studied the character. Before de Mauprat's entrance, the Cardinal has instructed Huguet to secrete himself behind a screen and to watch de Mauprat's bearing; should it be violent he was not to hesitate to use the carbine he carried. De Mauprat enters and during his scene with Richelieu resents being called trickster and thief and advances threateningly on His Eminence. Huguet at once appears and levels his carbine. Now, King turned in his chair and with his right hand seized the barrel of the carbine and held it at arm's length above his head while he declaimed: 'Not quite so quick, friend Huguet. Messire de Mauprat is a patient man and he can wait.' Stagey! Not at all good!

Booth picked up a pen—*the* pen 'that is mightier than the sword,' and with it deflected the barrel which was pointed at de Mauprat, across the table, towards the audience.

Still stagey! But better.

Irving never moved. He knew—the Cardinal Richelieu knew by de Mauprat's surprised start—that the Chevalier was covered by the spy, and as he noted and admired the young man's bearing he spoke the lines in that slow, dry way that was peculiar to him. The still figure was in striking contrast to the other who supplied the action. Irving not only thought himself—he was the cause of thought in others.

The speech that brings this act to a close was recited by Booth and declaimed by King. By Irving it was felt, and his patriotic fervour vibrated through the theatre and roused us to enthusiasm.

The difference in the method of the three actors was as strongly marked in the well-known passages with the sword in Act II. Booth's effort you regarded as a fine piece of acting and applauded as such. King, you felt, was fooling you, for King could not be weak, he always looked and always was strong. But to watch Irving trying to wield that weapon aroused your sympathy; it was obvious to anyone that he had not the strength and you were relieved when he gave up the attempt.

Again, the Cardinal's attitude towards the boy, François, as portrayed by the three actors, was in all cases most marked.

In the scene where the boy hastens to the Cardinal—*without the packet*—Booth austerely reproved him; King soundly rated him; Irving was as much concerned for the poor lad's feelings as for his failure.

The famous 'Curse of Rome' speech King thundered in his most impressive tones and finished the Act with too much fight left in him. Booth was given to rant this speech and he was certainly overacting when the scene closed. Irving delivered it with a respectful intensity as though he knew the dire effect that dreaded threat must have on those who opposed him. His portrayal of Richelieu's physical suffering and moral agony at the close of the Act were natural and convincing. The last Act was for the spectators a triumph both for the Cardinal and the Actor. The curtain fell on a memorable performance.

Irving's was a magnetic personality. I never left the theatre after seeing him play a part but I found myself thinking of it —and continuing to think of it. I thought of the Cardinal from his first entrance to the fall of the curtain. I thought of the play. I sometimes think of it still; but to recall Richelieu as played by either Booth or King is to tax my memory. Irving as the Cardinal I still remember vividly. Why? Because King declaimed him; Booth acted him; but Irving lived him.

I have always considered it to be his greatest impersonation. Those who never saw it missed a rare memory. I once heard an old actor friend declare that if it were possible to see Irving act once again the part he would choose to see him play would be Richelieu.

It is indeed a part that suited the great actor's distinctive powers; he presented a character study that from first to last held and interested the playgoer and satisfied the historian.

I never look at Champaign's portrait of Richelieu, a copy of which hangs in my study, but I think of Irving's performance of the great Cardinal.

H. HALLADAY-HOPE.

VIII

IRVING as PHILIP

Lyceum Theatre, 7th of February, 1874 :—

PHILIP

WRITTEN BY HAMILTON AIDË

Count Philip de Miraflore	MR. HENRY IRVING
Count Juan de Miraflore	MR. JOHN CLAYTON
Count de Flamarens	MR. H. B. CONWAY
Baron de Beauport	MR. F. CHARLES
Saint Aignan	MR. BRENNEND
Monsieur de Brimont	MR. BEAUMONT
Thibault	MR. JOHN CARTER
Count Kitchakoff	MR. HARWOOD
Count de Charente	MR. BRANSCOMBE
Marquis de Lallemont	MR. COLLETT
Monsieur Virey	MR. TAPPING
Servant	MR. A. LENEPVEN
Madame de Privoisin	MISS VIRGINIA FRANCIS
Countess de Miraflore	MISS G. PAUNCEFORT
Louise	MISS ST. ANGE
Inez	MISS J. HENRI
Marie	MISS ISABEL BATEMAN

ACT I. *Exterior of Ancient Moorish Castle in Andalusia. Parapet overlooking the Guadalquiver.* ACT II. *Salon of Madame de Privoisin in Paris.* ACT III. *Exterior of Château de St. Leon in Brittany.* ACT IV. *The Boudoir and Oratory of Madame de St. Leon.*

'ON the banks of the Guadalquiver.' How well I remember handsome John Clayton singing that—and Irving glowering as he listened. In fact I'm afraid poor Mr. Irving had to do a lot of glowering in this play. After *Charles the First*, *Richelieu*, and *Eugene Aram*, it seemed a play without much distinction, and I think was chosen rather to give Mr. Bateman's daughters, Isabel and Virginia, opportunities that so far they had not had. It was the only really modern society play, of the kind that became popular later at the Haymarket, that we ever saw at the Lyceum, and it gave Isabel Bateman a very fine emotional chance. She had had less than three years of leading parts at the Lyceum and only small experience previously in the provinces with her sister, Kate Bateman's (Mrs. Crowe) Company. And there was an amusing light part of a young French Countess for her sister, Virginia 'Francis.' Mr. Bateman took the theatre two and a half years earlier to make his pretty daughter a star, but the failure of *Fanchette* interfered; then came the stop-gap —the most wonderful stop-gap, I suppose, in all theatrical history: *The Bells*, and everything was changed. But now that the theatre was firmly established the opportunity came. Isabel had a part that was not overshadowed as all she had done had been up to this time.

But though the acting chances were effective, the story wasn't very attractive. Irving as Philip had a violent scene of jealousy with his brother Juan (John Clayton) over Marie (Isabel Bateman) and shot him, and thought he had murdered him. The public were by now so used to seeing Mr. Irving as a murderer—except in *Charles the First*—that I believe they were quite disappointed that he hadn't killed him. Anyhow, we were not supposed to know that yet.

Then years passed before Act II and the scene changed to Paris, and this was rather a disappointment, because we thought it was to be a Spanish play. In my album I have a charming water-colour by my friend Miss Corder of the first very beautiful scene in Andalusia, showing Isabel and the two brothers who were rivals for her love, Mr. Clayton very jovial with his guitar and Mr. Irving glowering, and we all knew how he could glower—his eyes seemed to smoulder!

Mr. Irving's remorse for the death—in this case of a man he hadn't killed—was very fine acting, but we had come to know him by now and we were not frightened as we had been in the last act of *Eugene Aram*.

We met him at the house of Mr. Archer, R.A., and my sisters and I were enthusiastic about *Charles the First*. I hadn't had the courage to see *The Bells*, for I had heard that the scene of mesmerism and the dream and trial were too terrifying. He asked me if I had seen it when we met at Mr. Archer's and I told him this and remember his smiling and saying: "You need not be frightened now that you've met me." I felt at ease with him from the first and we chatted together, and from that moment began the friendship that lasted till his death between him and my family, and all through my married life, for he and my dear husband became very great friends.

But to return to *Philip*. Irving was very fine in those scenes of love and remorse; he was at his best when he had to portray very strong passions—they gave him his biggest opportunities as well as his greatest difficulties, and I think he loved difficulties for the joy of overcoming them. Then Philip and Marie got married and went to live in his château in the South of France. The last act was a scene taken from Balzac. Juan, of course, was not dead after all and he returned in disguise and made love to Marie again. She was glad he was alive and wanted to be friends, and Philip grew suspicious and, at last, became certain that his wife was deceiving him, though of course she wasn't. Then Marie hid Juan in her oratory and Philip, guessing he was there, ordered the masons to wall up the doorway. This was a great thrill—or rather it wasn't, because it was never carried out. This scene, I came to realize as I got to know the theatre better, must always be a very dangerous one. It is either too horrible, so that the audience's mind revolts from it and remembers that it is 'only acting,' and then the illusion is all gone, or else if the walling-up is done—and it wasn't in this play—it seems, somehow, rather ridiculous. Anyhow, it seemed not to be convincing, in spite of being very finely acted. However, *Philip* did not run very long and then our beloved *Charles the First* was revived.

One day when Irving was driving down Piccadilly with us in a four-wheeler we told him we were getting up the last act of *Charles the First*. Could anything be more preposterous? But he, being a great lover of young people, listened attentively to all our plans and asked: "How about the costumes? Who is making them?" I, very proudly, said: "I have a real black velvet dress for Henrietta Maria, it belongs to my mother; the other costumes will be made at home of sateen by our artistic sister, Charlotte Dusa." He showed great interest at once and said: "Who does the King?" "Dusa, the sister who makes the costumes and the scenery." Princess Elizabeth and Prince Henry were to be played by my younger sisters, Vivie and Nina. Anyone less great than Irving would have pooh-poohed the arrogance of four girls daring to try to imitate a Lyceum production, but he said: "About the costumes, remember one thing—you will want a very high collar for Charles I, and it must stand up all round and not fall down! Cut the material twice the width of the collar, cut a piece of cardboard the right depth of the collar, and fold over the extra piece of material." This was done by Dusa and the collar never got out of place. He drew us out about our great undertaking and we assured him it was only to be performed before our father and mother and one or two members of the family and the servants, but he said: "I must come and see it. Mind you let me know when it is to be." And sure enough, when the day came—a Sunday afternoon—the great actor came with it. We were all in a state of nervousness, but after the curtain was drawn and the first few words spoken we felt quite at ease, for there was Irving, his long legs stretched out before him, listening to every word and showing that he was enjoying the performance. At the close of the act, when Big Ben was tolling the death of Charles I, Queen Henrietta Maria in tears, the children with backs to the audience looking out of the window 'at horses and soldiers, a bonny sight'—their father's words—Charles leaves the stage, holding up a pendant and looking at his wife says, 'Remember!' and the curtain falls. The audiences at the Lyceum, night after night, dissolved into tears, no one trying to dissemble either their feelings or their handkerchiefs. Our stage curtain had fallen, but in a moment Irving drew it aside, jumped on the stage, and said: "Where's the book?" He corrected one or two words, praised our rendering of the play, and said we had very well followed the Lyceum production. He did smile over our deep-voiced Cromwell (our younger brother, Emile, who hated acting as much as we loved it, but a good-natured boy) and then he added with a twinkle in his eye: "I should do away with the bell!" and he was right, for two saucepans clapped together were a poor substitute for Big Ben! Then he said: "You must do it again for Isabel." But we found it much more difficult to play before her than Irving; there was something so attractive, so drawing one towards him, so much of his sympathy going out to us that we forgot our nervousness because of his sweet nature and kindly help to young people.

Another instance of his love of youth—long after. I had been a happy married woman many years then. I was taking Pip, one of my younger boys, to Bournemouth for his first preparatory school; Irving was staying there and invited me and Pip to lunch. He captivated the schoolboy as he did all who came in contact with him. About two months later my husband and I were at a Lyceum first night, and at the reception on the stage afterwards in a crowd of admirers, artists, diplomats, Press people, scientists, and other society people, Irving left the group of which he was the centre to come to me and ask: "How does the little fellow like his school?" That 'little fellow's' brother, now a Vice-Admiral and a Knight, was allowed to stand in the wings at the Lyceum whenever he was home on leave.

On a certain occasion in 1875 we had asked Henry Irving to come to Cadogan Gardens to meet a few friends; he was always sure of a great welcome from young and old. With the utmost simplicity he asked my mother if she thought we would like to hear him recite Hood's poem, *The Dream of Eugene Aram*. We were astounded at his kind offer. He gave us the most wonderful performance of Eugene Aram telling an innocent schoolboy how he had followed and killed a man to get his gold, and when he sees the horror depicted on the boy's face he says, with a sad smile: 'Remember, gentle lad, this is nothing but a dream,' and goes on to tell how the murder was committed:

> 'Two sudden blows with a ragged stick
> And one with a heavy stone;
> One hurried gash with a hasty knife
> And then the deed was done.
> There was nothing lying at my feet
> But lifeless flesh and bone.
> Nothing but lifeless flesh and bone
> That could not do me ill,
> And yet I feared it all the more
> For lying there so still.
> There was a manhood in his look
> That murder could not kill.'

Anyone who ever heard Irving recite this weird and thrilling Dream can never forget how kindly and gently he spoke to the small boy when he saw the child's horror at the description of the murder, and in the most terrifying manner the schoolmaster's despair and remorse at the ghastly deed of which he had been guilty. He made you actually see the corpse of the murdered man—as though you were hypnotized. And the end:

> 'Two stern-faced men set out from Lynn
> Through the cold and heavy mist
> And Eugene Aram walked between
> With gyves upon his wrist.'

With no scenery to help, just sitting on a chair, he brought before his audience the murderer trying to get rid of the body by throwing it in the stream—'the depth was so extreme'; then next day he finds 'the river-bed was dry,' then he buries the corpse in a lonesome wood with heaps of leaves; when he next visits the haunted spot a mighty wind has swept the leaves away. All these scenes Irving brought before our eyes so intensely, so vividly, that to this day I can picture them. The interest gradually awakened, then the horror, the dread, the fear, and finally the relief that Eugene Aram was at last safe in the hands of the Law. I heard Irving recite *The Dream of Eugene Aram* many times in public, but the thrill of that first occasion, when he did it in my old home in Cadogan Gardens, is a memory I shall always carry with me.

MARIE DICKENS.

IX

IRVING as HAMLET

Lyceum Theatre, 31st of October, 1874 :—

HAMLET

WRITTEN BY WILLIAM SHAKESPEARE

Hamlet	MR. HENRY IRVING
King	MR. THOMAS SWINBOURNE
Polonius	MR. CHIPPENDALE
Laertes	MR. E. LEATHES
Horatio	MR. G. NEVILLE
Ghost	MR. THOMAS MEAD
Osric	MR. H. B. CONWAY
Rosencrantz	MR. WEBBER
Guildenstern	MR. BEAUMONT
Marcellus	MR. F. CLEMENTS
Bernardo	MR. TAPPING
Francisco	MR. HARWOOD
1st Actor	MR. BEVERIDGE
2nd Actor	MR. NORMAN
Priest	MR. COLLETT
Messenger	MR. BRANSCOMBE
1st Gravedigger	MR. COMPTON
2nd Gravedigger	MR. CHAPMAN
Gertrude	MISS G. PAUNCEFORT
Player Queen	MISS HAMPDEN
Ophelia	MISS ISABEL BATEMAN

ACT I, SCENE 1. *Elsinore. A Platform before the Castle ;* SCENE 2. *A Room of State in the Castle ;* SCENE 3. *A Room in Polonius's House ;* SCENE 4. *The Platform ;* SCENE 5. *A more remote part.* ACT II, Scene 1. *A Room in Polonius's House ;* SCENE 2. *A Room of State in the Castle ;* SCENE 3. *Another Room in the same.* ACT III, SCENE 1. *The same ;* SCENE 2. *A Room in the Castle ;* SCENE 3. *Another room in the same.* ACT IV, SCENE 1. *A Room in the Castle.* ACT V, SCENE 1. *A Churchyard ;* SCENE 2. *Outside the Castle ;* SCENE 3. *A Hall in the Castle.*

WHEN I was a young man—some five and fifty years ago—the Lyceum Theatre meant for me, and a thousand like me, the centre of metropolitan culture and the supreme artistic privilege within our power to enjoy. Other play-houses we also patronized, but the Lyceum when Irving reigned was different—the difference between a cathedral and all lesser places of worship. Upon a first night I seldom failed to join a patient throng in that covered alley-way leading from the Strand to the Lyceum pit door where, packed shoulder to shoulder, the faithful congregated with good will in somewhat strenuous physical conditions. Nor has half a century failed to dim the personal recollection of a rebuff once inflicted upon me—by no fellow-creature, but my own nervous system under stress. After certain hours, without a midday meal and within ten paltry minutes of the opening moment, I fainted, only to return to consciousness, too late, in a public-house near at hand, whither kindly souls must have conveyed me. So I did not see the first night of *Romeo and Juliet*.

When one thinks of Henry Irving, his profound intellectuality comes always uppermost. Intellect is not the watchword and sign-manual of the actor's profession, and few there have ever been among them who could claim it; but Irving was an embodied brain of the most subtle and radical clarity. His eyes alone proclaimed what homed behind them, and it was impossible for a face so steeped in the radiant quality of mind ever to escape that penetrating significance under any make-up. Consider his voice also. I have heard Salvini, Forbes-Robertson, Booth, the American, and many another famed for resonance and mellow purity of diction and intonation; but they were as singing birds to the bodeful and pregnant ring of intellect in Irving's staccato, raven croak. Elocution, after all, is the art of making your words and meaning absolutely clear, and he never failed to do that.

Yet the consciousness of such acute intelligence marred one's ideals sometimes. When, for example, I did see his Romeo, I knew that this was never the headstrong, hot-blooded, handsome boy that Shakespeare meant. This stern and adult man, with that voice and those eyes, would never have made a hopeless mess of his young life for love. It was impossible to suppose that he stood before us young and green, just as it was absurd to imagine that his Juliet still went in awe of her nurse. I never saw such a mature Romeo and Juliet before—or since.

Above all he was a master of irony, since that belonged intrinsically to his own character and is a product of pure intellect. It follows that to me such impersonations were the grandest. No Hamlet that ever I saw came within measurable distance of him.

At this distance of time one cannot regain all the thoughts inspired by his Hamlet, but certain impressions for ever persist,

IRVING *as* HAMLET

FROM A DRAWING BY CARAN D'ACHE
(Reproduced by kind permission of the Green Room Club)

accentuated by later experiences of other actors in the same part. I remember its amazing consistency in portrayal of those inconsistencies of which Hamlet is composed—a note maintained with steadfast perfection ; but the undying picture for me is that of great intellect hovering nearer and nearer to the brink —an intellect conscious of its own abstract grandeur, yet equally conscious of its concrete infirmity when faced with demand for action. Many from whom action was demanded have been similarly stultified by a habit of thought—that fatal disposition to balance one course against another which so often ends in failure to do anything at all. A mind too big to be made up is powerless to accomplish the definite, and accordingly we find men of great promise—in law, or art, or statecraft, or philosophy—come to nothing. They defeat themselves by their own opulence and many-sidedness, fail to reach an option between ' for ' and ' against,' and so remain static when dynamic deeds and decisions are called for. They know only too well meantime that opportunity is slipping away, sinister conditions rising to complicate the issue ; and the effect upon themselves of such dilemmas is swiftly apparent.

Irving's understanding of the psychical torment that resulted from Hamlet's failure to act, I still remember as a most wonderful thing ; for he showed how inward distraction and misery produced outward lapses, in his sardonic contempt for lesser men and his ultimate hatred of himself. From courteous and philosophic indifference to the affairs of the world outside his own little cosmos and the happiness he had planned, events emerge to change him, challenge him, sap his security, confound his vision and cry for those commonplace qualities of leadership and self-assertion that inferior men possess, but he lacks. The strain threatens his mind and he stands before us as a man of rare intellect confronted with just those problems that his supreme order of intelligence is powerless to solve. Hence the threat of madness hovering nearer and nearer, for he knows that his petty shifts are unworthy of him and such knowledge promises to unhinge his mind.

So I remember Irving's Hamlet and that unique and special magic of intuition it possessed. For me, therefore, it will always be the greatest stage impersonation in my memory. Hamlet was a genius, and Irving, being himself a genius, possessed the rare, vital quality to interpret him after a manner probably never before accomplished. He often overpowered one's personal conception of many a classic part, convincing me, against my own private conclusion, that he was right and I was mistaken. Nor could ever one see another actor afterwards to obliterate his reading. Perchance his own humanity and greatness of heart came between him and the realization of some characters. He felt the soul of goodness in things evil, or rather the human, latent possibility hid in the darkest villain, so that his impulse was often to awaken a sympathy opposed alike to the instinct of justice and the purpose of the dramatist. His Shylock was not Shakespeare's, and the intellectual element, combined with self-control and extraordinary dignity, clashed with the brutal facts of the Jew's purpose. You felt that his Shylock could never have experienced the ferine and frantic lust to kill that belongs to the part. He towered over the virtuous pygmies who tricked him and made their triumph cheap, their humour at his expense vulgar.

In other characters also his intense intellectualism negatived the intrinsic villainy of primitive souls; while his Iago, on the other hand, was an obvious villain and lacked the trustworthy bluff and seeming-honest exterior one imagines Othello's ancient to have exhibited to the world. Only in connection with a hearty and straightforward exterior can we get the full flavour of the soliloquies, when Iago lifts the mask at moments of solitude.

Had Irving played the terrible but shadowy abstractions of Greek tragedy and portrayed the plight of mighty agonists under those dooms and dilemmas that dwarf the more humanistic dramas of our own Golden Age, he had probably risen to stupendous heights of spiritual significance; but there was no audience for such art and doubtless the requirements of his public and the need to live denied him many tempting propositions. Apart from Shakespeare he never played in anything big enough to challenge his own powers, for there was no contemporary dramatist to meet him.

I never had the good fortune to see some of Irving's greatest comic parts, but his amazing sense of character must have enriched the humour that he brought to oddities and eccentrics. One creation I did indeed see: his Digby Grant in *Two Roses*—a delightful egotist; and a specially interesting performance, because I believe it was on the strength of it that Mr. Bateman, with prophetic eye, saw in Henry Irving a great Richelieu. In connection with Albery's pleasant comedy one remembers also that it introduced George Alexander to the professional stage.

His Richelieu I did not see, but many judges held it to be

among his highest triumphs. One can imagine him as Milton's Lucifer had that been possible, but the play in which he acted Mephistopheles was a thing of little more than commonplace melodrama.

Henry Irving always challenged and inspired young lovers of his art, awakening active criticism and personal enthusiasm such as no other actor in his time, or since, has aroused. I remember, when the late William Archer published a little book upon him, what waves of indignation troubled our coteries. Archer, who so nobly enriched our Theatre with Ibsen, decried Irving and proclaimed an intensely feminine streak in all that he did—an indictment which we denied and resented. But every great, creative artist is surely man, woman, and child rolled into one, and should he lack either ingredient, so much the worse for him. If there lurked the gentleness of woman in Irving's heart, it never intruded for an instant where no demand existed, and it was not femininity which made him offer a sentimental appeal to the sufferings of the evil-doer, but the deep humanity which feels all and forgives all.

Generous and often tender to a fault, he was yet a stern man in all concerning the conduct of his stage. One mildly wonders what he might have said to professional 'producers,' or answered, had it been suggested that another mind than his would achieve a finer ensemble unweighted by playing the lead. For my part, despite half a century of theatrical evolution, I cannot recall in my theatre-going days any productions or any stage-craft superior to his. None ever cast the great plays better with the material at his command; none sensed the power of his fellow artists more subtly; and none was more swift in recognition of talent, or quicker to reward promise. The tale of those who supported him and learned from him embraces nearly the whole of the last generation of eminent actors and actresses; and though the majority have joined him in the shades, those who delight us still are yet the most accomplished members of their profession and rich in traditions sprung of his greatness.

He brought learning and dignity—a new respect and exalted standards of performance—to the theatre, much enhanced its status in the Victorian world of culture, and left behind him affection, reverence, and great gratitude for all that he had given of ennobling pleasure through his lifetime of genius and devotion.

It is interesting to reflect how exceedingly rare the giants of the theatre have always been. Your lover of music can easily enumerate a hundred composers of utmost distinction; any reader knows a hundred supreme writers; the picture-lover can cite a hundred painters whose names are familiar to us all; but who will furnish a list of a hundred great actors, or mention more than half a dozen in the history of the British stage to be set beside that of Henry Irving?

EDEN PHILLPOTTS.

The first time I saw Henry Irving was at Leicester in 1878, when he was playing *Hamlet* for a week. As my parents were old-fashioned Puritans who regarded the theatre as one of the many avenues to Hell, I used to slip away after dinner every evening of the week, and return late, climbing over the back gate. I remember chiefly the extreme slowness of Irving's delivery in his great soliloquies, but the general impression has remained so fixed that whenever I read *Hamlet* I read it as Irving spoke it, and acted it, though I have seen every performance, except one, in London since. I did not see his Vanderdecken, but I broke every rule of Christ Church, Oxford, in order to see his Shylock about the same year, or perhaps in 1879.

I met Ellen Terry and Gordon Craig fairly often, but Irving only once off the stage. He came into the Savage Club when I was dining there, and his acting was superb, for he acted himself throughout. Next to Sarah he was the greatest actor I have ever seen.

HENRY W. NEVINSON.

X

IRVING as MACBETH

Lyceum Theatre, 18th of September, 1875 :—

MACBETH

WRITTEN BY WILLIAM SHAKESPEARE

Duncan	MR. HUNTLEY
Malcolm	MR. BROOKE
Donalbain	MISS CLAIR
Macbeth	MR. HENRY IRVING
Banquo	MR. FORRESTER
Macduff	MR. SWINBOURNE
Lennox	MR. STUART
Ross	MR. G. NEVILLE
Menteith	MR. MORDAUNT
Caithness	MR. SEYMOUR
Fleance	MISS W. BROWN
Siward	MR. HENRY
Young Siward	MR. SARGENT
Seyton	MR. NORMAN
Doctor	MR. BEAUMONT
Porter	MR. COLLETT
An Attendant	MR. BRANSCOMBE
Murderers	MESSRS. BUTLER AND TAPPING
Apparitions	MISS BROWN MR. HARWOOD MISS K. BROWNE
Lady Macbeth	MISS BATEMAN (MRS. CROWE)
Gentlewoman	MISS MARLBOROUGH
Hecate	MISS PAUNCEFORT
Witches	MR. MEAD MR. ARCHER MRS. HUNTLEY

ACT I, SCENE 1. *A Desert Place;* SCENE 2. *A Heath;* SCENE 3. *Palace at Forres;* SCENE 4. *Macbeth's Castle;* SCENE 5. *Exterior of Macbeth's Castle;* SCENE 6. *Macbeth's Castle.* ACT II, SCENE. *Court of Macbeth's Castle.* ACT III, SCENE 1. *Palace at Forres;* SCENE 2. *Park near the Palace;* SCENE 3. *Palace at Forres.* ACT IV, SCENE 1. *The Pit of Acheron;* SCENE 2. *England: A Lane;* SCENE 3. *Dunsinane: Ante-room in the Castle.* ACT V, SCENE 1. *Country near Dunsinane;* SCENE 2. *Dunsinane: Room in the Castle;* SCENE 3. *Birnam Wood;* SCENE 4. *Dunsinane Castle;* SCENE 5. *Dunsinane Hill;* SCENE 6. *Outer Court of the Castle.*

It was many years ago, during my school holidays, that my father and I were staying with an old college friend of his, an eminent barrister, at Chistlehurst: and one evening after dinner, our host, having recently visited the Lyceum Theatre, regaled us with his imitations of Henry Irving in *Macbeth*. One item selected for our entertainment was the speech 'I have done the deed.' There was a vogue prevalent about that time, I think, for certain folk (including, according to H. J. Hibbert, Sir James Barrie!) to entertain their circles with such parodies of the great actor. How easy it must have been to magnify and burlesque with various forms of walk, utterance, and extravagancies of facial contortion his outstanding and marked peculiarities.

I think that even at that early period I must have harboured some leaning towards the stage, because I remember having been much perturbed by our host's grotesque ravings and posturings and wondered how a great actor could be so belittled, and there remained with me for a long time a certain feeling of grievance and resentment.

Years later, having reached the age of maturity, I had the great happiness of seeing Henry Irving in many of his Lyceum productions: and when I saw *Macbeth* my mind went back to that drawing-room at Chistlehurst and as I heard Irving speak the words 'I have done the deed,' I can recall how relieved and grateful I felt that I was duly gripped and harrowed.

That Irving possessed many and varied mannerisms no one will deny: what actor has not? But these peculiarities of his, traits, call them what you will, were to me an added fascination of his personality, becoming almost embellishments, so that I could hardly have brought myself to spare a single one.

In the early days of his Lyceum reign, Irving had many detractors, notably among them being R. W. Lowe and William Archer, joint authors of that lamentable publication, *The Fashionable Tragedian*. Archer's vitriol became somewhat diluted as the years went by, and later on he developed into one of Irving's admirers, judicially so as he was bound to be, splendid critic as he was. Bernard Shaw has never been held to be over-prodigal in his appreciation of Henry Irving, therefore, it is comforting and intrinsically valuable to find him writing in his *Dramatic Opinions and Essays* of 1907: 'His Macbeth I thought fine and genuine.' There was a pamphlet published in 1875, duly recorded by Lowe, and which I have on my shelves, entitled *Macbeth at the Lyceum by Two Amateurs;* this was not a reply to *The Fashionable Tragedian* (the extravagance of which prevented it from carrying much weight), but preceded it. I believe the anonymity covered the identity of collaborators of some note, as it bears the mark of scholarship and is shrewdly and forcibly written, and it remains to-day a valuable testimony of the contemporary opinion of sixty-three years ago.

I can only recall, of course, the revival of 1888 or perhaps the succeeding one. This play of *Macbeth*, one of the greatest Shakespeare ever wrote, provided Irving with one of the most absorbing, and surely one of the most difficult of problems. In one of his addresses Irving quotes Voltaire as saying of the art of acting: 'The most difficult, the most rare and the most beautiful' and Irving undoubtedly realized this for us in his production of *Macbeth*—'the first occasion,' says Harker, 'on which I have known the piece to prove a box-office success.'

It is common knowledge that Henry Irving took intense pains over all his parts. Amongst other Irving relics in my possession is his copy of Hawkin's *Life of Edmund Kean* in two volumes, bearing his bookplate by Byam Shaw; and in the margins there remain the peculiarly characteristic markings and scorings, undoubtedly Irving's, beside the passages which describe Kean's reactions to the most vital moments in his Shakesperean *rôles*, notably those of Richard, Othello, and Macbeth. Significant indeed!

What treats those Lyceum evenings were! 'Lyceum nights of fond delights.' How well phrased!

I can recall Irving's first appearance at that revival of *Macbeth*. The tall lean figure of this most magnetic actor, armed and helmeted in the scene on the heath, a picture of eerie and beautiful significance, where he encounters the weird sisters; and as I watched that wonderful face and glittering eyes, and heard that haunting voice that was like no other actor's, I became aware in that early period of the play that tragedy was on the way; and undoubtedly it was that consciousness which enabled me to follow so clearly his subsequent reactions.

Duncan's arrival at the castle being greeted by Lady Macbeth:[1] can one ever forget it and Ellen Terry, the incomparable, with her bewitching and sinuous grace with all the *diablerie* that it implied, welcoming the old king at the summit of the slope. It was a scene pregnant with meaning, and could one fail to

[1] The writer is describing his impressions of Irving's performance in the revival of *Macbeth* under his own management, 29 December 1888, when Ellen Terry first appeared as Lady Macbeth.

acclaim the mind that had conceived it: but Irving always gave us superb and helpful settings.

The famous dagger scene was a triumph. The terrible suspense of the long waiting for the bell that was to be the signal for the murder: here Irving brought before us all the physical horrors and the dread prostration that possessed him at the contemplation of what was to follow: it was real and pitifully alive. That and the ensuing scene—'I have done the deed' where he staggered distraught and stricken, down the rough steps of the curved stairway from Duncan's chamber, these are both vivid and painfully memorable to me even now.

The banquet scene, though pictorially splendid, affected me in a less degree; but in the final scene where Macbeth at Dunsinane is confronted with Macduff, 'of all men else I have avoided thee,' was magnificent in its intensity: the tall soldierly figure, in bearing full of dignity and honour, was now transformed; his courage, which had failed him before and after the murder when he was *mentally* assailed, now asserted itself when faced with *bodily* peril. Conscious of doom but manfully resolved to meet it, his hair dishevelled, his features drawn and tense, looking like a gaunt, hungry, famished wolf, Irving was piteous and terrible to behold. What memories it all recalls!

In these few jottings, which is all they are, I have endeavoured, lamely I am aware, to set down some impressions which still remain with me of this great actor, and in surveying them I am conscious of my temerity.

The scope of *Macbeth* is tremendous. When one considers the immensity of the theme, the gigantic conception of its principal character, beset throughout with so many and varied and conflicting passions and emotions while all the time fate is bearing him along involuntarily to its appointed end.

Many there are living so much better qualified than myself to describe the effect that this play wrought upon an audience, yet none more conscious I avow, even after so many years, of the spell of Henry Irving.

Mr. Aria records that Irving when gazing at Clint's study of Edmund Kean as Hamlet remarked 'some fifty years hence some old fool will be saying "there never was an actor like Irving"', and well he prophesied. None of us shall see his like again. When we think of his long and honourable career, 428 parts in his first two and a half years upon the stage, followed by a wealth of illustrious successes and triumphs, until his untimely death on 13 October 1905 at Bradford, as it were 'with harness on his back.' His body was brought back to

London to the house of the Baroness and Mr. Burdett-Coutts in Stratton Street, Piccadilly, and there he lay in state, like a monarch that he was. The public funeral took place as we know in Westminster Abbey, magnificently symbolic of the respect of a nation: and it was hard to realize even through this impressive ceremony that this immense personage had been taken from us.

It can hardly be possible to convey with mere words, to anyone who had never seen Sir Henry Irving, the power of his extraordinary appeal. A grand, distinguished and compelling personality.

O. B. CLARENCE.

XI

IRVING as OTHELLO

Lyceum Theatre, 14th of February, 1876 :—

OTHELLO

WRITTEN BY WILLIAM SHAKESPEARE

Othello	MR. HENRY IRVING
Duke	MR. COLLETT
Brabantio	MR. MEAD
Roderigo	MR. CARTON
Gratiano	MR. HUNTLEY
Lodovico	MR. ARCHER
Cassio	MR. BROOKE
Iago	MR. FORRESTER
Montano	MR. BEAUMONT
Antonio	MR. SARGENT
Julio	MR. TAPPING
Marco	MR. HARWOOD
Paulo	MR. BUTLER
Desdemona	MISS ISABEL BATEMAN
Emilia	MISS BATEMAN (MRS. CROWE)

ACT I, SCENE 1. *A Street in Venice ;* SCENE 2. *Another Street in Venice ;* SCENE 3. *A Council Chamber.* ACT II, SCENE 1. *The Harbour at Cyprus ;* SCENE 2. *A Street in Cyprus ;* SCENE 3. *The Court of Guard.* ACT III, SCENE. *Othello's House.* ACT IV, SCENE 1. *Othello's House ;* SCENE 2. *A Street in Cyprus ;* SCENE 3. *Exterior of Iago's House.* ACT V, SCENE. *A Bedchamber.*

DURING my forty-nine years of theatre-going (1867–1916) I have seen two hundred performances of Shakespeare's thirty-six plays. I exclude, of course, the spurious *Titus Andronicus* which curiosity might have led me to witness had opportunity served. I must premise though that the acting version of *Pericles* was such a burlesque on Shakespeare's drama as to be unworthy of inclusion in my list. Just fifty of these representations were given under the direction of Henry Irving. In witnessing these two hundred performances I have experienced disappointment, some actual pain, keen interest, and much vivid delight, and I have found it quite the exception to leave the theatre without having gained some fresh idea, without some sidelight having been thrown on a character.

My first Shakespeare play was *Much Ado About Nothing,*

produced at the Adelphi Theatre, in August 1867, during Miss Kate Terry's farewell performances there. I was very young, and my recollections are confined to a perfectly natural and delightful Beatrice, and a manly, cheery Benedick—handsome young Harry Neville. Thirty-nine years later, at Ellen Terry's Jubilee Performance, I saw my first Benedick and Beatrice act together as Antonio and Ursula, in the first scene of the second act of the same play : the scene was like a ray of sunshine on a cloudy day, a bright five minutes charged with happy memories during an afternoon of sadness.

All who love our great dramatist must honour Phelps, who in the drama's blackest days kept the flag flying at Sadler's Wells for eighteen long years, and in his farewell speech on 15 March 1862, he claimed during that time to have produced thirty-four of Shakespeare's plays.

It is an extraordinary fact, however, that when Phelps revived *Richard* in 1861 he apostatized and used Cibber's balderdash ! In trying fairly to gauge Phelps's intellectual standing, we cannot ignore this surrender, or the extraordinary point of view which rendered him so indignant when cast for Macduff to Macready's Macbeth, that 'he and his manager were at daggers drawn from that moment,' and 'for the first night or two he did not attempt to act but merely walked through the part ! ' For an intelligent artist to take up such a position as this is to us incomprehensible.

In comedy, Phelps invariably gave me keen pleasure, but in tragedy he followed the old school, and his correct declamation and heroic postures failed to convince and merely wearied; he struck me as a first-rate comedian, but as being without special personal charm, and as not more than a sound, intelligent, well-trained and painstaking tragedian.

At the Princess's I saw performances of *Othello* and *Macbeth*, where Phelps and Creswick were starring. Of these, *Othello* was by far the better performance. In it, Phelps' Iago stood right out as of different rank to all else, the touches of dry humour were quite splendid, and the cold-blooded, deliberate slaughter of Roderigo unforgettable.

I saw Phelps as Wolsey at the Gaiety. He did not strike me as being more than sound and scholarly—nor did I feel otherwise about his Shylock. I wish it had been otherwise, as I never again saw Phelps in Shakespeare—he died on 6 November 1878.

The 3rd April 1875 was a red-letter day, for I then, at Drury Lane, saw Tommaso Salvini as Othello. The tragedy was acted in Italian, and there was nothing worth recording in it so far as the support was concerned. Signora Giavognoli was passable as Desdemona, the Iago of Signor Carboni was the conventional stage villain, but the Othello was in appearance, in carriage and speech, the realization of Shakespeare's Moor. At the opening of the play, he appeared middle-aged, noble, dignified, a leader of men, born to be obeyed. His splendid voice was capable of expressing every emotion without apparent exertion. The address to the Senators was a glorious bit of quiet declamation, and I had not before, and have not since, heard the 'farewell' speech spoken with such profound pathos. The overwhelming depth of his love for Desdemona culminated in the meeting at Cyprus, and the difficulty he experienced in mastering his anger in the scene of Cassio's degradation was finely expressed and led up to his uncontrollable rage in the subsequent scenes with Iago and Desdemona. In the later scenes, the veneer of civilization had disappeared, and he was merely a maddened wild animal completely mastered by frenzied jealousy. Such an exhibition of overwhelming passion had probably not been seen since the days of Edmund Kean, and with all its ferocity you felt the mirror was being held up to Nature, though whether the death scene was not too brutal in its wonderful realism is perhaps open to question. The dagger was driven into the left side of the neck and wrenched across the throat, Othello falling quivering from head to foot with the death agony. Salvini was strong where Irving was weak; he had a superb voice and magnificent physical strength, and his portrayal of Othello was an effort of genius. On 2 July (three nights after the two-hundredth performance of the same play at the Lyceum), I saw his Hamlet, and my disappointment almost balanced the delight I had felt in his Othello. In person, he was as unlike Hamlet as he was like the Moor, and I could find no reason which justified him in attempting the part. The representation was almost dull. Surely here is an example of an actor's limitations. No unprejudiced person will, I think, hesitate in agreeing with me that Salvini's Othello was much finer than Irving's, but while Irving's Hamlet was at least equal to the Italian's Othello, Irving's Othello was infinitely superior both in conception and execution to Salvini's Hamlet.

Then, on 9 March 1876, came Irving's third venture in Shakespeare—*Othello*. It is at first sight difficult to understand why he should have chosen so early in his career a part which had just previously been so superbly acted, for which he was not physically fitted and which would inevitably bring into prominence those foibles which were the delight of his enemies.

Irving, however, never lacked courage, and I think probably he was out of sympathy with the wild beast side of Salvini's Othello, and wished to present the more intellectual, more civilized, Moor—the reading that would naturally appeal to his cultured imagination. The Othello he presented in 1876, though finely conceived and intensely interesting, was full of defects and was but a first study for the finished picture of 1881. His acting of this part could never have been wholly satisfactory. He had not the necessary physical strength, but he succeeded, as ever, in conveying to the thinking portion of his audience his very beautiful conception of the character. Who that saw the performance can ever forget the meeting with Desdemona at Cyprus, or, later in the play, the pathos of the speech commencing: 'Oh! thou weed, who art so lovely fair'?

When Irving played Othello with Booth in 1881, the improvement he showed, as compared to the 1876 performance, was remarkable; his command over his resources had enormously increased. Unfortunately, fine actor as Edwin Booth undoubtedly was, his point of view and Irving's differed, and his performance was the only one not in harmony with the rest of the picture, not in sympathy with the dominating mind. It was as though a splash of crimson had been introduced in a delicate nocturne by Whistler. I would illustrate this by saying that his Iago brought down the final curtain standing over Othello, pointing triumphantly at the dead body and gazing up at the gallery with a malignant smile of satisfied hate.

In her delightful *Story of My Life*, Ellen Terry takes a view of Irving's performance that is enlightening as 'inside information'; to him and to her his performance was a complete failure: 'I think his failure as Othello was one of the unspoken bitternesses of Henry's life. When I say "failure" I am of course judging him by his own standard, and using the word to describe what he was to himself, not what he was to the public.' That reservation is well advanced; there was no sense of failure for me. But listen to this: 'Yet night after night he achieved in the speech to the Senate one of the most superb and beautiful bits of acting of his life. It was *wonderful*. He spoke the speech beaming on Desdemona all the time. The gallantry of the thing is indescribable.' The conclusion is typically Irving: 'On the last night he rolled up the clothes he had worn as the Moor, one by one, carefully laying one garment on top of the other, and then, half humorously and very deliberately, said: "*Never again*." Then he stretched himself with his arms above his head and gave a great sigh of relief.'

I had seen Irving in the previous September unfold his conception of the character of Macbeth. His point of view was original, and naturally the old school and the whole host of his enemies rose up and attempted to destroy him by ridicule. Instead of the generally accepted honest Scotch soldier striving to act justly, but o'erborne to his destruction by a wicked wife and the powers of evil, Irving presented the Macbeth in whose mind the thought of murder had found a place before his first entrance—murder which he rather fears to do than wishes should be undone; a sort of degenerate brother to Hamlet; tormenting himself with reflections—possessed with an abnormal imagination.

On that first night nothing gripped me more than his rendering of the character in the last act, his reading being founded on the lines:

> 'Some say he's mad;
> Others, that lesser hate him, do call it valiant fury.'

The desperate wildness of his despair during those final scenes—his hopelessness whenever he paused to think—was magnificently conceived and conveyed. As was his Hamlet so was his Macbeth, a living, suffering man, and the splendour of the conception and the greater part of the execution made one grieve the more that the work was blemished by mannerisms which in the banqueting scene bordered perilously upon the grotesque. When the play was revived some thirteen years later he had his resources under far better control.

No more bitter controversy was ever waged over a public man than that which raged round Henry Irving during the years following his triumph in *Hamlet*. No taunt was too vindictive, no gibe too unmannered to express the hatred felt for the actor by those who saw him growing assured of his exalted position in spite of their abuse. With the dignity and tact which were part of his nature, Irving took no notice of his assailants, excepting when a statement was printed that he suborned the Press, and again when a breach of good taste was committed so gross as to be unendurable by any man who respected either himself or his art. Irving quietly lived down this abuse, and although to the end plenty of people could understand nothing in his acting but its faults, the old cry that he was merely a mouthing mountebank became a thing of long ago, and those who admired him least as an actor acknowledged his greatness as a man.

As an actor, his strongest characteristics were an extraordinary intellect, marvellous imagination and wonderful personal magnetism, the keenest sense of humour, abnormal insight into, and sympathy with, the human mind, and unique power of conveying to an audience his conception of a character. To those qualities must be added indomitable courage and inexhaustible patience. His face was extraordinarily expressive, with mobile eyebrows and piercing eyes, and he had the most beautiful smile I ever saw. His hands were long and delicately shaped, and his dark hair fine as silk. (A lock of it is before me as I write.) He was gifted with the ability to take infinite pains, and above all, he was never satisfied with doing less than his utmost.

During the one hundred and eighty occasions on which I saw him act, he never once ceased to be the character he was representing.

Critics have said that Irving appealed to the intellect, not to the sympathies; that he spoke to his audience from brain to brain, not from heart to heart. Not from heart to heart? We are all constituted differently, but had those critics ever watched an audience leaving the Lyceum after a performance of *Charles the First?* Did they remember the drawing down of Horatio's head to Hamlet's dying lips, and had they forgotten the look on Mathias' face when his daughter bent over him, exclaiming: 'Dear father, how good you are!' Nothing that I have seen in dramatic art has equalled the pathos of that look of silent anguish and hopeless remorse.

Quite exceptional was what can only be described as the 'affection' existing between Irving and his audiences. During the last years of his career, at the end of the performance, after several recalls, he would say a few words almost nightly, and send the audience away contented and happy. There was nothing beyond personal charm in those few courteous, modest words, just an assurance that he was always their 'loyal, obedient and affectionate servant,' but no one could doubt the assurance. The audience knew that affection really existed.

RICHARD DICKINS.

XII

IRVING as PHILIP OF SPAIN

Lyceum Theatre, 18th of April, 1876 :—

QUEEN MARY

WRITTEN BY ALFRED TENNYSON

Philip of Spain	MR. HENRY IRVING
Gardiner	MR. SWINBOURNE
Simon Renard	MR. BROOKE
Le Sieur de Noailles	MR. WALTER BENTLEY
Edward Courtenay	MR. CARTON
Lord William Howard	MR. MEAD
Sir Thomas White	MR. HUNTLEY
Count de Feria	MR. BEAUMONT
Master of Woodstock	MR. COLLETT
Lord Petre	MR. STUART
Messenger	MR. SARGENT
Steward to Princess Elizabeth	MR. NORMAN
Attendant	MR. BRANSCOMBE
Mary of England	MISS BATEMAN (MRS. CROWE)
Princess Elizabeth	MISS VIRGINIA FRANCIS
Lady Clarence	MISS PAUNCEFORT
Lady Magdalen Dacres	MISS CLAIRE
Joan	MRS. HUNTLEY
Tib	MR. ARCHER
Maid of Honour	MISS HALL
Alice	MISS ISABEL BATEMAN

ACT I, SCENE. *An Apartment at Whitehall.* ACT II, SCENE 1. *The Guildhall;* SCENE 2. *The Gatehouse at Westminster.* ACT III, SCENE 1. *Apartment at Woodstock;* SCENE 2. *Whitehall.* ACT IV, SCENE 1. *Street in Smithfield;* SCENE 2. *Apartment at Whitehall.* ACT V, SCENE 1. *Mansion near London;* SCENE 2. *The Queen's Oratory.*

I SHOULD not be surprised to learn that I am among the oldest survivors of those who saw any of Henry Irving's performances in, or before, 1870. At that time I was a callow student at the Royal Academy of Music and few things were less likely than that I should ever be engaged in the traffic of the stage. I was, however, typically an enthusiastic pittite, and in that capacity had already seen Irving in some melodrama at the Old Queen's Theatre. What the play was I cannot remember, but I do remember that Irving's playing had aroused the pit's attention, and that we marked him as a coming man. Then, in 1870, came his Digby Grant in *Two Roses*. The pit (including myself) rose to him, and from that moment until his death I was an enthusiastic Irvingite, although I confess there were times when my enthusiasm had to carry me over trying intervals of doubt.

For instance, his young lover in *Fanchette* at the Lyceum, was discouraging and certainly gave no promise of triumphs that theatre was to see for the next thirty years, was, indeed, to see begin at once. *Fanchette* was produced in September 1871, and in November of the same year came the first night of *The Bells*, at which I was present, and which marked the bursting into full flower of Irving's glory. That was a First Night I shall never forget.

After that I took care to see everything Irving did. There were exceptions, as I presently had to make my own living away from London, but I saw the more important performances and came more and more under the great actor's spell.

The great actor's spell! Let me rather say, Henry Irving's Personal Magnetism, his hypnotism, his irresistible magic. It was this that created the blind enthusiasm of his followers. Anyone who escaped its power saw little or no charm in Irving's acting, but for ever remained more or less cold both to his art, and (what was more curious) even to his gifts as what we now call, a producer. The representative instance of this was William Archer, that level-headed Scotsman, who, as a dramatic critic was, at the time, about fifty years ahead of his colleagues, was unaffected by Irving's magic and judged his performances with the same judicial calm which he applied to the work of any other actor.

But to those in the power of the Irving spell—and they were the vast majority—Irving, as actor, producer, manager, and man, could do no wrong. That is putting it too mildly—he could do nothing less than the absolutely perfect, the absolutely true and the absolutely beautiful.

This spell of his affected far more than his own performances. It covered all the members of his company and persuaded us that each of them was a great actor or actress—only just not as great as himself, and—what was far more serious—it warped our judgment about all matters connected with the Lyceum. The house became a temple. Even the pit was holy ground. We were inclined to take our shoes off on entering; the people in the more expensive seats were obviously the cream of London, and the plays—ah, but this was a very mischievous effect of the spell!—the plays were all heaven-sent masterpieces, and were all equally great. We lost all sense of proportion. *The Corsican Brothers* seemed as notable as *Hamlet; The Lyons Mail* was as great as *Macbeth*, *Eugene Aram* as great as *Othello*, the most contemptible piece of stage carpentry was the equal of the noblest effort of genius, and we even accepted the unutterable malversion of *Faust* as rather better than Goethe's original. In this play, by the way, Irving did actually descend to grinning through a horse-collar, for one of his culminating effects was made by suddenly and without any reason whatever, pushing his head through a trap in the door of Marguerite's garden.

Amongst the least-known of Irving's plays, I witnessed his production of Tennyson's *Queen Mary* in which he played Philip of Spain. It is a fact that while I have vivid recollections of all the other plays he produced I recall nothing whatever of this particular play, except the figure of Philip standing before a great fireplace, sinister and terrifying, the very embodiment of a Velazquez. But what he said or did, or what the play was about (or who played in it), had so entirely gone from me that I had to read the play just now to remind myself of it. Small wonder I couldn't recall it; it is perverse as drama and a perversion of history. It was produced, of course, to exploit the eldest daughter of Mrs. Bateman, who had succeeded her husband in the management of the theatre, Mrs. Crowe, the famous 'Leah' Bateman, *Leah the Forsaken* being the title of the drama in which she drew all London to the Adelphi Theatre in 1863. Tennyson's *Queen Mary* was severely cut in order to make the part of the Queen more prominent. Tennyson wished Irving to play Cardinal Pole, but in the cutting that part, as well as Cranmer and Sir Ralph Bagenhall, the three best-drawn male characters in the play, disappeared, so Irving had to be content with the less important part of Philip of Spain. Of his performance John Oxenford said in *The Times*:

> 'Philip is only a subordinate character: he appears in but two scenes, that are curiously alike: in each he is required to rebuff the Queen's fondness and to express his resolve to leave England. As Philip, Mr. Irving secures an easy victory. Nothing indeed could be better than his performance of this character. He has carefully copied the traditional appearance of the King, and conveys very admirably his airs of frigid arrogance, heartless cruelty, and intense selfishness; the fanaticism and gross superstition which were also characteristic of Philip the author has not required the actor to demonstrate. Mr. Irving's happiest effort was perhaps contained in his scene with De Feria, where

> Philip hints at the prospect of the Queen's death, and, while toying with his poniard, suggests the punishment of his agent if he is not secret in the matter. Noting Mr. Irving's self-control and repose in his personation of Philip, we could not but deplore the lack of these qualities in certain of his more ambitious essays.'

Of Irving's first nights I saw only two, but they were memorable. The first—and I am very proud of that one—was the first night of *The Bells* (25 November 1871). His Digby Grant, in 1870, had put a handful of us young bloods on the *qui vive* to watch him; his fiasco as the young lover in (was it *Fanchette?*) at the Lyceum in '71 had, if anything, whetted our curiosity. The evening started depressingly; the theatre was not half full; it was cold; it looked and felt miserable; the critics lounged in, bored and evidently foreseeing another flop; the piece began as pieces translated from a foreign tongue always seem to begin, with a pointless conversation in that strange language —English in translation. I was in the front row of the pit and my heart sank into my boots. I felt that no actor, however great, could win that audience. They were not only dead heads, but dead all over.

And then Irving entered, and we sat up and took notice. Here was a new Irving, a new actor, a new and tremendous personality. He gripped us even before we had understood a word he said. We did not at first understand a word; we did not understand his walk; nor any of his movements; but he gripped us, he interested us, he excited us, and the excitement increased and increased, until, when the last curtain fell, we could only sit, gasping, stunned and silent. But after a moment we leapt to our feet, we leapt on to the benches, we shouted, we waved handkerchiefs, caps, anything that could be waved, and we then and there consecrated Irving the greatest actor of our time. And, from that moment onwards, for us the Irvingites, he could do no wrong.

The other first night I witnessed at the Lyceum was on the famous occasion when Irving 'offered the hospitality of his theatre' to the celebrated American tragedian, Edwin Booth. Booth had been playing to empty houses at the old Princess's in Oxford Street, such things as *Richelieu*, *The Fool's Revenge*, etc., and his season had been disastrous. He was a tired and discouraged man. Irving invited him to come to the Lyceum and they would play *Othello* together, each alternately playing Othello and Iago, with Ellen Terry as Desdemona.

This was heralded as an epoch-making event in dramatic

history. London was stirred to its depths, and although I was due at Sherborne for the beginning of a new term, I determined that I must be there, even if I risked my job by staying in London an extra night.

So I was at the pit door at 8 a.m. disgusted to find that some still earlier birds—one very fat—were already there. I remember the pit door was down a passage off the Strand (is it still there ?), a sort of yard, with most fortunately a door into a public-house on the right. This small space was soon chock-a-block, and the queue ultimately extended a long way down the Strand. We were a sociable crowd and passed the time with song and story, and with refreshments from the pub. Just before the pit door opened, the fat man in front of me went off into a dead faint. There was no way of getting him out through the crowd, so we hoisted him up and handed him out over our heads. I got his place, and presently found myself in the front row of the pit.

The contrast between the audience of this first night and that of *The Bells* was amazing. That had been shabby, listless, and trying to persuade itself it wasn't there. This was composed of the *élite*, the *fine fleur*, the top o' the basket of London. One could see by the expressions on their faces that every individual there was satisfied he or she was somebody. We, the pittites, encouraged this idea by bursting into frantic applause whenever a gentleman entered throwing out his chest, or a lady appeared who gave us that delightfully shy look which implied : 'Oh, *don't* applaud me ! '

We were all agog to welcome our Henry and our Ellen. Incidentally we were quite ready to be polite to our American guest ; but I think I can honestly say we never saw him. There was, to be sure, a pleasant gentleman representing Othello, but he was timid, he acted in corners ; he seemed to beg us not to look at him. And, indeed, it was difficult to see him as all the time our Henry was doing clever bits of by-play, eating grapes and spitting out the pips in a significant manner, which rendered Booth invisible. Oh, it was a great evening, and our enthusiasm rose to its wildest height for our Henry.

Afterwards I could not help asking myself whether to play with Irving on his own stage was really a wise thing for a foreign star to do. I also wondered, though I felt I was getting perilously near blasphemy, whether there might be a streak of cruelty in my divinity. I had heard, and I have constantly heard since, thrilling accounts of his wit ; of the quickness of his repartee; of his brilliance. But as time went on and I got more familiar with things theatrical, it struck me as peculiar that I never heard of his wit excepting in connection with alleged *bon mots* which must have scathed the objects of them, skinned them alive. I have quite a collection of his flashes and I am sorry I cannot print one of them, as the victims or their descendants may be alive. In all cases I either can't see the joke, or, when I can, I have to turn away my eyes because the joke is—to say the least—unkind, and makes me feel as we of the old school used to feel when somebody spoke an unseemly word in the presence of a lady. That feeling may not be experienced now that ladies themselves freely use even much stronger expressions. But after all this flaw was only a spot on our sun. The fact remained that Irving towered over all other actors, that his productions were artistic events of real importance, that we were thrilled when we were going to see one of them, that we were thrilled to the marrow when we saw it, and that when we saw him we were in a state of ecstasy. Do we get those thrills about anything or anybody in the theatre nowadays? Does a film 'première,' even attended by a countess, produce that tingle of expectation? Or that rapture of satisfaction? I ask for information in all humility.

LOUIS N. PARKER.

XIII

IRVING as DORICOURT

Lyceum Theatre, 11th of June, 1876 :—

THE BELLE'S STRATEGEM

WRITTEN BY MRS. COWLEY

Doricourt	MR. HENRY IRVING
Mr. Hardy	MR. J. ARCHER
Sir George Touchwood	MR. BEAUMONT
Flutter	MR. BROOKE
Saville	MR. BENTLEY
Villers	MR. CARTON
Courtall	MR. STUART
Letitia Hardy	MISS ISABEL BATEMAN
Mrs. Racket	MISS VIRGINIA FRANCIS
Lady Frances Touchwood	MISS LUCY BUCKSTONE

ACT I, SCENE 1. *Lincoln's Inn ;* SCENE 2. *An Apartment at Doricourt's ;* SCENE 3. *A Room in Hardy's House.* ACT II, SCENE. *Ballroom.* ACT III, SCENE 1. *Hardy's House ;* SCENE 2. *Doricourt's Bedchamber ;* SCENE 3. *Queen's Square ;* SCENE 4. *A Room in Hardy's House.*

THIS rollicking comedy is the story of a marriage which has been arranged between Letitia and Doricourt by their parents. The 'courtship began on their nurses' knees,' but when the play opens they had not met since childhood.

At the reunion Letitia's maidenly reserve disconcerts Doricourt and, to her great mortification, he appears to be indifferent while she confesses that she feels herself his slave.

With the aid of her friend, Mrs. Racket, she concocts a plot by which he will think her a rather silly country wench—a mere hoyden and impossible as his wife. Then later at a ball, under cover of mask and domino, she will show her bewitching self with all the charms she is well aware she possesses. This is done very delightfully and he becomes so enamoured that he begs her to unmask, swearing eternal love, but she will promise no more than that he shall see her 'at a time he least expects.'

His friends have observed this encounter and Flutter—an irresponsible chatterer—dumbfounds him by declaring her to be the mistress of some lord. But Doricourt, loath to believe this, seeks a means to cancel the marriage with Letitia and to this end pretends to be mad. To counter this, Letitia's friends decide on an immediate marriage, and to expedite matters old Hardy pretends to be dying, so the ceremony is performed and Doricourt, in a very gloomy state, joins his friends to whom, shortly afterwards, there enters the masked lady. She tells Doricourt she has come in fulfilment of her promise that he should see her when least expected. Saville remarks that the occasion is well chosen as Doricourt is just married. Old Hardy then suddenly reappears to Doricourt's amazement, Letitia unmasks, explains her little plot, and the curtain falls upon their happiness.

Irving appears to have played Doricourt for the first time on 6 October 1866, at the St. James's Theatre under the management of Miss Herbert. He had by then become 'an actor of recognized standing.' Miss Herbert herself played Letitia and Mr. Walter Lacey appeared as Flutter. Irving was also stage-manager.

After this performance, he said: 'I was cast for Doricourt, a part which I had never played before, and which I thought did not suit me; and I felt that this was the opinion of the audience soon after the play began. The house appeared to be indifferent, and I believed that failure was conclusively stamped upon my work, when suddenly, upon my exit after the Mad Scene, I was startled by a burst of applause, and so great was the enthusiasm of the audience that I was compelled to reappear upon the scene, a somewhat unusual thing, except upon the operatic stage,' though it happened every time Henry Neville played Charles Surface in the Screen Scene.

It was not until 1881 that Doricourt was accorded a more or less permanent place in the programme at the Lyceum, when it was revived on 16 April, being played in conjunction with Tennyson's tragedy, *The Cup*, and replacing *The Corsican Brothers*.

For years we had been accustomed to see Irving playing tragic and weird *rôles*, and to see him as a light comedian immediately following his graphic performance of Synorix on the same evening, was a revelation indeed. But he had graduated in a school that fostered and cherished the Old Comedy manner, which should be one of our Theatre's most valued possessions. Yet with the passing of Fred Terry, the last survivor of that famous Old Comedy management of Mr. and Mrs. Chippendale at the Haymarket, the tradition is for ever lost.

In *The Belle's Stratagem* the Mad Scene is, of course, the great moment of the play; and how remarkably Irving played it! Such lightness of touch, and never a point slurred or missed. It happens in Doricourt's bedroom, and Saville, his confidant, tells Flutter it always recurs at the full of the moon. Doricourt, hearing this, picks up his pillow, jumps on the bed and declares he holds the moon in his arms; he then flings it at Flutter and, drawing the bed curtains round him, puts his head through, almost exactly as in his final entrance after the Dream Scene in *The Bells*.

Many had tried to burlesque him, and it is an interesting thought that he may have decided to give them a lesson in mimicry by seizing this opportunity to burlesque himself! Personally I can conceive it well within the limits of his well-known sense of humour to play this little trick on audience and fellow-players alike. The result was received with laughter, such as had never before been heard at the Lyceum under his reign.

Writing of his performance in June 1876, Clement Scott says:

> 'Nearly ten years have elapsed since Miss Herbert, on reopening the St. James's Theatre, assigned to Mr. Irving, then chiefly known as an actor of repute in the provinces, the character of Doricourt. The value of the acquisition thus made was at once acknowledged, but, notwithstanding that his scene of mock madness in the comedy possessed some unusual vividness of colouring, it would have been a bold prophecy to then declare that the representative of the fastidious gentleman, whose admiration had to be secured by such whimsical devices, would before very long become capable, as Hamlet, of attracting audiences at another theatre for two hundred consecutive nights.'

The comedy was again performed on 19 July 1883, as one of a series of farewell performances, also on 25 July, the latter being an occasion none of us who was present is likely to forget. This was Irving's Farewell Benefit before his first visit to America. We had *Eugene Aram* arranged in one act, two songs by Herbert Sims Reeves, a monologue, *Trying a Magistrate*, by J. L. Toole, two songs by Sims Reeves, and *The Belle's Stratagem*. A feast, a banquet indeed! It is not for me to enlarge here upon that marvellous evening, but the enthusiasm and excitement were intense—the shouts for Irving!—God-speed!—*Bon Voyage!*—Speech! the waving of flags, Union Jacks, Stars and Stripes flung over the gallery rails—showers of bouquets and garlands on to the stage, and finally the gracious words of farewell, all left an indelible impression upon my youthful mind.

On this American tour the comedy was included in the repertoire and produced in New York on 20 November. William Winter, the leading American critic, wrote:

> 'The performance of this old work in seven brief and rapid scenes proved more enjoyable than the representation in all its acts has commonly been . . . the quintessence of the characters and the fun is preserved. Mr. Irving's Doricourt was of a superb aristocratic elegance, perfect manners, a fine dexterity in treating the somewhat trivial incidents. It has the distinct individuality of a luxurious polished man of the world. His crisp delivery of the text, particularly in the " aside " speeches, will be remembered as especially felicitous.'

Reference has already been made to Irving's perfect command of the Old Comedy manner and it is interesting to recall his other successes in that school. Bram Stoker, who became his manager and lifelong friend, first saw him play Captain Absolute with Miss Herbert at the Theatre Royal, Dublin, in 1867. Those were the days of the star system, when the stock company, being well soaked in traditional business, were prepared to support the star with perhaps one rehearsal. The 'adherence to standard business was so strict that no actor could venture to break it.' Irving had played the part during his three years at Edinburgh and knew that his only chance of scoring was to improve on the established lines within the traditional method; in fact, to impersonate the character to better advantage. Stoker goes on to say:

> 'The playing of Henry Irving as Captain Absolute was different from any performance of the same part which I had seen. What I saw was a patrician figure as real as the person of one's dreams, and endowed with the same poetic grace. A young soldier, handsome, distinguished, self-dependent; a man of quality who stood out as a being of another social world. A figure full of dash and fine irony, and whose ridicule seemed to *bite;* an inoffensive egoist even in his love-making; of supreme and unsurpassable insolence, veiled and shrouded in his fine quality of manner. Such a figure as could only be possible in an age when the answer to insolence was a sword thrust. The scenes which stand out most vividly are: his interview with Mrs. Malaprop in which she sets him to read his own intercepted letter to Lydia wherein he speaks of the old lady as " the old weather-beaten she-dragon " was simply a triumph of well-bred insolence. Again, when he makes repentant obedience to his father's will, his negative air of content as to his suggested wife

was inimitable. And the shocked appearance, manner and speech of his hypocritical submission was as enlightening to the audience as it was convincing to Sir Anthony. The scene, when in the presence of his father and Mrs. Malaprop he has to make love to Lydia in his own *persona*, was on the actor's part a masterpiece of emotion—the sort of thing to make an author grateful. There was no mistaking the emotions which came so fast—his mental perturbations; his sense of the ludicrous situation, his hurried, feeble, ill-conceived efforts to find a way out. And through them all the sincerity of his real affection for Lydia, coming straight and convincingly to the heart of the audience. But these scenes were all of acting a part. The reality of his character was in the scene of Sir Lucius's quarrel with him. Here he was real. Man to man the grace and truth of his character and bearing were based on no purpose or afterthought. Before a man his manhood was sincere; before a gallant gentleman his gallantry was without flaw, and outshone even the chivalry of that perfect gentleman, Sir Lucius O'Trigger.'

Irving also played Young Dornton and Young Marlow which he was to act again at the Queen's as well as Faulkland. And of his Joseph Surface, Clement Scott says:

'He gave an admirable reading, taking up the line on which I have ever insisted, that Joseph Surface is not a tragedian gone silly as the actors of old were determined he should be; but a good-looking light comedian, as young, as modern, and as up-to-date as his brother Charles; but a hypocritical, plausible fellow, as compared with the reckless daredevil spendthrift. Until Irving took up Joseph Surface the brother of Charles was, according to stage tradition, a prig in a wig; but he made him a handsome, cynical, sensuous, seductive betrayer of women, by means of his brain and his artifice.'

This agrees with Charles Lamb's description of the first Joseph Surface by 'Plausible Jack' Palmer, in 1777.

The reference by Bram Stoker to the traditional business of the Old Comedies is significant, for it brings home to us to-day that we possess no record of matters of such importance, a lasting disgrace to the English Stage. I believe that at the *Comédie Française*, Molière's original prompt books of all his comedies are treasured together with those of Racine and Corneille, and no departure from tradition as to text or business is permitted. This is also true of the standard plays of Victor Hugo, *Ruy Blas* and *Hernani*. However, should an artist of eminence, such as Got or Coquelin, Bernhardt or Bartet, suggest an alteration—naturally it is usually a comedian who tries to improve on tradition—the matter is debated in solemn conclave and if the suggestion is allowed, the *régisseur* is instructed to record the new business in the prompt book with the date and the name of the artist suggesting it, and this, of course, is counted an inestimable honour by all *sociétaires*.

A. Harding Steerman.

XIV

IRVING as RICHARD III

Lyceum Theatre, 29th of January, 1877 :—

RICHARD THE THIRD

WRITTEN BY WILLIAM SHAKESPEARE

King Edward IV	MR. BEAUMONT
Edward, Prince of Wales	MISS BROWN
Richard, Duke of York	MISS HARWOOD
George, Duke of Clarence	MR. WALTER BENTLEY
Richard, Duke of Gloucester	MR. HENRY IRVING
Henry, Earl of Richmond	MR. E. H. BROOKE
Cardinal Bourchier	MR. COLLETT
Duke of Buckingham	MR. T. SWINBOURNE
Duke of Norfolk	MR. HARWOOD
Lord Rivers	MR. CARTON
Lord Hastings	MR. R. C. LYONS
Lord Stanley	MR. A. W. PINERO
Lord Lovel	MR. SERJEANT
Marquis of Dorset	MR. SEYMOUR
Lord Grey	MR. ARTHUR DILLON
Sir Richard Ratcliff	MR. LOUTHER
Sir William Catesby	MR. J. ARCHER
Sir James Tyrrel	MR. A. STUART
Sir James Blunt	MR. BRANSCOMBE
Sir Robert Brackenbury	MR. H. SMYLES
Dr. Shaw	MR. TAPPING
Lord Mayor	MR. ALLEN
First Murderer	MR. T. MEAD
Second Murderer	MR. HUNTLEY
Queen Margaret	MISS BATEMAN
Queen Elizabeth	MISS PAUNCEFORT
Duchess of York	MRS. HUNTLEY
Lady Anne	MISS ISABEL BATEMAN

ACT I, SCENE. *A Street.* ACT II, SCENE 1. *King's Ante-Chamber ;* SCENE 2. *Prison in the Tower ;* SCENE 3. *Ante-Chamber.* ACT III, SCENE 1. *Chamber in the Tower ;* SCENE 2. *Hastings' House ;* SCENE 3. *Council Chamber in Baynard's Castle.* ACT IV, SCENE 1. *The Presence Chamber ;* SCENE 2. *Room in the Tower ;* SCENE 3. *Tower Hill.* ACT V, SCENE 1. *Richmond's Encampment ;* SCENE 2. *The Royal Tent ;* SCENE 3. *Richmond's Tent ;* SCENE 4. *The Battlefield.*

MANY abler pens than mine have written of the great Manager and the great Artist; I shall write of the man as I knew him.

Henry Irving was a very simple person to his friends, though no one would call him ingenuous; it was the simplicity of a very frank nature and though perhaps rarely suspected, of a deeply religious nature. Honest he was in all his dealings and of a princely generosity. He had no conception of the value of money except as a symbol; it flowed from him like water from the stricken rock in the desert for the necessities of his art or the entertainment of his friends, and also in a perpetual stream for the relief of those less fortunate than himself, though at the last he fell under a succession of cruel strokes which perhaps more thrift in the days of prosperity might have averted. But who can tell whether thrift might not have defeated the prosperity?

J. L. Toole, who was my manager and friend, had been Irving's devoted comrade for many years; they were, in fact, inseparable, but nothing could have been more remarkable, even ludicrous, than the contrast of their personalities: Irving, tall and ascetic, Toole with his large head and short legs, the typical comedian. I am sorry I missed seeing them as the two thieves in the old melodrama they had played together so often, Robert Macaire and Jacques Strop.

My friendship with Toole brought me often in contact with Irving, and as I was a lad my presence hardly restrained their confidences. Irving confided in very few, in fact, in the days I speak of, Toole was perhaps the only really intimate friend he had. He was a man of solitary habit and a deep sadness by reason of his estrangement from his sons, Harry and Laurence, who from their earliest childhood had been taught to dislike him. It was not until they were grown men and could reason for themselves that they learned to overcome this cruel inculcated prejudice. But this unnatural situation left its mark on the father's reserved and sensitive nature, a deep sorrow of which I am sure he never spoke to any but his old comrade, Toole, who was Laurence's godfather. His control was absolute; I suppose no man ever lived who had more complete command over expression both on and off the stage. But Toole was not so reticent and from him I knew of Irving's tragic disappointment. Had Irving been a general he would have been a master of stategy; as an archbishop, which would have become him well, a model of ecclesiasticism ; as a statesman, the fortunes of the Empire would have been in safe hands ; as an actor—yes, I see, I shall have to come to that.

In repose his face was beautiful ; he could transform it, and did, in every part he played. His natural expression was austere, but the smile was beautiful. Yes, it had the beauty of a sweetness passing that of the most lovely women, for it mirrored the essential goodness that was in him ; the charm of his manner was irresistible, yet he could be stern and, on occasion, cutting, with a whiplash sting that insolence could not forget : his speech was laconic, his humour dry, sardonic, yet never bitter without provocation. If you doubted that, you had only to watch his eye—the key was always there. His hands with their long tapering fingers were eloquent, and he used them with masterly and unerring effect on the stage ; the sleeves of his costumes were always cut to show them to full advantage.

When Irving made his first great successes public and Press were much divided in their judgment of him and controversy waxed high. Some saw only a peculiarity of gait and heard a curious staccato utterance ; others discerned the genius that raised him head and shoulders above his contemporaries. He had outgrown or put aside those mannerisms when I first saw him act. I say ' put aside ' because I believe they were deliberately affected or at least calculatingly exaggerated in his early days.

The stories told of him, mostly untrue, would fill a volume ; any joke that depended for its humour on a crisp concision was fathered on him.

Rumour had it once that the Baroness Burdett-Coutts was very attracted to him and idle tongues wagged maliciously of an ill-assorted marriage—remember that in those days the stigma of vagabond and rogue was still upon our calling. Anything more absurd could not have been invented. That great lady, whose benevolence was a legend, admired Irving's genius as deeply as anyone in London and that she did help him in the early days of his management to the extent of a loan of three thousand pounds is true, but neither she nor anyone was ever his backer. The loan was repaid almost immediately and that was the beginning and end of financial obligation between them, though not of friendship.

Irving's two sons were my intimate friends from the time they went on the stage. Both bore striking resemblance to their father, and yet were curiously unlike each other ; Harry was uncannily like the old man, especially at supper-time when he was happy with his friends. He was not perhaps quite so mannered as Laurence, in whom the resemblance in his work grew more and more marked as time went on. Had he lived he might have taken his father's place, many thought. Harry studied for the bar, in fact was 'called'. His great hobby was criminology and he never missed an important trial. Laurence was an actor born. In remembering him I am always happy to know that in a small way I helped his reconciliation with his father. At Toole's urgent request, I persuaded him on his twenty-first birthday to visit his father at Grafton Street. I waited for him outside the house for two hours. I am convinced that the interview altered Laurence's whole nature; what it meant to his father we can only surmise, but we may be sure that all the depths of tenderness in that profound nature were stirred to their utmost and the boy learned the extent of all he had missed in being so long deprived of that affection: his heart was much troubled but it was with a deep sense of pride that he showed me the gold watch his father had given him. From that hour a deep and affectionate comradeship grew between them, and the fact that Harry had also become reconciled and was now his father's most constant companion did much to soften the blows that were yet to fall upon the once triumphant manager.

I have tried to emphasize the gentle qualities of this great man as I knew him because I want to show by contrast how remarkable was his art in one of the greatest—if not the very greatest—of his impersonations. Lord Tennyson tells us that his father, the late Poet Laureate, 'always pronounced Irving's Philip of Spain in *Queen Mary* to be a consummate performance, ranking it with Salvini's Othello. He was further of the opinion that Philip and Richard III were Irving's best parts.' Philip of Spain I cannot judge; it was before my time, but having read the play I know that nothing short of genius could find scope for its display in such a part, but Richard I saw, and such a picture of evil I never witnessed before or since. It seemed inconceivable that the man I knew could exude such an atmosphere of malignity. Weird, sinister, sardonic all in turn and all together, grimly humorous and keenly intellectual. From the first moment of the play he struck the note of mocking villainy that was to be the predominant characteristic of his reading, the tyrant who is prepared to wade to eminence through rivers of blood if need be, with superb indifference as to whose blood it might be, friend's, accomplice's or enemy's; but always—always the Plantagenet air. 'I often wonder,' said Tennyson, when Irving first played the part in 1877, 'where he gets his distinctive *Plantagenet* look.'

It happened curiously that in the previous autumn Barry Sullivan was playing Richard at Drury Lane, but in the Colley Cibber version—or perversion. From the memories of an ardent Shakespearean student I quote the following :[1]

> 'I went to Drury Lane to see *Richard the Third*, innocently expecting to witness Shakespeare's play. Alas! the work presented was Cibber's travesty, and for the first quarter of an hour my bewilderment was complete and I seriously supposed the play had been changed. When at last some of Shakespeare's text was given my indignation increased. Every third line or so was mutilated, and hearing the lines one knew so well thus spoken was like receiving repeated slaps in the face. I need only add that Barry Sullivan was the Richard and I felt that I was never likely to see a coarser or worse performance; possibly, however, I was not in the frame of mind to judge charitably.'

I quote this to emphasize the contrast even in those days between the method of Irving and that of the old school—for Barry Sullivan was of the school of Macready and Phelps. Where they were ponderous Irving was incisive; where they used the broadsword he employed the rapier; where they relied on thunder he employed intellect and personal magnetism. The keynote of the character as portrayed by Irving was in the lines :

> 'Our aery buildeth in the cedar's top
> And dallies with the wind and scorns the sun.'

He walked with a limp and one shoulder higher than the other, but yet contrived a noble presence. He gloried in his mental superiority and the ease with which he could outwit his fellows. I felt that he lacked physical power in the fight scenes, yet in some respects his fight with Richmond was more *deadly* than any I have ever seen; after the death-stroke he clutched the fatal blade of his enemy with hands and teeth. The effect was ghastly.

But where he excelled was in the wooing of the Lady Anne. Anything more wonderful it would be difficult to imagine. The scene must always be an artificial one, but in the hands of Henry Irving it became absolutely believable and possible. The weird lighting; the tolling of the bell; the shadowy procession bearing the dead king to his tomb; the girl, shrinking

[1] *Forty Years of Shakespeare on the English Stage*, by Richard Dickins.

yet fascinated, like the frightened antelope who scents the python and has no strength—hardly the will—to flee.

The long soliloquy which opens the play was one of the most perfect elocutionary efforts I have ever heard, rivalled only, I have been told, by his delivery of ' To be or not to be.' Alas ! I never saw his Hamlet.

And what could be more wonderful than his handling of the Lord Mayor on the instigation of Buckingham, and the look of devilish triumph he threw to Buckingham at the end ?—or the craftiness in his scene with the little princes ?

' Splendidly satanic ' was the verdict of one eminent writer on his Richard, and remembering those scenes and the outburst against Hastings I cannot but echo the phrase.

In his tent before Bosworth I can only compare him with his own inimitable Mathias in *The Bells*. The intensity of foreboding that he put into the couplet :

> ' I have not that alacrity of spirit
> Nor cheer of mind that I was wont to have.'

It was not fear—nor despair—nor the prick of conscience, yet it suggested all ; he knew the end had come and made you know how he would face it. He never lost nobility, the nobility of Lucifer.

Irving was a mighty actor, a great gentleman, a loving friend.

SEYMOUR HICKS.

XV

IRVING as LESURQUES and DUBOSC

Lyceum Theatre, 19th of May, 1877 :—

THE LYONS MAIL

(*An adaptation of Le Courrier de Lyon by MM. Moreau, Siraudin and Delacour*)

WRITTEN BY CHARLES READE

Joseph Lesurques	MR. HENRY IRVING
Dubosc	MR. HENRY IRVING
Jerome Lesurques	MR. T. MEAD
Didier	MR. E. H. BROOKE
Joliquet	MISS LYDIA HOWARD
M. Dorval	MR. F. TYARS
Lambert	MR. LOUTHER
Guerneau	MR. GLYNDON
Postmaster at Montgeron	MR. COLLETT
Coco	MR. BRANSCOMBE
Garçon at Café	MR. TAPPING
Guard	MR. HARWOOD
Postillion	MR. ALLEN
Courriol	MR. R. C. LYONS
Choppard	MR. HUNTLEY
Fouinard	MR. J. ARCHER
Durochat	MR. HELPS
Julie	MISS VIRGINIA FRANCIS
Jeannette	MISS ISABEL BATEMAN

ACT I, SCENE 1. *Room in the Café, 17 Rue de Lac, Paris ;* SCENE 2. *Exterior of the Inn at Lieursaint, on the Lyons road.* ACT II, SCENE. *Salon in the House of M. Lesurques.* ACT III, SCENE 1. *Panelled Chamber overlooking the Garden in M. Lesurques' House ;* SCENE 2. *The Prison ;* SCENE 3. *First Floor of a Cabaret, overlooking the Place of Execution.*

THIS drama, originally produced in Paris in 1850 at the Théâtre de la Gaieté, with Lacressonière in the dual rôle, soon found its way to England. It was translated and played at the Standard Theatre, the Victoria, and the Adelphi, where Leigh Murray played the leading part, before the younger Kean produced Charles Reade's adaptation at the Princess's in 1854. It was then named *The Courier of Lyons*, but it was pointed out to Mrs. Bateman that in fact the French *courrier* is not translated into English by courier, that in fact there is no courier in the play and that the sense of the French title is correctly conveyed by *The Lyons Mail.* And so, when she arranged with Mr. Reade to produce his adaptation, the new title was adopted. It is founded on a well-known miscarriage of justice, a *cause célèbre* of the days of the Directoire in which the innocent M. Lesurques did in fact suffer the extreme penalty for the crime of Dubosc, leader of a gang of ruffians, *who bore no physical resemblance to him whatever.* Lesurques was a stalwart, flaxen-haired, fresh-complexioned Norman; Dubosc a mean, undersized, sallow Parisian of the apache type, but as he rode from the inn at Lieursaint after the crime, a maid at the post-house, who saw only his back view, swore away Lesurques' life because Dubosc was wearing a flowing tow wig. This servant-girl becomes, in the play, the boy Joliquet, the part I played with Irving in the 1891 and 1893 revivals and tours.

In Paris the audience so objected to the *dénouement*—the execution of Lesurques—that the authors wrote another ending which was played on alternate nights. If Lesurques was guillotined on Mondays, Wednesdays, and Fridays, he was reprieved on Tuesdays, Thursdays, and Saturdays, and Dubosc suffered in his stead. How they managed on Sundays I cannot say, but the odds are that Lesurques escaped, for Sunday is in Paris the popular theatre-going night of the week. But Charles Reade disdained compromise and in this country at least the innocent has not suffered for the guilty—in this instance anyhow. In the theatre, in popular drama, romance and a happy sequel must not be ignored; if facts are contradictory so much the worse for facts. The play itself is built on a contradiction of fact, namely, a resemblance between Lesurques and Dubosc, which did not exist, and it lives mainly to give the actor opportunity for a *tour de force* in playing the two totally dissimilar parts of the honest and respected citizen and the depraved ruffian. It has often been objected that in order to emphasize their versatility Irving and other actors enacting this dual *rôle*, including myself, have made the two characters so much unlike that there is no possibility of confusion between them, and that by emphasizing their dissimilarity the story of the play is nullified and defeated. The objectors forget that it is only at certain points in the story that the resemblance needs to be marked, for example, when Dubosc meets Jerome Lesurques in the posting-house and when the boy Joliquet faces Joseph Lesurques in the second act; in all other scenes it is an advantage that the two should be as dissimilar as possible. On those two occasions, since the same actor is actually playing the two parts, he must be a poor one indeed if he cannot contrive for those brief moments to look like himself in both cases.

But our interest is not so much in history or in the play, or in its traditions, its simplicities and its complexities, but in what Irving did with the parts, parts which he made his own and played continually for over twenty-eight years.

Lesurques, in his hands, bore very little resemblance to a hero of melodrama; he was typical of all that is implied by 'middle class respectability,' though perhaps a trifle too distinguished, and might very well have passed for a younger brother of Doctor Primrose, whom he more nearly resembled than any other of his impersonations. It was a singular trait of Irving's acting that the characters he created were so distinct that they did *not* remind you of his other creations. All may have reminded you of Irving—in fact they did—but never of each other. Lesurques did *not* remind you of Robert Landry despite the strong physical resemblance. Landry of the dead heart had no sort of affinity with Lesurques whose heart was very consciously alive, as we saw in his filial devotion and his tenderness to little Julie his daughter. And it is this dutiful, sensitive, law-abiding, conventional-mannered, respectable bourgeois who, in the midst of his peaceful, almost uneventful existence, is suddenly confronted with the accusation of robbery accompanied by most brutal murder. And what aggravates the terrible accusation is the appalling fact that his own father believes himself a witness of the crime and is prepared to testify against him; not voluntarily, but being a reputable citizen, if he should be called upon by the Law he cannot refuse to give evidence. And the evidence is damning for, as he believes, he has encountered his son on the scene of the crime and been struck down by him as he made his escape.

And how did Irving, as Lesurques, face this gruesome situation? Under the magistrate's examination I have seen upon him the mantling cheek, the smarting eyes and the sickly smile of the obviously *guilty*; superb touches, for (as an eminent judge has pointed out) the really innocent frequently appear the most guilty and the most downcast. But Irving's reaction comes when left alone with his father; Jerome offers him the escape of suicide. Indignantly he refuses to proclaim a guilt he does not bear; he puts aside the proferred pistol, and the old man, mistaking the motive of this gesture, denounces him for cowardice. Who that heard it can forget the solemn booming, like rolls of distant thunder, of old Tom Mead's *basso profundo* descending the octave with that thrice-repeated 'Coward!'

I can compare it only with the Boris Godounov of Chaliapine.

There is little more to be said of Lesurques, except for his scenes with Julie, scenes that recall the less tragic episodes between Olivia and her father; scenes of tender reassurance, despite his own mental agony, for the girl's despair. There remains only the one radiant smile when innocence is recognized and he is restored to his friends—but what that smile could be!

A friend who saw *The Lyons Mail* twenty-three times at the Lyceum assured me that Irving was at the top of his form as Lesurques seventeen times, as Dubosc only six. It is not to be supposed that he 'slacked' or shirked his work on any occasion—Irving was far too conscientious for that. Besides, his work was his life, he lived for nothing else. But apart from his masterly technique, which he never ceased to embellish and improve, there is a spiritual *drive* that inspires each performance, and in one of Irving's singleness of mind it was inevitable that when that spirit was at its purest Lesurques would gain and Dubosc that night would be played on technique; when the spirit was mischievous or excited—perhaps by some perfectly extraneous happening—he would revel in the wickedness of Dubosc, and technique would take care of Lesurques. There were, of course, magic occasions when the protean feat was inspired in both its manifestations, and then the result was staggering.

Yes, that is fact. I have known the audience 'stagger' on the first apparition of Dubosc. Lesurques is hardly out of sight when Dubosc is there in the doorway, grim, sinister, the embodiment of wicked intent. His accomplices cower as he comes among them chewing his straw, and regarding them with contemptuous, insolent tolerance. Then, peremptorily, he issues his orders and from that moment dominates. The robbery of the mail is planned and in the next scene carried out. The gang lie in wait near the post-house. The Mail approaches. The horses are forced back on their haunches, the postillion and guard are shot and the mail-bag rifled. The boy, Joliquet, locked in the cellar, witnesses this through an iron-barred grating. The scene is *macabre*. After killing the guard in cold blood and turning over the body to search for his papers, Irving was wont to emphasize Dubosc's callousness by humming a bar or so of *La Marseillaise*. One night in a fit of fantastic humour he almost shocked us by substituting 'Nearer, my God, to Thee!' The effect was appalling.

A brutal callousness is still the note of Dubosc's scene

with his mistress, Jeannette, a scene of purely conventional melodrama.

But it is the final scene that is the high spot of the play. A drunken Dubosc lies on his stomach, peering over the edge of the balcony into the place of execution below where the innocent Lesurques is to suffer for his crime. The scene is a low cabaret and the effect is that his room is a *mansarde* to which the hum of a great crowd comes up giving a most gruesome atmosphere to the scene. And what a performance of drunken malevolence he gave! His treatment of his jackal, Fouinard, would make the audience wince at its savage realism. It is no wonder the worm—in this case an adder—turns and stings. And here was a triumph of stage management. You were conscious by the careful gradation and graduation of the murmurs below of the exact moment when Fouinard, having reached the street and fought his way through the crowd to the scaffold, poured out his venomous tale and directed the mob's attention to the attic window where the murderer watched. Here, Irving's performance rose to the height of frenzy. The yells rose as they perceived him and he hurled imprecations and flower-pots in return. It was pandemonium. The wild beast, for he had become no less, was cornered; desperately he tried to barricade the door, and when a stalwart arm forced its way through the gap as the weight of the crowd without burst the bolt from its socket, he slashed at it with his long-bladed clasp-knife. The door gives, the mob surges in and Dubosc is overwhelmed and lost in their midst. The innocent Lesurques appears and the drama is over.

It is hardly possible to exaggerate the savagery of Irving's performance in that scene, yet never did he overstep the truth of nature and degenerate into extravagance. Dubosc though a monster was a credible human being and it was that fact that gave the play its lasting popularity. Had it been a mere display of melodramatic exaggeration such as the public were well accustomed to, the play would never have had that lasting appeal that attracted every class of playgoer to its performance.

Irving was always intellectual and his studies were psychologically observed. To the last he never relaxed in the perfecting of means to give his craft full effect. He *lived* Dubosc; he *was* Dubosc just as surely as he was Hamlet and Becket.

But *The Lyons Mail* is not only a one-part—or rather, not only a dual-*rôle*-play. The gang are all excellently drawn and admirably contrasted. Choppard, whose father 'bred Daddy-Long-legs,' was first played at the Lyceum by that grand actor, James

Fernandez. I call him that because the word expresses the nobility of his presence and the peculiar dignity of his art. He had been as Claudius a magnificent foil to Irving's Hamlet, an invaluable Nils, the pilot in *Vanderdecken*, and who can forget his Leonato? He had all the good qualities of the older school which he combined with a naturalness equal to that of 'Daddy' Howe. Yes, a grand actor. Fernandez was succeeded by dear old Sam Johnson, who had been a member of E. D. Davis's Company at Sunderland and had persuaded the manager that the youth Irving 'had something in him,' and so prevented his getting the 'sack'. Irving never forgot. Sam Johnson's reward was a thirty-years' engagement at the Lyceum, where his support was invaluable; his First Grave-Digger was excellent. No doubt he would have played many more important parts but that he had—shall I call it—an idiosyncrasy? Like many more old actors of his calibre, the wine of the country, any country, had an irresistible appeal for him, and Irving disliked taking risks.

The last Choppard was Charles Dodsworth, an actor of a very different type, dry and hard where the others had been unctuous and oily; but he made his effect, for Choppard is a fine part. In Paris, the great Paulin-Menier had made him the star part of the play.

Of Courriol, the dandy, on the first production Clement Scott wrote that it was a pity the small part was so inadequately cast. When I read that I was astonished, for in Terriss' hands it never struck me as a small part; his gallant bearing, his excellent grace and finish, his admirable comedy and the way that he wore his clothes as well as the authority of his manner gave the part equal importance with any in the play. And Fouinard, Jack Archer. Jack Archer was always Fouinard and how could he ever have been bettered?—though our dear old friend Tom Reynolds was as good on his rather different lines. Jack Archer was a pantomimist, and in his early days had 'worked the traps'; Fouinard's business with Dubosc in the garret gained enormously by his acrobatic experience as he took kickings and cuffings and did one astounding back-fall such as only a practised athlete could carry off. He was playing the part still in his eightieth year, despite his rheumatism. He had been in the cast as one of the Witches when Irving played Macbeth in 1875.

But apart from the leading character, the most striking part in the play is the father, Jerome Lesurques, and this was *acted* by our old friend, Tom Mead, a most striking personality and boon companion of Sam Johnson. Tom Mead had a voice like the sixteen-foot pipe of an organ and the complexion of a disinterred corpse, caused probably by his sedentary habits and the smoking of too many cheap cigars. He wrote charming verses and was quite accomplished as an artist in water-colour. He was, however, very absent-minded and liable strangely to misplace the words of his part. 'That is the sky,' he explained to Ellen Terry in *Iolanthe*, when the Princess has just received the gift of sight, 'the grand, the vaulted dome where we believe God hath his'—a long pause—'his—ah—apartments' (I think 'dwelling-place' was the text). The scene with his son in *The Lyons Mail* seemed to possess a maximum of 'snags' for slips of this kind. Convinced that his son is guilty of highway robbery and murder, he throws aside the testimony of other witnesses and exclaims with indignant emphasis: 'They have not seen you as *I* have, a dagger in one hand, a pistol in the other, and in the other——' Irving is said to have suggested in a savage stage whisper, 'a broomstick.' Again, in the same scene, aware that the few moments allowed him by the Chief of Police for a final interview with his son were rapidly passing, he pointed tragically to the clock and whispered: 'He gave us three minutes—barely ten are left.' But what a voice! To hear that sonorous organ from the steps of the high altar in the Church Scene in *Much Ado About Nothing* raised in passionate defence of Hero's innocence, was an experience never to be forgotten, and always brought the house down. Tom Mead was also an invaluable ghost in *Hamlet.*

Hamlet! I am convinced that he never even *thought* of the play without a sense of reverence—I am speaking, of course, of Irving. I was told, and I accepted it without question, that on the days he was to play Hamlet he fasted—as Dubosc, Collinson would bring him burnt brandy in the wings and he would gulp it, carelessly, and perhaps fling the glass away, not caring where it fell. But Hamlet! To him playing the part was a solemn ritual. Well, I suppose that is true of all of us. It is with a sense of responsibility that any sincere actor approaches that task, to interpret the greatest poetic creation of all time, the embodiment of Everyman to every man, for the cliché in this case is a living truth that in Hamlet each man sees himself. As we read we feel it; as we watch it in action we are confirmed in its truth.

He fasted, yes. And Bram Stoker told me that he also prayed—'if ever I prayed in my life,' he had said, and that lonely soul that was Henry Irving must often have found solace in prayer, for no man that I ever met was so truly lonely as he.

My first impression of him in the part—I was very young—was that he was grotesque; it seemed to me that he scribbled the interpolated lines of *The Mousetrap* in *The Murder of Gonzalo* leaning the script against a pillar, in letters a foot high. That ungainly gait; who compared it to trying to run quickly over a ploughed field? The simile was apt. Then the sudden pause and the stamp of the foot. A trick? A natural one, then. It begat an awful attention, which he never disappointed.

I was to play Osric with him later when I was able to form a more mature view of his conception. His Hamlet—it was his first essay in Shakespearean tragedy in London—was markedly individual in this: he was the first leading actor to combine tragic with character acting—the first to abandon the rhythmic beat of the verse and introduce naturalism into the classic. It was this that so inflamed certain critics against him. Dutton Cook writes of 'vulgarizing poetic tragedy which should occupy ground removed from the trivialities and the homeliness of ordinary life,' but I am inclined to question, not the truth, but the wisdom of the critic. It seems to me more important to popularize Shakespeare—to bring him nearer to the public's understanding—than to perpetuate that old notion of maintaining his aloofness. How many have I heard say that nothing would induce them to see *The Merchant of Venice* or *Julius Cæsar* in the theatre, having been so thoroughly sickened by those plays because of their use as text-books at school? If we can teach the people to love the reality, the homeliness of Shakespeare, we shall do a great work.

The note of Irving's Hamlet was his veneration for women, exemplified in his mother and Ophelia, and his horror, first at his mother's incestuous marriage, and later at what he conceived Ophelia's betrayal of himself. He had felt when he first played the part in London that his audience was not with him in the earlier scenes, nor till the scene with Ophelia was his original treatment of the part appreciated. From then onward his triumph was assured. He dwelt especially on the hysterical note in Hamlet's character, and this is where he departed most from the approved method of tragic acting. It was obvious that he must have pondered more upon the man Hamlet as a live creation than as the protagonist of a great tragedy, and this I take to be the sense of Dutton Cook's reference to 'homeliness.' I endeavour to see Irving's point of view, putting aside my own conception entirely, and it is impossible to withhold sincere tribute to a great actor's noblest creation. It was human, it was tragic, it was lovable, and in its last moments it had ineffable beauty.

JOHN MARTIN-HARVEY.

So much has been written of Henry Irving—so much still remains to be told, for he was a Leader of Men born. He would have taken that place in whichever calling it might have pleased him to adopt. This great personality, this great actor can never be forgotten by those who had the good fortune to see him in the exercise of his art.

My most vivid recollection of him is in *The Lyons Mail.* The amazing contrast he effected between the two parts of Lesurques and Dubosc was indeed a superlative achievement, the more so as it required the entire submergence of his own powerful individuality in both characters. The masterly effect of the gradually approached outburst of horror and bewilderment when Lesurques, the genial, unaffected, pleasant bourgeois finds himself accused of robbery and murder, and that accusation supported by his own father, was enhanced by touches of genius such as only a great actor could accomplish. Contrast with this the truculent figure of the successful ruffian Dubosc, who despite his villainy still could not fail to command admiration for his daredevil courage and never-failing resource—an absolute impersonation in which there was no perceptible trace of his own personality. By supreme art he raised this rather sordid melodrama to the level almost of a classic.

As a club acquaintance of some years and the father of one of my great friends, Harry Irving, I had full opportunities of gaining an insight to his more personal characteristics. In furthering the dignity of his calling he lost no opportunity, and it was common knowledge that those of his cloth who were less fortunate knew where to come in their distress. His heart was as great as his art.

It has been said, and it is undoubtedly true, that he had a caustic humour, but it was never wantonly cruel—unless the object of it had well deserved a trouncing. But always for those who knew him the eye would correct the bite of the tongue; he was incapable of a grudge, but he could hardly forbear to score when the object of his shaft had no sense of the joke. Knowing him well over some considerable time, one understood that most of his seeming bitterness had always a ring of humour round it; it was merely a veneer, perhaps to hide his generosity of heart, and a geniality that might have been mistaken for weakness.

He had undertaken a heavy work in trying to put his calling on a decent footing, hauling it out of the mire into which it had fallen, and in his time how triumphantly he succeeded.

As an example of his humour, always surging through his view of life, I remember an occasion when, having driven with him one night from the club back to his flat in Old Bond Street, the cabman looked at his fare and said: 'Rather a lot of money for this short job, Mr. Irving."

"What have I given you?" said Irving.

"Ten shillings," said the cabby.

"You're lucky it wasn't a sovereign," chuckled Irving, referring no doubt to the lateness of the hour.

After fifty years on the stage, one of my most cherished memories is to be able to say: I knew this man.

ALLAN AYNESWORTH.

IRVING *as* *DUBOSC*

FROM A DRAWING BY
SIR BERNARD PARTRIDGE

IRVING *As* *LOUIS XI*

FROM A DRAWING BY
SIR BERNARD PARTRIDGE

XVI

IRVING as LOUIS XI

Lyceum Theatre, 9th of March, 1878 :—

LOUIS THE ELEVENTH

(Adapted from Louis XI by Casimir Delavigne)

WRITTEN BY DION BOUCICAULT

Louis XI	MR. HENRY IRVING
Duke de Nemours	MR. F. TYARS
The Dauphin	MR. ANDREWS
Cardinal D'Alby	MR. COLLETT
Philip de Commines	MR. F. CLEMENTS
Count de Dreux	MR. PARKER
Jacques Coitier	MR. J. FERNANDEZ
Tristan l'Ermite	MR. W. BENTLEY
Oliver le Dain	MR. J. ARCHER
François de Paule	MR. T. MEAD
Monseigneur de Lude	MR. HOLLAND
The Count de Dunois	MR. LANETON
Marcel	MR. E. LYONS
Richard	MR. SMITH
Didier	MR. BRANSCOMBE
Officer of the Royal Guard	MR. HARWOOD
Montjoie	MR. CARTWRIGHT
Toison d'Or	MR. TAPPING
King's Attendants	MESSRS. EDWARDES AND SIMPSON
Marie	MISS VIRGINIA FRANCIS
Jeanne	MRS. ST. JOHN
Martha	MRS. CHIPPENDALE

ACT I. *Exterior of the Castle, Plessis-les-Tours.* ACT II. *Throne-room in the Castle.* ACT III. *A Forest Glade.* ACT IV. *The King's Bedchamber.* ACT V. *The Throne-room.*

FROM 1878 onwards the part of Louis XI was a favourite one with Henry Irving, and with the public. In his last season at Drury Lane in 1905, he acted it, and in the Bradford Theatre Royal he played it on the night before he died. We gather from Ellen Terry—and every word Ellen Terry wrote about acting is to be taken seriously—that it was one of the actor's easy parts. 'He could have played it three times a day "on his head," as the saying is,' she wrote in her autobiography. Well, all I will say on that point is that if Irving found it easy to act, a good many of us also found it easy to admire.

The play certainly is far from great. Whatever merits Casimir Delavigne's French original may have had, Dion Boucicault's English version certainly possessed few. From beginning to end there is hardly a moment in it of decent human feeling, and as a piece of literature it is ' cheap ' to a degree. Compared with it *The Bells* is a masterpiece. To a gifted actor, however, it certainly gave opportunities. The part of the old king hovering between earth and the next world was really the play. We saw him conscious of the near approach of death, fighting against it to the last; growing more evil as he became more senile; praying to his images at one moment, sneering at them in the next. The only other character of any interest in the play was the envoy, Nemours, who in one act bullied the old king in the throne-room, and in another frightened him almost to death in his bedchamber.

The play was in five acts. In the first nothing of any interest happened, the king did not appear, and the curtain used to fall on it to an almost silent audience. The second introduced us to the throne-room in the castle of Plessis-les-Tours, and, with the hobbling-in of the King, in his clothes of rusty green velvet and tight-fitting black cap, the scene suddenly became intensely alive. The third act took place in a forest glade, and gave the actor one of those scenes of ironic comedy in which he could be such a master. A buxom young peasant woman, recognising the old man as the King, but pretending not to do so, flattered him grossly; and the art with which Irving showed the old creature's senile delight, kept the audience in continual pause between a sort of laughter and a kind of shiver. Then came the bedchamber scene in which one saw the King seated before the fire planning his vengeance on Nemours, pausing to mumble his prayers to the holy images in his cap, and then muttering to them with an evil leer: ' If I thought ye knew all that's in my mind I'd burn ye ! '

It was in that act that Irving's rendering of a few very bald lines constituted the most thrilling piece of acting I ever saw. Seated in his chair in the gloomy room lit only by a single candle, and still mumbling his superstitions and his hates, he presently looked up and saw his enemy standing before him dim and ominous. He seemed to shrink into himself; and the following dialogue ensued:

> LOUIS: Ne-mours! Mer-ci-ful God!
> NEMOURS: Not a word!
> LOUIS: Si-lence! Si-lence! Mer-cy! Mer-cy!

The King breathed each syllable in a long whisper as in a paroxysm of fear. Under it the audience sat spellbound. Followed as it was by the wretched man's shrieks, prayers, grovellings, and final collapse to the floor, the curtain used to fall amid a veritable thunder of applause.

The fifth and last act was quite short. Again we saw the throne-room. Courtiers whispered to each other that the King was dying. Then someone came in to say that he was rising from his bed, declaring himself to be well and strong, and putting on the crown and the robes of State. Then a servant announced: 'His Majesty the King!' and presently, in the open doorway at the back stood a tall figure, with a face white and death-like, swaying to and fro in a long robe of light blue velvet embroidered with the fleur-de-lis, with the great gold crown of France upon his head, and clutching the sceptre. Saved from falling, and helped into a chair (near the footlights) he sank into it, muttering his resolve not to die, but to 'live by the strength of my own will.' At last the old man's head fell forward, the courtiers turned towards the young Dauphin, and sank upon their knees with their backs to the dead man in the chair; and to their softly spoken prayer, 'Long Live the King!' the curtain fell. As a play, *Louis the Eleventh* may cut a poor figure indeed, but Irving's performance in it was a very great one.

The fact that the same man could present such a Hamlet and such a Louis XI as Irving's is surely sufficient to justify his fame. It also seems to account for what I have long felt to be a rather interesting fact in the annals of art. I refer to the rarity in history of the supreme actor as compared with the supreme poet; the immense position which such men as Garrick, John Kemble, the elder Kean, Macready, and Irving occupied in the artistic life of England in the eighteenth and nineteenth centuries, and the unique appeal they made to multitudes of men and women in all classes from the highest to the humblest. Obviously there must be something unique in a genius such as that which caused Pope to watch Garrick's Richard III with eyes that 'shot and thrilled like lightning' through the actor's frame; that sent Byron into a sort of convulsive fit as he watched Kean in the part of Overreach; and that drew from Tennyson (who was by no means an ardent playgoer) the tribute that Irving's Hamlet had lifted Shakespeare's creation 'a degree nearer Heaven.'

I saw him in all his great *rôles*, and in most of them more than once, and I see and hear him still. In all his face played a great part. It could be that of a hero or the most craven of cowards, a saint or the vilest of sinners. It could be beautifully Hamlet and terribly Iago ; ideally the Vicar of Wakefield and repulsively Dubosc. Void of 'make-up,' its refinement was its most marked characteristic. I once heard a curious comment on this fact from a very able man, who was also a brother actor. One pre-war afternoon, as I was bidding good-bye to Sir Squire Bancroft after a visit to him, I noticed hanging in his hall an engraving of Millais' portrait of Irving, and remarked to my host upon the extreme refinement of the face. 'Yes,' he replied, 'but Irving wasn't always like that. I knew him when he was struggling and unknown, and his face was a very different one then. In every way, success refined him.' As he spoke I found myself studying Bancroft's own striking countenance, and I remembered that he, also, had emerged long before from the ranks of the strolling players. And, watching him, as he spoke in his impressive way, I thought his mouth the hardest I had ever looked upon. It set me musing on Tennyson's line : 'The abysmal deeps of personality.'

Was Bancroft right ? After all, I doubt it. Irving's 'success' really began with the first night of his Hamlet at the Lyceum, in the October of 1874. He was then still in his thirties, and we find the critics of that day referring to his 'exquisite refinement,' 'princely air,' and 'the beauty of the smile with which the dying Prince drew Horatio's face down and kissed it.' Years earlier, in Manchester, he had acted the same part and won praise for his 'delicate treatment of its poetry,' while in other characters the 'elegance' of his acting and its quality as 'that of a scholar and a gentleman' had been recognized. We also have Ellen Terry's written memory of her first meeting with him in 1867 : 'Better than his talent and his will, I remember his courtesy.' All of which seems to suggest that Irving's refinement was as innate as any other of his qualities, and was in no way a result of his 'success.'

I hope I have brought to young playgoers of to-day something of his Louis XI, though I know only too well that most of it is gone for ever. Some of it lives in Scott's novel, *Quentin Durward*, a book which may well have influenced Delavigne while he was writing his play. And visitors to that 'garden of France,' Touraine, may still find in the city of Tours a surviving scrap or two of that terrible castle of Plessis, and perhaps not far away a glade by the Loire which may suggest the one in which the old King was bamboozled by the young peasant woman. For those, however, who did not see Irving's performance and wish to gather some idea of it, the best course is to hark back to the newspapers and magazines of the day, and to the work of Bernard Partridge, James Pryde, Fred Barnard, William Nicholson, Alfred Bryan, William Rothenstein, and the scores of other splendid artists in black-and-white and in colour who made that period a Golden Age of illustration. To quote Ellen Terry once again: 'In those days all the painters loved the Lyceum'—and in their work Henry Irving's Louis XI and other impersonations are still almost as alive as ever.

H. M. WALBROOK.

The first time I saw Irving was as Mephistopheles in *Faust*. Though I was impressed, as no one could fail to be by any performance at the Lyceum, I had a feeling of disappointment. I had gone to see a tragedian and I saw a character actor in a performance, picturesque, and of a rare mocking humour, which I was too young and too unskilled a theatre-goer to appreciate.

A few weeks later I saw Irving as Louis XI, and was so fascinated that I went to see him again the following night. I saw him play it many times and to me it was the most completely satisfying of all his performances.

What distinguished Irving from all other actors was the extraordinary intellectuality he could impose on each and every character. It was a quality that made of him the master statesman, the master poet, and, in the lower scale, the master criminal. He made little things great and was no futurist seeking to see heaven in a blank wall. Added to this supreme intellectual suggestion was a complete mastery of his craft. Such as his tools were, he had entire control of them. In Louis XI all his physical defects fitted into the character. His rather inflexible staccato utterance, his restless eyebrows, his weakness at the knee, his thin, expressive hands. His technique extended to every part of the show business.

His first effect on his audience started in the street, with the poster. At a time when the walls were covered with luxurious lithos of virtuous maidens pursued by beautifully moustached villains, the Lyceum bills faced you, simple, austere. As you went up the red carpeted steps of the foyer you knew you had arrived—somewhere; some rare place. When you reached your seat you saw the frescoed line of the dress-circle with its clusters of candles, and the atmosphere began to affect you like the dim religious light of a cathedral. You were given a programme, simple and unpretentious, printed in the same colours as the poster which had attracted you; it was absolutely devoid of advertisement.

Irving knew, with the rest of the great fellowship of which he was the head, that nothing the author writes reaches the audience direct. Whatever his views, or his desires for propaganda, his words are simply those spoken by one character to another and entirely modified by the sympathy of the listener as it leans to one or the other. That is why Mr. Shaw's prefaces are so much more entertaining than his plays; we like him best to address us direct. Irving knew that not only must the dialogue be between the characters—and not sound as if it were indirectly aimed at a third person—but so must its delivery. The voice must be used so as to be heard distinctly in the gallery; the actor cannot afford to tire the listener. The voice must also produce no effect of shouting on the people in the stalls. This was an art, never too common. It has almost been destroyed by the microphone.

My friend, Julia Neilson, addressing some medical students on elocution, pointed out that reading aloud was the oldest known anæsthetic. Both Irving and Wyndham had a theory that each new sentence should have a different pace and different pitch. Frank Cooper told me that the old man (as he referred to Irving) sometimes carried this trait to ridiculous lengths. In a dull patch in *The Bells*, he would say in a low voice: 'It is a fine day' and then, in high, abrupt tones, 'but I think it will snow.' I am not quoting the exact words. Irving used this method with great success in Louis. He entered, pulling the ear of the farmer of customs who was stealing more than the conventional amount. . . . 'What, what, robbing my people . . . Robbing my people and me—especially me.' He slipped out the 'especially me' an octave lower and in what appeared to be the most casual manner, and the whole house roared with laughter, as the actor went on, apparently not having made the slightest effort; 'throwing the line away,' in modern stage parlance. It sounds easy, and so it is, if you don't mind being inaudible! Irving's gestures were individual, but we can gather there was nothing haphazard about them when he declared that the eye was so much quicker than the ear that he always delayed his gestures slightly to harmonize with his voice as it reached the audience.

In *Waterloo* he made up each separate finger to show the enlarged knuckles of age; in shabby clothes, with shambling walk, and careless manner he never lost his dignity. It was another instance of his stage-craft. Even in the act where he pretends to play the good man with his subjects they were never allowed to forget their respect, and communicated their respect to the public. When Irving entered as Dubosc, with the curiously nonchalant effect produced by chewing a long straw—Gillette did it with a cigar—he produced a feeling of terror in the audience. It was the feeling conveyed by his fellow criminals on the stage.

I have been dwelling a little on technicalities, because however great a man's gifts, he cannot convey them to the public without a mastery of his art. Irving's great achievement in Louis XI was to die slowly from the beginning of his performance to the end, and to give that death a spiritual significance.

Keats has described Edmund Kean, and Charlotte Brontë Rachel, in purple passages that produce the effect of a sunset at sea, a Canadian forest touched by frost, or the sudden Northern Lights. I am calling on Clement Scott to express what the great inarticulate public thought. Scott was less erudite than Walkley and Archer, but his sympathy was infallible. I am quoting loosely from memory an article Scott wrote fifty years ago for the *Illustrated London News*. It was entitled *Death Scenes I have Seen*. It was written at a time when Sarah Bernhardt was exploiting herself in Sardou's thrilling melodramas. A necessary concomitant was a violent death scene. The heroine chose the most virulent poison she could find and then exhibited her sufferings to a gasping public. Sarah would throw herself on a sofa, then wriggle on to the floor with a groan, and when she had exhausted the furniture, give her final flop.

Mrs. Bernard Beere, whom her admirers called 'the English Bernhardt' (she did not deserve the nickname for she was a fine actress in her own right) followed the vogue with a violent death scene in *As in a Looking Glass*. In the last act, when the poison gripped her vitals, Mrs. Beere uttered a scream that nearly made me jump out of my seat. Scott had no use for these acrobatic agonies. At the same time Mansfield caused quite a sensation in New York by his representation in *A Parisian Romance* of a man stricken by paralysis. Slowly one side of the man collapsed; one side of the face contorted, one arm, one leg. Scott dismissed it as a 'a case for the hospital and not the theatre.' He insisted that death on the stage must have a spiritual significance and not represent merely the physical fact. No one could forget the quiet grace of Aimée Desclès' final parting in *Frou-Frou*. We might have two opinions about Salvini's Hamlet, but only one about the lovely smile he gave

Horatio before he passed away. He might have added the pathos of Duse's '*Non voglio morire*' in *Adrienne Lecouvreur*—'the only hardship of death is to leave love behind.' Scott then points out the significance Irving gave to the last great exit in *Louis the Eleventh*. The King is lying motionless, inert, apparently alone, as he never was in life. The Dauphin enters and wonderingly lifts up the crown. Slowly the old King's eyes open, he takes the crown from the frightened boy, replaces it on his own head and tries to rise, leaning on his sceptre; but it is no support, his earthly grandeur cannot help him, and he sinks back for the last time into his throne.

It is not for me to speak of Irving's relations with his company. He engaged the best and paid them well, and generally managed to keep them in the background. He starred Ellen Terry, one of the most charming English actresses of all time. She shared with Ada Rehan the capacity of making blank verse sound absolutely conversational without sacrificing either rhythm or melody. But he showed too much or too little humour when he cast Ellen Terry for Lady Macbeth.

The only member of the company who could cope with Irving was Terriss. His calculated ingenuousness was too much for Irving. It was a tradition that no one should take a call but Irving and Ellen Terry. The first time Terriss played Nemours in *Louis the Eleventh* his admirers were in the gallery, and after the old man had been duly acclaimed, shouts arose for Terriss. Terriss advanced to take his call and the stage manager tried to stop him. Terriss drew his sword melodramatically: 'I kill the first man who tries to keep me from my public' and marched triumphantly on to the stage to meet Irving emerging from the other wing. Irving said nothing and from then on Terriss took his call.

Another example of Terriss's impudence occurred in the same play. In the scene where Louis is praying to the saints to intercede for him, to forgive him his sins and the little sin he is going to commit—namely, the killing of Nemours—Nemours, who has escaped from the prison, is standing unseen behind him. As the scene was arranged Irving was kneeling by the fire, with limelight from the fire on to his face to show up his agonized pleadings, when he discovers Nemours; Nemours standing like the Angel Gabriel, but in the dark. Just before he went on, Terriss went to the limelight man and said: "The Guv'nor says you are to put the lime on me." The limelight man gasped. "The Guv'nor says you are to put the lime on me," repeated Terriss. Terriss played the scene in shining armour, while Irving acted furiously in the gloom. When the curtain came down Irving exploded, but his anger melted before Terriss's ingenuous explanation: "Well, you see, Guv'nor, it was the only chance I had." Perhaps the old man felt the compliment was sincere, if not the explanation.

WILLIAM DEVEREUX.

IRVING *As SHYLOCK*

A CARICATURE BY
T. W. A. LINGARD

XVII

IRVING as VANDERDECKEN

Lyceum Theatre, 8th of June, 1878 :—

VANDERDECKEN

(*An adaptation of The Legend of The Flying Dutchman*)

WRITTEN BY W. G. WILLS AND PERCY FITZGERALD

Philip Vanderdecken	MR. HENRY IRVING
Nils	MR. JAMES FERNANDEZ
Olaf	MR. WALTER BENTLEY
Pastor Anders Been	MR. EDMUND LYONS
Alderman Jorgen	MR. A. W. PINERO
Jans Stoffen	MR. R. LYONS
Soreen	MR. ARCHER
Nurse Birgit	MISS PAUNCEFORT
Christine	MISS JONES
Jetty	MISS HARWOOD
Old Nancy	MISS ST. JOHN
Thekla	MISS ISABEL BATEMAN

ACT I. *Evening.* SCENE. *Cottage of Old Nils, the Pilot, near the entrance of the Christiania Fjord.* ACT II. *Daybreak.* SCENE 1. *Quay of the Fishing Village ;* SCENE 2. *Interior of the Cottage.* ACT III, SCENE. *Path leading by the Cliff to the Cottage of Nils ; distant view of the Skager Rack.* ACT IV, SCENE 1. *Interior of the Cottage ;* SCENE 2. *Deck of the Phantom Ship. The Haven.*

THE first time I saw Irving act was in *Uncle Dick's Darling* with Toole, and I think I saw everything he did after that, most of it many times. As Mr. Chevenix I can see him now, the typical aristocrat of the 'sixties in tightly buttoned frock-coat and silk hat, leaning on his umbrella as he talked to Michael Garner (Toole), bargaining with him, I think, for his daughter's hand, while the old showman sat on the shaft of his caravan, cleaning some harness.

Mr. Chevenix led to Digby Grant, Digby Grant to the Lyceum under Bateman, and then his own triumphant management.

Vanderdecken is interesting as being the last play produced there under the Bateman management. It was a bold experiment and reflected the greatest credit on Mrs. Bateman. It must have been no easy matter to decide on a successor to *The Lyons Mail* and *Louis the Eleventh*, two of Irving's greatest successes, for he had become the star and the main attraction in spite of the fact that the theatre had been taken to exploit Bateman's youngest daughter, Isabel. So far she had had no very great opportunity, except as the Queen in *Charles the First*, but this play, which Percy Fitzgerald had suggested to Irving some years before, contained a very beautifully drawn character of a young girl which gave her the chance to repeat her success, and something more, for it was touched with a very sweet and sensitive poetry and Miss Bateman's success in it was complete. Clement Scott wrote of her: 'We must congratulate Miss Bateman on her recital of the fine poem by Mr. Wills—that is, the legend of the Flying Dutchman—it struck the first note of the prelude to romance. So earnest, so absorbed, so rapt was the actress that she held the house.'

The story is, of course, founded on the same original as Wagner's opera, not the old Adelphi melodrama of Fitzball in which T. P. Cooke and afterwards the celebrated O. Smith ('Sweeny Tod') appeared as the Phantom Dutchman arising from the waves in blue fire, but the legend of the Dutch sailor who for an impious threat was condemned to sail the seas eternally, yet given the chance once in every seven years of redemption by a woman's love. Heine had found this love motif for Wagner, Fitzgerald adopted it for his romance and invited W. G. Wills to give it his poetic touch. But for Irving it had two disadvantages; while it offered him all possible scope for poetic expression and picturesque pose it lacked strength and variety of character. All his magnetism was brought into play, but the theme was that meanest of human obsessions, self-pity, and that, I believe, was the root cause of the play's failure. Audiences do not analyse, they feel, and self-pity is an emotion that has no appeal for them.

The production was ideal, the settings weird and atmospheric, the lighting a marvel of ingenuity. But the basic idea was not sympathetic and at the end of a month the play was withdrawn to make way for a revival of *The Bells*.

It must not be supposed that in any sense *Vanderdecken* was a crude melodrama. With the exception of the quarrel between the two men, Olaf, Thekla's rejected lover, and Vanderdecken, and the fight that ensued, there was little action; but for me, to hear the verse so excellently phrased and spoken was full compensation. Never was Irving more quiet, never—except perhaps as Philip of Spain—had he exercised such authority. Scott, in the notice from which I have quoted above, said: 'The greatest praise that can be given to Mr. Irving is contained in the fact that his presence and influence showed a Vanderdecken clear and distinct to the audience, a Vanderdecken of picturesque and romantic interest, a Vanderdecken haunted by the despair of an eternity of life and comforted by the possession of an eternity of love.' A great sentimentalist, Clement Scott.

We had become used to plays of action at the Lyceum; the static charm of this eerie romance was something new, and, of all groups of society, playgoers are the most conservative.

I will admit that I do not remember the detail very distinctly and that is why I turned up Scott's notice, but two things I do remember very clearly: Irving's first appearance; he didn't enter—he was there! A most weird effect, achieved by the lighting and the silent removal of a sail, and, in a ghostly mist, he stood before us. The second effect, after the fight when Olaf flung Vanderdecken's dead body from the cliff-top: Vanderdecken was presently washed up by a wave and rescued by Thekla, living, and I see the two together standing on board the ship at the end.

We saw Isabel Bateman afterwards at the Princess's in *Taken from Life* and in that most wonderful Adelphi success, *In the Ranks*, both with Charles Warner, who, with Irving and George Belmore, had been engaged by her father to support her when he opened the Lyceum. She left the stage eventually and became an Anglican nun. She died last year.

But it is pleasant to remember that Mrs. Edward Compton (Miss Virginia Bateman), the mother of Fay, Viola, and Ellen Compton and the novelist, Compton Mackenzie, is still with us. As Miss Virginia Francis she was the first to play Julie Lesurques in *The Lyons Mail* and Marie de Commines in *Louis the Eleventh* with Irving. She was also the Mrs. Racket in *The Belle's Strategem*, and as her husband's leading lady in the Compton Comedy Company we remember her in many parts at the Strand Theatre (where Aldwych tube station now stands), Lady Teazle, Kate Hardcastle, Lydia Languish, and Sophia in *The Road to Ruin*. I think I saw her, too, as Viola in *Twelfth Night*. Edward Compton himself was the last to play Richelieu in London; I also saw William Mollison and Murray Carson in the part, but none could compare with Irving.

Surely there was never an actor who had such a hold on the public as he. In all the years that I followed his career I know of no occasion when he lost his grip on the audience, though I do remember a first night when his entrance was greeted with unwelcome laughter. It was in the second act of *Ravenswood;* Ellen Terry as Lucy had rushed on the stage pursued, as she said, by a mad bull. A shot was heard and Irving rushed in, gun in hand, to a shout of laughter. To this day I cannot say exactly what was wrong, but I believe a slight alteration was made on subsequent nights.

Nor did he often make a slip, though I remember one occasion. In the scene with Ophelia, following 'To be or not to be,' speaking with intense passion Hamlet says: 'To a nunnery go and quickly too, Farewell!'—on this Irving rushed off the stage and immediately returned to go on with the words: 'If thou dost marry, etc.' Instead, he began again the speech he had just said, but pulled up short and went on to the right words.

On the last night of his farewell season at Drury Lane he came out on the arm of H. B. and in answer to the applause of the crowd outside the stage door he put his hand on H. B. as much as to say: 'Here is the new Irving!'

And they are all gone!

FRANK HALDEN MACEY.

THE FASHIONABLE TRAGEDIAN[1]

This is probably one of the most scurrilous pamphlets of the nineteenth century. The biting sarcasm of the very title reflects the intellectual snobbery and arrogance of its authors—two young men who had rashly decided that an actor who fills a draughty theatre to capacity must necessarily forfeit claim to recognition in the centrally heated mansions of art. I have read and re-read these twenty-four pages of adolescent invective, and I have searched in vain for any evidence that the authors had any more substantial grievance than that in 1877, when the pamphlet was written and published anonymously from Scotland, Henry Irving was the most overwhelmingly popular English actor of the day. Apparently, our two young pamphleteers, veiled in reckless anonymity, could not see what the theatre world generally had observed unerringly, that Irving's interpretations of Hamlet, Macbeth, Othello, and Richard III bore the unmistakable imprints of genius and presaged a renaissance of English histrionic art.

Irving's early triumphs appear to have completely flabbergasted his two young critics. Their contempt for his acting

[1] *The Fashionable Tragedian: A Criticism.* With Ten Illustrations. (Thomas Gray & Co., Edinburgh and Glasgow.) 1877.

only slightly exceeded their contempt for the public which willingly and eagerly paid hard cash for the privilege of seeing it. I do not think it will be difficult to prove that their contempt for both one and the other was contemptuous. And I propose partly to discharge this pleasant duty by quoting from the pamphlet itself:

> 'No actor of this, or indeed of any other age, has been so much and so indiscriminately belauded as Mr. Henry Irving. For more than five years he has been "the bright particular star" of the British dramatic firmament. Night after night has he filled the dingy old Lyceum, from the front row of the stalls to the back row of the gallery, with audiences which applauded every jerk, every spasm, every hysteric scream—we had almost said every convulsion—in which he chose to indulge. In the provinces he has met with the same success and the same laudation. Newspaper "critics" have ransacked and exhausted their by no means limited vocabulary in the search for words in which to express his greatness. He is, we are told, the resuscitator of all the past glories of the British drama, with the addition of new glories peculiarly his own. . . . Men of science, men of learning, poets, philosophers vie with each other in singing his praises. Bishops eulogise him in after-dinner speeches; statesmen "tap him on the shoulder" while walking down Bond Street and introduce themselves to him with expressions of enthusiastic admiration; peeresses engage the stage-box night after night to gaze at his contortions.'

If there exists anywhere in the whole of English literature a fragment of polemical writing that surpasses the foregoing quotation in either impudence or perversity I am fortunately unaware of it. To me, it is incredible that any man of any age in any age would dare to give the permanence of the printed word to submissions that outrage every letter in the alphabet of creative dramatic criticism. Even more incredible is the fact that the authors of *The Fashionable Tragedian* not only failed to see the advisability of blowing out their brains as a minimum atonement for their thuggery, but in later years actually enjoyed respectable and even respected public eminence as Mr. William Archer and Mr. Robert William Lowe. If the authors' unrighteous indignation and ruthless iconoclasm are accepted literally we must infer that two young and very inexperienced critics seriously imagined that philosophers, poets, statesmen, dramatic critics, and the poor old British public were being individually and collectively hypnotized by a charlatan. I think they must have had some slight realization of the fundamental weakness of their case, for they are at pains to point out that 'we are speaking of Mr. Henry Irving *as he is*, and as he has been for two or three years: not as he was before long runs, indiscriminate adulation and several other circumstances had exaggerated his inherent defects, and destroyed what he undoubtedly possessed—the germs of a good and even great actor. His Digby Grant was excellent. His first performances of Mathias were certainly wonderful. Even up to his first performances of Hamlet his faults had not grown upon him to any morbid extent. It is from the marvellous "200 nights' run" that his degeneration dates, and since then his course downhill has been rapid and fatal.'

I submit that this is *not* dramatic criticism. If it is anything at all within the range of human comprehension it is perverted omniscience caricaturing itself. Unfortunately, it cannot have failed to wound the sensibilities of the great actor whose heart and soul were absorbed in his art. And for that reason, if for no other, such an ill-natured attack, exceeding the bounds of fair and intelligent criticism, demands refutation in this Symposium. I cannot find words charged with sufficiently speedy momentum to overtake our authors' lightning verbal flashes of exaggeration and self-evident contradiction. I am content to posit one incontrovertible fact. It is this. Their pamphlet appeared in 1877—one year before the beginning of Henry Irving's twenty-one years' triumphant reign as 'Guv'nor' in the Lyceum Theatre. If one-tenth of the authors' statements against Irving, all of which implied that he was already a 'spent force' in the theatre, were true, is it conceivable that Irving could have filled his theatre with wildly enthusiastic audiences at every performance from 1878–1902? Irving's pre-eminence as a consistent 'box office' attraction has never been surpassed, and probably never equalled, in the annals of the English theatre. And, therefore, I find it impossible to believe that the British public has ever been so completely bereft of critical judgment as to support and acclaim an artist of whom our authors record that 'it is by no means difficult to prove, beyond the possibility of *rational* contradiction from any one who is not blinded by fashion, that Mr. Irving is in fact one of the worst actors that ever trod the British stage in so-called "leading characters."' In this connection it is germane to point out that because a person is rational is no sufficient reason for assuming that he is right!

I have previously suggested that our authors, when writing their thesis, were dimly aware that its public reception would be hostile except among a very small minority. They certainly displayed excessive anxiety to side-track any suggestion that their attack on Irving was actuated by either personal or professional animosity. 'We write,' they naïvely confess, 'entirely without personal feeling . . . we have no personal knowledge of Mr. Irving, have had no communication of any sort with him, and indeed never saw him except on the stage. Moreover, we have no professional connection with the stage: our knowledge of it is gained entirely from the front of the house.' I have no means of knowing what effect this admission had upon those members of the public who read the pamphlet on its appearance, but I am willing to confess that, when I read it, it staggered me. Here are two youngsters, barely out of their teens, self-confessedly without any pretensions to professional dramatic criticism, with no personal experience of the art of acting, who have so much brazen effrontery and intellectual pomposity as to see nothing ludicrous in their intention to animadvert both the Press and the public for its indulgence in hero-worship of a man who, whatever he was or was not, had certainly clearly won his spurs—and golden ones at that—in the Theatre.

It would be absurd for me, or for anyone else, to pretend at this distance of time that Irving, as actor and producer, was faultless. Indeed, this very Symposium to which I have the honour to contribute, does not fail to point out his occasional lapses and his insurmountable limitations. But I am not to be persuaded that Irving's immortality is spurious because of them, any more than I am capable of doubting the eternity of our Shakespearean heritage merely because some of our professors of English literature have discovered that Shakespeare sometimes jilted his own genius. I will make a present to Messrs. Archer and Lowe in the frank admission that their insistence on re-valuing almost all of Irving's assets as liabilities is staggeringly original in terms of æsthetic accountancy. Their procedure is quite elementary. In effect, they argue, if the verdict of the public and the Press is that this and that and the other are Irving's qualities and virtues as actor and producer, our duty as custodians of the nation's artistic conscience is as clear as the blood-red and sea-green lights of railway signals. All we need to do is to shout a discordant chorus of categorical Noes, and lo and behold the nation's verdict is null and void! And what are the 'alleged' great qualities in this grand personality which incense and outrage the mean minds of his anonymous detractors? They themselves do not scruple to enumerate them—

sticking them up like alley-skittles for the sheer joy of knocking them down again. Here they are:

I. Irving is the most intellectual of all actors.

II. He is original—does not cling to stage traditions, but invents new conceptions of character, new modes of expression, and new arrangements of text.

III. He is picturesque in attitude, motion and bearing, and vivid in expression.

IV. He is master of a psychological subtlety hitherto unknown in histrionic art. He lays bare the very quivering nerves of the characters he expounds and illuminates.

V. He elaborates his performances—every motion of the fingers, every elevation of the eyebrows, every protrusion of the lower jaw being carefully studied and contributing towards a well-defined end.

VI. He is possessed of a most delicate and exquisite taste which presents Shakespeare precisely as he should be presented —without superstitious adherence to text, and yet without Gothic mutilation of it.

If the eye-witness evidence contributed to this Symposium by those who acted with Irving and by those who saw him act can be accepted as reliable—and surely there can be no two opinions on this point—it will be conceded that the foregoing brief summary of Irving's major qualities as actor and producer is substantially incontestable. I need hardly add that the writers of the pamphlet have recalcitrant views on the subject. They are careful to warn their readers that 'it is not our purpose to examine these separate items of laudation very minutely. Some of them we think wholly unjustified, and others true only in a limited sense.'

I will now epitomize their case against *The Fashionable Tragedian*. Irving, they claim, could not walk—he limped. His natural voice was harsh. His stage voice 'was still more unpleasant by his trick of alternating between *basso profundo* and *falsetto*.' His pronunciation of English was impossible to represent with the ordinary letters of our alphabet—'we should have to invent new characters unknown even to the phonetic system.' His physical defects are caricatured with what I can only describe as vicious personal animus—'a weak, loosely built figure, face whose range of expression is very limited'; physical defects, in short, that 'utterly preclude the possibility of dignity, grace, or even ease.' Our authors pungently remind us that many other actors, particularly Edmund Kean and Garrick, have overcome physical defects by sheer force of genius—' in Mr. Irving there seems to be none of the divine flame.' His intellectuality is damned with faint praise—' it is very satisfactory, in the present low state of culture among actors, to possess a tragedian who can write in advanced reviews, read essays on the drama, make neat self-laudatory speeches at dinners and shine at temperance soirées and æsthetic teas.' But when all is said and done our authors admit, with painful reluctance, that there is no harm in granting Irving intellectual eminence because, in any case, that does not affect the argument that he is ' a very bad actor.' Again I contend that this is not criticism. It is spiteful, unbalanced, ill-mannered abuse. Why and how these youthful iconoclasts escaped a public birching surpasses my comprehension. On the face of it, if Irving commanded, as he did, the respect and admiration of men and women of culture, it follows that he received these attentions only because he was genuinely entitled to them.

Our authors proceed to dismiss Irving's originality, picturesqueness, and vividness as mere personal peculiarities. They ask readers to believe that the secret of his originality lies ' in the forehead, chin, neck, shoulders, and legs—no one possessed of these eccentric members could be other than original in his execution: that is to say, he must of necessity act as no one ever acted before, and, let us hope, as no one will ever act again. . . . People see a man moving, standing, and attitudinizing on the stage as no actor ever did before and they at once call him vivid and picturesque.' It is impossible to take a charitable view of such unlicensed vituperation. I confess I am mystified as to which precise specie of bee had made habitation in these juvenile critics' bonnets. It is inconceivable that Irving had at some time or other done them an injustice. On their own admission, they were strangers, and it is reasonably certain that Irving had never even heard of them. Irving, like all great men before and after him, had his critics, but I can discover nothing else in print so unmistakably irrelevant and, in the true sense, uncritical as the anonymous mud-slinging in this pamphlet. If there was any veracity in the censure I have just expounded then Irving on the stage cannot have been appreciably superior to a performing ape. That, not unfairly, is the logical deduction from the authors' so-called criticism.

But the panegyric that obviously threw our authors into a paroxysm of rage is that which credits Irving with the mental attribute of psychological subtlety. Apparently, a warm-hearted idiot had dared to write that Irving was a profound student of human nature, and to this our authors, from their pedestal of ludicrous isolation, protest—' he is merely condensing what hundreds of other critics have said before him.' This really is unbeatable whether considered as an example of blind obstinacy or as an indication of the intellectual myopia of little men when they make up their twisted minds to prey upon great ones. They are not content merely to swim against the tide of public and critical opinion. They insist that in their trickling tributary alone flow the limpid waters of histrionic art.

They admit grudgingly that Irving's studies of murder, mesmerism and nightmare possess psychological subtlety. His Shakespearean impersonations, however, are ' simply ghastly.' We are invited to believe that ' Hamlet, in his scene with Polonius, suggested nothing so strongly as a rude, overgrown schoolboy insulting his guardian,' while his approaches to Ophelia reminded one of ' the tyrannical guardian in a farce ordering off the innocent heroine to a boarding-school. His bullying of her was gratuitously ungentlemanly—we should be inclined to call it vulgar.' It is perhaps not without significance that our authors' criticism is frequently emphasized by similes that remind us of the place they themselves have so recently deserted—the classroom! Having icily dismissed Irving's Macbeth and Othello as performances that were beneath contempt, our pamphleteers run riot in a summing-up which, as creative criticism, manifests a maximum of heat and the minimum of light—' if it be Irving's psychological subtlety which makes of Hamlet a weak-minded puppy, of Macbeth a writhing poltroon and a Uriah Heep in chain armour, of Othello an " infuriated Sepoy," and of Richard III a cheap Mephistopheles, all we can say is, the less we have of psychological subtlety on the English stage the better.' Surely such ' criticism ' defeats itself? Not only is it impossible to imagine that Irving's acting remotely justified such libellous condemnation, but it is equally inconceivable that any actor of any age and of the meanest quality could survive on the English stage for five minutes if our critics' vituperative allegations were fundamentally true. Irving himself ignored this pamphlet, and this fact tempts me to suggest that there is no need to look further afield for evidence of his quintessential greatness as a man and of his supreme self-confidence as an artist.

My criticism of a criticism is reaching its journey's end. Two counts remain in *The Fashionable Tragedian* indictment. They concern Irving's artistic elaboration and taste. Of the former, our authors are graciously pleased to admit that ' it is the only virtue which we freely and without qualification concede to

Mr. Irving. To say that he elaborates his performances is merely to say that he does not insult the public by appearing in half-studied parts. It shows to what a low level British dramatic art has fallen when the merest commonplace conscientiousness is considered a perfect miracle.' It does indeed! It also demonstrates that our critics' views on what constitutes an *unqualified* admission are as unorthodox and illogical as their opinions on great acting. At the very best, the writers have handed out a double-edged compliment. At the worst, one more insult. It is not very difficult to concede that a man is a giant when you have first taken mighty good care to place him among pygmies.

The last claps of verbal thunder are reserved for Irving's much-lauded Taste. 'In the large,' they write, 'this quality must be granted him. But when we come to minor points—the points on which an actor's reputation must depend—the case is altered. Here his taste is questionable. We need not again refer to the grosser absurdities of his performances which proceed, perhaps, as much from physical necessity as from bad taste. His tendency to carry realism to a ludicrous extreme cannot, however, be excused. It proceeds from the bad taste of being unable to recognise the limits of his own powers. In the hands of a heaven-born actor like Salvini, realism is impressive . . . in the hands of Mr. Irving it became merely ludicrous.' Outside the pages of this pamphlet there is not a particle of evidence, either oral or verbal, which suggests that Irving—the actor and the man—was deficient in good taste. On the contrary, there is abundance of evidence in this very Symposium and elsewhere to support the claim that Irving's taste was impeccable. But when all is said and done, if there is one subject more than another upon which our critics would have been wise to remain silent it is surely on the question of other people's taste. Their pamphlet, from first page to last, reeks of bad taste and, if possible, worse judgment. Indiscriminate ridicule and personal abuse are unworthy substitutes for constructive and creative criticism. Irving's alleged extreme realism is ideal compared with our critics' extreme iconoclasm. From my own careful perusal of this pamphlet I carry away at least one lasting impression—a picture of three little boys (I make this belated acknowledgment to the artist-collaborator whose outrageously cruel and spiteful caricatures so faithfully interpreted the authors' text) poking fun, 'cocking a snook' at a man who had already convinced the majority of his contemporaries of his greatness, and who ultimately established his genius beyond any shadow of doubt in the minds of those best qualified to appraise and acclaim his achievements.

Messrs. Archer and Lowe end their 'hymn of hate' on a note of critical anticipation. They write: 'Our theory regarding Henry Irving may be summed-up as follows: when the first blush of fashionable fame is over, the generally received theory will be somewhat similar to our own.' And, mark you, this gem of fatuous prognostication was written on the eve of Irving's greatest triumphs—triumphs which transformed the English theatre in general and the Lyceum in particular into vital, living realities. That they must have been overwhelmingly convincing triumphs is beyond cavil, if for no more cogent reason than that our critics themselves were subsequently forced to eat their own words. In so short a space of time as six years after the first appearance of their verbal vendetta, William Archer could, and did, write: 'I believe that many other of Mr. Irving's critics have gone through similar phases of dislike and struggling respect, to end in what I hope I may call rational appreciation. Mr. Irving, in sum, has been lavishly endowed by nature with the constituent features of a magnetic personality. . . . Such a brilliant success, achieved and maintained by one man, is probably without precedence in the history of the stage.' And on that note of qualified, though none the less welcome, recantation I may, perhaps fittingly, lay down my pen.

CECIL PALMER.

XVIII

IRVING as CLAUDE MELNOTTE

Lyceum Theatre, 17th of April, 1879 :—

THE LADY OF LYONS

WRITTEN BY BULWER LYTTON

Claude Melnotte	MR. IRVING
Colonel Damas	MR. WALTER LACY
Beauseant	MR. FORRESTER
Glavis	MR. KYRLE BELLEW
Monsieur Deschappelles	MR. C. COOPER
Landlord	MR. S. JOHNSON
Gaspar	MR. TYARS
Captain Gervaise	MR. ELWOOD
Captain Dupont	MR. CARTWRIGHT
Major Desmoulins	MR. ANDREWS
Notary	MR. TAPPING
Servant	MR. BRANSCOMBE
Servant	MR. HOLLAND
Madame Deschappelles	MRS. CHIPPENDALE
Widow Melnotte	MISS PAUNCEFORT
Janet	MISS MAY SEDLEY
Marian	MISS HARWOOD
Pauline	MISS ELLEN TERRY

ACT I, SCENE 1. *A Room in the House of M. Deschappelles ;* SCENE 2. *The Exterior of The Golden Lion ;* SCENE 3. *The Interior of Melnotte's Cottage.* ACT II, SCENE. *The Gardens of M. Deschappelles.* ACT III, SCENE 1. *The Exterior of The Golden Lion ;* SCENE 2. *The Interior of Melnotte's Cottage.* ACT IV, SCENE. *The Cottage, as before.* ACT V (*two and a half years are supposed to have elapsed*), SCENE 1. *A Street in Lyons ;* SCENE 2. *A Room in the House of M. Deschappelles.*

HAMLET was the first part I saw Henry Irving play.

I was a young schoolboy at the time, having only recently arrived in London from Kingston, Jamaica, whither my father's family had migrated from Spain to escape the rigours of the Inquisition.

My father, who was devoted to the drama, used to take his vacations in New York, where he saw Edwin Booth, then in the full flush of his youth and his powers, in *Hamlet* and in most of his great parts, over and over again. Booth *was* Hamlet to him, and my father was deeply impressed by his performance.

When I was about nine he began reading the great *Hamlet* scenes to me and he made me read them after him, so that by the time I was eleven I knew them by heart.

When Irving took the Lyceum and opened it under his own management on 30 December 1878, I was there. Crowds had gathered for the pit hours before the doors opened. I arrived about three hours before opening time and found the queue stretching far up the Strand. That, however, did not worry me. The people in the public-house next door knew me by sight, by reason of my frequent attendance, and I was let in under the counter and allowed to clamber through a window which opened on the top of the passage where there was an iron grating which was given a wide berth by the crowd lest the weight of people standing and pushing on it might break it down. I dropped on to this grating and so was quite close to the door.

So dense was the crowd that it was impossible for anyone to get in to light the single gas lamp over the pit door, in spite of the cries for light, for it was pitch black, and that gas lamp was the only means of illumination in the passage. Being very small and light, two men hoisted me up, while I held my knee joints perfectly stiff, and giving me a box of matches, I turned on and lighted the gas—thus winning my first round of applause from a theatrical audience.

It was a night of triumph. Being his own Manager, Irving naturally could do what he liked. On 17 April 1879, he interrupted the run of *Hamlet* to produce *The Lady of Lyons* with himself as Claude Melnotte, which had become one of the great test parts for leading actors since it was produced by Macready over forty years earlier.

Again I was there, in the front row of the pit, at the doors of which I had waited some three hours and had squashed in, for there was no queue in those days and we had to fight and struggle to keep our feet and prevent our ribs being broken in the closely packed mob which stretched from the passage by the side of ' The Wellington ' to far up the Strand.

It was said that Irving produced the play to give Ellen Terry the opportunity to play a star part as she had had to be content with Ophelia when she opened as his leading lady. I discredit that altruistic motive. Consider the following facts.

The night after he made his *début* at the Royal Lyceum Theatre, Sunderland, he played the Second Officer, who appears only at the beginning of the last act. Two years later, while acting in Edinburgh, he announced a reading of the play in

Linlithgow during 'holiday week.' Nobody attended ! Nothing daunted, when he was leaving that city to go to the Princess's Theatre, London, he was given a benefit on 13 September 1859, and he chose to play Claude, and made a great success.

Three months later, on 19 December, he gave a reading of the play at Crosby Hall, and the chief London papers chronicled his remarkable success, while in Manchester on 4 April 1862 he again acted Claude and on 8 August 1863 he read the play in the ballroom at Buxton.

It is the fashion to say that *The Lady of Lyons* is 'fustian.' It is only fustian when treated in the wrong spirit, without conviction and enthusiasm. Actually it is a great *acting* vehicle, taxing all the actor's technical skill.

The son of the gardener employed by Monsieur and Madame Deschappelles falls in love with their beautiful proud daughter, Pauline. With artistic tastes far beyond his station, he has become adept with the small-sword and the musket, and has studied music, poetry, and painting so that he is able to paint from memory the portrait of the woman he adores.

The audience sees him first when he rushes into his mother's cottage, flushed with success at having won the local shooting match. Up to that time all the actors of Claude had worn the blue blouse of the French peasant and carried the gun which was the prize. Irving, with his keen sense of appropriateness and the picturesque, wore a shooting coat of brown velveteen with gaiters buttoned closely to his thighs and across his shoulders was slung the gun with which he had been shooting, while in his right hand, high above his head, was the prize, wreathed with brightly coloured ribbons.

According to the calendar, Irving was forty-one. The calendar lied, for Claude did not look a day over twenty-five. We did not need the opening line to tell us of his triumph, for the face that only a night or two before had been 'sicklied o'er with the pale cast of thought' was now radiant with youth, alive with excitement, alert with success. Unlike so many actors, Irving did not wait until he came on the stage to begin to act. His acting began where all acting should begin, in his imagination, in his dressing-room.

In spite of his almost boyish enthusiasm and joy in his victory, Irving, who probed every part he played for its psychological problems, gave a deep mental maturity to Claude.

The young hero is, however, not allowed to enjoy his triumph for long. The messenger who has taken his passionate verses to Pauline has been driven from the door with blows.

In her pride she has also rejected the addresses of a rich suitor, Beauseant. Both men are incensed to the point of seeking vengeance on her.

Beauseant's more subtle brain devises a plot to use Claude's frenzy to take a double vengeance on Pauline by offering him in a letter the opportunity to woo and win her in the disguise of an Italian prince. With that letter Irving made an effect which an actor less sure of himself would never have attempted. He read it, not once nor twice, but three times, as if he could not grasp the full possibilities of the proposal. On the third reading his expression blazed with comprehension and triumph and he achieved a wonderful *coup de théâtre*. The house rose at him.

As the Prince of Como, Claude makes passionate love to Pauline. In the garden of her home, by the light of the moon, he paints for her a picture of the home to which 'could love fulfill its prayers' he would lead her. Lying on a grassy bank he pours honey-sweet words into her love-raptured ears. As played by Irving it was the quintessence of love-making.

Although accepted by the family, Colonel Damas, Madame Deschappelle's cousin, mistrusts the supposed Prince of Como, but Claude, with bantering sarcasm, cleverly turns the tables on the old soldier, making him appear ridiculous. Such an insult cannot be allowed to pass. Damas challenges him to a duel then and there. Claude, expert with the small-sword as with the musket, disarms his adversary and hands him back his sword, whereon the old soldier, exclaiming: 'It's astonishing how much I like a man when I've fought with him!' declares himself Claude's friend for life.

Overcome at the apparent success of what he now realizes is a mean plot, Claude seeks out Beauseant and begs to be released from his part in it. Beauseant reminds him that the contract was sealed by oath and compels him to carry out its terms.

Claude marries Pauline and takes her, not to the palace he so eloquently described, but to his mother's humble cottage. She, all unconsciously, reveals the truth. As Pauline recoils from him, Claude's mental torture was expressed so forcibly as to become a great emotional triumph for Irving.

With her love betrayed, Pauline has still to drain the cup of bitterness. Her father and mother, shocked by the imposture of which they have now heard, arrive with Colonel Damas to demand a divorce for their daughter. In bitter humiliation, Claude consents, and to rid them of his presence announces his intention of joining the army, a detachment of which is passing through the village. The approaching band is playing the Marseillaise.

"Place me where France most needs a life," he begs of Damas, and the old officer replies: "There shall not be a forlorn hope without you."

Claude rushes from the room as the music swells, and, with men, women, and children following the band, the soldiers, four abreast, come marching in a never breaking line. Higher and higher grows the excitement; still the band plays; still the men come marching until, at length, with head held high, mouth set stern, eyes blazing with excitement, Claude passes the window and waving farewell to the little group in the cottage, the curtain comes down to thunderous applause.

Up it went. Down it came. Over and over and over again as we kept on applauding, applauding, applauding with a fevered, almost frenzied, tribute of admiration for a master of climax.

Two and a half years go by, and, in the last act, Claude who enlisted under the name of Morier returns with the rank of Colonel and the reputation of one of the bravest men in the army. As he came on the stage, Irving looked the image of Napoleon. The effect was electrical. It was not, of course, the Buonaparte of the later days when he had put on flesh, but the Buonaparte of the first Italian campaign . . . the Buonaparte of the set mouth, the eagle-like glance, the beautiful, thin face, which Josephine said was too handsome to be disfigured by a moustache.

The remarkable fact was that he was more like Napoleon then than when he played the Emperor himself in *Madame Sans-Gêne* in 1897.

The end of the play is, of course, obvious. With all Lyons talking of its hero, Pauline's romantic nature is fired with admiration for the man, and when she meets Morier and recognizes that he is her husband she goes joyfully to his embrace.

Magnificent as were Irving's climaxes, on which he always laid stress as part of his technique, there were critics who went to the extreme length of declaring that nature had placed a bar against his playing such parts, while others went further, saying they hoped he would never attempt Romeo.

Three years later, however, he not only attempted but played Romeo in such a way as to reveal new beauties in a part which he made a picture of passionate young manhood, instead of one of adolescent youth. The Earl of Lytton, speaking at a banquet given by Irving in celebration of the one hundredth performance of the play, said: ' Mr. Irving's eminence as an actor needs from me no individual recognition. It has long ago been established, and in connection with its manifestation, it has been reaffirmed with enthusiasm with a popular verdict, which supersedes all personal comment.'

In the early part of his career, as I have suggested, much stress was laid on the Irving mannerisms. On certain occasions and in certain parts he undoubtedly adopted a restlessness of demeanour, an abruptness of gait, a sharp staccato method of speech which, it was generally assumed, were inherent defects in his technical education. Were they? On one occasion, talking to Laurence Irving about his father's performances, he said to me: " My father once told me that when he resolved to play the great Shakespeare parts he realized he had not the physical force to act them in the way they were usually represented, so he translated them into a language of his own." Is it not possible that some of these ' mannerisms ' grew out of the ' Translation '? They certainly were wonderful adjuncts in his representations of such characters as Mathias, Dubosc, and Louis XI, three magnificent performances whose highest points were revelations, not only of the intimacies of the human mind, but also of the effect which a great actor can produce on ' a theatre of others.'

During the last run of *Hamlet* at the Lyceum, my father came to London.

" I'm going to give you the treat of your life," I said to him, " for I'm going to take you to see Irving play Hamlet."

I booked three seats in the stalls, with his money, and with a friend we went on the appointed evening. When the curtain had fallen on the first Act, I turned to my father and speaking with intense admiration, said: " What do you think of him? "

" My son, I have seen Edwin Booth play Hamlet," said my father.

I was crushed. Not another word did I speak until the curtain fell on the second Act, when, with even more *empressement* I asked: " Well, what do you think of him now? "

" My son, you have never seen Edwin Booth play Hamlet," replied my father, and there was a note of pity in his voice.

Silenced to sadness, I sat dumb. When, however, the curtain fell on the third Act at the end of the Play Scene, and Irving, who had been lying at Ophelia's feet, had leapt on to the dais and, picking up the peacock fan with which the Queen had been toying during the performance, held it high above his head, shouted :

> ' For thou dost know, O Damon dear,
> This Realm dismantled was
> Of Jove himself and now reigns here '

then, hurling the fan into the throne just vacated by the King :

> ' A very, very peacock.'

I turned to see my father standing in his place, beating his two hands together loudly above his head and shouting at the top of his voice : " Bravo ! bravo ! bravo!" utterly unconscious of the fact that scores of people had turned round and were staring at him. I caught him by the left arm, our friend caught him by the right, and we pulled him down into his seat.

" Well ? " I asked triumphantly.

" My God, Edwin Booth never did anything like that ! " he exclaimed.

Many years later, as I was leaving the Lyceum after one of the last performances of *The Bells*, followed by *Waterloo*, a friend stopped me and asked what I thought of it.

" If anyone had never seen the old man until to-night," I replied, " he would understand that Irving's feet stand where the heads of all other actors leave off."

I have seen many performances since. My opinion remains unchanged.

RUDOLPH DE CORDOVA.

XIX

IRVING as SIR EDWARD MORTIMER

Lyceum Theatre, 27th of September, 1879 :—

THE IRON CHEST

(Founded upon Caleb Williams by William Godwin)

WRITTEN BY GEORGE COLMAN THE YOUNGER

Sir Edward Mortimer	MR. IRVING
Captain Fitzharding	MR. J. H. BARNES
Wilford	MR. NORMAN FORBES
Adam Winterton	MR. J. CARTER
Rawbold	MR. MEAD
Samson Rawbold	MR. S. JOHNSON
Peter	MR. BRANSCOMBE
Gregory	MR. TAPPING
Armstrong	MR. F. TYARS
Orson	MR. C. COOPER
Robbers	MESSRS. FERRAND, CALVERT, HARWOOD, etc.
Robbers' Boy	MISS HARWOOD
Lady Helen	MISS FLORENCE TERRY
Blanche	MISS MYRA HOLME
Barbara	MISS ALMA MURRAY
Judith	MISS PAUNCEFORT

ACT I, SCENE 1. *Rawbold's Cottage ;* SCENE 2. *Hall in Sir Edward Mortimer's House ;* SCENE 3. *Ante-room in Sir Edward Mortimer's House ;* SCENE 4. *Sir Edward's Library.* ACT II, SCENE 1. *The Ante-room ;* SCENE 2. *The Library.* ACT III, SCENE 1. *Lady Helen's Cottage ;* SCENE 2. *A ruined Abbey.* ACT IV, SCENE 1. *The Library ;* SCENE 2. *The Hall ;* SCENE 3. *The Library.* PERIOD—1794.

MY earliest memories of Henry Irving are rather vague and diffuse. They begin in the mid-seventies, when I was a boy at Harrow and saw him in *The Bells* under the Bateman Management, which was the first play to make a strong impression upon me, if I exclude Charles Matthews in *Used Up* and the elder Sothern in *David Garrick*.

When I became articled to the Law in 1878 I haunted the gallery at the Bateman *matinées*, and saw Irving with dear little Florence Terry in *The Iron Chest.* This was a rather turgid melodrama, saved only by the charm of Florence Terry, who conveyed the idea all through it that she was obsessed by a mystery that the grim Mortimer would not disclose. When, at last, the Lover extracts the secret he is 'smashed' by it, and Irving had one of his typical effects, towering over him with the line: 'You sought this knowledge—I did not thrust it upon you'—in the limelight, of course, on a darkened stage.

It is curious to reflect that in practically every part that Irving played a single sentence remains vivid in one's mind after half a century; such as when he is counting his daughter's dower in *The Bells* and finds a blood-stained coin from the Jew's hoard—'For me—for me. Not for them!' in *Robert Macaire*—'I would embrace my son'; in *The Merchant of Venice*—'My turquoise, I had it of Leah when I was a bachelor.' All old playgoers will have such sentences printed upon their minds; they made 'high-lights' that are unforgettable.

Then came his grim performances in *Louis the Eleventh*, *Vanderdecken*, *The Lady of Lyons*, and his *tour de force* in *The Corsican Brothers* with William Terris as de Chateau-Renaud, and *The Cup*, which did not impress me. His Digby Grant in *Two Roses* stands out, and what impressed me and remains in my memory most vividly was his performances in Comedy. Irving pretending to be mad, prancing about on the bed in a flowered dressing-gown in *The Belle's Stratagem;* his Robert Macaire, with Weedon Grossmith as Jacques Strop; his Jingle, are never to be forgotten. His way of interlarding his rollicking fun with moments of exquisite pathos was thrilling to a young playgoer, and to the end of his life I regretted that his productions were so overloaded with elaborate details and scenic effects.

In private life he was always courteous and delightful to young people, though he never 'suffered fools gladly.' I remember an occasion at the Garrick Club, when a new member, anxious to claim familiar acquaintance with him, came up to him and said: "Hullo, Irving, an extraordinary thing has just happened to me. A total stranger stopped me in the street and said: 'God bless me, is that you?'" and Irving replied, in his characteristic staccato: "And—er—was it?" A tiresome lady broke into a conversation he was holding with a group of friends at one of Lady Jeune's receptions and said: "You have not seen me, Sir Henry," and Irving replied, testily: "And how did you know, Madam, that I had not seen you?" Personally, I have never seen anyone more completely crushed.

EDWARD HERON-ALLEN.

Such was my early upbringing that a visit to the theatre with the knowledge of my parents was out of the question, but one of my brothers, a year or two my senior, suggested that—on the principle that stolen fruit is sweetest—he and I should 'do' a play somehow.

I was about sixteen at the time, and although funds were not very flush we could manage the financial side of the question, but how to surmount the difficulty of a long evening's absence and a late return home was not so easy. I'm afraid our strict early training was put to a severe test, but the end seemed to justify the means, and we must have presented a plausible tale, for our delinquency was not discovered.

At that period there were few theatres, but the Lyceum was outstanding, and the name of Henry Irving, who had not long completed his phenomenal run of two hundred performances of *Hamlet*, was in all men's mouths. So the Lyceum it had to be.

In 1879 very little was attempted in the way of comfort for the humbler patrons of the theatre, but in one respect the Lyceum was ahead of the others; it did provide shelter for the waiting galleryites. At most other theatres the crowd waited in the street without any cover, and a mad rush ensued as soon as the doors were opened, and 'the Devil take the hindermost.' I have a vivid recollection of the long wait on a dimly lighted staircase; the early-comers naturally had the most favourable chance of choice of seats—if they were vigorous enough to withstand the pressure exerted from behind. It was a fight for position. What a fug it was on that staircase before the pay-box opened! The fact that hot air rises was amply demonstrated.

Once inside, the inconvenience was forgotten and we settled down to the play.

After the lapse of so many years my memory of detail is somewhat blurred, but I retain a general impression, and I recall the great scene vividly, though I know now, as I did not know then, that that great moment—the reason, in fact, for the play's existence—failed of its full effect, and it is all the more to Irving's credit that he did succeed in leaving on my mind the impression of tragic force that determined me to miss no opportunity of seeing him in other and more congenial *rôles*.

The story of *The Iron Chest* is both gloomy and sordid: the sole interest is in the character of Sir Edward Mortimer. George Colman the Younger, I believe, appropriated the plot from William Godwin's novel *Caleb Williams*.

It is difficult to understand anyone wishing to dramatize that lugubrious masterpiece, but the fascination of the character of Falkland, who becomes Sir Edward in the play, was likely to be irresistible to the actors of the old ponderous school, and George Colman fully appreciated this. On its first production at Covent Garden the play failed signally, and surely never was actor so berated and abused by an author as was John Philip Kemble. But Kemble survived it, and what is more curious, the play survived also, but only as many a better play has done—as a vehicle for a great actor's performance, in which he can succeed only if he has an overpowering personality.

It is recorded that the actor playing Wilford with Edmund Kean fled from the stage to his dressing-room in terror the first time he encountered Kean's appalling gaze when he surprised him at the open chest. It is doubtful if Macready succeeded in inspiring such awe; I am not sure whether Phelps attempted it, but I expect so, for he followed very closely in Macready's footsteps. It is unfortunate that Irving could not challenge comparison with his forerunners in the part or at all events in that particular situation, for by an error of judgment, so rare in him that I can recall only one other instance, he cast Wilford to an actor whose experience and ability did not warrant his being entrusted with a part so vitally important. I saw practically all Irving's productions from 1879 to the end, but I cannot remember another instance of so obvious a misfit.

I was, of course, unaware of this at the time, and thought that all was as it should be. Irving, in any case, was great; though lacking the support his performance demanded and deserved he did not arrive at the full stature I have known him to attain in other impersonations.

Sir Edward Mortimer has committed a murder and is haunted by the memory of it and racked by conscience, or rather injured pride, for it is not remorse that moves him. The crime was useless and the futility of it rankles in his proud spirit beyond appeasement, yet some morbid sense will not allow him to dispose of the evidence, a knife and some papers, which he keeps in an iron chest, always locked and always with him, as though to goad his memory; a self-inflicted torment. In the great scene he is surprised by his young secretary while morbidly gloating over these relics. The lad has entered the room inadvertently and is amazed, paralysed with fear, as he encounters the malevolence of his master's glance. Cowering, he is sworn to silence by an oath he dares not break. But Sir Edward's whole nature is changed by the incident; the fact that another shares his secret preys on his mind and he resorts to the expedient of the common criminal; he conveys the tell-tale evidence to the boy's own trunk and when discovery is imminent denounces him as the criminal. Wilford is dumb, bound by his oath. Sir Edward is dominant, triumphant. Then suddenly he breaks, and in an outburst of hysteria, confesses the truth and dies. The character is a study in morbid psychology, a pathological phenomenon. The play exists solely for the development of the character.

This sombre story is without relief of any kind save the graceful fluttering of Lady Helen like a caged bird in this house of gloom.

Irving realized every aspect of the character in a performance of concentrated brilliance; the vehemence of his passion did not disguise Sir Edward's intellectual qualities, and, marvellous to relate, in spite of the character he managed to retain our sympathy. It is a tribute to his art to be able to say this. That he appalled us by his terror in the scene of discovery, yet failed to reach the climax of horror by reason of the inadequacy of his fellow-player, was a tragedy within a tragedy.

It has been said that Irving showed us no more of his art and personality than had been already seen in Mathias and Eugene Aram. I do not doubt it, for in Sir Edward Mortimer are far fewer opportunities than in either of those plays, but to see this great actor on a *first visit* to *any* theatre was calculated to make, and did make, an indelible impression on my youthful mind.

I saw Irving in a number of his well-known impersonations, but the thrill of my first impression stands out. This is not to suggest that my admiration has been lessened in any way by familiarity. His Shylock remains in my memory a most vivid and convincing picture. To present the Jew as a dignified and imposing figure was a daring experiment and, in my opinion, was fully justified in the result.

His Cardinal Wolsey was again a departure from tradition; here was no typical son of a butcher, but a highly cultured, sensitive prelate of surpassing dignity. Historically incorrect, maybe, but histrionically triumphant. Who can forget that dominant figure presiding over the revels at York Place? What a picture it was! But the settings, costumes and stage appointments at the Lyceum were always perfectly applicable to the varied subjects and periods they were designed to illustrate.

To sum up: to have seen and heard Henry Irving and his associates, particularly that glorious actress Ellen Terry, was a delight to be remembered for a lifetime.

ERNEST E. PROBERT.

XX

IRVING as SHYLOCK

Lyceum Theatre, 1st of November, 1879 :—

THE MERCHANT OF VENICE

WRITTEN BY WILLIAM SHAKESPEARE

Shylock	MR. IRVING
Duke of Venice	MR. BEAUMONT
Prince of Morocco	MR. TYARS
Antonio	MR. FORRESTER
Bassanio	MR. BARNES
Salanio	MR. ELWOOD
Salarino	MR. PINERO
Gratiano	MR. F. COOPER
Lorenzo	MR. N. FORBES
Tubal	MR. J. CARTER
Launcelot Gobbo	MR. S. JOHNSON
Old Gobbo	MR. C. COOPER
Gaoler	MR. HUDSON
Leonardo	MR. BRANSCOMBE
Balthazar	MR. TAPPING
Stephano	MR. GANWORTHY
Clerk of the Court	MR. CALVERT
Nerissa	MISS FLORENCE TERRY
Jessica	MISS ALMA MURRAY
Portia	MISS ELLEN TERRY

ACT I, SCENE 1. *Venice—a Public Place ;* SCENE 2. *Belmont—Portia's House ;* SCENE 3. *Venice—a Public Place.* ACT II, SCENE 1. *A Street ;* SCENE 2. *Another Street ;* SCENE 3. *Shylock's House by a Bridge.* ACT III, SCENE 1. *Belmont—Room in Portia's House ;* SCENE 2. *Venice—a Street ;* SCENE 3. *Belmont—Room in Portia's House ;* SCENE 4. *Venice—a Street ;* SCENE 5. *Belmont—Room in Portia's House.* ACT IV, SCENE. *Venice—a Court of Justice.* ACT V, SCENE. *Belmont—Portia's Garden, with Terrace.*

SIR HENRY IRVING was the most remarkable actor I have ever seen, and I have seen a great many English and foreign actors in various countries, some of them admirable, two or three—I think of Coquelin, Lucien Guitry, Bassermann, Zacconi—really great in certain parts. Irving of course had mannerisms, some of them irritating. My father could not bear it when, as he said, Irving 'pawed the air.' I remember his taking me to see *The Bells* at Bristol when I was a boy. I was enthralled, and my father thought Irving wonderful as Mathias, but he said: "At times he's epileptic!" Oddly enough when, long afterwards, we both of us heard him read *Becket* in the Chapter House of Canterbury Cathedral, he dropped all his stage mannerisms, was absolutely natural and spoke all the lines perfectly.

But in all his parts, except King Lear, I lost sight of his mannerisms of both speech and manner in his greatness; in all his parts he had unforgettable moments such as very few actors ever have. He had them in *King Lear*. But in that *rôle* I failed to understand a great deal of what he said and felt like one being entirely submerged in a sea of mad incoherence.

I saw Irving in nearly everything he played and can even now remember exactly the sound of his voice when he spoke certain words. I can still hear him say in Tennyson's *Becket:* 'She died of leprosy'; in *The Bells*, when he was counting the money in his daughter's dowry and came upon a coin that had belonged to the murdered Polish Jew: 'Not for Annette!'; in *The Merchant of Venice:* 'I pray you, give me leave to go from hence; I am not well; send the deed after me and I will sign it.' His voice in the line from *Becket* gave me a terrible impression of all the incomprehensible tragedy of our world; in the line from *The Bells* the murderer's conscience seemed to be weeping over his crime; in the line from *The Merchant of Venice* —'I am not well'—the whole misery of the impotent Jew's heart seemed to be conveyed to me in four simple words. In all these moments Irving was great, and in many others. He towered above all other actors. One felt that one had to do with that rare bird, a genius.

Irving once told me where he found his model for Shylock. For he had a model. A long time before our conversation I went for a camping trip in Morocco with a friend, in days when Morocco was really wild and each night one had to be guarded by a circle of soldiers. On this journey we camped for several days in the plain that stretches towards the sea below Tetuan, which was then a filthy Moorish city containing a great number of Moorish Jews, many of whom visited our camp bringing their wares for sale. When I saw Irving as Shylock one of these Jews seemed to stand before me, impudent and cringing, insolent, cunning, and prone to self-pity when unable to get what he wanted. The likeness was quite amazing, and one night, when I was behind the scenes at the Lyceum Theatre with Irving, I spoke of it. I remember that I said:

"You are almost exactly like some of the Tetuan Jews I encountered long ago in Morocco."

He said:

"That's not surprising, as I took many ideas for my Shylock from a Moorish Jew I saw when I was yachting once and went ashore in Morocco. They are astonishing fellows."

Then I told Irving that he achieved almost a miracle with his Shylock. He asked me what the miracle was. I said:

"Whether you play for it or not, you walk away with nearly all the sympathy."

His hypnotic eyes twinkled and he said:

"I don't chance very much in my performances. No—not very much. One has to know what one's doing, why one's doing it, and exactly what effect it is certain to have upon an audience."

And he added something about the great danger in any part of repelling an audience too much. I can't remember exactly his words, so I can't quote them. But he left me with the impression that in planning out his performance of Shylock he had decided that, if he was to have a lasting success in it, which he did have, he must get all the sympathy that he could possibly obtain legitimately. Certainly I had more sympathy for his Shylock than for any other Shylock I have seen.

His Jew was no doubt often repulsive, but he had moments of sheer humanity, when one felt with him and almost, or quite, suffered with him. Something of the eternal man, subject to the striving and suffering which is the common lot of all human beings, pierced through the crust of his greedy Jewishness, prey-demanding, revengeful, and bitter, and went to the heart. One almost forgave him.

His aim throughout his performance was evidently to be immensely picturesque, which he was, and not to let the audience at any point actually loathe him. But he was far too much of an artist to play for illegitimate sympathy. His genius might possibly have been able to compel it, but it would have been followed by a reaction, even might have made an audience feel ashamed of itself.

A famous moment when he got my sympathy, and I think the sympathy of almost everyone in the audience, was when he made his exit from the Trial Scene, after speaking the lines I have quoted: 'I pray you give me leave to go from hence: I am not well'; he went out like a broken man, who, nevertheless, by will-power and because he knew many eyes were watching him, managed to keep some shreds of dignity, like rags to hide nakedness, about him. He was a great Shylock.

Irving had a remarkable power of impressing an audience in silence. He proved this in the scene of Shylock's return to his empty dwelling after his daughter had left it. It was an absolutely silent scene. One simply saw the figure of the Jew in the shadows walking slowly and alone to his house. But who that saw that figure can ever forget it? I at least cannot.

All great actors have a mysterious power of getting hold, of getting as it were a complete grip, of an audience, however large, directly they come upon stage or platform, either in make-up and costume with scenery to help them, or on a bare platform with no accessories and in ordinary dress. Chaliapine, the Russian opera singer, had this power. Not long before his death he gave a song recital in Zurich. As he walked on to the platform, with his eyes directed towards the crowded audience, he possessed them. They belonged to him. Irving had this power. At a great charity *matinée* in London he was put down to recite *The Dream of Eugene Aram* in the middle of a long programme. I shall never forget the immediate effect he produced as he walked slowly on to the stage, wearing a frock-coat and black tie, looking impassive. He faced the audience, and stood quite still for two or three minutes. No one dropped a pin, I suppose. But had anyone committed that outrage it surely must have been heard. Then he began to recite. But we were all his before he had opened his lips. He was the most mesmeric actor I have ever seen. In any assembly, and much more in any theatrical company, he stood out as an unique personality.

I thought of him once when at a private view of the Royal Academy I saw Cardinal Manning passing through the crowd, in it but not of it. What a marvellous Archbishop or Cardinal Irving could have been if he had not been an actor.

One night, when he was acting Shylock, I went behind the scenes to see him, I forget why. He had sent for me, I think, and when I came to him he was dressed and made up as the Jew. We were alone together in a room for a good while, and in the course of conversation the subject of drinking too much came up. Irving began to expatiate on the various effects drunkenness had on different types of men, some becoming excited and gay under the influence of alcohol, others angry and violent, others sinister, and others again merely lamentable and full of self-pity. And he acted several of these types in a quite marvellous way, passing from one to another with a completeness and instant ease that astounded me. I expressed my amazement.

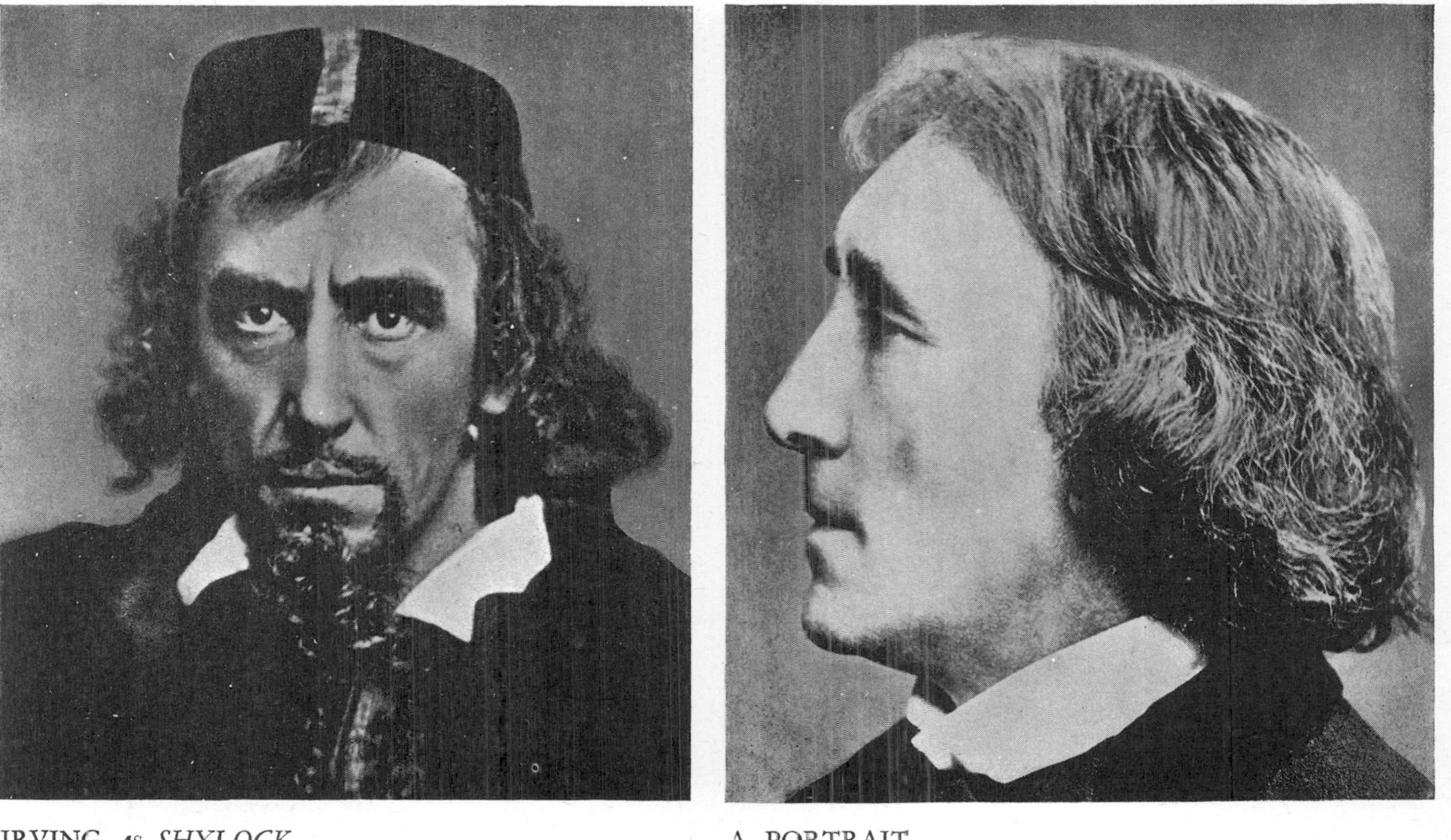

IRVING *as SHYLOCK*

A PORTRAIT

MR. HENRY IRVING preſents his compliments to

Mr. Christopher Bradshaw

and requeſts the pleaſure of his company at Supper in the Theatre, at Half-paſt Eleven o'Clock on the evening of Saturday, February the Fourteenth, 1880, to commemorate the One Hundredth repreſentation of "The Merchant of Venice."

LYCEUM THEATRE,
January, 1880.

ENTRANCE IN EXETER STREET.

PLEASE ANSWER.

"Ha!" he said. "Well, my boy, that's acting."

He had marvellous self-control.

One morning I had to see him on business and went to the Lyceum about eleven o'clock. I found him alone sitting at a table in his office. As I came in he looked up, smiled, and held out his hand. I sat down and there was a moment of silence. Then he said:

"I've just had a bad bit of news."

I said I was sorry and asked what it was.

"All the scenery of my many productions here was stored."

I believed he said: "Stored in an archway."

"It's all been burnt, every bit of it."

I was horrified and expressed my horror as well as I could.

"A pity—isn't it?" he said.

Then, after a slight pause, he began to discuss our business. I learnt later that the fire had cost him a fortune. The scenery wasn't insured.

People have told me that Irving could be cruel with his tongue, and I don't doubt it. But I never had anything but kindness from him, although he had, I'm afraid, little reason to like me, for I contributed to one of his very few failures. I think there was a great deal of nobility in the man, and I have always had an immense admiration for him. He was at times sardonic, and could, and did, make cutting remarks that were often terribly searching and also very amusing, except, I suppose, to the victims. A very famous American actor, now dead, told me a story of Irving which was hardly complimentary to him.

Irving was in America, and my American actor-friend was performing in a play written by Irving's son, Laurence, who persuaded his father to come and see it at a *matinée*. Irving came and sat in a stage box. Naturally, my American actor played up for all he was worth. When the final curtain came down Laurence hurried round to the box and asked his father what he thought of the actor's performance.

"Isn't he great? What did you think of it?"

Irving considered for a moment and then said:

"Audible, my boy! Audible!"

ROBERT HICHENS.

It is fifty-two years since I first met Sir Henry Irving, in New York. I had a letter of introduction to him from Jenny Lind.

I had just started on the stage and was a struggling—a *very* struggling!—actor. I was taken behind the scenes by Bram

Stoker, during the wonderful production of *The Merchant of Venice*.

Sir Henry received me as if I were a Royal Personage and introduced me to Miss Ellen Terry, who was equally kind and gracious. He promised to bear me in mind, when I should have finished my engagement with Daniel Bandmann. I have a dim remembrance of Sir Henry's attitude being one of gentle pity, and I suspect he foresaw that my adventures with the German tragedian might be unfortunate. His attitude was prophetic, for this is exactly what they turned out to be!

Irving must have been the first star actor to play Shylock for sympathy. It came as a great surprise and some critics resented it. I have been told that the old actor, Baddeley, who left a hundred pounds to Drury Lane Theatre, the interest on which was to provide a cake to be cut in the green-room every Twelfth Night (this grew to be a function and ultimately to be a supper-party), used to play Shylock as a comic character in a red wig. Edmund Kean, however, altered all that and established a new tradition with his deeply passionate, *human* performance. Irving, we know, was a great admirer of Kean, but he did not follow him in that. The sympathy he got for that hitherto entirely unsympathetic part was extraordinary, and yet of course he spoke Shakespeare's words, but gave them a new significance.

However, the public approved, and the revival ran for 250 nights on his first production of it, which was a record, and he went on playing the part to the last week of his life. He had played it on the Monday at Bradford (9 October 1905) and was to have played it on the Saturday, but that was an engagement he was unable to fulfil. The curtain had fallen on him the previous evening for the last time.

It is curious that the only time I played with Sir Henry should have been in the play that reminded me of my first meeting with him in New York. The occasion was a Benefit *matinée* at Drury Lane of *The Merchant of Venice* with an all-star cast. Sir Henry wanted me to play Gratiano but the cares of management made it too hard work at the time to master the part properly and so I contented myself with Old Gobbo.

I always had an enormous admiration for all Irving's work; his perfect timing, his instinct for the value of pause, his marvellous gentleness, all remain great and wonderful memories. I have never in all my long life had the feeling in any theatre that the enthralling atmosphere of the Lyceum gave. My wife, Winifred Emery, who acted in the Lyceum Company for so long, was full of enthusiasm for everything connected with it.

I became engaged to her in 1887; she was then, and for some years, Ellen Terry's understudy, though she was a great deal more than the ordinary understudy, for she played Ellen Terry's parts often and for quite long periods. Sir Henry gave Winifred a lovely travelling clock when we were married. She adored him and felt his death terribly.

I saw Sir Henry many times, more intimately when I was manager of the Haymarket, as he took a fancy to coming and sitting in my dressing-room. I remember well one day when he was there I was very anxious that he should take a keener interest than he did in the Actors' Orphanage, of which I was Chairman at the time and later President. I spoke to him at some length about this, holding forth with the greatest enthusiasm. I was making-up as I talked. He listened very politely and when I stopped said very gently: "Hm . . . yes . . . but you haven't rouged your ears."

Another story my wife used to tell was of old Tom Mead, one of Irving's oldest friends, for they had met in Sunderland. Tom had to approve somebody's conduct as meritorious, but on the first night, and in good rolling tones, he spoke of it as meri*o*torious. At rehearsal next morning, gently, as was his wont, Irving said: "My dear Tom, will you kindly say 'meritorious' as it is in the script, without the interpolated O."

When the cue came at night Tom's big bass voice resounded through the theatre: "The girl's conduct has been in every way meri*o*torious," and then in horror, on a yet deeper note, "Said it again, by God!"

When Irving died, I was one of the Committee who had the delicate task of arranging for his statue to be erected in London. I have a vivid recollection of confronting a great Civic Council of dignified City magnates. Old John Hare was to have stated our case, but at the last moment he was laid up with a cold, and to my horror it devolved on me. I felt very small—had rather an Alice-in-Wonderland complex—as I sat at the end of the great hall confronted by rows of City Elders. But the statue that stands behind the National Portrait Gallery in Charing Cross Road shows that we carried our case.

CYRIL MAUDE.

XXI

IRVING as COUNT TRISTAN

Lyceum Theatre, 20th of May, 1880 :—

IOLANTHE

(*Adapted from the Danish of Henrik Herz' Poem King René's Daughter*)

WRITTEN BY W. G. WILLS

Count Tristan	MR. IRVING
King René	MR. J. H. BARNES
Sir Geoffry of Orange	MR. COOPER
Sir Almeric	MR. N. FORBES
Ebn Jahia	MR. T. MEAD
Bertrand	MR. J. CARTER
Martha	MISS PAUNCEFORT
Iolanthe	MISS ELLEN TERRY

SCENE : *A Garden.*

THIS delightful fantasy appears to have been very much to the taste of the mid-Victorians. Mr. and Mrs. Charles Kean (Miss Ellen Tree) acted in an adaptation of it written by the Hon. Edmund Phipps at the St. James's Theatre in 1850. Sir Theodore Martin, who married Macready's leading lady, Miss Helen Faucit, wrote a new version for his wife and it was this version that Mrs. Bateman produced at the Lyceum Theatre on 23 June 1876 on the occasion of Miss Faucit's farewell to the stage. Irving then played Count Tristan de Vaudemont for the first time, and there is little doubt that the prospective manager, already maturing his plans for the future and having well decided who was to be his leading lady, had *Iolanthe* in his mind. It was then known as *King René's Daughter*, and Irving was already acquainted with it for he had acted the part of Sir Almeric in Edinburgh. But he appears not to have been satisfied with any of the existing adaptations and now that the opportunity occurred to do it under his own management, with the ideal fairy princess and an ideal setting, he commissioned W. G. Wills, who had already served him so well with *Charles the First* and *Eugene Aram*, to make a new adaptation.

The story is quite simply a fairy tale, none other in fact than the Sleeping Beauty.

Count Tristan finds the enchanted garden and within it the sleeping Princess. But Iolanthe's eyes are not only closed in sleep, she is blind. Daughter of King René of Provence, she has lost her sight in a fire which occurred in the palace in her infancy. She has no knowledge of her infirmity and it is to insure that such knowledge may not come to her that her father has kept her hidden in a miniature paradise. Those who know Lyceum tradition understand how to interpret those simple words on the programme, 'Scene; a Garden, painted by Hawes Craven,' a paradise it was.

The Moorish physician, Ebn Jahir, has promised to restore Iolanthe's sight, but he tells her father that it is an essential condition to the cure that she should desire to regain it. This means she must be told of her affliction and this the King dreads, being well aware that that of which the heart is not aware it does not covet, and what the eyes do not see they will not miss. But the Moor is inexorable. Ebn Jahir has all the paraphernalia of the medieval necromancer; amulets, potions, hypnotic passes and trances. The Princess is put to sleep, the amulet on her breast. She will not wake till it is removed and this is to happen with certain incantations at sunset.

Needless to say Tristan removes the amulet and she awakes and he is as much attracted by her beauty as she is by his presence and his voice. In the charming scene that ensues, her failure to distinguish between a red and a white rose discloses to both her state of blindness. Tristan goes sadly away.

This was certainly one of the simplest and most appealing of Ellen Terry's *ingénue* performances, and one still remembers the exquisite picture she made when, her sight restored, the garden is invaded by a hostile troop and, clinging to her father, she beholds the young Apollo of her dreams, resplendent in golden armour. Tristan has come to claim fulfilment of a bond of alliance with King René, who had sought to evade it on account of Iolanthe's blindness. The ending is obvious. It was certainly an act of self-abnegation on Irving's part to support his leading lady in such a *rôle* but, as always happened, he lent distinction by the weight and authority of his personality to a slight poem which might have had no substance at all but for his presence. Ellen Terry was exquisite grace, charm, and fantasy, the fairy princess of our dreams.

But what lives in my memory as the dominant figure is the Ebn Jahir of Tom Mead with his majestic bearing and the organ music of his voice.

Another play which Irving produced for Ellen Terry was a

'poetical fancy' (as the author called it) in thee acts, *The Amber Heart*, by Alfred C. Calmour. This was on 7 June 1887. Though Irving did not play in it himself he engaged a notable cast, including Beerbohm Tree, Allen Beaumont, Henry Kemble, and E. S. Willard: Cissy Grahame, Helen Forsyth, and M. A. Giffard. It was a slight and delicate little play, a graceful trifle that afforded Ellen Terry yet another opportunity to exercise her peculiar genius for suggesting ethereal—almost diaphanous charm. Actually I believe W. G. Wills was called in to give the little work the authentic touch of poetry and Hawes Craven provided another of his mystically beautiful settings.

The vogue for one-act plays, acted by players of standing and repute, seems to have passed, but it is interesting to note that another old associate of Irving's early days of struggle in Edinburgh owed his first chance as a playwright in London to him. On 20 September 1879, *The Bells* was followed by 'an original comedietta' called *Daisy's Escape*, by Arthur Wing Pinero; and a year later, on 18 September 1880, *The Corsican Brothers* was preceded by a very charming sentimental comedy called *Bygones* by the same author, who himself played the leading part of an old Italian professor. Irving had good cause to be grateful to the one-act play, both at the beginning and towards the end of his career at the Lyceum; *Raising the Wind* gave him Jeremy Diddler and *A Story of Waterloo* Corporal Brewster. But, as compensation, he had had to play Brown in *The Spitalfields Weaver* (Drury Lane, 1869). No leading actor could carry through that most ungrateful part, who exists only to be "scored off," without hating the exponent of the blatant Simmons, but as, in this case, it was his old friend Toole no doubt Irving was content to "feed" him.

The affection for each other of these two most dissimilar types is one of those mysteries to be explained only by the touchstone of personality. But it was very real, as those who remember Brighton front in the early years of the century can testify. Almost certainly, on any Sunday morning, they would see the grave and dignified figure of Irving pacing beside the bath-chair of the sad, paralysed cripple who outlived him and who would have made him a very rich man and spared him the terrible humiliation he suffered in his own *débâcle* had Toole passed out before him. Poor old Toole! his end was sad indeed. He had lost his wife, his son and his daughter, but the loss he felt as keenly as any was, I think, the loss of his hold on the public. They had outgrown his humour and indeed he had outgrown it also, though an occasional quip escaped him even in the depths of his infirmity. A stranger was introduced to him who said: "I believe you played *The Cricket on the Hearth* once?" "No," answered Toole, "twice." He had played Caleb Plummer more than two thousand times.

Irving and Toole had been friends since 1860. They met again at the old Queen's Theatre in Long Acre, which stood on the site now occupied by Odham's Press, in fact the façade, after seventy years, is practically unchanged. In the company were Lionel Brough, another staunch friend of Irving's, Charles Wyndham, and John Clayton, both destined to become prosperous managers. It was the beginning of what might be called the modern comedy period of Irving's career, starting with Bob Gassitt in *Dearer than Life*, a light comedy villain, and culminating with Digby Grant.

Though his personality was sturdily English there was no Saxon stolidity about Irving's art, in fact he had a *finesse*, a resilience that was essentially Gallic, and this, I think, he probably owed to an experience that I never remember to have heard dwelt upon but which I believe may have had great influence on his art. In the early summer of 1867 he went to Paris with E. A. Sothern to support him at the *Théâtre des Italiens* as the villainous Abel Murcott in *Our American Cousin*, but the Parisians did not care for Lord Dundreary so the venture failed and the company disbanded and returned to England. But Irving elected to remain behind to study the French stage. He lodged in a wretched garret, devoting all his means beyond the cost of bare necessities to visiting the theatres. There is no doubt that he saw the great Frédérick, but Lemaître was now in his sixty-seventh year, his powers were waning and especially his voice was losing its resonance, but nothing could disguise his amazing technique, and he was still playing Robert Macaire. Then there was Mélingue, fellow pupil with Fechter or Lemaître, the creator in the Theatre of D'Artagnan, Edmond Dantès, Chicot and Henri de Lagardère, who as Benvenuto Cellini used to model a nymph in clay at each performance; a great artist, sculptor, painter as well as actor; Rouvière, who had created Hamlet in Dumas's curious adaptation in which all the wicked except Claudius were bidden by the ghost of Hamlet's father to 'Repent and live.' Claudius was sent incontinently to hades; Lacressonière, whose Charles I in *Les Mousquetaires*[1] may well have given Irving the idea to invite

[1] *Twenty Years After*—English title of *Vingt Ans Après* from which *Les Mousquetaires* was adapted.

Wills to write his play on the Martyr King; in the last act they are almost identical. Ligier was perhaps still playing Louis XI, of which he was the original; Paulin-Menier, the great character actor, whose Choppard in *Le Courrier de Lyon* had outshone Lacressonière's performance of the dual *rôle;* Chilly, creator of Rodin in *Le Juif Errant* of Eugène Sue and Laferrière, the handsome juvenile; Chevalier d'Harmental, Anne of Austria's Buckingham and the Man in the Iron Mask. All these were children of the great Romantic Movement of the eighteen-thirties, fathered by Victor Hugo, Alexandre Dumas, Théophile Gautier, Casimir Delavigne, and inspired, in great part, by Byron and Sir Walter Scott. Their influence was very obvious in the breadth and sweep of Irving's art; he had a *panache*, especially in Hamlet, in Ravenswood, in Benedick, quite foreign to the English temperament.

He returned to London and took up his engagement at the Queen's Theatre, and there, in December, he made one more acquaintance who was to influence his career more profoundly perhaps than any other of his artistic associations. He was cast as Petruchio in David Garrick's adaptation of *The Taming of the Shrew* and the Katharine was Ellen Terry. In her delightful book, *The Story of My Life*, she refers to the meeting:

> 'His soul was not more surely in his body than in the theatre. He thought of nothing else, cared for nothing else; worked day and night; went without his dinner to buy a book that might be helpful in studying or a stage jewel that might be helpful to wear. Was Henry Irving impressive in those days? Yes and no. His fierce and indomitable will showed itself in his application to his work. Quite unconsciously I learned from him that to do work well the artist must spend his life in incessant labour and deny himself everything for that purpose.
>
> 'Henry Irving at first had everything against him as an actor. He could not speak, he could not walk, he could not look. He wanted to do things in a part and he could not do them. His amazing power was imprisoned, and only after long and weary years did he succeed in setting it free.'

Yet I wonder if that judgment is strictly accurate or just. Irving had been acting for over ten years. He had played 588 parts before he came to London: he was the stage-manager at the Queen's and was entrusted by the management with the leading part. It is difficult to credit that he was inarticulate as Miss Terry would have us believe, but no doubt she was speaking comparatively. Eleven years were to pass before she emerged from her retirement to become his leading lady at the Lyceum when it came under his management on 30 December 1878.

If ever there was an indefatigable worker it was Irving. How many actors would have been content, after his great triumph as Mathias, to play *The Bells* for the rest of his life? which suggests a story of the great American comedian, Joseph Jefferson, great as Bob Acres—the greatest, it was said, of his time. He 'struck oil' with Rip Van Winkle and thereafter played nothing else for the rest of his life. Writing to his friend, Laurence Hutton, 5 July 1905, he said:

> 'You are sure to see Sir Henry (Irving), tell him if you will that he is remembered here with much affection and give him my love and respect. I hope that he and I will act together in the other world if not in this,
>
> 'And on that last day when we leave those we love,
> And move in a mournful procession,
> I hope we'll both play star engagements above,
> For I'm sure they'll admit the profession.
> For myself, when I knock at the gate with some fear,
> I know that St. Peter will say:
> "Come in, young comedian, and act with us here,
> But for heaven's sake get a *new play!*"'

I must recall one other one-act play that Irving produced for Ellen Terry—*Nance Oldfield*, by Charles Reade—and in which she was supported by that admirable actor, T. N. Wenman, and her son, Gordon Craig. Some of us remember her performance as the most enchanting thing of all the enchantments she ever gave us, and we do not forget Juliet, Olivia, Beatrice, Portia, and Imogen.

I did not miss a first night at the Lyceum from 1879 to the end; the visits were something between a social duty and a religious rite, a delight incomparable, an experience quite apart and different from a visit to any other theatre. Undoubtedly, those first nights decided my choice of career.

In February 1893, dear old Henry Howe saw an announcement that the Irving Dramatic Club were playing *Cymbeline* at St. George's Hall. It was a play he had never seen, or, if he had done so, not for many years. I was playing Iachimo, and Howe went straight to Mr. Irving and mentioned me. The following week I had an offer from the Chief and was with him for over three years, until rheumatic fever in Boston put an end to my connection with the company. Dear Daddy Howe died in

Cincinnati whilst I was in hospital in Boston. Howe had one continuous engagement at the Haymarket for over thirty years. He had played the Second Officer to Macready's Claude Melnotte on the first production of *The Lady of Lyons* and subsequently acted every male part in the play.

F. Rawson-Buckley.

XXII

IRVING as FABIEN and LOUIS DEI FRANCHI

Lyceum Theatre, 18th of September, 1880 :—

THE CORSICAN BROTHERS

(*Adaptation of a play by MM. E. Gravé and Xavier de Montépin, founded upon Les Frères Corses by Alexandre Dumas*)

WRITTEN BY DION BOUCICAULT

M. Fabien dei Franchi *M. Louis dei Franchi*	} MR. HENRY IRVING
M. de Chateau-Renaud	MR. W. TERRISS
The Baron de Montgiron	MR. ELWOOD
M. Alfred Meynard	MR. PINERO
Colona	MR. JOHNSON
Orlando	MR. MEAD
Antonio Sanola	MR. TAPPING
Giordano Martelli	MR. TYARS
Griffo	MR. ARCHER
Boissec	MR. CARTER
M. Verner	MR. HUDSON
Tomaso	MR. HARWOOD
M. Beauchamp	MR. FERRAND
A Surgeon	MR. LOUTHER
Emilie de Lesparre	MISS FOWLER
Madame Savilia dei Franchi	MISS PAUNCEFORT
Marie	MISS HARWOOD
Coralie	MISS ALMA MURRAY
Celestine	MISS BARNETT
Estelle	MISS HOULISTON
Rose	MISS COLERIDGE
Eugenie	MISS MORELEY

ACT I, SCENE 1. *Corsica—Hall and Terrace of the Château of the Dei Franchi at Cullacaro. The Apparition. The Vision.* ACT II, SCENE 1. *Paris—Bal de l'Opera ;* SCENE 2. *Lobby of the Opera House ;* SCENE 3. *Salon in the House of Montgiron ;* SCENE 4. *The Forest of Fontainebleau. The Vision.* ACT III, SCENE. *Fontainebleau—Glade in the Forest. The Duel. The Vision.*

THE impression on a child is the only personal remembrance that I can give of Henry Irving as Fabien and Louis dei Franchi.

It is a vivid and unforgettable impression, but incomplete. Whether it is permissible to put it among the well-considered, comprehensive accounts that fill the pages of this book I am not sure—in fact I think it is *not*. So I am asking my friend, Graham Robertson, to expand and add to mine his personal memories of these enthralling and magnetic impersonations of Henry Irving.

Graham Robertson saw him often as the two brothers, and never, as he told me, did he lose the sense of thrill, the compelling hold that the performance exercised upon him. But he will tell you of this in his own words.

As I try to recall my sensations as I sat in the theatre a child of twelve or thirteen, I see a tall, picturesque, vital man coming through vineyards to meet his friend who has unexpectedly arrived in Corsica. But I am told now that I saw no vineyards and that Henry Irving, on the stage, came into a room through a door. He only said in words that he had come down from the hills through vineyards, but so strong was the influence of his imagination upon that of his audience that he compelled them to accompany him on that walk; letting them hear about it was not enough, they must have been actually with him in the country through which he has come. Irving didn't tell you things, he lived them on the stage. I never acted with any actor who, while you were with him on the stage, was so completely the character he was playing.

To go back to my impression of Fabien dei Franchi, I see a man who has the finger of Fate upon him; Fate seems to control his being. When he felt the stab of pain in his heart as he came down the mountain side, he never doubted that his twin brother was in danger. Throughout the scene Fabien's eyes have a look of suspense, of alert waiting for a call that he knows is coming. It is in the expression of his still, attractive face, in the quiet, nervous movement of his hands.

As I write, I see him vividly. He wears a short velvet coat, a wide, red belt studded with metal clasps, his breeches tucked into high gaiters, metal studded and fastening at the side. A semi-barbaric figure—a true Corsican.

There was great subtlety in the difference in character between the two brothers; a difference that was of the spirit, extraordinarily interesting in its shades and blended colours, wonderfully imaginative in its building up and significance.

In conveying Fatality he had no equal that I have seen.

My next remembrance is of him sitting at a table writing to his brother, Louis, by the light of a taper that he holds in his hand, the room having grown dark. The taper flickers and goes out. He so charged the air with suspense and mystery that you could not breathe; he held you literally spellbound. Then came the haunting music as, by the device of the sliding trap, the ghost of Louis dei Franchi stole across the stage to his brother, his hand upon the wound on his chest.

Irving's lighting effects were wonderful. No one ever realized more clearly than he did the power that lighting has upon the imagination of the audience. He only used gas and lime-lights, but with what perfection he blended colours, diffused light and created shadows. An old actor told me, the other day, that his effects from the use and control of light remain unsurpassed.

In the second act, his portrayal of Louis dei Franchi showed us a polished, courtly man, weaker in fibre than Fabien, like yet unlike his brother. He made you realize the similarity of their upbringing, and just what had been the effect on each nature of their experiences after they had separated.

Again I find that my remembrance of the play is not of what I actually saw, but was governed and created by Henry Irving imposing his imagination upon me.

In the last act, in the snow-clad wood outside Paris, where Fabien meets Chateau-Renaud and fights with him the duel that avenges Louis's death, I saw the coach bring on Chateau-Renaud and his second. There was no coach, but Henry Irving described it and so I saw it and saw, too, men get out of it. And probably so did every member of that audience, for Irving's imagination held us and made us see what he saw.

VIOLET VANBRUGH.

The Corsican Brothers, a crude melodrama with its dual *rôle* of twins, miraculously alike, its stilted language, its vendettas, its ghosts, its duel in the snow, would seem strange fare now to set before a London audience. And indeed in 1880, when it was revived at the Lyceum, it would have appeared almost equally old-fashioned had not Henry Irving been there to play Fabien and Louis dei Franchi.

Now when Irving took a fancy to a part and brought to it his overwhelming personality, it really mattered very little what the play was about or how it was written: the audience was completely carried away by the weird fascination and power of his presence; it was 'under spells' and could only follow where he led. Again and again he had wrought this wonder; in *The Bells* and *The Lyons Mail*, in *Louis the Eleventh* and *Eugene Aram* he had snatched a play from its spiritual home, the waste-paper basket, and had raised it into something terrible, something beautiful, something never to be forgotten.

And here he was, doing it again with *The Corsican Brothers*. As the curtain rose we were in the cool, dark hall of an old house in Corsica. It was used as a living-room, the walls hung with guns and hunters' trophies. In a recess at the back a great door stood open to the dazzling sunshine without.

A stranger is ushered in, a M. Alfred Meynard, who bears a letter to Madame dei Franchi from her son, Louis, in Paris. His hostess at once appears, greeting him kindly and telling him with what delight her son Fabien will welcome a friend of his brother.

On the first night of the Lyceum revival, Pinero, entering as Alfred Meynard, pale, bushy of eyebrow, and in a long overcoat much like that worn by Irving in *The Lyons Mail*, was mistaken by the audience for Irving himself, and, to his complete confusion, got Irving's reception. It was the forerunner of many tumultuous receptions in the future, to which he was legitimately entitled, but he did not know this at the time and the experience was a painful one.

When the real Irving appeared, a very different figure was seen. A slender youth, clad in rough mountaineering costume, came swinging through the sun-drenched garden. Swarthy and handsome, his thick black hair wind-blown, his rifle slung over his shoulder, he seemed to embody the spirit of his country, wild, lawless, and beautiful.

He receives the guest almost boisterously, snatching his brother's letter, and, as he reads it, his face falls. 'But this is dated three weeks ago—have you no later news?' he asks anxiously. 'How did you leave Louis?' Meynard, bewildered by the extraordinary likeness between the two brothers, tries to reassure him, but in vain.

Fabien explains that, during the last few days, he has been filled by a nameless dread, and the strange, sympathetic telepathy that is between the twins tells him that all is not well with Louis. If Louis is sad, he is sad, if Louis is in pain, he feels it, if Louis were dead—'Fabien!' interrupts his mother. 'If Louis were dead. . . .' 'I should know it,' replied Fabien. 'I should have seen him.'

By this time the actor has filled the dim hall with a boding horror, the shadow of death seems to hang over it. But now, with an effort, he flings away his melancholy and it is a gay young host who sits down to a supper which he probably enjoys more than do his mother and M. Meynard, for the table manners of the country-bred Fabien are not his strong point. He gobbles his food, gulps his wine, gnaws his bread, and speaks with his mouth full, but always without loss of dignity or charm.

After supper a crowd of peasants enter, summoned by Fabien to witness the end of an old vendetta between two families who have been industriously murdering each other for years on the strength of an absurd, long-ago quarrel. The scene is grotesque, roughly comic, but Irving shows Fabien as a man of peace, of kindliness and good nature: he sends the two old enemies away reconciled but, left alone, the dark cloud of foreboding descends upon him again. He calls his servant, telling him to be ready to ride at once with a letter to be dispatched to his brother and, as he sits down to write, the room darkens, the famous ghost appears, a dark stain on the breast of its white shirt. It lays a hand lightly on Fabien's shoulder—he turns—the quick and the dead are for a moment face to face—and the curtain falls.

It rises next upon a scene of wild gaiety, a Mask Ball at the Paris Opera House. The floor of the auditorium is cleared for dancers and parties of gaily dressed Maskers fill the boxes.

In this scene Irving often set aside his usual inflexible rule that no strangers were to be allowed on the stage, and would permit friends, duly masked and be-dominoed, to move among the crowd and to occupy the boxes. It is remembered that once Mr. Gladstone, ever an ardent theatre-goer, sat in one of the boxes and, on Irving's entrance, leaned forward so eagerly that the audience saw his face. There was a disconcerting burst of applause and strangers were not encouraged at the Mask Ball in future.

The staging was admirable; the colourful riot seemed absolutely spontaneous, and amidst its whirl and clamour the plot developed upon familiar lines.

The usual innocent lady brings her innocence to the Opera Ball to meet the usual professional seducer and duellist (in this case a M. Chateau-Renaud) in the hope that he will restore to her the usual love letters, and is much surprised to find that he 'has not them about him,' of which a glance at the exquisite fit of his evening coat should at once have convinced her.

But Chateau-Renaud has laid a wager that he will bring the lady that evening to a highly improper supper party at the house of his friend, Baron Montgiron, so he assures her that the letters await her at his own residence, if she will deign to accompany him thither. The lady, though innocent, is not intelligent and at once leaves the ball, leaning confidingly upon Chateau-Renaud's arm.

All did their best. The innocent lady was well played by Miss Fowler, whom Irving had engaged for the part more for her style and distinction than for her dramatic capabilities. William Terriss, looking splendidly handsome, lent himself to the villainies of Chateau-Renaud with the cheerful resignation of a thoroughly good-natured man; in fact the whole company did quite as much for the play as the author deserved.

But through this demoded world of well-worn theatrical commonplace moved a figure of strange vitality, living its mimic life with fullness and intensity, the figure of Louis dei Franchi, twin brother to the Fabien of Act I.

Irving sought no aid from make-up in creating the separate entities of the twins; Fabien and Louis were physically identical, yet, after the first glance, no one would have mistaken them. Fabien was the noble savage, Louis the finished product of civilization, exquisite in manners, meticulous in costume, gentle and courteous, chivalrous and charming.

He had learned the details of Chateau-Renaud's wager and had noted the lady, of whom he is an old friend and quondam suitor, leaving the ball with that gentleman. He hastens to the house of Baron Montgiron and arrives there in time to witness the entrance of the villain and his dupe and the discomfiture of the latter when she realizes the nature of the party to which she has been decoyed.

She appeals to M. dei Franchi to 'save her', which naturally leads to a quarrel with the deadly swordsman, Chateau Renaud, and to his inevitable challenge; and when Louis leaves the room, gallantly escorting the rescued fair, he goes to his death as surely as if he went to face a firing-squad.

And now came the last act, the act for which the play was written, the act that drew all London. And with it the play itself came to life, the tawdry trappings of melodrama fell away from it, and, as the frozen, moonlit glade near Fontainebleau was disclosed, the audience was held at strained attention by the deep hush, the snow stillness that wrapped them round. Nothing stirred, snow muffled all sound, yet there *was* a sound—perhaps a slight stirring of wind, a slight shifting of leafless branches. It was a single organ note held down, so soft as to be barely audible, more felt than heard; the voice of the great, sleeping forest, the sound that lies at the heart of silence.

Chateau-Renaud and his friend, Montgiron, appear; they are in flight from Paris, the former driven by a strange dread, a deadly foreboding of pursuing vengeance. Their carriage has broken down, most ominously, at the very scene of the duel. In superstitious panic they are hastening away when a dark figure bars their path and the moonbeams show the pale face of the dead Louis dei Franchi. But it is not Louis but Fabien, the Corsican, who stands there where Louis fell, demanding payment for his brother's blood.

He forces a duel upon Chateau-Renaud—it must be here and now. Montgiron objects—'We have no seconds, no weapons' —Fabien makes a sign and Alfred Meynard joins him, carrying two swords. Chateau Renaud cannot escape: he is no coward, but the place, the hour, the likeness between his challenger and his victim combine to unman him.

Through all the scene it is the absolute quiet of Fabien that is terrifying. He seems emptied of all human emotions, even of anger. He is Vengeance, he is Fate, irresistible, implacable.

The duel begins, Chateau-Renaud fighting wildly, exhausting himself; Fabien parrying his attacks without effort, almost without motion. Chateau-Renaud's sword breaks, the seconds interpose—the duel must stop. Fabien snaps his sword in half, binding the end of it to his hand with a kerchief and insisting upon his opponent doing the same. In a few moments all is over. Chateau-Renaud lies where his late victim lay and Fabien, his mission accomplished, and for the moment overcome, leans upon the shoulder of his second covering his face, and they pass together behind the bole of a great tree, upon the root of which Fabien sinks, weeping.

Again the shuddering violins are heard, as the forest glade with its dim figures grows more shadowy and in the darkness hangs the grim face of the ghost.

But as we gaze there comes a change. The face is no longer terrible, it softens, the eyes grow luminous and loving, it glows with a radiant and unearthly beauty as the pale lips part on a soft whisper of farewell and hope—and the curtain steals down and hides it.

We left the theatre in awe, in something of fear, in strange perturbation of spirit. We had come to see a play called *The Corsican Brothers*, but we had actually seen the transfigured face of Henry Irving, and we shall see it to the end of our days.

W. GRAHAM ROBERTSON.

About fifty years ago I sat in the pit of the Lyceum (a 2s. 6d. seat then). *The Corsican Brothers* was the play.

Just before, I had seen Kyrle Bellew in the same character at the Grand Theatre, Leeds. K. B. was a fine elocutionist; had an imposing stage presence.

Henry Irving was high-shouldered, walked stagily and gurgled annoyingly.

Sitting next to me was a Cockney, to whom I said: "Don't think much of your Irving."

"Ho!" he said. "Just wite a mo, young fellah."

I 'wited' until the scene of the duel in the snow. Irving was writing to his twin by the light of a single candle. He looked up, and in a vision saw his brother fall—pierced by his adversary's sword.

The expression on Irving's features and his horror-stricken cry, caused me to stiffen on my seat and groan: "My God!"

"Yayss," said my Cockney, "that's 'Enery Hirving hall ovah. 'E bores yer for twenty minutes and e' paraloises yer for foive."

J. H. Corbett.

XXIII

IRVING as SYNORIX

Lyceum Theatre, 3rd of January, 1881 :—

THE CUP

WRITTEN BY ALFRED TENNYSON

GALATIANS :

Synorix	MR. HENRY IRVING
Sinnatus	MR. TERRISS
Attendant	MR. HARWOOD
Boy	MISS BROWN
Maid	MISS HARWOOD
Phoebe	MISS PAUNCEFORT
Camma	MISS ELLEN TERRY

ROMANS :

Antonius	MR. TYARS
Publius	MR. HUDSON
Nobleman	MR. MATTHISON
Herald	MR. ARCHER

ACT I, SCENE 1. *Distant view of a City in Galatia (Afternoon)* ; SCENE 2. *A Room in the Tetrarch's House (Evening)* ; SCENE 3. *Distant view of a City of Galatia (Dawn). Half a year is supposed to elapse between the acts.* ACT II, SCENE. *Interior of the Temple of Artemis. The scene is laid in Galatia, a province of Asia Minor.*

THE CUP, a tragedy in two acts by Lord (then Mr.) Tennyson, is based on the vengeance wreaked by a priestess of the Temple of Artemis, on the murderer of her husband. She first pretends to yield to his advances and accepts him as a lover and then poisons the sacred cup from which he must drink at the marriage ceremony.

That much I remember. But after a lapse of fifty-eight years, impressions tend to become blurred. For this reason, I have thought it well to refresh my memory by reading some contemporary criticisms of the play, in addition to consulting authentic records. *The Daily Telegraph*, always a strong supporter of the drama, provided its readers with a characteristic and highly ornate description of the initial performance, which it appears was graced by the presence of Mr. and Mrs. Gladstone.

After a glowing account of the opening scene which is enacted before the Temple of Artemis, we learn that a wicked Galatian called Synorix is madly in love with the beauteous Camma, who is wedded to an honest-to-goodness hunter-husband, named Sinnatus. By a subterfuge, Synorix succeeds in luring the lady to the threshold of the Temple and there makes it clear that he has designs upon her virtue. His passionate avowals are overheard by the husband, who has unexpectedly returned from the chase, and, according to *The Daily Telegraph*, he thereupon brands Synorix as a seducer and taunts him with the opprobrious words—'adulterous dog.' Such an expression would, nowadays, be cheerfully employed by the head of almost any Central European State when exchanging compliments with a neighbour, but Synorix lived three hundred years B.C. and was not so advanced in his views. He was sadly uncivilized.

Highly incensed, he sticks the husband with a dagger which he snatches from Camma who has come provided with this weapon, presumably to protect her virtue. Camma, having now withdrawn into the Temple, Synorix, to quote again from *The Daily Telegraph*, proceeds to soliloquize over the dead body, with 'cool and cruel emphasis.' Substitute Dollfuss for Sinnatus, and we have quite a modern note here.

In Ellen Terry's *The Story of My Life* she speaks of *The Cup* as a great little play. Its chief fault in her view being that it was too short to justify such an elaborate production. She recounts how Tennyson read the play to them at Eaton Place in a 'monotonous low note.' We also learn that Tennyson wished to call the play *The Senator's Wife*, but they all finally agreed on *The Cup*. She states that she regards the production as one of the most beautiful things that Irving ever accomplished and she, like Bram Stoker in his *Henry Irving*, has a great deal to say about the interior of the Temple of Artemis in which the Second Act passes.

Stoker relates that James Knowles reconstructed a Temple of Artemis on the ground plan of the great Temple of Diana, and the late Dr. Alexander Murray, then assistant keeper of the Greek section of the British Museum, helped greatly with his researches among Etruscan designs. It may well be that some eye for effect decided that the priestesses and votaries, hitherto always seen in white, should wear colours and embroideries, and they greatly enhanced the general effect. Lighting played an important part. The gigantic figure of the many-breasted Artemis, placed far back in the scene dock, loomed through a blue mist, while the foreground of the picture was in yellow light; an exquisite effect.

When Dr. Murray came to see the play he was greatly concerned because a great Amphora, borne by two girls, displayed red figures on a black ground, instead of black figures on a red ground. This sight so affected Dr. Murray that the subsequent proceedings failed to interest him. He did not swoon. But there is no doubt that he suffered a severe mental shock.

The Cup originally formed the second item in a double bill; *The Corsican Brothers* occupied the first portion of the programme. Irving had revived *The Corsican Brothers*, in which he doubled the parts of Louis and Fabian dei Franchi, in the preceding autumn. He was anxious to attempt the dual *rôle* rendered famous in this country by Charles Kean and Fechter, and as Miss Terry's services were not then immediately available, he took the opportunity of adding the play to his repertory. On Miss Terry's return he added *The Cup* to the programme in order to provide her with an effective part in which to reappear. But the two plays together made the bill overlong. Later in the same year (16 April 1881) *The Belle's Stratagem* replaced *The Corsican Brothers*, and this constituted a more compact and better contrasted programme.

The Corsican Brothers, old-fashioned and stilted even in those days, came to life in Irving's hands. He gave it pulse and colour and mounted and dressed it magnificently. I remember it very well. As a youthful playgoer it both thrilled and stirred me.

A scene that remains in my mind is the duel *à outrance* between Fabien dei Franchi and de Chateau Renaud in the Forest of Fontainebleau. A winter dawn is breaking. Snow is everywhere, glistening on the trees, and lying deep on the ground. So deep that the two men have to kick it aside before taking up their positions. I still see the two figures as they faced each other sharply defined against the background of trees. I hear the slow music that heralded the apparition of the brother. Over everything there hung a sense of dread. One was fearful, expectant. Wonderful that after all these years I can recall that moment so vividly. It is a tribute to a magician who could conjure with our emotions, and bend us to his will.

If in *The Cup* I recall Irving's Synorix more clearly than Miss Terry's Camma, it is because the actor's personality was overwhelming. It stamped itself indelibly on the memory.

In *The Cup*, the first scene represented a mountain-side with distant views of the surrounding country. Irving entered along a rough path. He was then a man about forty-three, upright and vigorous. There was no dragging of the leg in those days. His wig was red, bound by a gilt circlet. He wore a slight moustache and a chin-piece. His face was pale with thin red lips. The face of a sensualist. A cruel face. He was clad in gold armour and a short cloak of tiger-skin fell from his shoulders. I wish that I could recall Camma with equal distinctness. But alas! the portrait has faded. I cannot even remember the toga on which the actress set such store. This garment, its colour and its texture, exercised the minds of the Lyceum staff for many days. Ultimately two people claimed to have discovered the right material for it. Bram Stoker, Irving's general manager, asserts that he discovered it at Liberty's. An Indian tissue of loosely woven cloth, the wrong side of which gave the desired effect.

On the other hand Ellen Terry claims that she herself found it. A piece of saffron silk with a design woven into it by hand. It was declared to be perfect but it cost twelve guineas a yard. Too costly, even for the Lyceum!

It was left to the ever resourceful Arnott, the property master, actually to solve the problem. He undertook to provide an imitation not to be distinguished from the original. And he was as good as his word. Ellen Terry was enchanted with the result. Mention of Arnott recalls a tale of Irving that used to be cherished in the old days by the back-stage staff.

In one of Irving's later productions a large cage of canaries formed a prominent feature in one of the scenes. When the cage was produced at rehearsal, Irving, who had a passion for detail, examined it with meticulous care.

After a lengthy scrutiny he sent for the property master.

"Oh, Arnott," he said, "this cage—um—not quite right. Eh? No.—Floor is a little too clean, Arnott—birds will be birds—um?—Yes—like all living creatures—they have their needs—make it a little less tidy, Arnott."

Arnott obediently removed the cage and splashed the floor rather copiously with white paint.

When it was returned to the stage, Irving examined Arnott's additions with much interest.

Presently he remarked in his never-to-be-forgotten tones:

"This cage, Arnott—um—is to be occupied by canaries—*not eagles!*"

. . . . . .

My personal contacts with Irving began many years later. They arose in the first place from my position as honorary secretary of the Irving Dramatic Club. This club, which commenced operations in 1879 with a performance of *Hamlet*, always received the approval and support of the Lyceum chief. Each season there was an elaborate Shakespearean revival. The club's most successful effort was undoubtedly a production of *Henry IV* (Part 1). So favourable were the accounts concerning it, that Irving offered to lend his theatre, in order that the play might be repeated for the benefit of the Actors' Benevolent Fund. Accordingly a *matinée* was arranged for Saturday, 29 March 1890, when Henry Irving and Ellen Terry occupied a box.

Like most actors of the old school, Irving did not look too kindly on the amateur histrion, though, as I have said, he was genuinely interested in the club that bore his name. Maybe his own youthful experiences did not predispose him too favourably in that direction. For Irving himself once appeared as an amateur and went to the length of paying three guineas for the privilege of playing Romeo at the Royal Soho Theatre (now the Royalty). That was on Monday, 11 August 1856.

The performance that he saw at the Lyceum did not belie the good reports he had heard concerning it, and he was considerably impressed. Among a company of capable players the acting honours were carried off by Frank Macey, as Harry Hotspur. His work stood out so remarkably that Irving invited him to join the Lyceum company.

Frank Macey was, and is at the age of eighty-three, a most accomplished actor. But being a man of sound common sense he preferred to stick to a prosperous business rather than to risk the hazards of the stage. He, therefore, respectfully declined this very flattering offer, which was afterwards renewed, when later on they met at dinner at the Augustus Littletons'. But Macey stuck to his guns and he has not regretted it.

Most members of the Irving Club tried to look like their President. I was at a disadvantage because my hair began to thin at an early age. But I remember that one of our number called Wellesley Forbes succeeded in training his abundant locks well over the collar of his coat. This accomplishment filled us all with envy.

It is very difficult to-day for people to realize the position that the Lyceum held in the public estimation in the 'eighties and 'nineties of the last century. It was not then so much a theatre as a temple to be entered with bated breath. There was a sacerdotal air about the entire building. The entrance hall was covered with sombre hangings. The lighting was dim. Small boys like acolytes distributed the programmes. When you entered the precincts you at once absorbed this rarified atmosphere. A high priest, in the shape of Mr. Joseph Hurst, sat remotely in a box office. If he smiled when rendering your change, it was a thing to be remembered.

Everyone who served under the Lyceum banner had to subordinate himself to the Chief. He insisted on implicit obedience. Many of the older actors like Tyars, Mead, Archer, and Howe looked upon their salaries as life annuities. Henry Howe received £500 a year, whether acting or not, till the day of his death. A useful old-age pension.

Years later, I was to share with Frank Macey the honour of appearing before the Lyceum Chief, but my efforts were less successful.

The occasion was a performance arranged by the late Mrs. Aria and her sister, Mrs. Frankau, both now dead. The idea was to exploit Mrs. Aria's daughter Nita in the character of Viola in *Twelfth Night*. Mrs. Aria was a great friend of Irving's and, greatly daring, she invited him to witness the performance. I am afraid we were not very good, and the whole affair must have been exceedingly depressing. Happily it was followed by a supper and dance, when the audience speedily recovered their spirits. We were naturally extremely anxious to know what the Chief thought about us, but he was not to be drawn. It was not till some days later that Laurence Irving managed to extract the great man's real opinion.

" What did you think of the amateurs ? " Laurence asked his father at point-blank range.

Irving frowned.

" What did I think of them ? " he cried. " What did I think of them ? My boy, I don't want to think of them."

HERBERT SWEARS.

XXIV

IRVING as IAGO

Lyceum Theatre, 2nd of May, 1881 :—

OTHELLO

WRITTEN BY WILLIAM SHAKESPEARE

Othello	MR. EDWIN BOOTH
Iago	MR. HENRY IRVING
Cassio	MR. W. TERRISS
Brabantio	MR. MEAD
Roderigo	MR. PINERO
Duke	MR. BEAUMONT
Montano	MR. TYARS
Gratiano	MR. CARTER
Ludovico	MR. HUDSON
Messenger	MR. MATTHISON
Paulo	MR. FERRAND
Antonio	MR. CLIFFORD
Julio	MR. LOUTHER
Marco	MR. HARWOOD
Emilia	MISS PAUNCEFORT
Desdemona	MISS ELLEN TERRY

ACT I, SCENE 1. *A Street in Venice* ; SCENE 2. *Another Street in Venice* ; SCENE 3. *A Council Chamber*. ACT II, SCENE 1. *The Harbour at Cyprus* ; SCENE 2. *A Street in Cyprus* ; SCENE 3. *The Court of Guard*. ACT III, SCENE. *Othello's House*. ACT IV, SCENE 1. *Othello's House* ; SCENE 2. *A Street in Cyprus* ; SCENE 3. *Exterior of Iago's House*. ACT V, SCENE. *A Bedchamber*.

IT is, I believe, acknowledged that in matters of art the criticism of a layman, unprejudiced and tolerably well informed, sometimes has interest. The only excuse that I can offer for the few remarks that follow is that, with something of a distaste for the theatre, I have a tolerable familiarity with the whole range of English dramatic literature. Nor, though as a rule I do not care for theatre-going, am I so little of a theatre-goer as to experience the attraction of mere novelty. I have seen (not often, it is true, but I have seen) most, if not all, of the more famous actors and actresses of the last quarter of a century.[1] Also I know my

[1] i.e. 1855–80. I began with Charles Kean in *Louis the Eleventh* and Marie Wilton in her very earliest stage, ' gagging ' something about Blink Bonny's Derby.

Shakespeare as well as I do the multiplication table.[1] But though I have written on most subjects, I have never hitherto[2] written a word of dramatic criticism in my life, and it was something of an accident which made me a not wholly willing spectator at the Lyceum on the second night of the performance of *Othello*.

The play is, on the whole, my own favourite among Shakespeare's graver works,[3] and the character of Iago is the character in it of which I have formed the clearest and the highest idea. That idea has never been in accordance with the traditional notion of Iago given either by the stage or by literature. A well-known passage of Macaulay's essay on Macchiavelli, and Hazlitt's formal criticism, may be said to embody this tradition (of course in rather different forms) well enough. According to it, Iago is a sort of human fiend, or rather a kind of Mephistopheles-monkey who delights in mischief, if not absolutely for its own sake, yet with only the faintest occasion or excuse. He is a person who says : ' Evil, be thou my good,' and who has a spontaneous and quite genuine pleasure in harming and hurting and debasing everything and everybody he comes across. I do not so read Shakespeare. It seems to me that, in the first place, Iago is a gentleman. He is known to Lodovico as ' a very valiant person.' He is treated as an equal by everyone, and ' three great ones of the city ' sued Othello for his lieutenancy. Venetian magnificoes did not usually interest themselves for kinless loons. In the second place, he is not a middle-aged villain, but a young man ; he gives us his age, eight and twenty. He has evidently a blameless reputation with those who have known him long, and must have had plenty of opportunities for observing any innate diabolism of character in him. No doubt he is something of a soldier of fortune, and the camp has a little tarnished both his breeding and his morality. Probably his means were not equal to his birth, and he had no doubt got into an easy habit of ' making his fool his purse,' a habit not unknown in other armies besides the Venetian. To estimate his character, it is very important to scrutinize narrowly the part of Emilia,[4] a part much curtailed, and, as it seems to me,

[1] In the same sense, of course. God forbid that I should pretend, or ever have pretended, to ' know ' him in any other.

[2] Or since.

[3] Not including *Antony and Cleopatra*, where the glory counts the gravity out.

[4] She, like Maria in *Twelfth Night* and others, suffers from the constant modern forgetfulness that such parts are those of ' ladies-in-waiting,' not ' ladies' maids.'

badly conceived in the acting version. Emilia is a little afraid of Iago, somewhat suspicious of him, vexed at his cavalier treatment of her, but it is by no means clear that she suspects him of any positive villainy, or thinks him capable of anything worse than waywardness. Her surprise when the Moor tells her who is his informant shows this, and that the passage (sometimes taken as a hint at Iago's underhand dealings) in which she suggests that Othello must have had his mind poisoned by somebody does not point in that direction is shown by the words, ' Some such squire he was,' etc., which would be absurd if she had been referring to her husband himself.

Therefore I think it is fair to suppose that, up to the time of the Cyprus voyage, no one knew anything of a serious kind against Iago. Now incarnate devils, doing harm for harm's sake, do not live till eight and twenty without giving some sample of their disposition. Iago appears to me to have been a person with a strong sense of humour, darkening into cynicism, no sense of morality, an Italian tendency to revenge and self-indulgence, and an extraordinary subtlety of brain. He is mortally offended by the putting of Cassio over his head, and he is certainly jealous, if only in a general and suspicious way, of Cassio and Othello himself. Those who believe this jealousy to have been a mere figment not only overlook Emilia's reference to it, but also forget the additional poetic value given to the play by the fact of Iago communicating his own disease to Othello. Despairing of inflicting the direct *peine du talion* (though he seems to have had some notion of that, too) on his general, he will at least make him feel what he has himself felt.

The motives, then, in his mind at first reduce themselves to a desire to exploit Roderigo to the uttermost, a wish to avenge himself on Cassio and Othello for the slight put upon him in the matter of lieutenancy, and for their supposed relations to Emilia, and perhaps also a kind of cynical anger with Desdemona for what must have seemed to him her *bête* purity and innocence. To turn Cassio out, to bubble Roderigo of as much money as possible, to plague the Moor, to discredit Desdemona, and perhaps to gain some influence over her, may be said to sum up his earlier objects.

But the means to do ill deeds present themselves with almost bewildering facility, and the pleasure of playing the game, the sense of his superiority to his victims, and the completeness of the revenge obtainable, by degrees overmasters him. He plays for ever higher and bloodier stakes. He loses some of the cautiousness which would hardly have deserted a simple amateur of devilry. He confesses to himself that 'this is the night that either makes him or foredoes him quite,' and only positive hatred and revengefulness could have blinded him to the fact that the chances of his being foredone were much the greater. At last he loses, and he pays the stake with the coolness of a veteran gambler. He neither cringes, nor snarls at his foes, nor gloats over the evil he has done with the clumsy glee of a stage villain. He has won the game, if he has lost the rubber, and he dies in silence. All Cassio's tortures, if that good-natured person ever really brought himself to carry out Lodovico's threats, did not, we may feel sure, make Iago quail.

This, in the main, is the conception I have formed of the character in many years' reading of the play, and this, to my great delight, was the conception which, as it seemed to me, Mr. Irving carried out in the main. Of course there were differences, but the tenor was the same. I had heard a good deal of Mr. Irving's mannerisms of speech, and though they were certainly perceivable, they did not seem to me to interfere much with the part. Probably the truth is that, mine ancient's language being, as usual with Shakespeare, somewhat of the euphuist kind, a certain artificiality in its utterance does it no harm. The outward presentment of the part pleased me particularly. The rich dress, bought, doubtless, with some of the unlucky 'snipe's' gold and jewels, was exactly that befitting a gentleman-adventurer. The manner, at first merely scornful, and with a slight touch of soldier-like brag about it, hardening gradually into that of the conspirator, yet without any affection of mystery or stage fiendishness, was equally appropriate. Mine ancient, as is but too well known, was loose in his language, as persons conversant with camps, and not remarkable for gravity or piety, are too frequently wont to be; and Mr. Irving kept just enough of this in his version to season the presentment of a man destitute of principle, eager for pleasure, profit, and the indulgence of the luxury of revenge, not already or inevitably a villain, but capable of villainy at almost any moment when the opportunity came.

The set *tirades* of a part are, I suppose, never its really difficult passages; but few things could have been better than the 'put money in thy purse' harangue. Generally, indeed, Mr. Irving's manner in the Roderigo scenes, the rapid and fantastic oratory with which he bewilders the poor chuff, his lavishness of gesture and pantomime—all calculated to distract his hearer's attention and keep it from unpleasant despondency and still more unpleasant inquiries as to the employment of the money he spends so freely—appeared to me masterly. The well-known scene with Desdemona on the port, with the matchless character of woman which sums up in half a dozen lines everything libellous that had been said from Simonides to the Fabliau-writers, was equally good.

In the development of the plot, it seemed to me that Mr. Irving might have been a good deal hampered by the excision (usual, I believe, on the stage) of the Bianca scenes. Without these the stages of deception and intrigue follow each other somewhat too rapidly; many of the confirmatory incidents, which best show Iago's skill, and most excuse Othello's weakness, are left out; and the plot, to read (though I have never read it in this form), would, I should say, lose much of its plausibility. It is all the more credit to the actor that no lack of such plausibility was actually felt. There was no time to feel it: the various actions of the machinator following each other as easily and speciously as possible.

Specially remarkable, as it seemed to me, were Mr. Irving's soliloquies. These much abused things are, of course, the only chance a dramatist has of giving his audience direct intimation of the workings of his characters' minds: and though both dramatists and actors ought, no doubt, to supplement this with much indirect information, it cannot be omitted. At the same time, the folly of a certain kind of soliloquy, in which the speaker kindly describes to himself his own motives and intentions very much after the fashion of that Scotch act of worship which has been described as 'informing the deity of his own attributes,' is notorious and nauseous enough. Mr. Irving makes the very utmost of the soliloquies of Iago, and the successive stages of the 'monstrous birth' are made absolutely clear.

My readers would not thank me if I were to go through the play, scene for scene. There are two, however, which deserve especial comment. The feigned consolation of Desdemona which brings upon Iago the unintentional weight of his wife's violent language is a very trying one. Nowhere is he more morally detestable, nowhere is he intellectually greater. He does not 'protest too much,' his speeches are brief and almost constrained in mere words, though those words are admirably chosen. The actor thus has to throw in a great deal of expression, and yet to remember that Iago is 'honest Iago,' a plain, bluff sort of person, not a fawning wheedling courtier. Mr. Irving does this consummately, and the single genuine utterance of the scene, the short 'You're a fool; go to!' to Emilia, is given at once with such an apparent pooh-poohing of the absurd suggestion of there being a 'cogging knave' somewhere, and, at the same time, such a hearty intensity of double meaning, as to make it admirable. Yet, again, in the last scene of all, when the game is up and he is at bay, the short retort to Othello: 'I bleed, sir, but not killed,' is equally admirable. Stoical composure, outward preservation of respect to the general, and yet a covert suggestion of the same ironic kind as that which Othello himself had made on the futility of his wrath, are all implied in it.

I can only say in conclusion that I rather hope Mr. Irving will not give us many more impersonations of this force. I should have to take to going regularly to the theatre, which would cost me a great deal of time, some trouble, and not a little money.

GEORGE SAINTSBURY.

Reprinted from the late Professor George Saintsbury's *A Second Scrap Book* by permission of his executors and with the kindly concurrence of his publishers, Messrs. Macmillan & Co., Ltd.

XXV

IRVING as MODUS

Lyceum Theatre, 23rd of July, 1881 :—

THE HUNCHBACK

WRITTEN BY JAMES SHERIDAN KNOWLES

Modus	MR. HENRY IRVING
Helen	MISS ELLEN TERRY

SCENE : *Library in Master Walter's House.*

THIS occasion upon which Irving played Modus 'for one night only' was his benefit, the last night of that highly successful season during which he had revived *The Corsican Brothers*, which had run for over two hundred nights, produced the Laureate's play, *The Cup*, revived *The Belle's Stratagem* and invited Edwin Booth to alternate the parts of Othello and Iago, a policy which had filled the theatre to overflowing at double prices for the month of May.

On 15 June *Othello* was acted for the last time at the Lyceum, 'for the benefit of Miss Ellen Terry,' Booth making his last appearance in the title *rôle* ; Irving also said good-bye to Iago. It is interesting to note that it was just twenty years since the two celebrated actors had first acted together in Manchester, when Irving had played Laertes to Booth's Hamlet.

The programme, of which the scene from *The Hunchback* formed a part, consisted also of *The Bells* and *The Birthplace of Podgers*, John Hollingshead's farce which J. L. Toole had first acted at the Lyceum in 1858. It was now revived for this performance only.

Of *The Hunchback* scenes, Clement Scott wrote that Ellen Terry was a Helen 'who wooed her student cousin with enchanting grace and coquetry,' and of Irving as the student of Ovid's Art of Love, that he was a Modus who 'with infinite variety and humour realized that happy condition when with "a touch, a kiss, the charm was snapt!"'

Those who know these delightful scenes of light comedy will have no difficulty in picturing the ideal Beatrice and Benedick in the parts of Helen and Modus. Though I was not present I can see them 'in my mind's eye.'

A reminiscence of another genius, the greatest after Irving of my time, which relates to these *Hunchback* scenes and concerns Irving is told in a letter written by Clement Scott nearly fifty years ago, of which the following is an extract:

'Yes, of course—but as a rule success does not attend so venturesome a step. In this instance however the entire circumstance is so unique that I doubt if the word failure could possibly have entered into it. You have merely got hold of a flimsy bit of the story. This is what really happened—and this is *how* it happened.

'Henry Irving cannot tolerate being caricatured, that you *do* know. Well, hearing of Fred Leslie's startlingly accurate imitation of him at the theatre immediately opposite in the new Gaiety musical show—as a matter of fact, Leslie actually appeared on the stage as Irving, dressed in woman's clothes, and oh, sir! fie, sir! in attenuated ballet skirts and extra scanty at that—very naughty-naughty, but oh, so funny, and so clever. Here is a copy of Irving's letter protesting against such an indignity . . . this letter Leslie found on his dressing-table after the curtain had been rung down on the final tableau of *Ruy Blas, or the Blasé Roué* and his counterfeit of Henry Irving.

"LYCEUM THEATRE,
23 *September* 1889.

DEAR MR. LESLIE,

I see that in your new burlesque I am put by you into woman's clothes, and I hope that you will at once withdraw such an exhibition.

Whether or not you are doing this thing by your manager's desire I cannot tell, but it seems to me that no consideration should tempt an artist to such an act.

Very truly yours,
HENRY IRVING.

Fred Leslie, Esq."

'I give you Irving's message *ad literatim* as it is jolly interesting and you'll be glad to read it. It nearly drove poor Leslie mad; he wouldn't wittingly hurt a fly, and he pranced about like a lunatic until he managed somehow or other to secure an interview with Henry Irving himself. Just think of it—and now for a huge surprise.

'Irving the aloof, Irving the consistently frigid, Irving the singularly unimpressionable master of his art, fell a victim to the natural charm and earnestness of Leslie, and this first interview made a flowery pathway for many others. Then Leslie made his confession, and told how he longed to act in serious drama.

' " I'm not feverish with Hamlet disease, I'm wholly free from that bacillus at the moment, but years ago, at one of your farewell performances at the Lyceum, you appeared in a scene from *The Hunchback*—you were Modus, and Helen, your adorable leading lady Miss Ellen Terry, and I . . ."

' Here Irving interrupted his visitor, and anticipating his desire gave him one of his wisest looks, which meant more than a hundred words from anyone else.

' " And you can see yourself as Modus ? Eh, well," here Irving chortled, " why not ? I'll make you an offer, Mr. Leslie. Come round to my theatre to-morrow morning, bring your Helen with you, and if you are sincere in your ambition I'll help you."

' Doesn't this fairly stop you breathing ? But I'm not through yet. Irving rehearsed Leslie and his Helen, the dainty, graceful, and slenderly beautiful Kate Vaughan, and then, when it came to the question of an engagement, Leslie developed a bad fit of the darkest blue funk. He became absolutely morbid with nervous apprehension and firmly made up his mind that his public which he had trained to scream and shriek with laughter would never accept him in the light of a legitimate stage artist.

' At last an idea came to him of how to overcome the difficulty. Leslie and Kate Vaughan were due to appear at a charity *matinée* at the Vaudeville Theatre, and instead of his own name being billed in the programme, he adopted the identical pseudonym which had served his purposes for years in topping and tailing every song he composed and every comic entertainment he ever designed, viz. A. C. Tor. Do you recognize the alias ?

' A gigantic go, and as everybody played for nothing (there were no free seats and no Press) nobody dreamed that Leslie had made his professional debut in straight drama, trained and perfected by Henry Irving.'

In 1892, nearing Christmas time, this great genius, his hopes unfulfilled, his ambitions unrealized, died of typhoid fever, in the hey-day of his manhood, at the age of thirty-six. His place in the theatre world still remains a void. It would be difficult to find Fred Leslie's rival—his equal—never.

A Lyceumite.

It was at the house of Charles Lamb Kenney, dramatic critic of *The Daily Telegraph*, that I first met Mrs. Irving. She was a tall, fair woman, with a touch of red in the gold of her hair and a bearing that proclaimed her nationality (you must have noticed the women in Sackville Street) as surely as it also left no doubt that she was 'Army.' If any doubt existed for a moment you had but to cast a glance at that other dominating lady who stood beside her, obviously her mother, who had the gait and glance of typical military bearing. In fact, they were the daughter and wife of Surgeon-General Daniel O'Callaghan, late of the Indian Army, decorated in the Mutiny for his conduct at the Siege of Delhi and later Inspector-General of Hospitals. He retired in 1872. Henry Irving and he had been and remained great friends, in spite of the fact that in that same year, 1872, Irving and his wife separated.

The story of this separation has been variously told, or perhaps I should say hinted at, for the suggestion that a marriage *could* be anything but perfectly happy was in itself a scandal in the eighteen-seventies. Incompatibility was not recognized as a possibility and it is beyond question that endless misery resulted from this narrow outlook. I think there is no doubt that Mrs. Irving admired her husband's great talent, though at the time of their marriage (15 July 1869) he had not yet had the opportunity of showing more than a little of his powers. He had not yet even played Digby Grant, and at the time of the marriage was acting at the Haymarket in a Comedy by his old friend Miss Le Thière, for which he did not even receive his salary for the last week. The title of the Comedy was *All for Money ;* that was certainly not the motive of the marriage. Irving was a typical Bohemian. He had struggled and starved for ten years in the provinces before he came to London ; he had the actor's habits and set way of life. His heart was in the Theatre ; in fact, to use a *cliché*, he was 'wedded to his art'—the kind who never should marry, though he loved children and was always popular with young people. He was indefatigable ; ready to work all day in the theatre, but his relaxation began with the fall of the curtain and, like all actors of his time, he seldom went to bed before four o'clock in the morning. This was not likely to fit in at all with the ideas and upbringing of Florence O'Callaghan, and I am quite sure—one glance was sufficient to tell me that—would be diametrically opposed to all Mrs. O'Callaghan's notions of decorum. Florence was not exactly a hard woman. She had great charm, an ingratiating manner, but was perhaps a little like H. G. Wells's Dolores—one who can concede nothing, allow nothing, nor forgive anything.

The story of their parting has been variously reported. I am disinclined to accept Bram Stoker's version of it, namely, that having returned home with his old friend Lionel Brough, while in quiet enjoyment of a smoke and a drink, Mrs. Irving appeared at the door (I think, candle in hand) and, ignoring the visitor, said: "It's time you were in bed, Henry," and left the room. Whereupon Irving said to Brough: "Can you give me a shakedown for the night, Lal?" "Yes, but——" "Come on, then——" and they left the house together. Irving not only did not return, but *never mentioned* his wife again.

His son, Laurence, was at this time three months old; he was born 21 December 1871, and Harry—known to all the world simply as 'H. B.'—about eighteen months (born 13 August 1870).

A far more likely tale, the one, indeed, which I am myself disposed to credit, is that Irving had returned home very late for several nights in succession. His wife, prompted undoubtedly by her mother, had told him: "If you can't come home at a respectable hour you'll find the door locked." He found the door locked—and never again sought admittance.

I was told that after that he lived some few months with the Batemans—H. L. Bateman was still living at that time—then moved to his rooms in Grafton Street, where he remained till the crash in 1899. Mrs. Irving was suitably provided for, in fact, handsomely; every expense of their sons' education was borne by Irving, whom they were taught to dislike and in fact never met until they were out of their teens.

My aunt, Josephine St. Ange, was Isabel Bateman's understudy and played the *ingénue* parts in the repertory of farces and light comedies that in those days always preceded and followed the chief play of the evening. It is not generally noticed that *The Bells* on its first production was preceded by a Farce and followed by a revised edition, in three Acts, of Albery's adaptation of *Pickwick*, which had failed to attract when it was produced a month earlier in its four-act form. The public expected the curtain to rise at 7 p.m. in those days and it seldom fell till after 11.30.

My young cousin and I had the *entrée* to the theatre at all times, and from the time I was seven till about seventeen I saw every play produced there, not once but a dozen times. *Much Ado About Nothing* is the first I remember. I was, of course, enchanted with everything. I did not attempt to criticize. It was amusing though to notice the very strong feeling Irving's style and manner evoked. Those accustomed to the older fashion of reading Shakespeare, following the tradition of Macready, such as Charles Kean and Samuel Phelps, were little short of scandalized by Irving's more naturalistic method.

A friend of my own was sent to await her father, who had

gone to a political meeting, in the stalls. Her father was a stern Macreadyite and knew exactly how Shakespeare should be spoken. He arrived at the theatre before the end of the second Act and stood at the end of the row waiting for the curtain to fall. But Irving's delivery of the text was too much for him and after listening to a speech which Macready had been wont to deliver as an oration, treated by Irving as a simple and natural piece of human emotion, he shouted: "Agnes, come out! The man's a fraud!" to the horror of the whole audience.

My aunt was a great friend of the Kenneys. I was a constant visitor at their house and of course they all worshipped Irving. Charles Lamb Kenney was supposed to have *made* Irving by his notice of *The Bells*, but then so many claimed to have discovered Irving. To my mind he simply discovered himself and nothing could have stopped him. You either adored him or you hated him, and there were many on both sides, though the worshippers were the majority. It was the solid goodness of the man that shone out, his extraordinary benevolence. No one ever appealed to him in vain. Irving's gratitude towards Mr. Kenney was evident from his generosity to Mrs. Kenney after her husband's death. He extended his benevolence to many pensioners. Anyone who had ever acted with him in the past seemed to be on his salary list, and I liked very much one story that is told of such a one. He had appealed to Irving saying they had once shared a bed. "Do you remember?" asked the old actor. "Yes, I remember," said Irving. And he was placed on the salary list, like the rest. After walking on in three productions he began to realize that he was not earning his very liberal salary, so he waylaid the Chief and asked him point-blank for a part in the next play. "We must consult the author," said Irving. When the cast was published the old actor looked in vain for his name. The play ran its course and a new one was announced. Once more Irving was waylaid and again he answered: "We must consult the author." This pathetic comedy was acted again—and yet again.

At last, a revival of *Hamlet* was to be put in rehearsal. And again our friend approached the Chief. Irving was just stepping into his hansom. "Lots of parts in the next production, Guv'nor. What do I play?" "We must consult the author." "But *Hamlet*, sir. The author's dead!" "Ah, well, we must respect his memory," said Irving.

Undoubtedly he had a sardonic humour, and I like better the story of Harry Stanford. H. B. Stanford went with him to

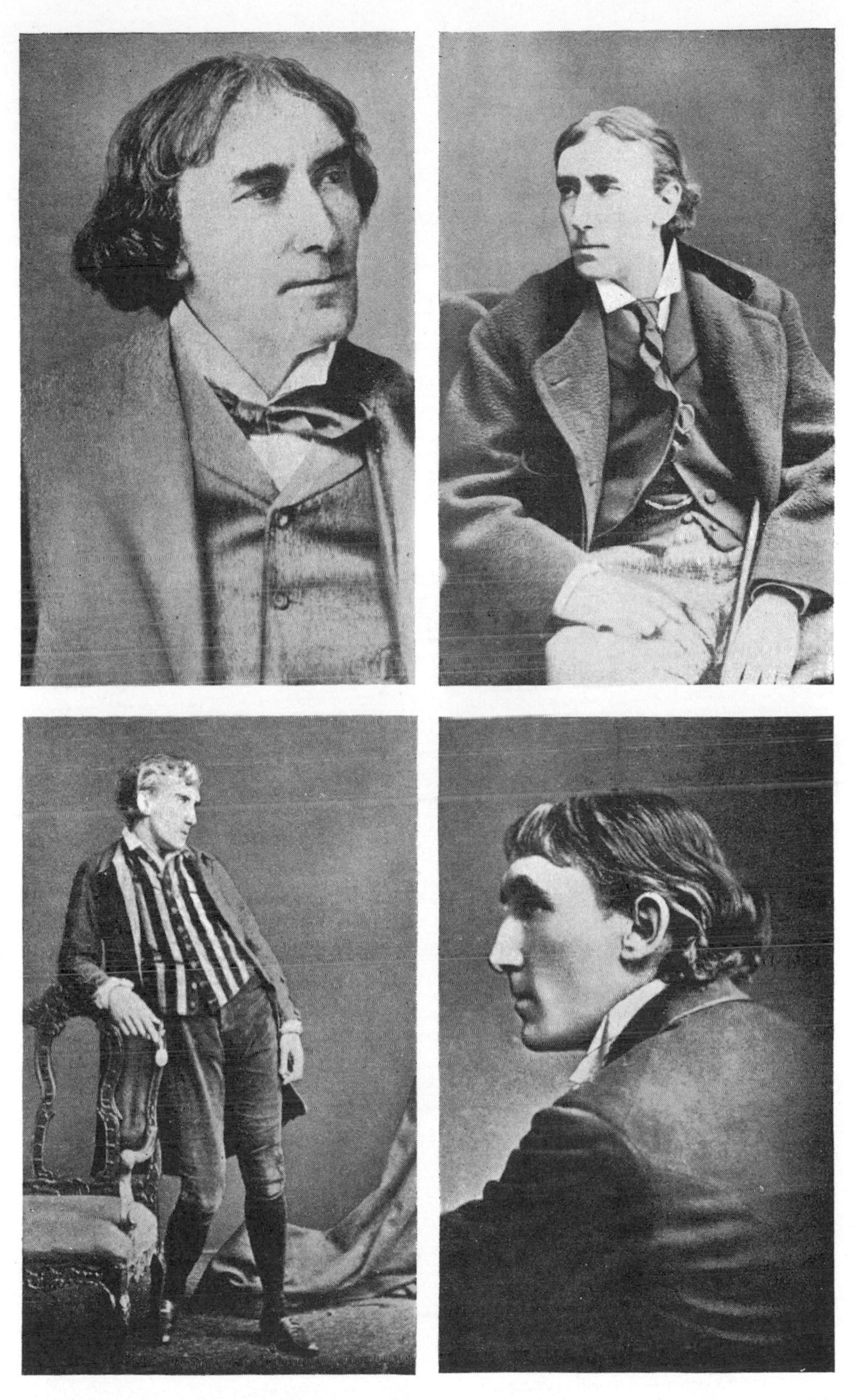

(*Top left*), IRVING *IN* 1875. (*Top right*), IRVING *IN* 1866.
(*Bottom left*), IRVING *AS MATHIAS*. (*Bottom right*), IRVING *IN* 1881.

America playing the juvenile parts. He was very good-looking and very attractive. He attracted the attention of an American manager—I forget who, though I think it must have been Frohman who was producing a dramatic version of Maurice Hewlett's *Forest Lovers*. Stanford asked for an interview with the Chief and very hesitatingly put his case. It was a big chance for him; he was to be starred in a beautiful part and a wonderful production, with, I think, Maude Adams as Isault.

Irving was making-up and listened patiently. When Harry had finished his story there was silence. At last: "What salary do they offer you, my boy, eh? What salary?" said Irving. "Three hundred dollars a week, sir," said Stanford, hopefully. "No, no, my boy, I'm sorry. I can't release you." And Stanford turned mournfully away. As he reached the door, Irving beckoned him back and said: "Tell them to make it four hundred and I'll let you go." And four hundred dollars it was.

RITA TREKELLE.

Although, as a young man, I had the good fortune to see our greatest actor play many parts, it never occurred to me that later on I should write plays for his son Harry, who became one of my dearest friends. I had no critical faculty whatever, but I can affirm this. What was on the surface, certain disabilities, physical not mental, appeared to me negligible. In a song of the seventies, Abdullah Bulbul Ameer, that 'haughty Mameluke,' could (among other accomplishments) imitate Irving. Years afterwards an American actor had the impudence to imitate to his face the great man. After the imitation, he addressed Sir Henry. "How is that?" he asked. Sir Henry replied calmly: "One of us, my boy, is rotten."

It was easy to imitate voice, walk, and gesture; but who could present the overpowering personality? I believe that an Italian not knowing a word of English would have surrendered unconditionally to Irving's genius, even as I, knowing so little Italian, bowed my knee to Salvini. Coquelin *cadet* is another example of this triumph of personality. In a London drawing-room, I heard Coquelin recite 'Je n'ai jamais vu Carcassone.' He held spellbound a crowd of fashionable folk, the 'rather nicers' of Mayfair, and I detected tears in the eyes of men and women.

A few days ago I sat next to a lady at luncheon who came to

this planet about the same time as I did, and who has a knowledge of and interest in the theatre greater than my own. Knowing that she had seen Henry Irving in nearly all his parts I asked her in which of them he had pleased her most? She replied without hesitation: "*The Bells*," adding, with a sly smile, "and his triumph in a bad play was to me the hall-mark of his incomparable powers as an actor." Many will say the same, or think it if they do not say it. Sir Henry's son—indeed both his sons—told me that a great part was a greater thing to their father than the whole. The divine Sarah must have ranked the part greater than the whole when she played Fedora and La Tosca.

It is significant that Irving overlooked nothing that might enhance the playing of a part. The late Joe Comyns Carr told me that a gorgeous cloak had been designed for Ellen Terry. She wore it only once at a rehearsal. Irving shot one keen glance at the garment and said: "Yes, yes, very arresting, take it to my dressing-room."

I shall never forget his Mephistopheles, another outstanding part in a play none too good. With all his arts and crafts as an actor Beerbohm Tree, in the revival of the play, failed to convey the diabolical subtlety and sardonic malice of Irving. I never saw him play Jingle, but Bram Stoker (I think) assured me that his Chief had almost curious affection for that part.

I never cared for his presentment of Romeo.

I saw him twice as Hamlet. The production cost him many thousands of pounds and it is likely that my eyes were too blinkingly aware of the setting. The same scenery and properties were used by H. B. when he played Hamlet for some six weeks at the Savoy Theatre. H. B. made a remark worthy of his father, when he said: "Hamlet has become a dictionary of quotations." *Punch* made a joke out of this. For my part I must admit that I have seen too many actors play Hamlet. Each, of course, beholds the melancholy Dane as a sort of personal possession or obsession. Each superimposes his own individuality. I repeat that I never attempted any technical criticism of actors when I was a young man. I have no regrets. I was a theatre 'fan' till I began to write plays; I could enjoy a bad play. Knowledge of technique impinges disastrously upon a playgoer's enjoyment of the Fourth Dimension. On several occasions, sitting next to a critic at a *première*, his too caustic comments have spoiled the evening's entertainment for me.

Again, even now—whan a certain detachment can be achieved

—I cannot discriminate between Sir Henry's presentment of Louis XI, Shylock, Charles I, Becket, and Benedick. I wish that I could. I have no shadow of doubt whatever that Sir Charles Wyndham was at his best in *David Garrick*. I could name the parts which most pleased me played by Sir George Alexander, Sir Charles Hawtrey, and Sir Herbert Beerbohm Tree. But Irving, unlike other knights of the buskin, appeared to soar above himself into an empyrean remote from ordinary criticism.

Off the stage, he cast the same spell. He could not enter a room without challenging and arresting uncanny attention. At the pre-war suppers at the Garrick Club he was invariably the monarch, slightly intimidating to the younger members. He was intimidating to his sons. He came to Harry's dressing-room after a performance of *The Admirable Crichton* and stood in the doorway. After a pause he said drily; "Irene very good, very good indeed, but you—do you like acting, my boy?"

This sub-acid edge to his tongue had to be accepted by all who came in contact with him as natural, part of his mental equipment. His heart—as thousands could testify—was softer than his head. His old dresser (and valet) Walter told me that his master's trouser pockets were replenished each morning with gold pieces, sovereigns and half-sovereigns. They were empty at night. He was incapable of resisting the importunity of any old actor who had known happier days. I was told, shortly after his death, that nearly a million pounds had slipped through his fingers. On one occasion, he came upon the stage at rehearsal to find Mrs. Sterling (I think) without a pair of horn spectacles.

"Where are your spectacles?" he snapped.

"Broken, Mr. Irving."

"Why haven't you another pair?"

"I—I don't know; I haven't."

There and then, despite the protests of his stage manager, Irving insisted that a gross of pairs of horn spectacles should be bought instantly.

H. B. told me that on another occasion a large quantity of jack-boots were displayed for inspection. They were new.

"Take them away, put them outside, let them get sodden with rain, bespatter them with mud. Then, and not till then, they will be fit to be seen."

Unless my memory fails me (which is distressingly possible)

Irving was the first actor who became a member of the Athenæum Club. H. B. was a member when I had the honour of being elected in 1912. Like his father, 'wine' was a synonym for champagne. On a hot day, Harry liked to drink champagne at luncheon. I suggested to him that the bishops might be offended. "We must run that risk," said H. B., with his father's chuckle.

Negligible though my opinion is, it was shared by many playgoers thirty years ago. A man had come from the people with none of the adventitious prerogatives bestowed upon the young patricians of his day; and he had made a lasting impact upon millions of his fellow-countrymen.

I have been constrained against my judgment to make this small contribution to a book designed to set forth a great actor in his particular parts, because I had the privilege of a too slight acquaintance with him and because I enjoyed the friendship of his two sons. Possibly, I achieved a deeper knowledge of the father because his elder son, Harry—apart from the physical resemblance—was so like his sire. The son had the same profound respect for the dignity of his profession. I recall telling H. B. that I was planning to write a novel dealing with the Stage as I knew it; he pressed my arm. "Don't," he urged, "write anything unkind about us!" Perhaps the greatest regret of the son's too brief life was expressed when he told me that he had never known his father as he wished to know him.

It was difficult to know Henry Irving. He towered above his contemporaries. He had one of the attributes of genius; the capacity for taking infinite pains. He descended to earth when he was smoking a good cigar or drinking a glass of wine. He inspired loyalty in all who worked with him and under him. In many ways he was unapproachable. This, perhaps, is as it should be. Divinity does hedge a king; and familiarity with the great too often breeds not contempt but a subconscious devaluation. The author of *The Lives of the Chancellors* once said to me whimsically: "Great men are so disappointing, because their greatness is not on the surface." A lover of Liszt made an enlightening remark: "When he plays, I shut my eyes, because I hate to see the warts on his fine face."

The fact that Irving played many parts is nothing. How he played them is everything. What is termed a 'foolproof' part may have appealed to an overworked actor, but he poured himself into every part, making it better than he found it. I recall my youthful hatred of Shylock till Irving transmuted hatred into pity. Irving must have felt pity for Louis XI. He could move to tears those who heard him recite *Eugene Aram.* Had he played the part of such a miscreant as Charles Peace, he would have quickened pity in us rather than reprobation.

It is impossible for the Man in the Street to acclaim Irving as supreme in one part because he appeared to be supreme in so many.

Off the stage his wit and sardonic humour recalled to mind Smollett instead of Henry Fielding. Who dares to say what Irving might have accomplished in another walk of life? It is indisputable that H. B. (with robuster health) might have become a distinguished advocate specializing (as Edward Marshall Hall did) in criminology. Had the father taken Orders, he might have worn Swift's mantle. Somebody—Clement Scott or Walkley—said that he would have made a great Showman. It is still disputable whether or not he did the modern theatre a service when he introduced expensive settings. He never foresaw the possibility that after his death over-production would imperil the life of a good play. Had a seer assured him that a play playing to £1200 a week would have to be taken off, he would have been shocked.

Here in Bath we have a remarkable *Irvingiana* collection. Many of his magnificent costumes can be seen at Stafford House. I looked long at them a few days ago. It is significant that the resplendent trappings of the outward man were to most of us merely accessories. Indeed, I had forgotten them. They served their purpose. So did the gorgeous curtain at the Lyceum, presented by Lady Coutts, which somehow aroused an expectation in every part of the house which the MAN behind it never failed to satisfy. He had this in common with Charles Dickens. Our greatest novelist triumphed gloriously over the prejudices and inhibitions of what was then called high society. So did Henry Irving. In the seventies it was as easy to parody Dickens as it was to imitate Irving, but the parodies and imitations were mildly amusing and nothing more.

Irving's statue, behind the National Gallery, is, I submit, the authentic presentment of him. How often Harry and I have stood bare-headed in front of it!

HORACE ANNESLEY VACHELL.

I saw Sir Henry Irving on the stage, but I never saw him act. I saw him take his final bow to the audience in front of the curtains at the Theatre Royal, Bradford, at the conclusion of *Becket* on the night of 13 October 1905.

I had recently joined the Beerbohm Tree Company as touring manager; one of his companies was playing at Leeds, and we were coming to Bradford—the following week I think—with *The Tempest.* It was a very heavy production, and being young and full of energy I thought it might be helpful if I slipped over to Bradford and had a conference with the local management.

I reached Bradford too late to see the performance at the theatre, so after a late dinner at the hotel, I strolled over to the theatre to arrange my plans for the following day.

"The curtain is just coming down," the manager told me, just as I had concluded my arrangements for the next morning. "Slip up to the back of the circle and hear the marvellous reception."

I then saw Sir Henry Irving for the first and last time on the stage—saw a majestic, but very exhausted figure bowing good-bye.

I must see this performance through to-morrow, I promised myself, I must not lose this opportunity, but alas! the opportunity had gone for ever. Under the same roof where I slept that night one of the greatest actors in the world passed away.

I shall never forget the shock that I received the next morning at breakfast when the head waiter told me that Sir Henry was dead.

I felt personally part of the great tragedy that had fallen on the artistic and theatre-loving world.

Yes, I saw Irving on the stage, but I only saw him take a call—his final curtain.

STANLEY BELL.

A SONNET TO HENRY IRVING

Here where your statue stands amid the throng
Of London which paid homage to your art
And you with it, I come with grateful heart
To lay my tribute which will last as long
As life, remembering the thrall and thong
With which, spellbound, you held us with each part;
Now stirring us to laughter, now to start
With horror, thrilling, crepitating, strong.

MODUS

Though dumb the voice that Shakespeare's language spoke,
Ashes the form that his creations woke
From sleeping words to living, vital men,
You live for us who ne'er shall look again
Upon your like, for on our modern stage
You kinged it,—Garrick, Roscius of your age.

R. de C.

XXVI

IRVING as DIGBY GRANT

Lyceum Theatre, 26th of December, 1881 :—

TWO ROSES

WRITTEN BY JAMES ALBERY

Mr. Digby Grant	MR. HENRY IRVING
Mr. Furnival	MR. H. HOWE
Jack Wyatt	MR. W. TERRISS
Caleb Deecie	MR. G. ALEXANDER
Footman	MR. HARBURY
Our Mr. Jenkins	MR. DAVID JAMES
Ida	MISS HELEN MATTHEWS
Mrs. Cupps	MISS C. EWELL
Our Mrs. Jenkins	MISS PAUNCEFORT
Lottie	MISS WINIFRED EMERY

ACT I, SCENE. *Mr. Digby Grant's Cottage.* ACT II, SCENE. *Jack Wyatt's Lodgings.* ACT III, SCENE. *Vassalwick Grange.*

WHEN Macready retired from the stage in 1851 an eminent critic wrote : 'His departure left a blank. There was no successor.' For just on two decades the void in the theatre world remained a social and artistic gap. The stage passively existed, but deprived of the dynamic force of any towering, outstanding personality. Of capable players there was no lack, but of capable dramatists there was none but Tom Robertson and H. J. Byron. The trail of Bulwer Lytton's *Lady of Lyons* hung about the proscenium arch, although *Money* revived the author's languishing fame as dramatist, but there was an absence of intellectual verdure and the stream of dramatic poetry had been scorched into nothingness by an indifferent public. Tom Taylor was adapter-in-chief of French Farce and Melodrama on which playgoers fed, enlivened by opera-bouffe.

The Nonconformist backbone was stiff in the land and middle-class England regarded the Pit Door as the open gate to Hell. Salaries of actors were of such modest proportions that the majority were just able to live, from hand to mouth. They dwelt for the most part in furnished rooms in Bloomsbury and Holborn. Chiswick was country and Hampstead an adventure. The omnibus was painfully slow, ill-lighted, and dirty; night journeys to and from the suburbs were ever a dismal experience. The enterprising playgoer after a tiresome journey found pit seats as wooden and uncomfortable as school forms, while the gallery in most theatres was a medieval monstrosity.

Such were the general conditions when Henry Irving was a young actor struggling for a position on the London stage. Success was not liberal in its entertainment and it was not until the production of H. J. Byron's *Dearer than Life* at the Queen's, Long Acre, in 1868, in which he played Bob Gassitt, that he achieved a popular success. Frank Archer in his *An Actor's Notebooks* speaks of it as 'a masterpiece of character acting.' It is interesting to note that Irving's associates in that play included J. L. Toole, John Clayton, Lionel Brough, and Charles Wyndham.

In 1870 the newly built Vaudeville Theatre was opened under the direction of Tom Thorne, David James and H. J. Montague. After a qualified initial success they produced James Albery's *Two Roses*, on 4 June of the same year. Probably it was Irving's success at the Queen's which led to his engagement for the character part of Digby Grant. *Two Roses* was the author's most signal success, and doubtless Irving contributed his full share towards that acceptable result, although the dramatic critics of the day were not overripe in praise.

A year or two later, in 1873, James Albery in a letter to Frank Archer, gives his opinion of Irving on seeing him in a performance of *Richelieu* at the Lyceum, then under the management of Colonel Bateman. He writes:

> 'Richelieu is a good but not a great performance. What it lacks, no study on Irving's part could give it. It wants that tone that comes from brain *power*. I mean a sort of mental physique, a moral toughness that affects the voice, look, manner. Suppose, for instance, Gladstone, who possesses the quality to a wonderful extent, was dramatised. I mean the character. Irving could not play it. Ungoverned rage, sorrow, dread he can depict, but not pure mental force. He well expresses the emotion of a mind acted on but not of a mind acting on others. He lacks what one may call the muscle and sinew of the brain.'

At the end of the successful run of *Two Roses*, Irving moved along the Strand to the Lyceum where Colonel Bateman was meeting with indifferent success, so indifferent that Irving found no great objection to his recommendation of Leopold Lewis's adaptation of *Le Juif Polonais* which was soon to be acclaimed as *The Bells*, in which, as Mathias, Irving won world fame in a night. It did more. It gave Irving a position in which his voice carried weight with his Manager. *The Bells* rang in *Hamlet*, for we may justly entertain the conclusion that the ambitious young actor had visualized himself in the famous *rôle* in which the great representatives of his art in the past had achieved national distinction. So we may regard *The Bells* as the harbinger of the series of Shakespearean Revivals at the once famous playhouse in Wellington Street.

It was now conceived that the gap occasioned by the retirement of Macready was about to be filled. The production of *Hamlet* in 1874 changed the surmise into certainty.

To a little remote village in east Kent there came wondrous reports of this new Prince of Denmark which sent an inquisitive youth to the family Shakespeare, and when that youth came to London he was drawn to the Lyceum where Irving had installed himself as lessee and manager, inaugurating his reign in December 1878 with a revival of the greatest of all poetic melodramas.

A rare and priceless possession of the playgoer is his tablet of memories. In middle and old age the raw enthusiasm of youth has mellowed into calm approval, but still we look back upon the hot-house exuberance of youth with a jealous longing, a hungry desire to recapture the burning fires of adolescence. But if the instant way is forbidden we can call up from the vasty depths of the past vivid memories of playhouse scenes, of gorgeous pictures indelibly inscribed on the mind's parchment.

As a youth of nineteen I saw Irving's *Hamlet*. In my mind's eye, I can recall certain scenes with a vividness and reality as though they were of yesterday and not a vision of sixty years ago.

I see Irving, sitting downstage, pondering the problem of existence, the ' to be, or not to be ' of human endeavour, many and eloquent pauses, but with Irving's pauses there was no cessation of dramatic action, his speaking eyes, his features aglow with thought, carried on the action. I see him, prone on the stage, watching with hectic eyes and spasmodic limbs the effect of the players on the King and Queen until the guilty couple flee in terror and the figure on the floor leaps to its feet alive with triumphant realization. Precious indeed, are thy tablets, Memory!

Irving's next revival, *The Corsican Brothers*, preceded his Vaudeville success, *Two Roses*. This was evidently marking time pending the production of his next Shakespearean venture *Romeo and Juliet*. In the cast of *Two Roses* were George Alexander (making his West End *début*), William Terriss, David James, Winifred Emery and, of course, himself in his original character, Digby Grant.

Tom Robertson had made pleasant London's tea-tables with his ' cup and saucer ' comedies at the little bandbox of a theatre just off the Tottenham Court Road which, with extraordinary self-confidence, Marie Wilton had taken, and from which she took a husband in the handsome figure of Squire Bancroft. *Two Roses* was of the family of *Caste* and *Ours* and it has ever been my opinion that Albery based his Digby Grant on Charles Dickens's Father of the Marshalsea, William Dorrit. In both characters there is the same hypocritical servility in poverty, the same arrogance in affluence.

The author introduces us to Digby Grant as the occupant, with his two daughters Lottie and Ivy, of a modest cottage in Kent. We see him as one of those dignified, self-satisfied imposters, without a shilling, imposing on those who enter his domestic circle, the importance of his birth and family connections. It is his belief, he maintains, that no disgrace attends, or arises from the impossibility of payment for debts contracted for necessary and assured wants, and advances with much stateliness the theory that the acknowledgment of a debt is almost as good as its discharge. At the same time he is not too proud to take pecuniary advantage of those better situated than himself. The two young men, his daughters' admirers, are distinctly not of his class, but he displays no scruples about accepting, with gracious condescension, occasional cash offerings. He extends the same liberality of sentiment to the genial commercial traveller, and also premises a tender regard for the widow, Mrs. Cupps, who has ' obliged ' towards the family exchequer.

Then comes the news that owing to the disappearance of the direct heir, Digby is the inheritor of an estate worth £10,000 per annum. We see now the other side of the man's character. No longer the complaisant attitude of the victim of circumstances ; his world has widened, he sees himself the centre figure in the glittering arena of Society. The cord is cut that has held him in durance ; the irritating disabilities of his cottage existence vanish from his mind, the cheque book he holds is the magic wand which will waft him into the empyrean of a new and brilliant life. Those who have humoured his petty foibles and eased him in his difficulties must be for him as though they never were. Cheque-book in hand, he calls them to his side, and one by one he discharges his obligations with a superior and distant indication that no welcome will await them in his new abode.

This cheque scene is the central spot of the play and the one that remains most distinctly visible in my mind. Those, and those only, who saw Irving in the shabby old dressing-gown, his heart bursting with self-adulation, handing to each of his former friends, with superb condescension, 'a little cheque,' are able to appreciate Irving's subtle and complete realisation of the character. Indeed, I imagine it must have been a surprise to the author himself, and may have accounted for the veiled hostility of the criticism quoted above on the actor's Richelieu. Voice, gesture, deportment are in perfect accord, each word is given its significant accent, each gesture is a studied exposition of the situation, each glance an indication of thus far shall you go and no farther. Never for a moment does the actor degenerate into caricature. The 'muscle and sinew of the brain' covertly and openly are exercising their power and potency not only on the actors concerned, but on the audience beyond the footlights. As we talk of a balanced meal so we may speak of Irving's Digby Grant as a perfectly balanced interpretation of a character that desires the appearance of magnanimity and only succeeds in displaying the repellent factors of a base and distorted mind.

Did any of those who saw Digby Grant foresee that it was the forerunner of other and more splendid character parts, Wolsey, Benedick, Shylock, culminating in Becket? Most probably not, for there was much to be revealed in Irving's creative 'make-up.' Whatever diverse opinions may be held as to his merits as a Tragedian there can be no question as to his incomparable gift and accomplishment as a character actor. That is why I attach such importance to his Digby Grant. It was the personality and craft of the actor that gave brain and substance to the author's creation, that has caused Digby Grant to remain, for me, a living figure during five or more crowded decades of playgoing, that it is impressed on my mind as one of the cardinal features of Irving's great moments.

The genius of a famous actor perishes with him and the number of those who saw Irving in his prime and can testify to his greatness is diminishing yearly and, likely enough, their words fall on the captious ears of a world removed by an eternity from the world of Henry Irving's Lyceum. Throughout sixty years of uninterrupted playgoing I saw all the 'stars' of the Victorian-Edwardian periods and . . . I have seen their successors.

What were the foundations of Irving's art as a character actor? In my opinion it was his intense, penetrative mind which could value the meaning of the slightest word, so that when engaged in the mental conception of a character that conception became so materialized that its transition to the corporeal in representation was a matter of comparative ease. Irving's facial play was ever indicative of the working of his mind whether attuned to the tragic introspection of a Hamlet or the infinite jest of a Benedick.

'A little cheque.' As common a phrase as 'a little cheese,' but had you seen Irving's facial expression, heard the vocal intonation, observed the sinuous movement of the nervous hands, you would have seen as in a looking-glass the material embodiment of a spirit destitute of all the finer qualities, and the reflection of a nature inexpressibly pitiful in its sordid attitude to his fellow-men and the world in general.

It is scarcely necessary to add that the missing heir proves to be one of the young men who were sent about their business by Digby on his succession to the transitory wealth.

By the Pinero-Jones standard *Two Roses* is poor drama, but it will live in the annals of the stage as the medium which first revealed to the Lyceum public the inimitable gifts of characterization, the fine comedy quality of the greatest actor of his time—Henry Irving.

B. W. FINDON.

XXVII

IRVING as ROMEO

Lyceum Theatre, 8th of March, 1882 :—

ROMEO AND JULIET

WRITTEN BY WILLIAM SHAKESPEARE

Romeo	MR. HENRY IRVING
Mercutio	MR. WILLIAM TERRISS
Tybalt	MR. CHARLES GLENNEY
Paris	MR. GEORGE ALEXANDER
Capulet	MR. HOWE
Montague	MR. HARBURY
Friar Laurence	MR. FERNANDEZ
Apothecary	MR. MEAD
Prince Escalus	MR. TYARS
Benvolio	MR. CHILD
Gregory	MR. CARTER
Sampson	MR. ARCHER
Abraham	MR. LOUTHER
Balthasar	MR. HUDSON
Peter	MR. ANDREWS
Friar John	MR. BLACK
Citizen	MR. HARWOOD
Chorus	MR. HOWARD RUSSELL
Page	MISS KATE BROWN
Nurse	MRS. STIRLING
Lady Montague	MISS H. MATTHEWS
Lady Capulet	MISS L. PAYNE
Juliet	MISS ELLEN TERRY

ACT I, SCENE 1. *Verona—The Market Place;* SCENE 2. *Verona—Loggia of Capulet's House;* SCENE 3. *Verona—Before Capulet's House;* SCENE 4. *A Hall in Capulet's House.* ACT II, SCENE 1. *Verona—Wall of Capulet's Garden;* SCENE 2. *Verona—The Garden;* SCENE 3. *Verona—The Monastery;* SCENE 4. *Verona—Outside the City;* SCENE 5. *Verona—Terrace of Capulet's Garden;* SCENE 6. *Verona—The Cloisters.* ACT III, SCENE 1. *Verona—A Public Place;* SCENE 2. *Verona—The Loggia;* SCENE 3. *Verona—A Secret Place in the Monastery;* SCENE 4. *Verona—Capulet's House;* SCENE 5. *Verona—Juliet's Chamber.* ACT IV, SCENE 1. *Verona—The Friar's Cell;* SCENE 2. *Verona—Juliet's Chamber (Night);* SCENE 3. *Verona—The Same (Morning).* ACT V, SCENE 1. *Mantua—A Street;* SCENE 2. *Verona—The Friar's Cell;* SCENE 3. *Verona—Churchyard with the Tomb of the Capulets;* SCENE 4. *Verona—The Tomb.*

VERONA.

City of Dread.

Here every man goes in terror of his life, for the partisans of the two rival Houses are forever on the watch; at street-corners and in dark alley-ways dark deeds are done. Secret raids, betrayals, ambushes, assassinations, and who knows whether it was a Capulet or a Montague who did the deed? A vendetta in which all the city takes a part: 'Who is not for me is against me! Kill! Kill! Kill!'

> 'Three civil brawls, bred of an airy word
> By thee, old Capulet, and Montague,
> Have thrice disturbed the quiet of our streets.'

Those were pitched battles in broad daylight, like that we are presently to see. It is a miniature civil war.

That I take to be the background, the atmosphere Irving imagined when he produced this tragedy, for he knew that it is a tragedy, the only manager who in my seventy years of play-going seems to have appreciated the fact. They have made it charming, effective, or pretty, and sometimes dramatic, but Irving only made it tragic.

'Wherefore are THOU Romeo?' asked *Punch*.

Ellen Terry supplied the answer: 'He had the power to portray *Italian* passions—the passions of lovely, treacherous people who will either sing you a love song or stab you in the back.' There is the answer: he had *passion*, passion that could blaze, the passion of tragic fire.

Is Romeo necessarily a callow youth, pink and white, of full cheek and clear eye, of shapely limb and rounded contours? The male love-bird? The pretty, if manly, boy? We have seen since that day a succession of beautiful people play the part; William Terriss, Kyrle Bellew, E. H. Vanderfelt, Matheson Lang, Harcourt Williams, Laurence Olivier, John Gielgud, Ivor Novello; all these were very pleasing to the eye, graceful, and gallant, but which of them had the soul of Romeo?—save perhaps Vanderfelt and Harcourt Williams they had been better Mercutios. All these were lucky lovers; one felt it, whom tragedy could never touch—heroes of a fairy tale who win their princesses and live happy ever after. But it happens that *Romeo and Juliet* is indeed a tragedy, no duet of bill and coo, no love poem, but a tale springing not from the wrangle of two quarrelsome neighbours but from the Italianate hatred of two virile races. The blood-feud, the ruthless vendetta declared between Montague and Capulet through the generations had infected all Verona : it is ' to the death ! '

Shakespeare establishes this in the first scene. The brawl that starts between the servants of the rival Houses leads to a bloody encounter between the kinsfolk of their heads. It requires the Prince in person to quell it, and his charge to the heads themselves leaves no doubt of the gravity of its importance :

> ' If ever you disturb our streets again,
> Your *lives* shall pay the forfeit of the peace.'

The atmosphere is established. This is no mere scuffle with Tom and Dick joining in for the fun of a row ; this is war—bitter, venomous, bloody ! And from this springs our play. What kind of protagonists do you expect to see ? Juliet with a skipping rope ? Romeo with a tennis racket ? Hardly. The seal of a tragic fate is surely upon them both. Their heads are in the stars ; they are fate-ridden, fate-driven, it must be so from the first.

Calamity predestinate.

We see him first ecstatic in adoration of his Rosaline ; he even kisses the Capulet's letter that is to reach her hands. He has no sense of humour, this Romeo, yet we have seen all the star actors strain for the laugh so easily wrung—and, as I maintain, wrongly wrung—from the lines. A kittenish Juliet is unthinkable—if one thinks. Yet whom have you seen play her without snatching at an easy guffaw for " —and with a silk thread plucks it back again."

We may smile, or even laugh (if our manners are bad or we have no mind for tragedy) at Romeo's extravagancies in the garden, but let him *play* for those laughs and he is no Romeo. They may be laughs at his lack of humour, his utter want of a sense of logic or proportion, but never because he is consciously humorous in his declarations :

> ' O that I were a glove upon that hand,
> That I might touch that cheek ! '

That is dead earnest, unequivocal. Give it a touch of comic intent and it is no longer Romeo.

Remember this : if Romeo be taken in that garden he won't be beaten and locked up till morning in the tool-shed ; he will be horridly butchered. If that is not in your mind, the stage manager has misunderstood his job.

From the first Irving's head was in the stars ; his instinct was unerring. He knew. Smarting from the indifference of

Rosaline he was ripe for a new infection. He penetrates, masked, into his enemy's house; he sees Juliet. The instant of their first meeting is tragic, and from that moment they move swiftly to their doom. 'Star-cross'd lovers!' Indeed, yes, for fatal Tybalt dogs them and will light on Romeo, the appointed agent of his fate.

Then we saw Irving blaze. There was not a nerve, not a muscle of him that did not quiver in passion.

> 'Away to heaven, respective lenity
> And fire-eyed fury be my conduct now!'

His eyes darted fire! His rapier was a whip. No hope for Tybalt; Romeo was past his guard in a flash.

> 'O I am fortune's fool!'

If Irving failed to carry all his audience in that scene of bewildered despair in Friar Laurence's cell, it was because of that natural tendency of the English to suppress emotion, the frank and abandoned expression of it embarrasses them; the snigger was self-conscious. A foreign audience would never have misunderstood—never even thought of smiling at such exhibition of abject despair.

The parting of those wedded lovers in the dawn in Juliet's bed-chamber; the beauty—the despair. And the imagination that produced that marvellous dawn! I was a hardened playgoer when I saw this play. At Drury Lane, the Princess's, the Adelphi, I had seen many beautiful productions; it was a time of most elaborate scenic display, and the theatres rivalled each other in this matter; but never anywhere, before or since, have I seen such exquisite scenery; such dignity—such imagination.

And then Mantua. I think Iriving reached his top note of tragedy in this scene. His first entrance in *Macbeth* against a blood-red sunset created an effect of doom upon me that I have never forgotten. His first appearance as Glo'ster through the arches of that old London street full of deep shadows, watching the funeral procession of Henry VI passing, ghostly, as it emerged from the darkness into a patch of light. Richard limped into sight, an evil vulture poised to strike, the embodiment of malevolence. These are moments to remember. Yet more clearly still—at least, more poignantly, do I remember that stricken man's utter despair as he murmured:

> 'Then, I defy you, stars!'

That line alone was *Punch's* answer.

I think we all sat numbed for the final scene. The iron crowbar; the swift fight and death of Paris; the entrance of Romeo dragging Paris's body from the earth-level down to the vault below where Juliet lies, throned in death—as he thinks—and there he joins her. And so to the final sacrifice.

Then the surge of the torch-lit crowd and reconciliation of the Houses.

Memories that are fresh and green after fifty-six years! We get no such first nights at the theatre now.

I first saw Irving as Digby Grant at the Vaudeville in 1870; 'a little cheque!' And Jingle! One would have thought Dickens must have seen him first and then put him into *Pickwick Papers*. Nothing could be funnier (for Irving was a great comedian) than his mock mad scene as Doricourt in *The Belle's Strategem*, and when you compare that with his abject fear in the bedroom scene of *Louis the Eleventh;* I think that was the very biggest thrill I ever had in a theatre. His head was bent as he leaned over his knees talking to the leaden images of the Saints on his hat lying in his lap; then he saw Nemours' shadow in the patch of moonlight on the floor. Any other actor would have started and looked up at Terriss. Not Irving. He concentrated on that shadow as the fear grew in him and fell on his knees, abject, grovelling, as he hoarsely gasped: "Mercy! Mercy!"

The nearest approach to it was when Eugene Aram saw his accomplice entering at the window and, with a muffled scream, cried: "Houseman!" There is no actor to-day who gives you anything like that to remember.

I saw him play Hamlet seven times, and if I start to talk about it I shall not know when to stop, but I must refer to the dynamic effect of the end of the Play Scene. However prepared you were for it, though you knew it must come, its thrill was never lessened, the shock hit you and lifted you out of your seat. That is literal, for it never failed, and at least half the audience stood to cheer him.

The modern Hamlets are very nice but they don't get over the footlights. I think his son, H. B., the best of those I have seen since. His sudden spring forward as he cried:

> 'O, what a rogue and peasant slave am I!'

had something of the electric effect of his father.

With Forbes-Robertson one felt that though he spoke it all beautifully, he was weary; he *had* to go through with it.

Wilson Barrett was never *real* and his striving for new readings worried me:

> 'The air bites shrewdly. *Is* it very cold?'

Tree I avoided. I didn't want to shudder. I never liked him in Shakespeare.

Yes, H. B. was the best since his father, who, however, was not encouraging to him, so the story goes. There were flares in braziers on the battlements, and he ' set it down in his tablets ' by the light of one of them. When he asked his father what he thought afterwards, Irving said : " I noticed the road was up in the Ghost scene." He was always ready with a quip, but there was no malice in him. He couldn't have wrung your heart as he did, in *Becket*, if there had been.

I was talking to a friend about him the other day ; he is a great playgoer and, of course, thinks a lot of his present-day favourites. I told him if he'd never seen Irving he didn't know what acting really is. Then his young daughter chimed in with : " I expect Clark Gable's as good."

I wanted to spank her.

HENRY R. PETTITT.

XXVIII

IRVING as BENEDICK

Lyceum Theatre, 11th of October, 1882 :—

MUCH ADO ABOUT NOTHING

WRITTEN BY WILLIAM SHAKESPEARE

Benedick	MR. HENRY IRVING
Don Pedro	MR. W. TERRISS
Don John	MR. C. GLENNEY
Claudio	MR. FORBES-ROBERTSON
Leonato	MR. FERNANDEZ
Antonio	MR. H. HOWE
Balthazar	MR. J. ROBERTSON
Borachio	MR. F. TYARS
Conrade	MR. HUDSON
Friar Francis	MR. MEAD
Dogberry	MR. S. JOHNSON
Verges	MR. STANILAUS CALHAEM
Seacoal	MR. ARCHER
Oatcake	MR. HARBURY
A Sexton	MR. CARTER
A Messenger	MR. HAVILAND
A Boy	MISS K. BROWN
Hero	MISS MILLWARD
Margaret	MISS HARWOOD
Ursula	MISS L. PAYNE
Beatrice	MISS ELLEN TERRY

ACT I, SCENE. *Leonato's House.* ACT II, SCENE 1. *Before Leonato's House ;* SCENE 2. *Hall in Leonato's House.* ACT III, SCENE 1. *Before Leonato's House ;* SCENE 2. *Leonato's Garden (Evening) ;* SCENE 3. *Leonato's Garden (Morning) ;* SCENE 4. *The Cedar Walk ;* SCENE 5. *A Street.* ACT IV, SCENE. *Inside a Church.* ACT V, SCENE 1. *A Prison ;* SCENE 2. *Leonato's Garden ;* SCENE 3. *The Monument of Leonato ;* SCENE 4. *Hall in Leonato's House.*

THIS delightful comedy was surely the progenitor and direct begetter of the Cloak-and-sword drama that so delighted our immediate ancestors. It has the joyous ring of *The Three Musketeers*. It might conceivably have inspired Anthony Hope and Stanley Weyman to give us *The Prisoner of Zenda*, *Under the Red Robe*, *A Gentleman of France ;* perhaps it did. But to expose all the facets of its brilliance to best advantage it must be most carefully cast and stage-managed ; it is not a play that acts itself. Especially the rather painful sub-plot—which, since it gives the play its title, may well have been designed as its main interest—must be most carefully dealt with ; for though Don John's slander of Hero, unfounded as it soon proves to be, would not to-day be accounted so trivial, since no actual harm comes from it, it may be said indeed to be 'much ado about nothing.' Yet this part of the play, treated unskilfully, must leave a rather unsavoury impression in our minds, if judged by modern standards. But the reward is rich, and the results happy, when interest is concentrated almost exclusively on the love-duel between Benedick and Beatrice, as Irving's production proved.

Beatrice is a character so rare and happy, and so entirely sympathetic in every aspect, that for any accomplished actress it is a gift, or, as the old actors used to say, a very, very 'fat' part. It is beyond all question that Ellen Terry suited it to absolute perfection ; neither a word nor a glance was thrown away, and there was the maximum of effect in every phrase and look ; in her passages of wit with Benedick, of gallantry with Don Pedro (William Terriss was at his consummate best in this part) ; in her tenderness with her cousin Hero, she was everywhere at the high-water mark of her fascinating personality and most skilful technique.

But the crux of this play is Benedick. If he be merely another of Shakespeare's young men who, though definitely characterized as all of them are, have generally a deplorable similarity in the theatre, the play is merely a pleasant one *if* the Hero scenes are not unduly stressed, and read in this sense the character of Benedick becomes merely an oafish young man who enjoys bickering with his host's pretty niece as Mercutio teases Juliet's nurse. And, indeed, Professor George Brandes speaks of Benedick as *Mercutio redivivus*. With the utmost respect to the Professor, I submit that Benedick is no such thing. True, both are soldiers and both are gentlemen, and there the semblance ends. What can be found common to them in temperament ? Mercutio is a light-hearted, hot-headed, devil-may-care, and certainly nothing of a misogamist ; Benedick, though a wit, is of a distinctly graver turn, a good comrade among his fellows, but, as he styles himself, 'a professed tyrant' of the other sex. It is his persistent indifference to women rather than his hatred of them that so galls Beatrice, for that attitude is vastly more tantalizing. No woman of her temper can believe that a man can truly entertain for her such tepid sentiment, and it is this indifference of his that goads her to her most pungent sallies; a mere woman-hater would never provoke her to the same extravagance. Extravagance is, I believe, the exact word, for before the Lyceum production a custom had developed of playing these two parts as sheer boor and virago, so that their scenes together became mere slanging matches. They were embellished on occasion by the art of the players, when an apt and even topical impromptu occurred to them, in utter disregard of Hamlet's sage advice: 'Let your clowns say no more than is set down for them,' and, *apropos*, how many topical 'gags' are printed, even in the first folio? Possibly not even Hemynge nor Condell could answer.

But Irving discarded as many old traditions as he created new ones, and in his reading of Benedick set up a standard that none, to my knowledge, has since attempted to emulate. Since his day I have seen many renderings of the part; his own stands out as the one illuminating performance. He conceived the character on completely new lines and gave the play a new vitality. His Benedick was an eccentric, a fantastic, an oddity, but *preux chevalier* always. There was no unseemly wrangling between a bully and a termagant, but a quick exchange of rapier thrusts barbed with humour, parried with wit, quarte and tierce, sparkle and flash and '*alla stoccata* carries it away!' the polished gallant and the nimble-tongued amazon who might well have graduated at Queen Marguerite's Court of Navarre. Thus the gloom, and, to more modern notions, irredeemably bad taste of Claudio's 'rotten orange' denunciation of Hero at the altar—mainspring though it be of the future action—took its place as a cog in the machinery and the play danced with the wit, the gaiety, the poetry of Shakespeare and sped with the *verve*, the *élan* of Dumas. This we owed to the ease and sureness of this Benedick, so unostentatious, assimilating so perfectly with his fellow-players—surely the most brilliant cast ever assembled at the Lyceum—yet rising so dazzlingly above them.

The characterization came, too, so surprisingly after his rugged Romeo, a fate-ridden, haggard, smouldering-eyed Romeo, no puling love-stricken boy, but a tragic 'fortune's fool,' as Shakespeare designed him. And now this feather-weight gallant, full of suavity, subtlety, and humorous quip, yet touched to a sudden fire, inspired by Beatrice's 'Kill Claudio!' to the quick of action, a slim rapier flashing like a flame. And so he dominated the whole, not by that supreme exercise of his art which he saved for Hamlet and Becket, but by a special and peculiar treatment that I cannot remember he duplicated in any other of his impersonations. How we hung upon his specious self-communing: 'I'll not swear love may not transform me to an oyster.' The amiable misogamist was caught in the toils of his friends' intrigue. Was it possible he could come scathless through the ordeal? No, the trap was too subtly baited. And how we rose to him at the climax: 'I'll go get her picture!' None but a great artist could so move his audience with the sense and power of such perfect assurance.

The settings were the most sumptuous and picturesque. I can remember none more beautiful even at the Lyceum; the Bay of Messina with Leonato's Marble Palace; the Garden; the Church; the Ballroom—never was mounting more appropriate and helpful, and the result was triumphant. As I have heard others say, and as I have always myself maintained: 'The most completely satisfying entertainment I have ever known in any theatre.'

It was not till many years later that I joined the Lyceum company and learned that all his effects were the result of the most careful study; nothing, absolutely nothing, did he leave to chance. He would rehearse again and again the simplest piece of business until fumbling was an impossibility, and then continue to rehearse till it had the ease of second nature.

I had a letter of recommendation to Irving from Canon Rowsell, one of the Queen's chaplains, but was too overawed to make use of the opportunity. Many years later I had another introduction to him from Madame Modjeska, the great Polish actress, but though it led to a pleasant meeting and an invitation to see his production of *Henry the Eighth*, no engagement followed. When I did join his company it was through Laurence Irving recommending me to play one of his friends in *Dante*.

I played the Colonel with him in *A Story of Waterloo* for two years. On one occasion I sat next to Sir Johnston Forbes-Robertson in the stalls at the Lyceum when *Waterloo* was an item of the bill and Sir Johnston said to me: "The most magnificent rendering of senility. What a performance!"

What impressed me as a member of his company was his gentleness, his consideration, and his kindly smile. So much has been written of his gait and his peculiarities of speech; how much of this was sheer characterization? It was never noticeable off the stage nor on it in his later years. But whatever the criticism be, the one word 'compelling' best describes his acting. This word does sum up his genius—the play of his features—the values he gave his lines where he had to express strong emotion as in Lesurques—his affection for his daughter; the beautiful delivery of the lines describing the deserted nest in *Becket*, ' the eggs were cold.'

Stories of Irving's subtle and sometimes caustic wit have been told many times. I will not repeat them. But I can tell stories that illustrate his love for his work, his upholding of a high standard of acting in his company, and his kindness and generosity to all his players.

" You're late," said Sir Henry once, to a member of the company. " I am never late."

While an old actor was interviewing Mr. Irving (as he then was) about a job, the question of salary arose.

" What salary do you ask ? " said Irving.

" Six pounds a week."

" H'm ! Are you married ? "

" Yes."

" Any children ? "

" Yes."

" And you ask six pounds a week ? You can live on that ? "

" Oh, yes," replied the old actor, eagerly.

" Ah ! Well, I'm damned if I should like to do it. Your salary will be ten pounds."

When Irving went back to the Lyceum under the Syndicate young men appeared in the small parts.

" Who are these young men ? " said Irving to Comyns Carr.

" Oh, this young man was at the St. James's—that one at the Haymarket," and so on.

" Ah ! " said the great Chief. " A lot of damned impostors. Get some *actors*."

This story was told me by one of the ' impostors ' who managed to get by. I helped him to do so. During our American tour one of the actors fell ill and had to be left behind. Sir Henry sent for his wife, who was playing small parts.

" You had better be with your husband and nurse him," he said.

Their salaries were sent to them while the actor was ill. When he rejoined the company, the actor asked Sir Henry if he could speak to him privately.

" Certainly, my boy. Come into my room."

" You have been so kind, Sir Henry," said the actor, " I feel I ought to tell you we are not legally married."

" Yes, I knew that," replied the Chief. " She's a very charming woman. Why *don't* you marry her ? " He did.

The morning after his passing at Bradford we all walked past the bed whereon Sir Henry lay. Never shall I forget those wonderful features—beautiful in death. He died as he would have wished to die—at the end of his day's work.

VINCENT STERNROYD.

Most of us who saw Henry Irving act must have done so in our salad days, and in recalling impressions that were born in an atmosphere of glamour and romance it is difficult to be either critical or precise in our judgment. But it is an incontrovertible fact that he was a great actor and a man of exceptional magnetic power. How else could he have risen to an eminence that was almost princely in its implication and a popularity that will leave its mark in the history of the Theatre?

In setting down my impressions of two of the parts out of the many which I saw him act, one is bound to be a little personal, and perhaps it is more valuable to record his effect upon a single individual than to speak generally.

I first saw Irving in the part of Becket when I was thirteen years old. Young as I was, I shall never forget the wonder of that afternoon. Without a doubt it altered my whole life, or maybe released desires that were already in my being. I don't only mean that the experience led me to the theatre as a craftsman, but it opened my mind to an unexpected world of beauty.

Two years later, when I was free to move about on my own responsibility, I haunted the Lyceum and became extremely familiar with the passage that runs up to the pit entrance from the Strand. The faint odour of stale beer wafted from an adjacent 'pub,' and the smell of oranges, which were still the stand-by of the pittite, took on a glory from the mysterious temple within. In those days Irving was giving revivals from his repertory before sailing for America, and so I had the opportunity of seeing many of the earlier plays. I still have the opera glasses from which I bit much of the paint during moments of intense excitement.

It was the original production of *Becket* that I saw, and I could write down most of the names in the cast without any reference to the programme. Irving's pose as he gazed out over the plains of Normandy, William Terriss's vault over the chess table, are indelibly imprinted on my memory. So, too, is the dim religious scene when Ellen Terry as Rosamund entered like golden sunshine to beg sanctuary of the Archbishop in London.

When recalling my experiences at the Lyceum this is exactly what happens to my memory. The conception of a character, the technique of acting escape me as, of course, at that time I was incapable of appreciating any such subtleties; but I do remember very vividly Irving's delivery of certain sentences, and particularly things he did. No one knew better how to turn an important phrase, or to time to a hair's breadth a piece of stage 'business.' He had an unfailing flair for the invention of the latter when he was building up the characterization of a part.

Recently at the Centenary *Matinée* given in Irving's honour several excerpts were given from what may be called the poorer material in which he successfully exploited one side of his genius. A young actor, who was cast for one of these parts, went in despair to one who had been a distinguished member of the Lyceum company, and flourishing the script, cried:

"But there is nothing here?"

To which the actress replied: "Exactly!"

In Shakespeare the case was different, and though Irving may have been censured for manipulating the text to suit the needs of his 'production,' it must be remembered that, following in the footsteps of Charles Kean, he was largely responsible for restoring the pure text and scrapping the abominations that had been popular in the past. Such stage business as he introduced was of an explanatory nature and never held up the action of the play, as became the fashion after his time. He has been blamed for one piece of business, and quite unjustly, because it has always been copied in the wrong way. I refer to the return of Shylock across the deserted stage to his empty house after the flight of his daughter. This is usually stage-managed by the plagiarists immediately after the exit of Lorenzo and Jessica, some three minutes after Shylock has departed, which makes it appear that he has left the Christian's feast as soon as he arrived, or not been there at all! Irving's way was to bring the curtain down on the elopement and make his return on the curtain call, which thus allowed for a passage of time.

But to return to my recollection of things that Irving did. The *Much Ado About Nothing* that I saw was a revival. How well I remember Benedick's first entrance. The almost sickening anticipation of his coming, and the impatience to see beyond the Prince of Aragon—he was Frank Cooper and Claudio was Ben Webster. With what a manner Irving trod the steps, elegant from his feathered hat to his embroidered gloves and spurred trim boots. He always wore his clothes superbly, and one never questioned but that Benedick was a man of breeding. There was something of the greyhound about his bearing, and his first scene with Beatrice was played with high comedy and good fellowship. Possibly Ellen Terry set the mood of the scene, which never developed into the exhibition of cattish repartee it too often becomes. On both sides there was a graciousness which made their sallies witty and good-humoured.

If I am to be honest I cannot dissociate Henry Irving from Ellen Terry to any great extent when they were playing together. It was too successful, too intimate an association ; and when they were both in a play they maintained a perfect balance.

Benedick's soliloquies in the garden gave me intense pleasure, though I cannot for the life of me record how he gave them, but I do recall the impishness of ' The world must be peopled,' and the solemnity of ' When I said I would die a bachelor, I did not think that I should live till I were married.'

The Church scene was the *pièce de résistance* as far as scenery was concerned. It was, indeed, a fine example of realistic stage setting, and Sir Johnston Forbes-Robertson's well-known painting of the scene confirms my impression. The scene opened in silence save for the distant notes of the organ. The dim recesses of the building seemed full of blue mysterious mists and the smell of incense pervaded the atmosphere. The characters entered one by one, removed their hats, crossed themselves with holy water, genuflected to the altar, and stood about in groups whispering to their friends. Irving knew exactly how to handle this kind of thing.

Of the famous scene between Benedick and Beatrice I remember only Ellen Terry, but that may be because, later in life, I acted Claudio with her, and the picture of what she did and how she did it is clear cut. Irving, whose high comedy was as brilliant as his tragic moments were terrifying, played the ' toothache ' scene superbly. I think Benedick must have been the first comedy part that I had seen Irving play. Probably Becket, Mathias, and other *rôles* had given me the impression that he was a tragedian only, wedded to a certain sombre dignity. Benedick took me completely by surprise and swept me off my feet with delight. When he spoke the concluding words of the play with a sparkling liveliness, ' Strike up, pipers ! ' and moved forward to begin the dance as though a master of the art, I was lifted out of my pit seat with admiration, to totter out into the Strand and quaff ginger pop to my hero before I made my way to my home in the suburbs. Fortunately, the traffic in those days presented little danger, otherwise I wonder how I ever reached home at all after those Lyceum nights, in such a dream world did I live for hours after. Well, fifteen is a great age to be.

I saw the original production of *Cymbeline*. By that time I was an old hand—a Lyceum *habitué*, and what I did not know about Irving and Ellen Terry was not worth knowing! It was a lovely production. Much has been said against realistic scenery, and there certainly is a good deal to be said against it. But if it is to be used at all, and in Irving's day it was an enormous improvement on the crude canvas wings that had gone before, his genius used it to its best advantage. He understood the effects to be obtained by good lighting and got masterly results without a quarter of the advantages of our modern elaborate electrical installations. Moreover, he was guided by the taste and the artistic brains of Ellen Terry. For this particular production he called in Alma-Tadema, the celebrated painter of classical subjects. No doubt he was responsible for the lovely folds of Irving's Roman toga. My mother and I tried to copy it, using a sheet for the purpose, so that I could wear it as Jupiter in my school play. This happened to be a burlesque, but I played my part as much on the lines of Iachimo as the puzzled author would let me.

The scene between Iachimo and Imogen is unforgetable. The subtlety of his approach, the Mephistophelian glint in his eye as he spoke the words: 'I dedicate myself to your sweet pleasure'; and with what craft, a second later, he bent to kiss her hand, before venturing on the next step, 'Let me my service tender on your lips.' Then came Imogen's wrath swift and beautiful, and Iachimo's swifter shifting of his ground, and the devilish tact by which he persuaded her to forgive him and allow his chest of valuables to be placed in her bedroom. Iachimo is but a shadow of Iago, but Irving contrived to put some of the divinity of hell into his acting of the part, and mixed it with a malicious twist of humour; as, for example, when he was lifting the lid of the chest in the bedroom scene, slowly—bit by bit—in a way that was half horrifying and half funny. His bearing throughout this scene was a mixture of craft, grotesque humour, and lustfulness. (I may say that I was warned by an aunt of the period that this scene brought some discredit on the Lyceum management as it was not suitable for the young. I am glad to say I braved the danger.)

When Iachimo at the conclusion of the scene stated that 'hell was here,' one believed him, absolutely, and then followed the tense listening while counting the clock—slow, deliberate—'One, two, three,' and the sudden incisive bite on the words, 'Time, time!' as the scene closed.

Another vivid memory I have of Iachimo is the end of the

scene after he has returned to Rome with Imogen's bracelet and ring, and so wins the wager against her husband. Philario, a mutual friend, says :

> 'You have won : . . . .
> Let's follow him and pervert the present wrath
> He hath against himself.'

' With all my heart,' replies Iachimo. Irving, allowing Philario to go before him, lagged a few paces behind as he held out his left hand and let his eyes rest upon the ring. Into that glance Irving put the cunning of the trickster and the gambler's greedy, malicious triumph.

But Irving's eyes ! Set beneath those strange overhanging eyebrows in a pale long face, what power they had. They were his strongest cards. What could he not do with them ? A letter appeared in the Press lately which recounted a happening on Leatherhead station, I think it was. Some boys were amused by his long hair and kept chanting ' Get your hair cut ! ' At last Irving went up to them and, with the words ' Get your tongues cut ! ' gave them a look that reduced them to a silent, frightened group at the end of the platform.

It is said that Ristori could thrill an audience with a single gesture. Irving could with his eyes. He could hold an audience of two thousand people spellbound by a glance.

. . . . . .

Alas, this tells those who knew not Pharaoh nothing. Strange how difficult it is to give life to a memory. I cry with Cleopatra, ' Think you, there was, or might be, such a man as this I dream'd of ? ' and should the disbeliever answer, no, I cry again, ' You lie, up to the hearing of the gods.'

Henry Irving as an actor and as a man of the Theatre, whose distinction and renown did more for the profession of the actor than perhaps any other, is a significant influence in the lives of those Victorians who love the Theatre. And yet, for my part, I find I cannot re-create in words the things that made his greatness. My desire is frustrated by infelicitous phrases and memories that are more general than particular. But that he was a great man may still be seen, by those who have eyes to see, in the wonder that he has put into the hearts of those who worship him.

HARCOURT WILLIAMS.

XXIX

IRVING as ROBERT MACAIRE

Lyceum Theatre, 14th of June, 1883 :—

ROBERT MACAIRE

(*An adaptation of L'Auberge des Adrets by MM. Benjamin, Saint-Amand and Paulyanthe*)

WRITTEN BY CHARLES SELBY AND PALGRAVE SIMPSON

Marie	MISS ADA CAVENDISH
Clementine	MISS ELLEN TERRY
Germeuil	MR. H. HOWE
Dumont	MR. FERNANDEZ
Charles	MR. TERRISS
Pierre	MR. THOMAS THORNE
Sergeant Loupy	MR. BANCROFT
Louis	MR. ANDREWS
François	MR. ARCHER
Jacques Strop	MR. J. L. TOOLE
Robert Macaire	MR. HENRY IRVING

Soldiers, Musicians, Villagers, etc.

ACT I. *Exterior of the Roadside Inn.* ACT II. *Interior of the Roadside Inn.*

I HAD unique opportunities for seeing all the giants of the Stage before I was twenty, and my memories of Henry Irving are many. Irving had the faculty of impressing himself upon an audience more vividly than any actor I can remember.

I can recall, now, details of Irving's performances more clearly than those of actors in plays I have seen within the last few months.

One of my outstanding memories is the entrance of Irving as Louis XI ; the cruel face and cunning eyes, the hesitant voice and manner ; irony, passion, and hypocrisy alternated . . . first he would bully and then he would whine.

Mathias in *The Bells*, Mephistopheles, Shylock, Robert Landry in *The Dead Heart* are all clearly etched in my memory, but Robert Macaire comes more clearly to my mind than any in the great gallery of Irving characters. My memory may be at fault, but I believe it was the first play in which I saw him. I know I was very young and was taken to the Lyceum by an old lady with whom I was staying in London.

Later in life I frequently saw the superb pantomimists, Paul and Alfred Martinetti, play Macaire and Jacques Strop. Extravagant as were the Martinetti performances, it seems to me, over this long distance of time, Irving's was scarcely less so in the early scenes. Even to-day I never see a drunken scene on the stage without recalling Irving's Macaire. He was miserable and merry, thumping and generally ill-treating poor, frightened Jacques Strop. His pockets were stuffed with stolen property, and the comic business of dropping things, while odd articles slipped from under his tightly buttoned coat, set the house in roars of laughter. It was sheer, broad low comedy, with a masterly touch.

At the end of the play Macaire is shot, which provided Irving with what must have been one of his most powerful melodramatic scenes. I think Irving's Macaire made as strong an impression upon my old friend, James Pryde, as it did on me; his portrait of Irving in this character is one of the best things he has done in a long career of distinguished work.

I only met Irving three times. The first occasion was at Pittsburg, Pennsylvania, when I had the privilege of being the third at a supper party given in the private Pullman car of Richard Mansfield, who was my employer at the time. Mansfield had played at Irving's Lyceum Theatre some years before. The season had not been successful and some misunderstanding had arisen between Irving, the landlord, and Mansfield, the tenant. The night in Pittsburg was the first time they had met since then. I don't think the matter was mentioned at the supper, nor did there seem to be any sign of an estrangement between them. Irving was in good spirits and talked slowly and deliberately of London and his experiences in the United States. Mansfield, on this occasion, proved a good listener. With a wicked twinkle of his eye Irving told us that he had bought a play from every dramatic critic in America.

I drove with him to his hotel and he graciously invited me to call upon him when I returned to London. Twice I had occasion to do so. Each time an appointment was promptly arranged, and I was most courteously received. In one instance he gave me some extremely good advice which was of enormous assistance to me. In his room at the Lyceum he seemed to me to be the kindliest of monarchs, and I left with the impression of having been greatly honoured by an audience.

CHARLES B. COCHRAN.

When I got into the street I found myself wiping the sweat from my brow. It's over fifty years ago, but that fact I remember distinctly. I know now that the play is one of the crudest of melodramas, but then it was terribly real to me. It was a wonderful evening; first we had had *The Amber Heart* with Ellen Terry, a sweet poetical romance, enchanting in its simplicity and grace and then—by what I now realize was a masterstroke of managerial policy—the violent contrast of *Robert Macaire*. Anticipation was at fever heat, for I was to see Irving for the first time! What I expected I cannot exactly describe; I had heard of Irving's reputation as Hamlet, Shylock, Othello, Macbeth, Richard III. What I saw was inevitably a shock; a gaunt shabby figure in rusty black with a battered hat and a black patch over one eye, with the manner of a sinister Jingle, grotesque as a painting by Dégas. I soon realized that I was seeing the most wonderful dramatic personality that I had ever seen or was ever likely to see. He took my breath away. I sat spellbound.

I have since learned the strange history of the play. It took three French authors to create the original which was produced in 1823 at the *Ambigu-Comique* in Paris. It became notorious, for in it the great French actor Frédérick Lemaître laid the foundation of his fame. It was his first part at the *Ambigu* and he was in despair about it, for it was nothing but a very ordinary 'heavy' part without a novel effect or situation in it. Then an idea struck him, and he took the comedian Firmin, who was cast for Bertrand, that is, Jacques Strop, into his confidence with the result that on the first night everybody—manager, authors, and actors as well as the audience—was astounded by the weird apparition of the two thieves. Firmin was wearing an overcoat far too long for him, so that its skirts trailed on the ground, an impossible hat on the back of his head and carrying the remnants of a bottle-green umbrella which looked as though its staves would scatter at the first attempt to open it, and Lemaître like a Cruikshank drawing—very like Irving no doubt, for he established a tradition by his make-up that is as much part of the play as its situations. Success was instantaneous and MM. Benjamin and Saint-Amand were as delighted as the manager, but it is said that Doctor Paulyanthe was horrified at what he regarded as desecration of the work to which he had contributed his share.

Charles Selby, the actor who adapted scores of plays from the French, must have seen the great Frédérick; he made an English adaptation which was produced at Covent Garden in 1834 with Wallack as Macaire and Vale as Jacques Strop. It became a favourite piece with all the leading actors. Palgrave

Simpson made a more scholarly version called *The Roadside Inn* for Fechter, who played it at the Lyceum in the early 'sixties, preserving most of the extravagant farcical episodes of the first Act. It was this version, with perhaps slight variations, that Irving used.

I did not see the extraordinary star cast which supported Irving on his first revival at the Lyceum. Dear old Toole was missing and Weedon Grossmith took his place, but what did that matter? Irving was there and wherever he was he was all-sufficient.

The buffoonery in Act I was as near burlesque as I have ever seen in drama, but Irving carried it off with such enjoyment, and with such an air of conviction, that you accepted it without question. His business with the wooden snuff-box that creaked and squeaked a warning when Jacques Strop's indiscretions threatened detection, had the air of inevitability that he gave always to the merest trifle. His dancing in the quadrille at the end of Act II, and the wild finale, were the apotheosis of extravagance.

Then in Act II came the scene with his wife, the unfortunate Marie, an exhibition of the grossest callousness. The technical skill—which I am now able to judge—in reconciling this side of the character with the grotesque demeanour of the thief in the earlier scenes, was a lesson I have never forgotten. This was paving the way to the end. The touch of humanity when he realizes that Charles is his son and longs to beg his forgiveness, even to touch his hand, and how he contrives it, turning the episode again to burlesque—master-strokes all. The thieves are discovered and arrested, Jacques Strop trembling, Macaire sullen and defiant. Suddenly he hurls the gendarmes from him and himself through the window. A volley is fired and he staggers back, bleeding, dying, to fall headlong down the staircase. All the batteries of his art were brought into requisition. Irving never spared himself as I learned in the years that followed, whether he played Mathias, Charles I, Lesurques, Dubosc, Louis XI, Becket, King Arthur, Napoleon or Corporal Brewster, you were always sure of getting his best. Other actors, even stars who knew they had the whole weight of the play on their shoulders, would slack and 'play down' if they were not in the mood, or crack jokes in whispers with the company, thereby 'guying' the scene and puzzling and often irritating the audience. But you ran no such risk on a visit to the Lyceum. Irving's work was his religion and as devoutly practised. His death scene as Macaire was a revelation; a mingling of despair and defiance, a thief, a murderer, passing unrepentant: 'I have foiled you, I shall die like a man'—terror and bravado—a gasp, a convulsive tremor, a choking sigh, and the wicked soul had fled.

That is why I wiped the sweat from my forehead as I left the theatre.

FEWLASS LLEWELLYN.

XXX

IRVING as MALVOLIO

Lyceum Theatre, 8th of July, 1884 :—

TWELFTH NIGHT

WRITTEN BY WILLIAM SHAKESPEARE

Malvolio	MR. HENRY IRVING
The Duke Orsino	MR. TERRISS
Sir Toby Belch	MR. DAVID FISHER
Sir Andrew Aguecheek	MR. FRANCIS WYATT
Fabian	MR. ANDREWS
Clown	MR. S. CALHAEM
Sebastian	MR. FRED TERRY
Antonio	MR. H. HOWE
A Sea Captain	MR. TYARS
Valentine	MR. HAVILAND
Curio	MR. MELLISH
A Friar	MR. HARBURY
1st Officer	MR. ARCHER
2nd Officer	MR. HARWOOD
Olivia	MISS ROSE LECLERCQ
Maria	MISS L. PAYNE
Viola	MISS ELLEN TERRY

SCENE. *A City in Illyria and the Sea-coast near it.* ACT I, SCENE 1. *The Sea-coast ;* SCENE 2. *The Courtyard of Olivia's House ;* SCENE 3. *Orsino's Palace.* ACT II, SCENE 1. *Terrace of Olivia's House ;* SCENE 2. *Road near the same ;* SCENE 3. *Olivia's House—the Hall.* ACT III, SCENE 1. *Orsino's Palace ;* SCENE 2. *Another part of the Sea-coast ;* SCENE 3. *Olivia's Garden.* ACT IV, SCENE 1. *The Market Place ;* SCENE 2. *Court-yard of Olivia's House ;* SCENE 3. *Olivia's Garden ;* SCENE 4. *The Orchard End ;* SCENE 5. *Olivia's House—the Dark Room.* ACT V, SCENE 1. *Olivia's House—the Cloisters ;* SCENE 2. *Before Olivia's House.*

IRVING had far too strong a personality for Malvolio. To the best of my recollection his Malvolio was distinctly a gentleman, not a buffoon ; he was dignified, not heavy. It was inconceivable that that commanding presence should be a mere steward. He looked like some great Spanish hidalgo—a painting of Velazquez ; never could he have become the butt of his fellow-servants. For surely Malvolio graduated in the kitchen or the buttery ; he is an old retainer, privileged as old servants are and abusing that privilege as so often they do, domineering over the rest of the staff till he provokes them to revolt. He apes the manners of his superiors with the inevitably grotesque results. With Irving one felt it impossible that he could have superiors. There is no element of greatness in Malvolio, only meanness; there is no intellect, merely a numskull, he is a proper butt for the rest of the household. But in Irving's hands the part became so transmuted that you marvelled how they dared, and no doubt having some such notion in his mind, he cast the play unfortunately; the ladies were too mature and, what was almost equally disastrous, the comedians were not funny; the sprightly Feste was played as a decrepit old man and Fabian was the brightest spark of the plotters. They were indeed a pusillanimous crowd who, one felt, would shrink abashed at the frown of this majestic Malvolio; one could never imagine him their gull. His scenes with Olivia were marked of course with the most courtly grace; with Cesario he was duly arrogant, but with his fellow-servants he was so masterful as to defeat comedy altogether. In the final scene: 'I'll be revenged on the whole pack of ye!' one felt he would, and the whole gossamer fabric of the play was rent. Malvolio should gain sympathy, for mere peacocking hardly deserved the humiliation he suffered, but this is no case for tragic intensity and Irving in a passion suggested no less. But, though possibly marred by the elaboration of eccentric touches, it was an excellent performance.

At the end of the performance on the first night there was an unusual demonstration. Strong as the anti-Irvingites were, I do not believe that there was anything in the nature of an organized opposition. I believe that the pit and gallery were frankly bored with the performance and disappointed to see their favourite actor in a part so inadequate and one, moreover, that could never suit him, and they expressed their dissatisfaction in the usual ill-mannered way, though I am bound to say I prefer that to the stony silence that greets failure across the Atlantic and across the Channel.

Irving for once was irritated out of his calm and in his perfectly dignified speech of remonstrance—though he had done better to have faced the situation in smiling silence—he used an illuminating phrase; he spoke of his company 'having exercised their abilities on *one of the most difficult of Shakespeare's plays*.' I cannot help thinking that it was the very simplicity of *Twelfth Night* that baffled Irving; he had prepared it looking all the time for profundities that he imagined must be eluding him. He was always at his best when faced with introspective and psychological difficulties; he sought them in vain in *Twelfth Night* for the simple reason that they are not there.

I have felt it very keenly being 'at odds', so to speak, with my old manager and most venerated Chief, so I have looked up old verdicts of professional critics hoping to find one well argued in opposition to my own opinion and I think I have found it in Mr. William Winter's review of the production when it had reached New York. Mr. Winter wrote:

> 'The formalism of Malvolio, his scrupulous cleanliness, his precise demeanour, his constitutional habit of routine, his inordinate self-complacency—over which, nevertheless, his judgment keeps a kind of watch—his sensitiveness of self-love, his condition of being real in all that he feels and suffers—these attributes Mr. Irving combined into a distinct and rounded personality, of which the humour is—as it should be—wholly unconscious. His sustained preservation of the identity was especially impressive, and he was most characteristic in his dry, distinctly articulated, unconsciously pompous delivery of the text.'

This compares feebly with Charles Lamb's panegyric on Bensley in the part, but I always felt that the mild humours of *Twelfth Night* and the gentlemanly puritanism of Bensley's Malvolio were just of a piece with the smiling spirit of the gentle Elia; the subdued chuckle becomes him; it is impossible to conceive him indulging the vulgarity of a guffaw.

I have said above that I did not consider Malvolio worthy of Irving. That is the fact. He was, to use a metaphor, so great an athlete that only the highest hurdle, the broadest ditch was worthy of his attempting. He needed stimulating by difficulties, easy conquests were beneath him: the complexities of a Glo'ster or an Iago challenged all his intellectual forces and ensured his greatest triumphs; the purely physical was beyond him and my metaphor of the athlete cannot be literally applied; the madness of Lear out-thundering the storm; the call to arms by Macbeth, the towering rage of Othello were beyond his physical strength. But who could surpass him in tenderness to Cordelia? Whoever has more subtly indicated the disintegration of spirit in Macbeth?—or shown us the innate nobility of the Moor in his defence before the Senate? It was so always with Irving; no matter what part he attempted he gave you always something to think about, there was always some one great outstanding point of originality if not of inspiration in his performance. It is for that reason that his memory lives; that even in these days when the theatre tosses like a rudderless ship in stormy seas without a chart and without a skipper we still remember him who guided her fortunes so skilfully and steered her into the happy haven of respect and dignity.

His artistic conscience was more highly developed than that of any of his predecessors. His singleness of purpose, his profound respect for his calling, taught the world to respect it also, and under his leadership it gained a higher place in the world's estimation than it had ever known or is like to know again. He identified himself with all that was finest, all that was most artistic, all that was most progressive in an age of remarkable expansions and developments. He brought the Theatre into line with the other arts by his association with artists, writers, and musicians, such as Rossetti and Burne-Jones, Tennyson and Swinburne, Sullivan and German.

My first introduction to him was characteristic. He had come to see our performance of the Agamemnon. " This Greek play of yours," said Irving, " was most interesting and if you will let me say so remarkably carried out. Should you think seriously of the stage as a profession I will do my best for you." What had appealed to him was the selflessness of the players and the simplicity of the production. When I decided shortly afterwards to try my fortunes in the theatre I went to him and the result was my appearance as Paris in *Romeo and Juliet*. From the first I was impressed by his dynamic force. Nobody could work with him without catching the spirit of his enthusiasm, which penetrated to every department. He was indefatigable. In the days when I knew him first he lived not only *for* the theatre (that was true of all his life) but *in* the theatre. No detail escaped him and no detail was insignificant.

In truth Irving *was* the Lyceum; his complete knowledge of his craft and of its every tradition gave him an authority that no one ever attempted to dispute.

To return to Malvolio: Ellen Terry says in her book that Irving's performance was ' fine and dignified, but not good for the play,' which corresponds exactly with my own impression. All that Irving did was ' fine,' so fine that, at times, it came near to defeating his end. Doctor Primrose, for example, was too fine for a country parson; Lesurques again was too fine for the bourgeois son of a village postmaster in the same way that Malvolio was certainly too fine for the servants' hall. His dignity pervaded his personality—exuded from it, and for many made him unapproachable. This was their loss, for it deprived them of knowledge of the man—of his innate gentleness and kindliness, qualities that made him so staunch a friend and won for him the reputation not only of a great actor but a manager, reliable, just and liberal in all his dealings.

Nothing impressed me more than the story of Ellen Terry's interview after the Abbey Service in October 1905. "What have you to say of him?" asked the interviewer. "He was a great actor, a great friend and a good man," she answered. "What more is there to say?" What more indeed!

FRANK BENSON.

XXXI

IRVING as DOCTOR PRIMROSE

Lyceum Theatre, 28th of May, 1885 :—

OLIVIA

(*Adapted from Oliver Goldsmith's The Vicar of Wakefield*)

WRITTEN BY W. G. WILLS

Dr. Primrose	MR. IRVING
Moses	MR. NORMAN FORBES
Squire Thornhill	MR. TERRISS
Mr. Burchell	MR. WENMAN
Leigh	MR. TYARS
Farmer Flamborough	MR. H. HOWE
Polly Flamborough	MISS COLERIDGE
Phœbe	MISS MILLS
Gipsy Woman	MISS BARNETT
Mrs. Primrose	MISS L. PAYNE
Dick and Bill	MISSES F. AND M. HOLLAND
Sophia	MISS WINIFRED EMERY
Olivia	MISS ELLEN TERRY

ACT I, SCENE. *The Vicarage Garden—Autumn.* ACT II, SCENE. *The Vicarage Parlour.* ACT III, SCENE. *The Dragon Inn.* ACT IV, SCENE 1. *The Vicarage Garden (Winter)* ; SCENE 2. *The Vicarage Parlour.*

I HAVE lately taken a great dislike to the term genius ; it is used so loosely that it has lost its meaning. Genius should surely be attributed only to a person of great mental and spiritual gifts, and to these Henry Irving could certainly lay claim.

In spite of many handicaps, his bad enunciation and harsh voice, his halting and ungainly walk, he was always the central figure. A proud, reserved man, he never lost those attributes on the stage, yet whatever part he played these seemed essential to the character.

I should say he possessed no actual technique, yet he was never wrong in any of his methods ; a master of mime but almost unconsciously, for always he did the right thing, exactly fitting the gesture to the word, and that, I think, proves the greatness of his genius.

What struck me so greatly about Doctor Primrose was his dignity ; it seemed a dignity of the soul. One felt he was living beyond this world, looking into the hereafter, inspired by the greatness and aloofness of another world. His delicate hands and the nervous movement of his fingers seemed to speak a dormant energy that might at any moment dominate and make the old man a creature of passion and vengeance.

Although in private life Irving gave the impression of harshness—almost cruelty—it was a false one for there never was a man more generous and tender, and it was these qualities that went to make his performance of Doctor Primrose the thing of beauty it was.

I started my stage career under his management and to criticize so great an artist may savour somewhat of presumption. I submit my recollections in all humility for what they are worth.

As Doctor Primrose his shortcomings were less apparent than in the more severely classical *rôles*, yet if he did not fit the part he made the part fit him. This impression he invariably left with me after watching one of his performances. It is difficult when one is so completely carried away by a great personality to see his faults.

As a very young girl I was allotted the *rôle* of a speechless page at the Lyceum and well I remember his gentleness and quiet humour. I had to run on and deliver a paper to the great man, and I had been told most emphatically by Mr. Loveday to be sure to keep on the knee nearest the audience. I was swollen with pride but quaking with fear; on I rushed and plopped down at Irving's feet, but in my terror of nervousness I feared I was on the wrong knee and so shifted from right to left and back again continuously. Irving stood gazing at my antics and then coldly remarked: "Perhaps you will go off when you've finished your Russian dance!"

A marvellous personality. 'We shall not look upon his like again.'

CONSTANCE BENSON.

Alas! I only met Sir Henry on a few occasions . . . once at the house of my sister-in-law (Mrs. Arthur Lewis), again at Mrs. William Morris's (Florence Terry), and once at the Lyceum Theatre when I went there to visit my sister-in-law, Ellen Terry.

I think the outstanding memory I have of Sir Henry as an actor is his performance of Doctor Primrose in *Olivia*—I shall never forget the tenderness and the dignity with which he invested this character. We were all so surprised at Irving's decision to play Doctor Primrose. He had been associated always with such entirely different parts, Hamlet, Shylock, Macbeth, Richard III, Charles I, Louis XI, and the melodramas, *The Bells* and *The Lyons Mail*, that for him to play the gentle Vicar of Wakefield seemed all wrong. Ellen, of course, had played Olivia at the Court Theatre with Herman Vezin as the Vicar, whom I always thought a fine actor, but hard.

What would Irving do with it? Everybody wondered. And then, as generally happened, he astonished us; his sweetness, his tenderness, and fatherly devotion were exquisite. And the pathos when he discovered his darling had fled: 'She came between me and my God. I am justly punished.'

In the beautiful scene with Olivia at the Dragon Inn the two great artists—for Ellen Terry was at her very best as Olivia—had the house in tears; in fact, it was said that never were more tears shed over any scene in the theatre, and that alone was enough to make the fortune of the play.

Fred, my husband, considered him a giant in his profession, a genius as a producer and actor. He was engaged to play Sebastian in *Twelfth Night* because of the strong family likeness to his sister Ellen who was Viola, when he was quite a young actor, and I remember his telling me of an incident at some early rehearsal. Fred had to draw his sword, just that—but Irving sent him back and back again, till finally Fred got exasperated and drew out the sword with a colossal swing and flourish and ripped a big hole in a new back-cloth, saying: "Is *that* what you want?"

Irving, with his characteristic calm, looked at Fred with that quizzical smile of his, and said: "H'm, yes, very good, my boy, very good, but—" (with a glance at the ripped back-cloth) "don't do it again!"

I also remember a piece of advice given to me in my young days. Ellen took me into the great man's dressing-room during a performance of *The Merchant of Venice*.

"I see you are going to play Constance, *crying* Constance," he said. "Well—let yourself go!"

I hope I profited by it. I think I did. *King John* was one of the biggest successes we had at His Majesty's.

JULIA NEILSON-TERRY.

In paying tribute, after the lapse of many years, to the revered memory of the great leader and head of our profession, my endeavour will be to give the impression he made upon me the first time I saw him as Doctor Primrose.

The occasion was a revival of *Olivia;* it was also my first visit to a London theatre and for me a memorable evening.

Before the curtain rose there was a buzz around me as notabilities of the day moved to their seats in the stalls below. There was a tingling of my own senses while awaiting the rise of the curtain in anticipation of seeing the great actor of whom I had heard so much.

The scene which quickened my interest was played in the living-room of the Vicarage on the evening when the Vicar's daughter steals quietly away to keep tryst for her elopement. Even now it comes vividly before me. The Vicar was seated beside the fire smoking his churchwarden pipe in restful, contemplative mood. On the opposite side of the room, music was being played by a trio, consisting of spinet, flute, and a stringed instrument. The Vicar's wife sat at the centre table plying her needles, mending woollen stockings. But it was the figure of Irving that arrested: it struck the note of prelude to the drama that was to follow. The repose of Irving was eloquent and the magic of his spell enveloped me.

In the scene I have attempted to sketch, Ellen Terry, as Olivia, unobtrusively left the group to prepare for the secret departure, while those on the stage remained apparently unconscious of her absence, Irving in masterly repose being still the dominant figure, and the pulsing accompaniment of this added to the acute anticipation of what was to follow.

Later, Ellen Terry was seen crossing the lawn and approaching the low casement window, which she quietly opened and with fingers to lips blew a kiss of farewell. An exquisite touch, poignant in its beauty, never to be forgotten. Ellen Terry having passed the window, my eyes were riveted on Irving who, still motionless, dominated the stage.

Then, as the story moved on, leading to the disquiet of the Vicar concerning his daughter and the rapid accumulative emotions that followed, Irving was the commanding figure throughout. He carried us with him, while we listened and watched in breathless interest. Our pulses throbbed in unison to the throbbing of his own agonized heart. Yes. Here was actuality, realism in Art: true in conception, nobly sincere in its simplicity.

That was the impression Irving left upon me in my eighteenth year at a time when I knew nothing of the technique of acting. Even when I took up the stage as a profession and witnessed

Irving many times in what was, in his day, our National Theatre, I was solely held by his intense sincerity in all his creations.

Conjuring up in my mind the vision of those glorious days of the Lyceum under Irving's management, I hold to the firm belief that it was through his sincerity that Irving held the world under the spell of his powerful magnetism.

Finally, I pay homage to the memory of Irving by quoting the words of a beloved Past President of the Green Room Club —the late Fred Terry. Courteously and inspiringly, when correcting a young member of the club, Fred Terry used these words: "In my opinion, sir, the term 'great' as applied to actors of the English stage can only be attributed to Garrick, Kean, and Irving."

D. J. WILLIAMS.

When I talk of Irving to actors of the younger generation they endure me for a few minutes, but soon they grow restive. Thus, they say in effect: ' It is one of the many bad habits of the middle-aged to have on constant tap a flood of eulogy of achievements in acting which exist only in the middle-aged mind's eye."

Alas, my masters, I never had the joy of seeing Irving until I was in the late twenties, and he was an old man. I had seen much good, and even great acting, but nothing like his. If ever again I see and hear anything so good and true which grips heart and brain with a magic like unto Irving's, I shall know it and be the readiest to cry 'Hail!' With deep love and respect for the high accomplishments of many actors of this age, fire cannot melt out my conviction that there has not yet appeared a successor to the throne left vacant by Henry Brodribb Irving, knight, actor.

The young overlords who pen their verdicts on the acting of to-day are so befogged when they have to touch on Irving. A well-known critic wrote of a recent revival of Wills's *Faust*: 'It is not easy to understand how Irving successfully frightened audiences into the Lyceum for sixteen months on end with this play in 1885.' Just so! It is not easy for us who never saw the miracle to understand the turning of the water into wine. 'Genius,' said William Archer, 'is not the faculty of making bricks without straw, but of utilizing superbly the bricks by observation and experience.'

Let me try and reconstruct my first impression of Irving the Great. Long hours of waiting, squeezed in a bulging queue, had won for me a seat in the extra early pit. I am to see Irving! Irving who has filled so many hours of my dreams. The curtain rises. A vicarage garden giving a peep of a house at 'stage right.' Some preliminaries of which no memory remains. There enters from the house a sweet old gentleman in white wig, rusty black suit, with knee breeches. Two thousand pairs of hands beat out a long fusilade of applause. The old gentleman appears quite unaware that we are making this noise for him. He is not concerned with or interested in us. He is busy with some more important family affairs. Presently he speaks, but not to us. There is no indication that he knows we are watching him. I have waited many long years for this moment. I am expecting some overpowering manifestation of acting—conscious acting, but here is a simple, benign old clergyman who does not care twopence whether I or any of that great audience listens to him or not. But I do listen as with, it seems, a new sense awakened. Soon the knowledge comes that this is the real thing. An illusion of life so perfect that all apparent effort is merged in art. Before this I had never known a point of admiration beyond thinking how finely this or that actor was doing his part. Until Irving no one ever made me forget he was acting. Years later Sarah Bernhardt gave me something of the same experience in *La Dame aux Camélias*, so did Duse in *The Lady from the Sea;* also, very recently, Werner Krauss in Hauptmann's play, *Before Sunset*.

As on that memorable first occasion so it was in each of the dozen parts I saw him play. Irving was POSSESSED—the capitals are needed—by the character; and every faculty, every limb and muscle was subdued to its actuality. Therein lay the magic and the glory.

Among other ineffable memories of *Olivia* two stand out. Olivia and Sophia have had their fortunes told by the Gypsy. They tell the Vicar what she has predicted for them 'What,' he exclaims, 'only lords for husbands! Why, my dears, I could have promised you princes at least, with equal confidence, for your sixpence.' The gentle, whimsical irony with which Irving said this! No other part allowed him so full scope for the expression of gracious and lovable traits of character. He must thoroughly have enjoyed depicting a personality which he had read, studied, and felt since childhood.

The other memory is the vicarage parlour on the night of Olivia's flight. 'The vicar is dreaming happily over the fire, his wife is at her sewing, the young ones are singing together at the old harpsichord, with Moses accompanying with his flute.'

The wayward, love-enthralled Olivia has stolen from the room and her white face is seen at the lattice window as she kisses farewell to her home. Still sits the vicar by the fire ; the cuckoo clock announces the hour. It is the heavenly calm just before the cruel storm which wrecks the happiness of that home and breaks the father's heart.

It was over Doctor Primrose that Mr. Bernard Shaw had one of the many spasms of his life-long malevolence against Henry Irving.

Herman Vezin had played the part many years before at the Court Theatre. During Irving's serious illness in 1897 he engaged Vezin to take this character in a short revival of *Olivia.* Mr. Shaw used Herman Vezin's acting as a whip for the invalided manager of the Lyceum. He went into critical ecstasies proclaiming that Vezin as Doctor Primrose far surpassed Irving. It is true that Herman Vezin was a very good actor, otherwise he would not have been engaged by Henry Irving in an effort to keep his theatre open during a personal disaster. Vezin was a man of immense virility and rather short in stature. His playing of the Vicar of Wakefield was on the conventional lines of the heavy, kindly father ; his interpretation lacked almost entirely resilience and humour. That did not matter to Mr. Shaw. Probably in his view, whoever had deputized for the part, would have been better than the hated Irving.

An illustration from another art may serve here. Browning's *Andrea del Sarto* proved that in one instance he could draw more correctly than Rafael, but admitted that the soul, 'the insight and the stretch' of Rafael were quite beyond him. Herman Vezin's elocution and precision of technique were, in one or two particulars, as I can testify from personal recollection, more correct than Henry Irving's. Vezin might have surpassed Irving had he also possessed Irving's soul, 'the insight and the stretch' of genius.

I have never fully realized the romance of Irving's life as when one day some years ago I stood in his birthplace at Keinton Mandeville. The village has hardly one touch of outward romance but its folk are lovable and very kind. The cottage where John Henry Brodribb was born in 1838 is a plain building on the roadside. It had entered into the good heart of Sir John Martin-Harvey, ever proud of his fourteen years apprenticeship under his chief, to engineer the placing of a permanent memorial over that lowly doorway. Sir George Frampton wrought a chaste tablet in metal and many leaders of the stage gave subscriptions to the cost. It happened, to my unspeakable surprise, that I was the only member of the acting profession present in the small audience. It numbered about two hundred and was made up of local gentry and friends from the surrounding district. Two old men were there who had played with Irving as a child. Sir John performed a simple ceremony of unveiling. A wire, a nobly long one, from Sir Arthur Pinero, was the only manifestation of London's interest.

There is no story of the stage so wonderful as Irving's. His father was a jobbing tailor. Hard times actually brought John Henry first to London. He was obliged to go to daily hard work at an age when nowadays most working men's children are still at school. He was always, so Irving said of himself, having to bluff his way along to cover up his defects in education. He really got his first experience of his art in an elocution class. Fancy having the boy Irving as a pupil! There was none to cherish, guide, and help him towards his kingdom, as he truly deserved and needed. Yet that youthful frame enshrined the rarest combination of gifts ever destined to be devoted to the English theatre. Compare Irving with Garrick and Kean, in so far as we know of them by published records. Irving was probably exceeded by Garrick in protean ability, and by Kean in flashes of sublime tragic splendour. In eerie powers and compelling intensity it is reasonable to believe that Irving was greater than both these other mighty men. Certainly he far surpassed them in character and intellect. If we also consider such services as raising the social status of the acting profession to a degree it never before enjoyed, the splendour of his homage to Shakespeare, then the record of Henry Irving is unique in the annals of the stage.

The splendid significance of Irving's final words upon the stage: 'Into Thy Hands, O Lord!' has often been dwelt upon. I like better to remind young folk of his *first* words upon the stage. He was then a painfully self-conscious boy of eighteen with a heart beating too fast for clear utterance. The place was Sunderland and the date, Monday, 29 September 1856. The play was Lytton's *Richelieu* and the words were 'Here's to our enterprise!'

JAMES BERNARD.

XXXII

IRVING as MEPHISTOPHELES

Lyceum Theatre, 19th of December, 1885 :—

FAUST

(*An adaptation from Goethe's Faust*)

WRITTEN BY W. G. WILLS

MORTALS

Faust	MR. CONWAY
Valentine	MR. ALEXANDER
Frosch	MR. HARBURY
Altmayer	MR. HAVILAND
Brander	MR. F. TYARS
Siebel	MR. JOHNSON
Student	MR. N. FORBES
Burgomaster	MR. H. HOWE
Citizens	MR. HELMSLEY MR. LOUTHER
Soldier	MR. M. HARVEY
Martha	MRS. STIRLING
Bessy	MISS L. PAYNE
Ida	MISS BARNETT
Alice	MISS COLERIDGE
Catherin	MISS MILLS
Margaret	MISS ELLEN TERRY

SPIRITS

Mephistopheles	MR. HENRY IRVING
Witches	MR. MEAD MR. CARTER MR. ARCHER MR. CLIFFORD

ACT I, SCENE 1. *Faust's Study*; SCENE 2. *The Witches' Kitchen*; SCENE 3. *Nuremberg—St. Lorenz Platz*. ACT II, SCENE 1. *Nuremberg—Margaret's Chamber*; SCENE 2. *Nuremberg—The City Wall*; SCENE 3. *Nuremberg —Martha's House*; SCENE 4. *Nuremberg—Martha's Garden*; SCENE 5. *Trees and Mountains*; SCENE 6. *Nuremberg—Margaret's Garden*. ACT III, SCENE. *Nuremberg—Street by Church*. ACT IV, SCENE. *Summit of the Brocken*. ACT V, SCENE. *Nuremberg—Dungeon*.

ON a cold Saturday evening in the late autumn, over fifty years ago, I stood in a dark passage leading to the gallery of the Lyceum Theatre. Above my head a gas-jet flickered, protected by a wire globe. I was hemmed in with a mass of humanity, full of excitement and expectation, who spent the waiting hours recalling previous plays in which they had seen Irving act, and anticipating the new wonders that they knew they were about to enjoy. At last there was a movement from above; the doors were opening; the crowd jammed into a compact mass, that with difficulty stumbled up the stone stairway. I clutched my shilling tightly in my hand—there would be no room to reach a pocket when I got to the pay-box, where it would be exchanged for a ticket.

After a great deal of good-humoured jostling, I found myself seated—I won't say comfortably—in the fourth row of the 'gods.'

There was a semi-sacred atmosphere about the old Lyceum; a sort of electric current that charged the audience and held them enthralled.

The play was *Faust*, and I remember I sat waiting with eyes glued on the proscenium. The house filled, the hum of expectancy died down as the orchestra swelled and the curtain rose on Faust's study. A death-like stillness pervaded the theatre. The soft lighting, George Alexander's mellow voice and the choir of students singing without, held the audience spell-bound. Suddenly we heard a roll of thunder; not of the tea-tray brand—the old-fashioned thunder-sheet which had done service at most theatres for years—but an awe-inspiring rumble that seemed to reverberate round the whole building.

Gradually, the stage darkened; the fire in the arched fireplace died down; there was nothing but a faint glint in the grate which was now emitting clouds of steam in the midst of which we became aware of a grey mask, pale and sinister, a malevolent rictus, embodying the whole spirit of evil. Such was Irving's first appearance and from that moment he held us in his grip.

How vivid are the pictures still! I see him beguiling old Martha in the garden and the diabolical cynicism of the oft-quoted line: 'I wonder where she'll go to when she's dead; I won't have her!' The sunset in that garden was the most perfectly realistic of any ever seen in a theatre. The Street in Nuremberg and the duel between Faust and Valentine, Mephistopheles intervening and striking sparks from the blades. Though Irving would have no electric lighting, he did not despise electric effects, as when he fondled the monkey in the Brocken scene, stroking flashes of fire from its head, an astounding effect as it then appeared. But we had had other thrills before that.

That evil leer that would change on the instant to Satanic Majesty. The concentrated fury of his outburst:

> 'Ere that should be I'ld tear you limb from limb,
> Your blood I'd dash
> Upon the wind like rain
> And all the gobbets of your mangled flesh
> I'ld seize up in a whirlwind
> And hurl them worlds away
> With your crushed, quivering spirit under them.'

and the sudden change to terror as the church bells peal and he leans cringing against the corner of the house with hands pressed tight over his ears.

Through a series of exquisite pictures, especially Telbin's Trees and Mountains that perhaps holds the palm even for that great scenic artist's work, we came at last to the Summit of the Brocken, a vision of vast antres, peaks and abysses, which might have been conceived by Gustave Doré at his imaginative best; Mephistopheles dominating the satanic revels, the whole suggesting a scene from Dante's Inferno.

Great as Irving's performance of Mephistopheles undoubtedly was, I never felt the part gave his genius sufficient scope and variety; in *Faust* he shone for me as a brilliant stage producer, and as my own bent was in that direction I thought how wonderful it would be to be associated with such a chief and in such a theatre. Many a time since I have stood on that stage, and, gazing up to my place in the gallery, my thoughts have carried me back to that memorable evening.

From that night I became a constant worshipper at the shrine of Henry Irving. Such notable performances as Macbeth, Robert Landry, Edgar of Ravenswood, Wolsey, and the saintly Becket, are forever indelibly written on the tablets of my memory.

Later, when I adopted the Sock and Buskin, I was engaged by Laurence Irving as stage manager for his first essay in management.

One day, in the spring of 1899, I met Laurence in the Strand. I had had some years' experience of the lighter side of theatrical entertainment in the meantime. Laurence seemed pleased to see me and asked if I would care to join the Lyceum Company; his father was producing *Robespierre* by Sardou, and there was a part in it, he said, that would suit me. I jumped at the idea, naturally, was taken to the Chief, and engaged then and there.

On returning home after the first rehearsal, full of enthusiasm, I found a telegram. 'Come to theatre 10.30 to-morrow. Irving.' My heart fell into my boots; it meant the sack, I was sure, and I spent a restless night. Anxious to know my fate, I arrived at the theatre on time. Old Barry, the Irish commissionaire stage-door keeper, with his palpably dyed whiskers and rich Irish brogue, greeted me with: "The Chief's waiting on ye in his office," and I was shown into the presence.

"Sit down, my boy," staccatoed the Chief. I subsided into a chair, fearing the worst. "My son tells me that you stage-manage?" he inquired.

"Only pantomime and light plays," I said apologetically.

"That's what I want," he replied. "*Robespierre* is spectacular. Loveday is ill. Here is the script. Help my son with the production."

I could scarcely get my breath, and I went out of that room in the clouds.

The Lyceum Theatre of those days was a most dignified institution; everything there was taken very seriously. During rehearsals no one would have dreamed of lighting a cigarette or reading a newspaper, everyone spoke with bated breath. The Chief was an autocrat, but he came to rehearsal with every detail worked out to the last iota so that there was no time wasted on experiments.

I know of only two people who had the temerity to stand up to him; one was William Terriss, who would, when reminded of some 'business' that interfered with the Chief, carry on as usual, and apologize for a lapse of memory so continually that Irving got tired of reminding him of it. The other was Walter Collinson, his dresser. Walter could do what he liked with the great man but he never, to my knowledge, abused his power. Irving's dressing-room was at the top of a flight of stairs at the side of the stage, and one evening when I was about to make my accustomed visit before the performance, I found Walter sitting on the top stair and heard the Chief's voice from his dressing-room saying: "Don't be a fool, Walter; come in."

"Not till you apologize," replied Walter, and there on the stairs he stuck. The altercation continued for some time, but at last H. I. called out: "Oh, all right, I apologize." Then Walter, with great dignity, rose and entered the room. No one but their two selves ever knew the details of that story.

Irving would never use electric lighting; he argued rightly that when you dim an incandescent lamp you obtain an orange-red effect, whereas the argand burner (a circular flame protected by a glass chimney) could be easily controlled and to its last flicker is blue. The calcium, or limelight, too, is soft and mellow and can be concentrated at will. Scenes lit by Irving had always the effect of oil-paintings, the boundaries lost in shade, high-lights focussing the points of greatest interest.

Calcium was obtained by two small jets of gas, one oxygen, the other hydrogen, playing on a piece of lime about the size and shape of a cotton reel, set in a square box at one end of which was a powerful lens. A special operator always followed the Chief's face with a small 'pin' light of steel-blue; however dark the scene was you always saw Irving's face. *Apropos* of this; we arrived in Kansas City after a tedious journey from Cincinnati. Several press men were waiting on the platform to interview Irving, but being tired he managed to escape them, went to his hotel and took refuge in the Turkish bath—only to find the press men there also!—but they got nothing from him.

Next morning I was standing at the stage door waiting for a rehearsal of supers, when a man came up, explained he was a member of the local press, and asked if I would allow him to be present at the rehearsal. I respectfully declined. While we were talking a lorry was discharging a load of long metal cylinders—addressed to Sir Henry Irving—dumping them at the stage door. The press man, seeing the label, asked what they were. I replied: "Cylinders of oxygen," and the press man disappeared.

That night passed off with the usual furore, but next morning when I went into the hall of my hotel for letters: "I'm sorry to hear about your Chief," said the clerk. "Sorry? Why?" I asked, and he handed me a newspaper in which I read:

IRVING DYING

While audience is cheering the Great Actor is being rushed to a caulked dressing-room to inhale
OXYGEN.

The Chief thought it a huge joke, but he felt it necessary for once to show himself, so he did a very unusual thing for him, for he was seldom to be seen walking—except in Bond Street. I accompanied him through the principal streets of Kansas City at midday so that the populace could give the lie to the Press.

In every production Irving surrounded himself with experts, artistic and practical, so no one could question any detail. Such men as Alma-Tadema, Abbey, and Seymour Lucas were generally in evidence during rehearsals, supervising scenery, costumes, etc.

Irving was profligate with regard to artists' terms; he usually gave them what they asked and very often more than they expected. Edward German, then unknown, whose music for Richard Mansfield's *Richard the Third* had taken his fancy, was commissioned to write the music for *Henry the Eighth*. He was conducting a final rehearsal. Irving was sitting on the stage superintending. Suddenly he turned to German and asked if terms had been arranged for his music. "No, sir," said German. Calling Bram Stoker, Irving asked: "What did we give Sullivan for *The Merchant of Venice* music?" "Five hundred guineas," Stoker said. "Then make out a cheque for the same amount for Mr. German," said the Chief. The unknown was paid the same fee as the celebrity.

I feel very privileged to have served in an official capacity under the banners of both Sir Henry Irving and Sir Herbert Tree. I was stage manager to both and can therefore review their separate qualities from a practical point of view. Tree was a different proposition altogether from Irving, very sentimental, a dreamer, vague, very vague as to his ideas and requirements. In youth he had affected a vacant manner that in later years it was difficult to throw off; it had become second nature. He was a very dear friend but during production he was impossible —childish and fretful. While his officials were trying to fathom what was in his mind they suffered the tortures of the damned until they lighted on the thing they thought he wanted. There was the difference. Irving knew what he wanted; Tree knew only what he *didn't* want—and sometimes got it.

Rehearsals for *Carnac Sahib*, a play by Henry Arthur Jones, had been dragging on for weeks. The scene was an Indian bazaar and Tree was indulging one of his usual fits of abstraction. "Here," he murmured, "I think we'll have a little tom-tom!" A loud voice came from the front of the house: "We'll have a little acting, if you don't mind, Tree. I haven't seen any yet!" It was the author speaking. It brought Tree down to earth with a bump. He lost his temper, ordered the author out of the theatre, and Jones never returned. The play ran five nights.

As I have said, Irving's productions were like oil-paintings; Tree's were like rich oleographs. Tree was a vacillating, emotional artist, witty, peevish, and undecided about everything. He had a certain authority but lacked dignity. Henry Irving was a genius—there's no doubt about that. I am sure he would have excelled equally as Prime Minister. He possessed a wonderful majesty. If he spoke to you casually, you felt you

IRVING *as MEPHISTOPHELES* *FROM A DRAWING BY PHIL MAY*

(Reproduced by kind permission of the Savage Club)

had been given a present. In life he stood alone, isolated, supreme. His death, practically in harness, was as he would have wished it.

PERCY NASH.

I first saw Henry Irving in the 'eighties when he played Louis XI: it was a tremendous performance. In New Haven, in *The Bells*, he held the audience spell-bound. Also in New York I saw him give a sumptuous performance of *The Merchant of Venice*. I thought him at his best in melodrama and that he reached the very heights of histrionic power in *The Lyons Mail*, *The Bells*, and *Louis the Eleventh*.

On a Saturday *matinée* in New York in 1887 I saw his spectacular and impressive performance of *Faust*; on the same evening I heard *Faust* in the Thalia Theatre in German with the great German actor, Ernst von Prossart, the greatest Mephisto of his day. The contrast between the two conceptions was marked—Irving's ironic, tragic, terrible; Prossart's roguish. Later, Herr Prossart told me a magnificent story concerning this simultaneous appearance of Irving and himself. The German company put on *Prolog im Himmel* as well as *Vorspiel auf dem Theater*. God appeared on the stage as well as the Archangels. Irving, wishing to show courtesy, sent an emissary over to the Thalia Theatre with a huge wreath, telling him that when the play began he was to walk on the stage and present it to Herr Prossart. But the emissary, who had been accustomed to seeing the play open in Faust's study, saw instead God and the three Archangels. He went back and reported to Irving that as they were not playing *Faust* that night he had withheld the wreath!

I saw Irving in a number of other plays and I think Sir James Barrie was right when he told me in conversation: "Whenever Irving is on the stage you don't see anybody else. He absolutely dominates every scene in which he appears. No matter who else is there, no matter who else speaks, one looks only at Irving."

M. LYON PHELPS.

XXXIII
IRVING as WERNER

Lyceum Theatre, 1st of June, 1887 :—

WERNER

WRITTEN BY LORD BYRON

Werner (Count Siegendorf)	MR. HENRY IRVING
Ulric	MR. GEORGE ALEXANDER
Gabor	MR. T. N. WENMAN
Baron Stralenheim	MR. C. GLENNEY
Idenstein	MR. HOWE
Rodolph	MR. HAVILAND
Fritz	MR. J. CARTER
Henrick	MR. ARCHER
Eric	MR. CALVERT
Arnheim	MR. CLIFFORD
Ludwig	MR. HARVEY
Josephine	MISS ELLEN TERRY
Ida Stralenheim	MISS WINIFRED EMERY

ACT I, SCENE. *Hall of Palace in Silesia.* ACT II, SCENE 1. *Exterior of Palace ;* SCENE 2. *Hall of the same ;* SCENE 3. *Secret Passage ;* SCENE 4. *Garden.* ACT III, SCENE. *Hall in Castle near Prague.* ACT IV, SCENE. *The Same.* PERIOD 1648—*Close of the Thirty Years' War.*

I FIRST saw Irving on his birthday, 6 February 1886, when he was forty-eight and I was not yet seventeen. That was in *Faust*, and on that evening, like ' some watcher of the skies ' a new planet swam into my ken. Not once in all the years which followed did I meet him or speak to him, but I have ceased to regret that now. In my adolescence and my early manhood he was a potent influence for good. I owed him delight, happiness, and culture. When I came away from the Lyceum after an evening with Irving and Ellen Terry I was as one lifted up to a plane above my rather dreary youth. And now I still owe him vivid and glowing memories, with which he solaces my age. Even if I offend Mr. Shaw I say that Irving radiated genius.

I saw everything in which he acted thereafter. Someone was speaking lately of *Raising the Wind.* There were three characters which I saw Irving act which had a family resemblance : Jeremy Diddler, Jingle, and Robert Macaire. To me the memory of

Jeremy is obscured by Jingle. He did not act Jingle—he *was* Jingle, raised to life. And at times that shabby, sardonic humorist, with the evil oozing from him—Robert Macaire—made one (like Mulvaney) 'crawl wid invijious apprehension.' I can see him now, slapping poor little Weedon Grossmith's dirty face with a wine-sop.

A year later (on 23 February 1887) Irving read *Hamlet* at the Birbeck Institution in aid of its building fund. I had never seen his Hamlet, and Fate had it that I never should, as he did not again, to my knowledge, play it in London. I would have lied or stolen to be at that reading—perhaps I did one of them—but anyhow I was there, and here are the notes I made that evening when I returned home.

The small theatre of the Institution was crammed when I arrived. No drop curtain, but the stage fitted with crimson baize; covered screens arranged in half of an ellipse. Presently a burst of cheering arose as Miss Terry took her seat in the front row of the stalls. She was popping up every minute or two, to speak to someone, or send someone on an errand, or to smile at someone with that dear familiar gesture—the pushing back of her sleeves from the graceful waving arms.

The hangings shook, then opened, and the great actor appeared, in evening dress, carrying a crimson bound book in his left hand. A roar of acclamation greeted him as he walked up to the reading desk, thin lips pressed together, and piercing eyes gleaming from under bushy brows. Opening the book, he bowed again and again until the applause ceased, and then spoke. "Ladies and gentlemen, I am about to read to you, or to attempt to read to you this evening Shakespeare's tragedy of *Hamlet*, or at least such part of it as may be compressed in the time at command." Then the characters and other preliminary details. And then: "Ha-a-a! who's there?" a warning movement of the right hand across the stand, and Irving was reading *Hamlet*—to me!

The charm of the affair was that it was like being admitted into an audience of the reader's friends, listening rather to a poem than an acted play. There was no standing-out of the Hamlet like a giant above all the other characters; no failing of any performer in his part; every character was lifted to the level of the central one. There were no waits, no changing of scenes, no properties, no prompting: although it was called a reading the book was only appealed to twice in the whole evening. Not once did he leave the desk to illustrate the text by any action: an uplifting of the arm, with an eerie laugh, at:

'Why, let the stricken deer go weep!' At 'Swear by my sword' an imaginary sword was held out; in the churchyard scene he crossed from one side of the desk to the other at 'Here lies the water, good! here stands the man—good!' striking either side of the desk in a comical deliberate manner. In the fencing bout, Irving, on giving the stage directions 'They play' and 'They play again,' made a movement of the right hand as though fencing. Now and again, for clearness, he said: 'Exit So-and-so' or 'Enter So-and-so' but nothing beyond this, merely mentioning the scene and where it was laid.

Claudius was a wayward, handsome, sometimes petulant fellow, who would have loved Hamlet. Horatio was splendid, as too was the water-fly, Osric. The two grave-diggers were alive and real—the First Grave-digger especially. Over the snatches of song he at first seemed rather nervous, but after that he crooned them out in a cracked old voice. Perhaps the best of the minor characters was Polonius, which was splendidly done. The little raisings of the brows and shruggings of the shoulders came in with great effect, and the gold eye-glasses ever and anon raised, quietly emphasized the age of the character. Polonius was emphatically not a doddering old imbecile, as he so often is represented to be, but a kindly, vain, whimsical but withal shrewd and worldly-wise old man, to whom Hamlet is a representative of the newer generation, hard to be understood by prejudiced age. Then Hamlet's remarks about the barber and the beard were not flung at him as gratuitous insults, but were rather half-laughing jibes to one for whom Hamlet had a certain good-humoured tolerance. They were followed by a puzzled look as the old man strove to keep pace with the Prince's wit.

And, above all, in the scene with Ophelia Hamlet was the lover instead of the bully. The words were not aimed like bludgeons; anger was not the only passion at work, but rather bitter disappointed love at finding that Ophelia is—as he thinks—as false and fickle as other women.

The soliloquies were superb, and especially was I struck by the speeches of the First Player, about the Siege of Troy. The whole of the fourth Act was omitted, partly for lack of time, but probably chiefly because of the presence in the audience of 'the fair Ophelia' herself.

The death was magnificent. He stood perfectly still and upright, with one hand on the desk, and without a movement spoke the well-remembered words. Not a sound could be heard but his voice; everybody bent forward entranced, and as

Hamlet's last deep sigh was almost sobbed out, it was echoed all over the house. Then, as the book was closed, everyone, the tension released, began to cheer, and again and again he was called out, amidst cheers and cries of 'Thank you, sir!'

Then out into the vestibule, where Kate Terry came out first, followed by an official, and behind him, tripping impatiently along with her hands raised to press forward, and a smile on her lovely face, came Miss Terry, in crimson cloak, beaming around, and now and then turning her head to speak a merry word, her beautiful hair waving like golden floss, and her mouth (too large, as all your criticasters agree, for perfect beauty, but yet so perfect, in its beauty—and bedamned to all criticasters!) trembling with happy smiles. Then, behind her, Irving, with tiger-like stride stretching lithely along, his hands clasped behind him, his head bent, his face relaxed in a smile, and his gleaming eyes looking amusedly up and around from under the bushy eyebrows, and his long hair pushed back. Amid a storm of cheers they got outside and drove off. That wonderful evening was over.

The 2 June 1887 was another occasion when it was vitally necessary for another of my relatives to die so that I might escape from the office to be at a *matinée* of Byron's *Werner* which Irving was to give for the benefit of a playwright of older days, Dr. Westland Marston, the author of *The Patrician's Daughter*, *Anne Blake*, and other now forgotten dramas of the Macready and Charles Kean periods.

The following is from notes I made next day. A house packed with notable people. Lord and Lady Randolph Churchill, Browning, Wilfrid Lawson, Johnny Toole, Willard, Arthur Cecil, John Clayton, the Beerbohm Trees—and me!

The curtain rose slowly, and as it rose so rose the applause, as tier after tier caught sight of the occupants of the stage. I can believe Byron in saying that he never intended this play for the stage. No modern dramatist would have 'discovered' his chief character, robbing the actor of an effective first entrance.

At a table, R.C., resting the right arm on it and looking straight across the house with fathomless, sorrowful eyes, sat Werner, and behind him Josephine. He had grey hair, whitening here and there, his face marble white and set, and he wore a small moustache, the ends inclining upwards. Josephine's sunny locks were hidden beneath a grey wig, giving quite a Widow Capet effect.

Such a reception! My faith, we made a row! At last it subsided. Werner rose and began to pace the scene with hurried, broken steps, and Josephine broke the silence with: 'Be calm, my love!' and it went ahead.

There was nothing to indicate that it was a first performance, unless it were the audience. All went smoothly and easily. Irving was nervous at first; his voice quavered slightly, but it passed quickly. Not once was the prompter heard. The only slip I noticed was in the last act, when Siegendorf calls Gabor out of the turret. Gabor answers: 'Who calls?' and Irving answered: 'I, Stralenheim!' instead of 'I, Siegendorf!'

The first Act passed off quietly, the only exciting parts being at the altercation between Stralenheim and Werner, up to the striking climax: 'Left one thing undone—Thank God for it!'

The second Act was the one for which all were waiting, to see upon what sort of wires Frank Marshall had strung Byron's dry bones. The curtain rose on a beautifully painted back-cloth, representing the castle on a hill, seen from the grounds. The scene in the hall between Idenstein and Fritz was cut, and the rest of the scene transferred to the outside of the castle. George Alexander was well received, everybody remembering kindly his success in *Faust* after Harry Conway had failed. Scene two was the scene of the first Act again, in the castle. A long scene this. It was the last scene of Byron's second Act and the first of his third Act lumped into one. Werner's three speeches, beginning: 'Before you dare despise your father' were given splendidly. The scene between Ulric, Stralenheim, and Gabor excellent.

Scene three: the Secret Passage. A great grey stone arch, stretching right across the stage, as dark as Erebus, gloom all round, and a misty background. Gabor discovered soliloquizing dismally in the dark. Now for it! Exit Gabor in search of the keyhole, and then the back of the scene fades in the wonderful way in which they manage that sort of thing here, and discovers a room, which we correctly assume to be Stralenheim's 'chambers'—these sort of people don't have mere 'rooms.' It was, in effect, a scene within a scene. Centre: a bed with crimson hangings; R. a door; L. another door; L.C. (we discover later) is the secret panel. Seen through gauze. Ulric enters L., soliloquizing most reprehensibly, calling his father a 'weak fool,' and incidentally mentioning his determination to settle Stralenheim's claim to the vague 'estates' in the twinkling of a dagger. Pulls aside the hangings, announces his fell intention, and stabs at the bed. 'Orrid groans! Ulric climbs up on the bed, spits on his hands, and gives another prod to prevent unpleasant mistakes. More groans from the bed, and an arm (a plump one—Glenny's to wit) flops out. Exit Ulric stealthily. Hish! Secret panel comes open and enter Gabor, with a crick in his back. He also opines correctly that the room is Stralenheim's. Thinks he'd like to take one look at the (very sarcastically!) 'noble Lord.' Pulls open the hangings, and Glenny falls half out, with a hole in his shirt-front and all over rose-pink. Gabor recognizes that appearances are against him, and looking off R., also recognizes Ulric. Exit rapidly in trepidation through panel. Enter Ulric R., stealthily, stage darkens, and scene changes. In fact the whole scene which Gabor describes in Byron's last act is put on the stage. Clever, I thought.

Act three, which is Byron's fourth Act, began with the entrance of Ulric and Rudolph. At the end of this Act also there was an alteration. Siegendorf and Ida are alone, and he confesses that he once defrauded her father of a sum of money. He then gives her the purse he stole from her father's bedroom Act one, and tells her to spend it in masses for her father's soul. A kindly —and thrifty!—thought.

Act four: same scene. I rather think this was the best played Act of the lot. They were all well warmed up to the work. The 'liar and fiend!' episode produced almost for the first time in this play the thrill one always confidently anticipates at the Lyceum. The scene from there on was excellent. Wenman was perfect, and Irving at his best of the afternoon. Alexander, in the succeeding scene with Werner, was at *his* best of the afternoon, but even that did not take one's breath away.

The play ended like Macready's version, with the death of Siegendorf, and this, of course, was the high spot of the afternoon. An impressive picture: the background of golden hills, bathed in sunlight, seen between slight columns; at the back, the guards, two of whom grasp Ulric, who gnaws his moustache in contempt and rage; and in front—the object which all eyes see only—the dying Siegendorf, with sad white face and silvery hair, his misty eyes looking out yearningly, and the last sigh rattling in his throat. Then slowly the heavy body slips from the arms of the grey-haired, kneeling Josephine, the remorseless green curtain descends, and the floats rise.

Three times the curtain was called up, discovering the chief characters on the stage, and then again on Irving and our Ellen. Then he appeared alone, to be succeeded by Dr. Westland Marston, the beneficiary, a jolly-looking old fellow with a pleasant red face. Enter later O.P., in response to continued cheering, Irving alone, who mentioned with sarcastic regret that he could not announce *Werner* for a run, but he thanked them for their approval which he was happy to note seemed unqualified—which it was. Exit H. I., and exit slowly the distinguished audience.

Irving was, of course, the best of all, but the character is not good. There is no backbone to it; it arouses no sympathy in anyone; his griefs don't stir one's pulse, and when he dies one finds one's self rather relieved. Besides: there is no *reason* for his dying. However, without the death the ending would have been fearfully tame, while with it it is inconsequent. He *might* have made Werner stab himself, or like Mr. Wilkins Flasher's acquaintance, say 'make away with himself' to escape his shame, but as it was, it was flat. Irving looked superb. He was, as usual, made up splendidly. He wore a dark, close-fitting coat of Polish fashion, trimmed with fur; fur-topped boots, and a fur-lined cloak over all.

Wenman was the next best, and really made the hit of the afternoon, making Gabor the best-defined character in the play. Glenny was good, too, though more nervous than the rest.

Miss Terry, of course, had only a very small part in Josephine: unworthy of her, but even as it was she did not seem inclined to make much of it. It seemed odd and sad to see her flitting on now and then at the back, with a line or two, and then off again, like a shadow, with no semblance of a character to play. However, it was all for charity!

I see that the papers this morning speak well of the production, but dubiously (if even so well) of the play. Even Clement Scott, in *The Telegraph*, is not so grandiferous as usual, although he does speak of the magic of Irving's method of production, and the skill of Frank Marshall's adaptation. Mr. Irving's standard is so high that I do not think this character would ever add much to his reputation.

A. E. Pain.

XXXIV

IRVING as ROBERT LANDRY

Lyceum Theatre, 28th of September, 1889 :—

THE DEAD HEART

WRITTEN BY WATTS PHILLIPS

Robert Landry	MR. HENRY IRVING
The Abbé Latour	MR. BANCROFT
The Count de St. Valery	MR. HAVILAND
Arthur de St. Valery	MR. GORDON CRAIG
Legrand	MR. ARTHUR STIRLING
Toupet	MR. EDWARD RIGHTON
Reboul	MR. F. TYARS
Michel	MR. CLIFFORD
Jean	MR. HARVEY
Pierre	MR. TAYLOR
Jocrisse	MR. ARCHER
Guiscard	MR. BLACK
A Smith	MR. RAYNOR
A Crier	MR. DAVIS
A Woman	MRS. CARTER
Cerisette	MISS KATE PHILLIPS
Rose	MISS COLERIDGE
Catherine Duval	MISS ELLEN TERRY

PROLOGUE (1771), SCENE 1. *The Garden of the Café de la Belle Jardinière ;* SCENE 2. *A Street ;* SCENE 3. *Bedchamber of Catherine Duval.* ACT I (1789), SCENE 1. *The Bastille. Tableau Curtain ;* SCENE 2. *Apartment in the Hôtel St. Valery. Tableau Curtain ;* SCENE 3. *The Café Jocrisse.* ACT II (1794), SCENE 1. *Entrance to the Prison of the Conciergerie ;* SCENE 2. *Corridor in the Prison ;* SCENE 3. *Room in the Prison.* ACT III (1794), SCENE 1. *The Guillotine ;* SCENE 2. *Room in the Prison.*

WHEN my grandfather, Benjamin Webster, produced *The Dead Heart* at the New Adelphi Theatre on the 12 November 1859 the play was already more than three years old, that is to say, he had bought it from Watts Phillips in June 1856. This did not prevent a charge of plagiarism when Tom Taylor's adaptation of *A Tale of Two Cities* was produced by Madame Celeste at the Lyceum Theatre on the 18 January 1860. This in spite of the fact that we know *A Tale of Two Cities* was suggested to Dickens by Wilkie Collins's play, *The Frozen*

Deep, in which Dickens had acted the chief part of Geoffrey Wardour in a private house with an amateur company. This was in 1857. Geoffrey Wardour suggested Sidney Carton. But even so, the main incident of a man 'laying down his life for his friend' by going in his place to the guillotine was no novelty, for Alexandre Dumas had used it in *Le Chevalier de la Maison Rouge*, which he dramatized himself and produced at the Théâtre Historique in 1847, with Mélingue, fellow pupil with Fechter of the great Frédérick Lemaître, in the part of Lorin. Boucicault made an adaptation of this which was produced at the Olympic under the title of *Geneviève, or the Reign of Terror* in 1853, with a cast that included both Madame Celeste and Benjamin Webster as Lorin; Alfred Wigan played Maurice, for whom Lorin sacrifices his life. All this is stage history which it may be interesting to recall in the light of the fact that poor Watts Phillips, the author of so many original dramas, and in his time quite an 'advanced' dramatist, was quite seriously branded as a literary thief owing to the colossal reputation of Dickens. It is quite safe to say that there was no plagiarism in the case at all; merely coincidence.

But none of these considerations affected the revival at the Lyceum, though there was much surprise that Irving should resuscitate a thirty-year-old melodrama of this type. The centenary of the taking of the Bastille was a good excuse so far as the general public was concerned, but it did not satisfy artistic conscience, and there was much shaking of heads and whispering of lowered prestige, but the end justified the experiment, both artistically and financially. Irving's special gift of giving dignity to any form of drama was again evident. Just as his treatment of *The Lyons Mail* and *The Bells* had raised them almost to the importance of classics, so he was able to perform the miracle once more. As to stage management, it is safe to say that never was such an amazing example of realism as the taking of the Bastille seen in a theatre. The spaciousness of the setting was extraordinary; one felt oneself transported to Paris on that fatal fourteenth of July, a participator in the drama; the heat, the dust, the rolling clouds of smoke from the cannon were present and actual. It was an experience lived, rather than merely witnessed.

The story is simple as all the great popular stories are: the inconvenient lover removed by the *lettre de cachet;* the prisoner released bent on revenge and, at the moment of its fulfilment, relenting and of free will entering the trap set for his victim—no more than that.

And Irving——? Never did that curious aloofness he could so well assume serve him to better purpose; as Vanderdecken, perhaps, and as Philip of Spain he used it, but not with greater effect. After the Prologue he stood, literally alone; martyr, avenger, hero.

It would be a simple matter to record the action scene by scene, but with Irving that would be to tell only half the story. He characterized unerringly, and it is worth noting that his young sculptor of the Prologue bore no trace of resemblance to Hamlet or Romeo, and even less, if possible, to Benedick; his light comedy did not remind you of Jingle or Jeremy Diddler or Macaire. The shrivelled fragment of humanity borne from the Bastille and placed upon a gun-carriage was a being unearthly, in whose faintly dawning reason there was infinite pathos, for returning reason must mean remembrance and remembrance only pain. That, at least, is what Robert Landry's friends fear for him, but in his case the reaction is more terrible, all human sense is dead in him, and when he faces the woman he had loved, who had betrayed him, he created in his audience a superlative emotion because in him there was none. Irving's treatment of this scene alone justified the revival. With icy formality he receives the Abbé Latour, the engineer of the intrigue that has condemned him; as coldly he signs the order for Citizen Latour's release and hands him the sword that is his key to freedom—if he can win past the sword in his own hand. Irving's duels were famous, but even the celebrated encounter in *The Corsican Brothers* lacked something in comparison with this, perhaps because Latour lives more vitally and is a more malignant agent of evil than M. de Chateau-Renaud. 'That man attempted my life and I killed him. Remove the body of the Citizen Latour'; passionless, bloodless words from the frozen lips of a corpse, for so at that moment he seemed, a corpse so far as concerned the affairs of this world, animated only for vengeance.

The change of purpose in the touching penultimate scene before the dawn at the foot of the guillotine, I need not dwell upon, but the glory, the beauty of him as he stood on the steps of the guillotine in the first rays of the rising sun is a memory to cherish. That serenity that seemed a fundamental quality with Irving was never used to better purpose, but it was not that alone, the eyes had their message of hope—of peace—of love.

A simple play. Very homely and very moving. No wonder the highbrows scoffed, but what they wanted precisely was never made clear. No doubt they wished to put on him a responsibility that he would never accept, the responsibility of producing the uncommercial drama, forgetting that he was manager as well as actor and not likely to turn altruistic to his commercial disadvantage.

Robert Landry was a great performance, but no one would for one moment compare it artistically with his highest, though he gave his best to every part he attempted. The production bore the hall-mark of Irving, which meant a faultless knowledge of all that was vital to the effectiveness of the play, but there was no scene that lives in one's memory in comparison with the exquisite pathos of his farewell in *Charles the First:* the revelation in the depths of tragedy that overwhelmed Romeo in the Mantua scene; the incarnate devilry of Dubosc and some wonderful moments of Macbeth; and the grandeur and dignity of Becket. These things are the treasures of our dramatic experiences for which one is always grateful.

To revert to *The Dead Heart:* a small incident at its first rehearsal always strikes me as an excellent example of that sardonic humour of Irving's that was so often misunderstood by those who did not know him; they failed to detect the unmistakable strain of impishness that was in him as well as to appreciate the innate kindliness of the man. Irving came on the stage and greeted the assembled company with that courtly grace of his that had nothing of condescension or patronage in it—but his eagle glance missed nothing: he noticed that old Arthur Stirling, who was to play Legrand, alone of all the company had no part in his hand. He went up to him:

"Good morning, Arthur. Haven't they sent you the—er—the part?"

"Impossible to rehearse properly with the part in one's hand," replied Stirling, patting his pocket.

"Ha! H'm! Yes. *Ex*-cellent! *Ex*-cellent! You know it, eh? What a—h'm—what an example to these younger ones—ha?"

And so the rehearsal started, and Legrand's first cue came—and there was silence!

PROMPTER (*whispering*): That's you, Mr. Stirling—your cue.

STIRLING: Ha! H'm! Er—er—— 'Here's a health to the bride and bridegroom—er—to be.'

PROMPTER: Elect.

STIRLING: Eh? Oh, 'elect,' exactly. 'Here's a health to the bride and bridegroom *elect*.'

And the rehearsal progressed till it came to Legrand's next speech—and again there was silence!

PROMPTER: That's your cue, Mr. Stirling.

STIRLING: Er—eh?—h'm—— and the old actor began to fumble in his pocket for his part. Said Irving: "Going to read it, Arthur? H'm, that's a pity. You got on so well with the first half of the first line."

BEN WEBSTER.

XXXV

IRVING as EDGAR OF RAVENSWOOD

Lyceum Theatre, 20th of September, 1890 :—

RAVENSWOOD

(*An adaptation of The Bride of Lammermoor by Sir Walter Scott*)

WRITTEN BY HERMAN C. MERIVALE

Edgar	MR. HENRY IRVING
Hayston of Bucklaw	MR. TERRISS
Caleb Balderstone	MR. MACKINTOSH
Craigengelt	MR. WENMAN
Sir William Ashton	MR. ALFRED BISHOP
The Marquis of Athole	MR. MACKLIN
Bide-the-Bent	MR. H. HOWE
Henry Ashton	MR. GORDON CRAIG
Moncrieff	MR. TYARS
Thornton	MR. HAVILAND
A Priest	MR. LACY
Lockhard	MR. DAVIES
Lady Ashton	MISS LE THIÈRE
Ailsie Gourlay	MISS MARRIOTT
Annie Winnie	MRS. PAUNCEFORT
Lucy Ashton	MISS ELLEN TERRY

ACT I, SCENE. *The Chapel Bounds.* ACT II, SCENE 1. *Ravenswood—the Library;* SCENE 2. *Tod's Den;* SCENE 3. *The Wolf's Crag.* ACT III, SCENE. *The Mermaid's Well.* (*An Interval of one year.*) ACT IV, SCENE 1. *Ravenswood—a Room;* SCENE 2. *The Sea-coast;* SCENE 3. *The same;* SCENE 4. *The Kelpie's Flow.*

BRAM STOKER, Irving's friend, business manager, and chronicler, thus describes the reading of this play :

'I heard him read through a good many plays in the course of a quarter of a century of work together and it was always enlightening. He had a way of conveying the *cachet* of each character by inflection or trick of voice and manner; and his face was always, consciously or unconsciously, expressive. I have heard him read in public in a large hall both *Hamlet* and *Macbeth*, and his characterization was so marked that after he had read the entries of the various characters he did not require to refer to them by name. On this occasion he seemed familiar

> with every character, and, I doubt not, could have played any of them, so far as his equipment fitted him for the work within a short time. Naturally, the most effective part was that of Edgar of Ravenswood. Not only is it the most prominent part in the cast, but it was that he was to play himself and to which he had given most special attention. In it he brought out all the note of destiny which rules in both novel and play. Manifestly Edgar is a man foredoomed, but not till the text sounded the note of doom in the weird and deathly utterances of Ailsie Gourlay could one tell that all must end awfully. Throughout the tragic note was paramount. Well Edgar knew it : the doom that wrapped him even in the moment of triumphant love was a birth-gift. As Irving read it that night and as he acted it afterwards, there was throughout infinite and touching pathos. But not this character alone, but all the rest were given with great and convincing power. The very excellence of the rendering made each to help the other ; variety and juxtaposition brought the full effect. The prophecies, because of their multiplication, became of added import on Edgar's gloom, and toned the high spirit of Hayston of Bucklaw. Lucy's sweetness was intensified by the harsh domination of Lady Ashton. The suffering of the faithful Caleb under the lash of Ailsie's prophecy only increased its force.'

Here, then, were high hopes of success, yet the play proved too gloomy in performance, despite its literary graces and the exceptionally beautiful setting that Irving gave it. The leisurely charm of Sir Walter Scott's novel was not to be captured in the theatre where continuous action is essential. The interrupted funeral in the First Act made a strongly dramatic start, but the development did not fulfil its promise. The shooting of the mad bull which attacks Lucy was an unfortunate incident in Act Two. Why this should be so it is not easy to explain, but the fact remains that somehow it was not dramatic. I suppose there is nothing heroic in shooting a mad bull. However, any shortcoming was amply atoned by the exquisite love scene in the next Act. I heard a remark : 'He may be fifty-two but he can teach all the young ones to make love.' Again a most exquisite setting for the Mermaiden's Well and a touchingly beautiful performance by Ellen Terry : also a very powerful one by Miss Marriott as the old crone, Ailsie Gourlay. Terriss as Hayston of Bucklaw gave a gallant picture of the gentlemanly bravo, and the duel in the last Act between Irving and him was well up to the level of the many fights I have seen on the Lyceum stage.

As for Irving himself as the seventeenth-century Orestes he

was as ever picturesque, intense, and entirely convincing, but he could make no headway against the inherent gloom of the story. Even *Hamlet* has its episodes of comedy; in *Ravenswood* there was no relief.

What remains in our minds and must, I am certain, linger in the memory of everyone who witnessed it, was the Turneresque beauty of the final scene. Surely there was never a more lovely picture seen on any stage than that sunset on the quicksands of Kelpie's Flow. The old servant Caleb Balderstone's solitary figure gazing out over the waste and the single black feather from Edgar's bonnet marking the spot where he has disappeared; it was in perfect keeping with this mournful tragedy, a fitting close to this story of Scott's fate-ridden hero, but none the less we left the theatre with a sense of dissatisfaction. Irving had had no scope.

And it was Irving we went to see. We knew the company, the scenery, the production would be the best that London could show us; the only question was, would the play give him sufficient opportunity? That, I believe, was the attitude of mind of nine-tenths of the audiences that crowded the Lyceum for twenty years.

Hamlet I never saw; he had given up playing it before my time. He was wise, I suppose, if, as they said, he felt he was now too old to play it, but seeing him as Edgar of Ravenswood, a part in some ways so like it, made me wish that I had been in time.

But I did see *Macbeth*, and it left a deep impression. It was a reading so different from all one's preconceived ideas, so unlike all that report tells us of the older school. A strongly imaginative Macbeth, a man foredoomed. A brave murderer; it is a mistake, I'm sure, to assume that murderers are necessarily cowards. He was under his wife's influence, but he didn't need that to urge him to 'do the deed,' for he had determined on that before the play began.

The Bells, of course, I saw, but there is nothing new to be said of Mathias, nor of Louis the Eleventh, nor Lesurques and Dubosc. But *The Corsican Brothers* has an interest of its own—or rather, an interest in its relation to Irving. He was, I believe, the only man who ever attempted a dual *rôle* in that or any other play that afforded such opportunity, who used no make-up at all for either part, but relied entirely upon his acting to mark the difference between the twins, and how strongly marked that difference was it is difficult to convey to anyone who missed it. But there was no possibility whatever of confusing Fabien, who was content to stay at home and manage his estate in Corsica, with his brother Louis who preferred life in Paris. For gentle charm Louis dei Franchi was one of Irving's most touching performances. Whereas Fabien was terrible. The swordsmanship in the celebrated duel in the snow had the usual Lyceum excellence, and again Irving was matched against Terriss as M. de Chateau-Renaud, and a truly wonderful fight it was from the moment they crossed swords till de Chateau-Renaud fell, pierced dagger-wise with Fabien's broken sword-blade.

What contrast were all these with the gentle Vicar of Wakefield—and with Wolsey, and what contrast between these two churchmen!

But there was another Cardinal who for me had a stronger fascination than perhaps any part he played, yet I would be loth to lose the memory of any one I saw; Richelieu, who combines all the subtlety of Louis with the authority of Wolsey—the cunning of Mephistopheles with the dignity of Charles I; a great part and to my mind a very great performance.

Another Churchman of a very different stamp was Becket—*Becket*, that exquisite poem of martyrdom on which all the laudatory adjectives in the language have been exhausted.

I think Shylock was my favourite of all. How wonderful he always was in it! It seems impossible to say anything new about it, for when he first played it he created a new tradition, and from his first production of it he played it till his death. Having seen Irving's reading it is difficult to understand how there ever could have been any other.

The last new production I saw at the Lyceum was *Coriolanus*, a very beautiful reconstruction of Ancient Rome, by Alma Tadema, but I regret to say the play made very little impression on me and I fear the public shared my view, for it was not a success. What I do recall is that the crowd effects were exceptional, even for the Lyceum. I seldom think of it except to recall a rather cruel story, redeemed only by its humour. Irving would have no loafers among his supers; they were all decent small people in their way and independent of the Theatre as a livelihood, and most of them keen critics. Among them was a newspaper-seller who had a small stand outside Gatti's in the Strand. After one particularly long and trying rehearsal of *Coriolanus*, about three o'clock in the morning, Sir Henry Irving, Sir Alma-Tadema, and Sir Alexander Mackenzie, who had composed the music, were standing talking together on the stage, and our friend, looking at them, remarked : " Yes, three bloomin' knights, and that's abaht as long as the bloomin' piece'll run." Unhappily his prophecy was fulfilled, although not quite literally ; it lasted only for thirty-six performances.

HENRY CROCKER.

IRVING *As WOLSEY*

XXXVI

IRVING as CARDINAL WOLSEY

Lyceum Theatre, 5th of January, 1892 :—

KING HENRY THE EIGHTH

WRITTEN BY WILLIAM SHAKESPEARE

King Henry VIII	MR. WILLIAM TERRISS
Cardinal Wolsey	MR. HENRY IRVING
Cardinal Campeius	MR. BEAUMONT
Capucius	MR. TABB
Cranmer	MR. ARTHUR STIRLING
Duke of Norfolk	MR. NEWMAN
Duke of Buckingham	MR. FORBES ROBERTSON
Duke of Suffolk	MR. TYARS
Earl of Surrey	MR. CLARENCE HAGUE
Lord Chamberlain	MR. ALFRED BISHOP
Gardiner	MR. LACY
Lord Sands	MR. GILBERT FARQUHAR
Sir Henry Guildford	MR. HARVEY
Sir Thomas Lovell	MR. STEWART
Sir Anthony Denny	MR. DAVIS
Sir Nicholas Vaux	MR. SEYMOUR
Cromwell	MR. GORDON CRAIG
Griffith	MR. HOWE
Gentlemen	{ MR. JOHNSON MR. ARCHER
Garter King-at-Arms	MR. BELMORE
Surveyor to the Duke of Buckingham	MR. ACTON BOND
Brandon	MR. SELDON
Sergeant-at-Arms	MR. POWELL
A Messenger	MR. LORRISS
A Scribe	MR. REYNOLDS
A Secretary	MR. CUSHING
Queen Katherine	MISS ELLEN TERRY
Anne Bullen	MISS VIOLET VANBRUGH
An Old Lady	MISS LE THIÉRE
Patience	MRS. PAUNCEFORT

ACT I, SCENE 1. *London—the Palace at Bridewell;* SCENE 2. *Outside the Palace;* SCENE 3. *The Council Chamber in the Palace;* SCENE 4. *A Courtyard;* SCENE 5. *A Hall in York Place.* ACT II, SCENE 1. *The King's Stairs, Westminster;* SCENE 2. *An Ante-chamber in the Palace;* SCENE 3. *A Garden in the Palace;* SCENE 4. *A Hall in Blackfriars.* ACT III, SCENE 1. *The Queen's Apartment;* SCENE 2. *The Palace at Bridewell.* ACT IV, SCENE 1. *A Street in Westminster;* SCENE 2. *Kimbolton.* ACT V, SCENE. *Greenwich—Church of the Grey Friars.*

It is a long time ago since Irving's revival of *King Henry the Eighth* at the Lyceum Theatre and unfortunately my memory for details is not as good as it was, but that revival contained scenes and pictures which are unforgettable.

In the days before the Great War I was walking along Piccadilly one evening with Forestier, the artist, when he suddenly said: "I think, of all the historic productions I have ever seen in the Theatre, nothing has ever compared for beauty and correctness with Irving's *Henry the Eighth*. How magnificently it was mounted! How finely the costumes were designed, and what a wonderful Wolsey he made. How grand Miss Ellen Terry was as Queen Katherine, and Forbes-Robertson's Buckingham—did you ever in your life see anything finer than Forbes-Robertson's Buckingham?"

As he spoke the words a door behind him opened and Forbes-Roberston's head appeared over his shoulder. The face was illumined by a green light from a fan-light, and it reminded me uncannily of Julius Cæsar's ghost at Philippi. Forestier remained quite unaware of the vision he had conjured up; his back was turned to it. But I simply gasped feebly, with astonishment. I was so surprised I never even spoke to the owner of the face. Later on, when I told Forbes-Robertson of the incident, he said that we must have been standing on his sister's doorstep and he was just returning from paying her a visit. It was a very strange coincidence, following on Forestier's splendid summing-up and truthful criticism of a marvellous production.

The Tudor scenery, painted by Telbin, Hawes Craven, and Joe Harker, was superb. It was never too prominent, never killed the faces of the actors, but was always just the appropriate background. Seymour Lucas, master of historic knowledge, designed the beautiful dresses. I remember, a few days after Sir Henry's death, seeing an album in his rooms in Stratton Street in which the lovely drawings were all collected. I wonder who bought that album at the sale of Irving relics?

Surely no play was ever better cast, with, I think, one exception—the King. Much as I admired William Terriss in certain parts, I did not think he was suited to play the Tudor monarch. He had not the great, brutal physique; he was far too good-looking, and he wore some rather pretty curls, regardless of the great original's huge bladder-of-lard forehead. Seymour Lucas also told me that William Terriss would add little bits to his dress which were not in keeping with the character. This was very unnecessary, for surely no finer set of costumes was ever made for any actor. Irving paid as much as fifteen guineas a yard for real cloth of gold for them, and this was covered again with hundreds of seed pearls. One of these dresses, still in existence, is as good as new after all these years.

But there were two scenes in which Terriss was superb—the trial of Katherine of Aragon and the disgrace of the Cardinal. The end of the trial scene might be described as an exhibition of magnificent bad temper. First came the Queen's scathing attack on Wolsey's pride, her refusal to be judged by the Cardinals, and her appeal to be allowed to bring her cause before the Pope. 'The Queen is obstinate,' says old Campeius, as Katherine and the Ladies left the room. This was followed by Henry's fury with the Judges he had appointed.

> 'I may perceive
> These Cardinals trifle with me: I abhor
> This dilatory sloth—'

—a vicious kick and the footstool flew across the stage. The King rose.

> 'Break up the Court
> I say, set on!'

And His Majesty strode from the throne.

The Cardinals, none too pleased with these two snubs, rose to make their exit, Wolsey especially indignant. Little Campeius, who certainly had the right to precede the other, was going out first, but Wolsey, touching him on the shoulder, flung out yards of scarlet train to be caught by waiting pages, and swept out in front of him. Truly, a magnificent curtain!

In the disgrace scene, Henry's 'Read o'er *this* and after *this* and then to breakfast with what appetite you have,' was never to be forgotten.

Miss Ellen Terry's Queen Katherine was the epitome of stately dignity and sweetness. She won all our sympathy, even though the little minx, Anne Bullen, was played by Miss Violet Vanbrugh, then a very young actress.

But the great Cardinal is the real subject of this slight sketch. If there was one class of part in which Irving excelled it was as the grand cleric. Witness his Becket and his Richelieu. Charming as he was as dear old Doctor Primrose, one always had a lurking feeling that he should have been Archbishop of Canterbury and not a mere humble Vicar of Wakefield. His first appearance as Wolsey was a superb picture; far too fine, I fear, for the real Wolsey. There was nothing of the 'Butcher's ketch' about him. A slow procession entered the palace of Bridewell, under a carved oak screen, when he met his enemy Buckingham. First came guards, then the silver pillars, secretaries, the purse borne before him, and then the scarlet figure complete in Capa Magna[1] carried by pages, then more guards. A pause as the procession halted. The two men eyed each other; a snake-like look came into Wolsey's eyes as he said:

> 'The Duke of Buckingham's surveyor, ha!
> Where's his examination?
> Here, so please you.
> Well, we shall then know more; and Buckingham
> Shall lessen this big look.'

The procession swept on, and you knew poor Buckingham was already doomed.

The next most vivid memory is of the scene of the great banquet at York House; the entrance of the dancers. For the first time we heard the now famous 'Three dances for Henry VIII' by German. I can still see the Cardinal on his high seat on the right of the stage, his long, scarlet train covering the steps. His polite boredom as he watches the first two dances; then the sudden gleam in his eye as he notices the King among the shepherds in the final dance; his change of demeanour, his intense interest as he follows every movement, beating time with his fingers, then, watching King Henry's evident attraction towards Anne Bullen, with some misgiving. This leads up, in a later scene, to his arrogant: 'The French King's sister: he shall marry her. Anne Bullen! No. I'll no Anne Bullens for him. There's more in't than fair visage.'

This arrogance leads to the disgrace which speedily follows, and Wolsey's horror as he glances at the unfortunate papers which he has included in his intercepted packet to the Pope. After that came the finest scene of all, as Norfolk, Suffolk, and Surrey jeer at the fallen minister.

I have watched various renderings of this scene. In one case it became a vulgar wrangling match in which the Cardinal was more vulgar even than the rest, but in Irving's rendering you only thought of a crowd of jackals yapping round a dying lion. This was followed by the deep pathos of his last farewell—

> 'O Cromwell, Cromwell!
> Had I but served my God with half the zeal
> I served my King, He would not in mine age
> Have left me naked to mine enemies.'

[1] Made from silk especially woven at Marseilles and dyed in Rome.

After that, what mattered? A beautiful procession for the minx, Anne Bullen, fresh from her coronation. Then, old Griffith, Katherine's gentleman usher, beautifully played by Howe, telling of Wolsey's last journey from York to Leicester, where, arriving at the abbey, he says: 'An old man broken by the storms of State has come to lay his weary bones among ye,' to be quickly followed by the pathetic death of the old Queen, accompanied by a 'flight of angels.'

The play ended with a fine spectacle of the christening of the infant Elizabeth, and some prophetic flattery by Archbishop Cranmer recording her future greatness. But all this did not matter much, for Wolsey was no more. There was still, however, one actor in this great production whom I have not mentioned in detail. For once, if at no other time, Irving was rivalled in his own theatre by another performance at least as beautiful as his own. Whoever, among those who were fortunate enough to see and hear Forbes-Robertson's farewell to the people before poor Buckingham took boat to the Tower, with the axe's edge turned towards him, can fail to remember it? I think it was the most beautiful piece of elocution I ever heard in my life.

My father told me that in those days there lived two old clerks in Hull who were the local critics. They attended the theatre every Monday night, and what they said about the play for the week—went! If they praised a play it was a success; if they damned a play it was damned. They had never been to London, but when Irving produced *King Henry the Eighth* they determined to make a special journey to see it, and him. When they returned they were asked how they enjoyed the performance and what they thought of it, and him. "Eh, it was fine," they said, and they liked Irving well enough, but

> "Bookin'am—the chap that played
> Bookin'am—yon's the chap for our mooney."

TOM HESLEWOOD.

I did not know Henry Irving off the stage, but I saw him in a round of characterizations when he was in America in 1883. The repleteness of his stage mountings and the masterly direction of his casts, apparent in every play he produced, surpassed anything American theatre patrons had ever seen. This was generally acknowledged, and throughout the acting profession here he was hailed as 'a great stage artist.'

It was the common impression that Nature made Henry Irving unique, and there was never any need for him to put himself 'into the trick of singularity,' not even in the *rôle* of Malvolio, from which I quote. I saw him in all of his repertoire, except *Hamlet*, and my most vivid memory of his personations is that of Eugene Aram in the play of that name. His gaunt body, his mystic mien, captured my sympathetic attention upon his first entrance, before he spoke—and he was the tragic scholar-suspect to the life throughout the play's unfolding.

In the summer of 1892 the Comic Opera comedian, De Wolfe Hopper, and I went to Europe together. It was the first voyage across the Atlantic for each of us. Our destination was Vienna, where an international theatrical congress was being held. But the hospitality of the Green Room Club members was so agreeably incessant that we failed entirely to reach Austria. One Monday I suggested to Hopper that we had better curtail our socialities lest we departed from London without seeing some of the things we shouldn't miss.

"For instance?" he queried.

"Wouldn't you like to see Henry Irving's production of *Henry the Eighth* at the Lyceum?" I said.

"Yes, of course, by all means, if we're free and there is room for us. It's almost a duty, my boy, to see the best England can do in our own line of business," he replied with emphasis.

"Thursday is open, and we can go *then*," said I.

"How do you know we can get seats?" he asked.

"I'll write Mr. Irving," I replied.

"You'll do *what?* Oh, no, he'd think we have a monumental nerve," suggested Mr. Hopper.

"No," I murmured, "I'll write the note and show it to you before it's posted." I did that, and, Mr. Hopper agreeing, I sent it off.

A messenger arrived at our hotel on Wednesday with a reservation slip from the Lyceum Theatre booking office, showing that seats would be awaiting us on Thursday, as per request, but—*mirabile dictu*—across the face of the slip his own handwriting appeared: 'With Mr. Irving's love.'

We were both touched to the heart . . . stunned. Hopper spoke first:

"My boy," he rambled, "can you *beat that?* Why, if any producing manager in the United States, actor or layman, were to do a thing like that to me I'm sure I'd drop dead!"

Naturally, I related the episode with fervour a number of times after our return to New York, and there was always some cynic present who tried to dampen my ardour. "Don't you know," he would say, "that Henry Irving was a long-headed promoter? Didn't he have the celebrated Clement Scott, *littérateur* and dramatic critic, over here, visiting all our cities, for more than a year, and laying pipe in preparation for the advent of his organization in America? Take it from me, those stall seats sent you, when he was playing to capacity business, were in contemplation of future returns when he re-visits us."

At the moment I could only say that I didn't believe it.

England's Queen honoured the most illustrious figure of his country's Theatre with Knighthood in 1895, and in 1898, when he came back to us as Sir Henry Irving, I learned of a happening during his tour that enabled me to confute the cynic's suspicions for ever after.

Sir Henry was filling an engagement in an Ohio city. On his way to dress for a performance he stepped into the box office for a word with his representative there. Among other papers he was handed a note in which the writer, an actor sojourning in the place between engagements, requested seats as a professional courtesy. The house treasurer, when asked, identified the applicant as one who, while not exactly a theatrical luminary, was a competent and reliable follower of the actor's calling.

"Gratify his wishes, with my compliments," said Sir Henry.

"But, sir, we shall sell out!" protested the representative.

"Ah, then, we can better *afford* to extend a little fraternal hospitality," countered Sir Henry, kindly.

In 1881, when our revered Edwin Booth ended an unprosperous engagement in London, Henry Irving persuaded him to play a joint engagement in which they alternated in acting *rôles* such as Othello and Iago. Irving's motive was to aid a colleague to recoup some of his losses, and it was noble of him—not selfish. Too many of us are incredulous when true greatness of character reveals itself. No doubting Thomas, however, could impute to Sir Henry Irving any baseness when he provided Richard Mansfield with a large sum of money after he had come a cropper in London, and could not get himself, company, scenery, or effects back to the United States, without aid.

The production of Shakespeare's *Henry the Eighth* that De Wolfe Hopper and I saw, by courtesy, in 1892, made a lasting impression on us. We had never before seen a theatrical presentation wherein the auditorium, stage settings, the cast, and the spectators were so completely in agreement. Between the acts we read in the programme folder the announcement of a special performance to be given in a few days to aid the Actors' Benevolent Fund—the beneficent Sir Henry and his staff would have charge of it in the Lyceum Theatre, and we felt a grateful urge to attend. In fact we deferred visiting Paris, as planned, to do so. Luckily we were able to purchase good seats, for it was a superb bill including all the most highly accomplished dramatic artists in England.

In the spring of 1898 Phœbe Davis and I did a scene from *Way Down East* in the annual bill to aid the Actors' Fund of America, at the then Broadway Theatre. Sir Henry, in *Waterloo*, was a feature of the programme. Of course, Hopper and I had sent him a note of appreciation, six years before in London, but I was sorely tempted to recall the experience and tender him more thanks orally. But I refrained. His place on the bill was the second following us, and by hastily changing, after coming off the stage, I succeeded in getting around to the standing-room space of the auditorium, whence I saw *Waterloo*, and discerned the fine art in the portrayal of the old soldier.

Isn't it interesting to consider the varying degrees of power with which different notable actors impress an audience, mindful, of course, that *all* auditors do not have quite the same measure of receptivecapacity?

Ten yearsago, when the radio as a means of public expression was in the experimental stage in New York, I was retained as a broadcaster to help in popularizing it. The microphones were placed on the top floor of a high building. On one occasion I launched *Waterloo* upon the ether, essaying Sir Henry Irving's *rôle*, the old soldier, myself. The dialect was clearly shown in the little book of the play I held, and I had no desire to imitate the grand characterization I had beheld thirty years before, yet despite that, the portrayal by Sir Henry was reincarnated beside me throughout my interpretation.

Now I had seen Sir Beerbohm Tree as Gringoire, in *The Ballad Monger*, on the Actors' Benevolent Fund programme in 1892 and enjoyed it greatly. But when I broadcast Gringoire myself I was not haunted by any wraith.

Sir Henry Irving's great qualities as a man and an artist won him the first invitation ever extended to an actor to speak at Oxford University. All of his colleagues of the English-speaking Theatre, who love and respect their calling, realize that such recognition of it, through him, as an important cultural force in civilization, raised their social status immeasurably.

We should all glorify his memory for ever and for aye!

Howard Kyle.

XXXVII

IRVING as KING LEAR

Lyceum Theatre, 10th of November, 1892 :—

KING LEAR

WRITTEN BY WILLIAM SHAKESPEARE

Lear	MR. IRVING
Edgar	MR. WILLIAM TERRISS
Edmund	MR. FRANK COOPER
Earl of Glo'ster	MR. ALFRED BISHOP
Earl of Kent	MR. W. J. HOLLOWAY
Duke of Cornwall	MR. HAGUE
Duke of Albany	MR. TYARS
King of France	MR. PERCIVAL
Duke of Burgundy	MR. BOND
Curan	MR. HARVEY
Old Man	MR. HOWE
Fool	MR. HAVILAND
Oswald	MR. GORDON CRAIG
Physician	MR. LACY
A Knight	MR. TABB
A Gentleman	MR. IAN ROBERTSON
An Officer	MR. LORRISS
A Herald	MR. BELMORE
A Messenger	MR. POWELL
Goneril	MISS ADA DYAS
Regan	MISS MAUD MILTON
Cordelia	MISS ELLEN TERRY

ACT I, SCENE 1. *King Lear's Palace ;* SCENE 2. *Earl of Glo'ster's Castle ;* SCENE 3. *Duke of Albany's Castle.* ACT II, SCENE 1. *Court within Glo'ster Castle ;* SCENE 2. *Open Country ;* SCENE 3, *Court within Castle.* ACT III, SCENE 1. *A Heath ;* SCENE 2. *Another part of the Heath ;* SCENE 3. *A Farm-house.* ACT IV, SCENE 1. *Albany Castle ;* SCENE 2. *Open Country ;* SCENE 3. *Country near Dover ;* SCENE 4. *French Camp ;* SCENE 5. *Tent in the French Camp.* ACT V, SCENE 1. *British Camp near Dover ;* SCENE 2. *The same.* SCENE. *Britain.*

WHENEVER I think of Irving's King Lear I vividly remember the reading of the play in the foyer of the old Lyceum Theatre, two or three days before we commenced rehearsing on the stage. The whole cast read their parts sitting around informally, with the Chief unhurriedly explaining and illuminating the text, scene by scene. A word here, a word there, as to the characterization and conception of the whole play for his already prepared production.

His reading of the old King was magnificent, voice, speech, both his servants during those early days. He conveyed the overwhelming tragedy of the play without apparent effort. In consequence, we had the privilege of listening to a superb mental conception unimpeded by first-night nervousness, or any sense of physical discomfort during even the scenes of the greatest strain, thus demonstrating that he was equal to the demands that Shakespeare asks of the actor who plays his great, if not his greatest, creation.

The turbulent, masterful King of the early scenes, with a distinct suggestion of incipient madness; the great curse scene; then the mad scenes, culminating, I believe, in the most beautiful scene in all Shakespeare—Lear's awakening to reason with Cordelia at his side, which closes with the words 'forget and forgive, I am old and foolish.'

Irving's reading of Lear has remained with me as an unforgettable memory. I join issue with some of the conclusions of Austin Brereton when writing of *King Lear*, in his Life of Irving. He says:

> 'Irving's knowledge of his limitations as an actor was never used more to his advantage than in the revival of *King Lear*. He knew, none so well, that he could not realize, as other actors had endeavoured to do, the colossal terror of the tragedy. He had not the physical means to make his voice sound like thunder in the very rafters of the theatre. He could not shout and storm and stamp as Ernesto Rossi had done a few years before at the old theatre, Her Majesty's, in the Haymarket. Nor could he approach the fine but physical delineation of Tommaso Salvini the greater of the two Italian actors—who laid stress upon the robust side of the character and made the King Lear of the earlier part of the play a typical sportsman, hunter, and rider, of sound constitution and without any suggestion, in the first act, of approaching insanity.'

Brereton mentions other outstanding Lears in the history of the Stage—Garrick (one of his great parts); Edmund Kean (restoring the Shakespeare text); Macready (reinstating the Fool); also Samuel Phelps (during his production of the thirty-four Shakespearean plays), and Charles Kean (with an elaborate production at the old Princess's).

Irving took his own view of what Swinburne calls 'the most terrible work of human genius.' I quote again from Brereton's Life to give his remembrance of the latter part of the play: 'and although it was impossible for him to realize completely the terrific nature of the character, no one who witnessed the performance could forget the infinite pathos of the later scenes between King Lear and Cordelia.

'In Miss Ellen Terry he had a Cordelia of matchless sympathy, but he so filled the old King and father with a wealth of tenderness that the conciliation scene between " the very foolish fond old man " and his daughter was one of the most profoundly beautiful passages ever seen, even on the stage of the Lyceum.'

Brereton reminds us that, as he himself said, in after years, of a welcome given to him, 'it is a fragrant memory.' It was one of the finest moments in the acting of Miss Terry, for she was doubly inspired by her own view of the character, and by the sublimity of Irving. She shed real tears, and when Lear asked: " Be your tears wet? " and touched her with his long, wan fingers, and put the salt drops to his lips before he made reply, " Yes, faith," the spectators were also moved to tears. It was a scene which can only be described by the one word—exquisite. Men far less in intellect, though robust in stature, and with voices like the peal of an organ, have given the commanding and terrific side to Lear, but no other Lear has so touched the heart.

When Brereton says that 'Irving could not realize, as other actors had endeavoured to do, the colossal terror of the tragedy,' he seems to me to be unconsciously belittling a man who had always full realization of any of the characters he prepared for the stage. Although his voice could not actually convey a sense of thunder, he did, at the reading and subsequently during the run, suggest the man capable of great flights, even of physical power.

It is worth noting that the Lyceum production of *King Lear* ran for three months, seventy-two consecutive performances.

A number of these performances I saw from the O.P. Corner. Irving was good enough to grant me that privilege. For it was a privilege for a young actor to be able to watch the development of a character as it was built up, by a master of his art, night by night on the stage, by innumerable subtle touches, the give and take of the voice according to the necessity of the scenes, his fine sense of timing, pausing, sometimes a little on the slow side, but always significant. We have been told that on the first night a good deal of the text was inaudible; also, it has been alleged, that Irving did an amazing thing on the first night. He decided to give almost a new interpretation from the one he had rehearsed. I cannot say personally about the one or the other allegation for, though I had a small part only in one scene, there was no opportunity for a member of the cast to see the performance on the first night from any part of the house.

I can only speak of those inestimable opportunities I had of seeing Irving, from the privileged corner, develop his performance of Lear. Other plays I witnessed in this way were *Henry the Eighth* and *Becket*, but neither of them was built up after the early performances as Lear was.

To me, as I watched the play, Irving's Lear, before the end of the run, became one of his greatest performances.

The heath scenes, whether in presentation on the stage or as dramatic readings, which I organized as Director of the B.E.S.S. in London and in many places in the kingdom, have always proved a difficult proposition. When the voice could, more or less, outdo the thunder, the mind often was not able to convey the mighty conception of the tragedy.

During my first touring days I was in a minor production of *Lear*—the mad scenes then gave all of us plenty to think and talk about. The talking and thinking still goes on—I would not have it otherwise. The severe voice test that starts with the curse speech that comes early in the play, then the heath scenes almost continuously until nearly the end of the Fourth Act, is an accumulating strain on the actor, quite apart from the mental and psychological aspects of the character. The heath scenes with Edgar as ' Poor Tom's a cold ' feigning madness and in consequence deliberately making considerable noise; the bursts of passion and anger from the mad Lear himself, the chorus-like comments of the Fool, including Gloucester and Kent, contribute respectively to the titanic creation of this overwhelming tragedy.

In Ellen Terry's *Memoirs* we read: ' Henry Irving is hard at work studying Lear. That is what only a great man would do at such a moment in the hottest flush of success.' (This was referring to the success of *Henry the Eighth*.) ' No swelled head —only fervent endeavour to do better work. The fools hardly conceive what he is.' Apparently, Ellen Terry did not agree with the allegation that Irving changed his conception of Lear on the first night. She says: ' Henry was just marvellous, but indistinct from nervousness. Terriss, as Edgar, spoke out, but who cared? Haviland, as Fool, was very good. My Ted (Gordon Craig) was splendid in the little bit he had to do as Oswald. I was rather good to-night. Cordelia *is* a wee part but a fine one all the same.' To me, her Cordelia was one of her loveliest performances. The last scenes between Lear and Cordelia have fragrant memories which will never leave me.

I must speak of Irving's striking appearance as Lear in the first scene of the play, the make-up and costume cleverly suggesting a man of wider proportions than he himself possessed, the ample robe-like dress was very full and magnificent: in fact, as the text suggests, he looked 'every inch a king.' Bernard Partridge, in the Lyceum Souvenir of *Lear*, gave a fine, faithful 'counterfeit presentment' of Irving as the King. Whenever I see this picture I recall the performances as clearly as though the run was in the immediate past instead of over forty years ago. A largeness of conception permeated the whole production and, whenever and wherever I directed a dramatic reading of *King Lear* during my twenty-one years as Director of the British Empire Shakespeare Society, I constantly kept in mind the precepts of the Chief.

It would not be easy to write all that my two years at the Lyceum have meant to me as actor, producer, and teacher, but I can state with all sincerity that I could not have played many of the leading Shakespearean and other parts without the experience I gained at the Lyceum in the great days under Irving. I am ever his grateful pupil.

A. ACTON-BOND.

XXXVIII

IRVING as THOMAS BECKET

Lyceum Theatre, 6th of February, 1893 :—

BECKET

WRITTEN BY ALFRED, LORD TENNYSON
(*Adapted for the stage by Henry Irving*)

Thomas Becket	MR. IRVING
Henry II	MR. WILLIAM TERRISS
King Louis of France	MR. BOND
Gilbert Foliot	MR. LACY
Roger	MR. BEAUMONT
Bishop of Hereford	MR. CUSHING
Hilary	MR. ARCHER
John of Salisbury	MR. BISHOP
Herbert of Bosham	MR. HAVILAND
Edward Grim	MR. W. J. HOLLOWAY
Sir Reginald Fitzurse	MR. FRANK COOPER
Sir Richard de Brito	MR. TYARS
Sir William de Tracy	MR. HAGUE
Sir Hugh de Morville	MR. PERCIVAL
De Broc	MR. TABB
Richard de Hastings	MR. SELDON
The Youngest Knight Templar	MR. GORDON CRAIG
Lord Leicester	MR. HARVEY
Philip de Eleemosyna	MR. HOWE
Herald	MR. L. BELMORE
Geoffrey	MASTER LEO BYRNE
Retainers	MR. YELDHAM MR. LORRISS
Countrymen	MR. JOHNSON MR. REYNOLDS
John of Oxford	MR. IAN ROBERTSON
Servant	MR. DAVIS
Eleanor of Aquitaine	MISS GENEVIÈVE WARD
Margery	MISS KATE PHILLIPS
Rosamund de Clifford	MISS ELLEN TERRY

PROLOGUE, SCENE 1. *A Castle in Normandy;* SCENE 2. *The Same.* ACT I, SCENE 1. *Becket's House in London;* SCENE 2. *Street in Northampton leading to the Castle;* SCENE 3. *The Same;* SCENE 4. *The Hall in Northampton Castle.* ACT II, SCENE. *Rosamund's Bower.* ACT III, SCENE 1. *Montmirail—'The Meeting of the Kings';* SCENE 2. *Outside the Wood near Rosamund's Bower;* SCENE 3. *Rosamund's Bower.* ACT IV, SCENE 1. *Castle in Normandy;—King's Chamber;* SCENE 2. *A Room in Canterbury Monastery;* SCENE 3. *North Transept of Canterbury Cathedral.*

THERE are six men, great in their work, whom I have had the privilege of really knowing, and whose influence on my life has had a positive effect. One of them is Henry Irving.

It is curious that I should be able to speak of Irving as really knowing him, because I was only ten to fifteen years of age when I used to feel the touch of his hand on my shoulder, and was conscious of his charm and penetrating understanding. My father, the Rev. Reginald Barnes, was a friend of Irving's ; and, indeed, Irving gave my sister, Violet Vanbrugh, her first big chance.

I suppose Irving realized how genuinely thrilled I was by the plays at the Lyceum, for he told me that if I wrote him a letter in my own hand he would always give me two seats for any of his productions. Naturally, I did not overlook this 'fairy godfather' offer. I was at an impressionable age. I can remember the states of absorption and transport which Irving and the plays at the Lyceum created in me.

I use the word 'transport' because there was something in the atmosphere which took me completely out of myself and riveted attention. On looking back I realize that these sensations were created by Irving's imagination, that I had been magnetized, taken up and carried along with his personality. I have never since experienced in the theatre such complete detachment from myself and absorption in what was taking place on the stage.

I remember an occasion upon which he let me stand in the prompt box throughout a performance of *Faust*. I had heard of the Brocken scene, which signalized the triumph of Mephistopheles, and he asked me whether I would like to come and see how it was done. I can still smell the sulphurous fumes, and hear the thunder, and see the golden rain falling from the flies, and I still remember the touch of Irving's hand, clothed in scarlet, as he came to me at the end of the play and took me along to see Ellen Terry.

It is amazing how many passages in Irving's productions still remain vividly in my imagination after so many years. The last time I saw him act was as Becket, the year before he died. I was at the back of the pit, a long way from the stage, and I remember enjoying Irving's performance more on that occasion than I had when I had first seen the play. He expressed in the character not only the dignity required for it but the weariness which a great man must feel when approaching the end of his struggle in life.

IRVING *as* BECKET

There was a wonderful, almost infinite, pathos in his rendering of the later scenes of the play, and his eyes seemed to be looking straight across the auditorium at me; and no doubt hundreds in the auditorium had the same impression.

In his eyes and his hands Irving showed himself to be an absolute master of dramatic expression; every look and every movement conveyed the inner thought and feeling of the character. His voice was not a perfect instrument for an actor, he was inclined to increase the tone in a way that would not be approved by the best masters of voice production; and when he was putting in these overtones his speech was not always as distinct as it should have been, but when he used his voice without this additional force it had a fine carrying power, and his diction came to the ear as perfect.

This last performance of Becket struck me as quieter than the one I had previously seen; and I remember, on coming away, that from the back of the pit I had been able to hear every word he spoke. I shall never forget his rendering of the speech:

> 'Am I the man? That rang
> Within my head last night, and when I slept
> Methought I stood in Canterbury Minster,
> And spake to the Lord God, and said, "O Lord,
> Am I the man?" And the Lord answer'd me,
> "Thou art the man, and all the more the man."'

It made a deep impression on me. I had a strong conviction that this was the last time I should see Irving on the stage, and it was; although I saw him once again a little later at the Garrick Club, just before he started on his last tour, and we spoke of the days when, as a little boy, I used to go to the Lyceum as his guest.

In *Becket*, his great achievement was not only as an actor but as a man of the Theatre, because he had been able to transform a play which, in itself, was inclined to be unwieldy and in parts tedious, despite the magnificent passages in it, into a noble work of dramatic art. Bram Stoker records in his book the amount of work that Irving had to do on the script to give the play any chance of success on the stage; and how Tennyson had given him a free hand. This could only have been done by a creative artist of first-class talent.

Irving gave to Becket, as indeed he did to all the characters he impersonated, not only vitality, but stature; and this he accomplished, without physical advantages, through the power of his imagination and his technique. As Becket he had to achieve the stature of a saint, and he did so to the full ; and with this sense of power he combined acute tenderness of feeling. There is an absence of this quality of stature among actors of the present day. They are apt, perhaps, to confuse stature with what is known as ' ham acting ' ; but there never was any stature in ham acting, which is superficially put on from outside, whereas an impression of stature must come from within, and magnify not the actor's self but the character he is acting.

I think it is untrue to say that Irving shaped his theatrical productions around himself. He realized, of course, that the central figure would be the pivot of the play, and that he himself would have the responsibility of being the central figure ; but in his mind he shaped his productions as a great man of the Theatre, and not as a selfish leading actor. His aim was to give the public a whole performance that would appeal, and would elevate, and there is no doubt that he accomplished this work as nobody since him has accomplished it on the English Stage.

He had the power of appealing not only to the emotions, but to the intellect of his audiences. He was able to magnify the human personality ; even when he was interpreting the murderer Mathias in *The Bells* he conveyed somehow the greatness of the human soul as only a genius could have done.

Oh ! for another Irving, say I !

KENNETH R. BARNES.

I well remember the impression Irving made upon me when I first saw him as Becket.

He strode across the stage, an immense figure swinging his great cloak of scarlet—he was the centre of the stage, all else was dimmed by the magnificence, the tremendous personality of Becket, and when Becket spoke, the audience was stilled. The power and intensity of thought penetrated, vibrated, and, conveyed by his magnetic force, set tingling every nerve. Irving dominated ; he was not passive or statuesque ; he had the quality of greatness to command and to compel attention.

Irving *was* Becket. His mind was so absorbed in the character that you felt you were actually in the presence of this mighty man, this great saint, whose voice, harsh and terrible, was shattering in the great scene where Becket is asked or commanded to sign the document. Irving, robed in a black cassock, his mind set on martyrdom, drew himself up to his full height—taller, thinner, and yet taller ; he paused, and then rapped out in a mad frenzy of ever-rising crescendo : " And that I will not sign—and that I will not sign." It was as though a blizzard had swept through the theatre. We in the gallery felt icy, shivering and exhausted, and when the end came the spell was not broken; even though we shouted ourselves hoarse, the picture remained, and will remain as long as life lasts.

Soon after—at a public luncheon given to commemorate the name of Sarah Siddons, after the unveiling of her statue in Paddington—I met Irving, the man. The magnificence had gone. The courtier took my hand, bowing, not towering, and he spoke in a soft, low voice, kindly and gently. When he addressed the audience Irving spoke as a suppliant, almost apologetically. . . . 'Your humble servant.' Irving was the actor, the great artist on and off the stage.

LILLAH MACCARTHY.

Extract from the Rev. Stopford A. Brooke's letter to Gerald Lawrence.

1 MANCHESTER SQUARE, W.
20th May, 1905.

I had not seen *Becket* since its first night seven years ago and I was delighted to see it again. It is most remarkable what Irving has made of the play which as it stands in Tennyson's work can scarcely be called drama. As it has been brought together by Sir Henry, it makes a fine thing, with the exception of the scenes between Rosamund and the King in the bower and the Eleanor and Rosamund part. I cannot endure those scenes. Tennyson ought to have written them well. They are, I think, the most inadequate and irritating things, both in conception and execution that he ever did. I wish they were excised and the play left only as the struggle between the crown and the church—between Henry and Becket.

I was profoundly moved and impressed by Sir Henry. When I saw him long ago I thought his representation one of the finest things I had ever seen, and his intellectual conception of the church and its aims and power in Becket as great as his passionate representation of the man himself possessed with the impassionating idea which fills his soul and I admired as much the emergence through this, at certain times, of the natural tenderness and grace of the man who moved beneath the priest.

But this time it was better. All the nobility of the representation was greater, more dignified, solemn and thoughtful than it was some years ago. It was a very noble and solemn thing to see: and the last scene was magnificently done and staged. But the man was infinitely finer than the staging.

Very sincerely yours,

STOPFORD A. BROOKE.

In the prompt copy of an address spoken by Henry Irving at Oxford on 26 June 1886, corrected, signed, and presented by him to me, Irving, whilst proudly acknowledging the honour of the invitation he had received from the ' Distinguished Vice-Chancellor ' to lecture before members of ' this great University,' replied that he could only say something about his own ' Profession.'

The word ' Profession ' he has, however, deleted, and in the margin, in his own unmistakable handwriting, Irving has substituted for ' Profession '—' CALLING '—and as such he invariably alluded to the Art he worshipped—the Art to which he dedicated his life, the Art he raised to the highest pinnacle of dignity and refinement, the Art he tasselled and threaded with endless gems that must remain for ever ' beaded ' in the rosary of remembrance encircling the amazing reign of Henry Irving at the Lyceum Theatre.

From the instant that Lord Tennyson suggested Thomas à Becket, Statesman, Chancellor of England, Archbishop of Canterbury, martyr and saint, as the foundation of a fine tragedy, Henry Irving became obsessed with the idea. His pulses throbbed and tingled with excitement. To give a study of this whole galaxy of characters merged into one seemed to him to be the crowning point of his every ambition.

He had frozen his audiences stiff with the weird, mysterious, and psychological side of nature—he had astounded them with the artistry of his senile, his drunken, his diabolically cruel and fantastic figures, every study a mastery of detail, and perfectly finished—but no ideal from dreamland could rival in his imagination the beauty of Becket and its calmly exquisite simplicity.

Though not exactly a misogynist—I certainly think that in early life Irving must have qualified for the part—he had always pictured himself in such a character as the Becket his fancy had painted, that of a pale, cultured, refined, and highly intellectual ascetic.

Strange as it may appear, Irving had the very gravest objection to being called a character actor, arguing that every part he played must of necessity be a character, and that before assuming the ' skin ' of another man, personal individuality should be entirely shed.

Bram Stoker—Irving's lusty red-haired Irish henchman—the most faithful, loyal, and devoted servitor Henry Irving ever had, ushered me into the ' Chief's ' dressing-room one evening before the play had started. He urged me gently round the tall screen, draped as usual with the costliest brocades and embroideries.

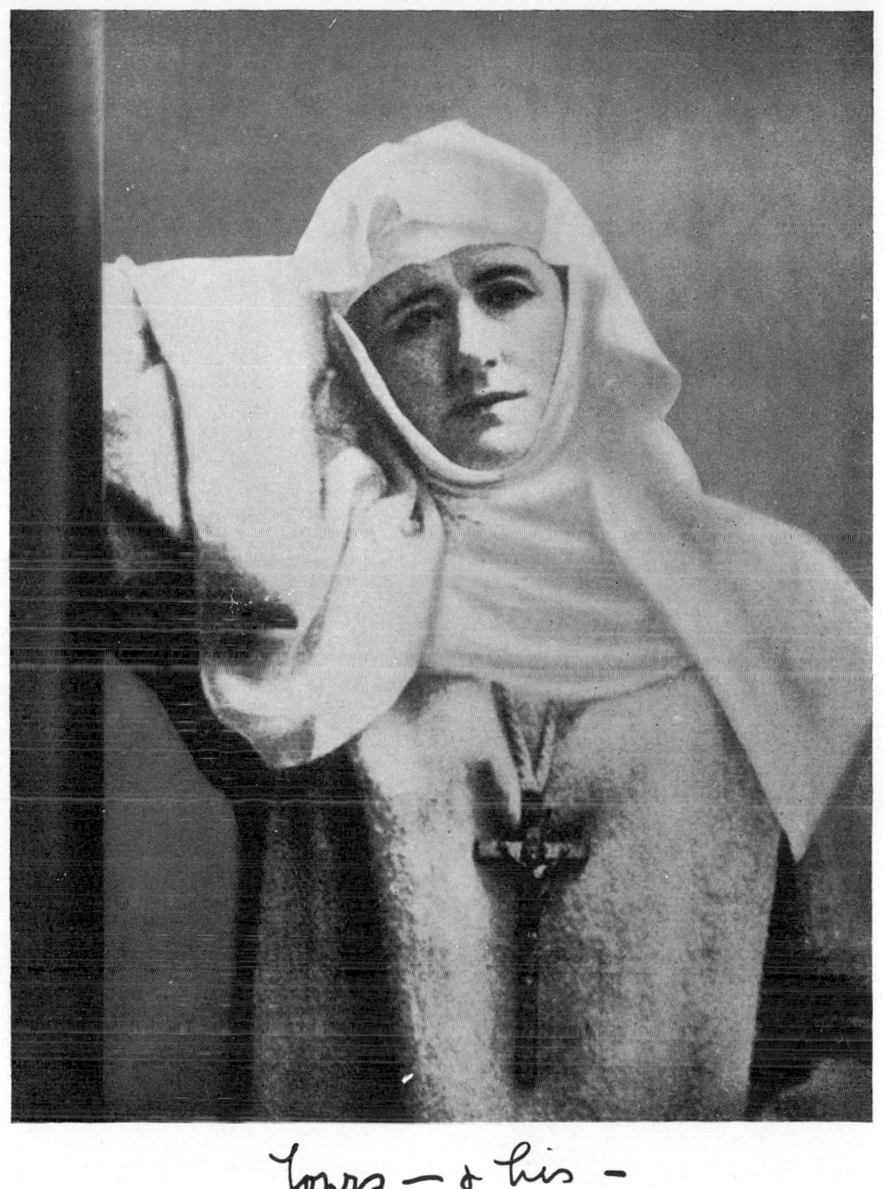

ELLEN TERRY *as Fair Rosamund in BECKET*

Seated before a long mirror in a high-backed regal-looking chair, I discovered Henry Irving holding a powder-puff. I laughed—I simply couldn't help it.

"What is amusing you?" Irving asked quite seriously.

"To see you powdering your face, I suppose."

"I am not doing anything of the kind. I am going to paint a picture. A picture of Goethe's Mephisto—my face is merely the empty canvas on which I do my work."

And his words set me thinking. Henry Irving always did make you think. If he only said a little, he made you think a lot. But Henry Irving was a great man, he had genuinely great ideas—and beautiful ideas—and he held to them, and did immense good with them, and a man must be great who can have the ideas Irving had and carry them through to success as he undoubtedly did.

To return to Becket. Unfortunately, the ennobling vision Irving, with his imaginative brain, had conjured up and the one Tennyson had fashioned did not harmonize at all. Discordant notes jarred and jangled—where you expected sweet melody, ear-cracking minor chords crashed and tore your nerves to pieces. But Irving swept all his fears into the background and bade Tennyson send the MS. for him to read.

And thus, for the first time, and that as far back as 1879—fourteen or fifteen years before the production of the play—the vast handwritten manuscript numbering endless acts and still more endless scenes, passed over the threshold of the Lyceum Theatre into Irving's room, and there it remained, occupying a fairly large portion of the apartment. Both Irving and Stoker were staggered at this monster bale of literature—they walked up to it—paused before it—glared at it—grunted and moved on—both of them feeling too weak to cut the rope and let poor Thomas free. Finally, the Poet Laureate became impatient. He wrote and begged for news of Becket. Directly the cord released the bulge—Irving knew from a glance at the first few pages how insurmountable were the obstacles and difficulties facing him.

Tennyson had no theatre sense whatever, but, as a rule, he would listen to those who did have it, and in this capacity Henry Irving had no peer. Still yearning for Becket, Irving deftly tried diplomacy. With the subtlety of a Richelieu he insinuated a few judicious touches which might twist Becket into somewhat more the shape he pictured him. The poet, discreetly non-committal, did not answer yea or nay to the hints thrown out to him.

His persuasive powers running dry, the actor then centred his attention on the beauties of simplicity—of expression—and, finally, on the dangers of over-elaboration. Once more the arguments fell on dead soil. He could make no impression whatever on the self-important author, so Irving changed his tactics completely.

He could not visualize any other artist in England being seriously interested in Becket, and, odd as it may seem, one and all of the friends to whom he had spoken of the play failed to see eye to eye with Irving.

This being the case—Irving argued—why worry? All the same he felt more determined than ever, to conquer at any price, and so with the utmost delicacy and perfect discretion, Irving 'hedged.'

"*Becket* is too long as it is," he remarked musingly to Tennyson, "at least for my theatre—but the arrangement of it is so good that *I personally dare not touch it*—but—will you try and do me something shorter? I want a very dramatic, powerful, and picturesque story to follow *The Corsican Brothers*. If you feel inclined—write me the drama I suggest—and I'll accept it."

The Poet Laureate, only too keen to have any work of his running at the Lyceum Theatre, wrote to order and in his own incomparable verse evolved *The Cup*, a superbly sumptuous production in which Ellen Terry looked her very loveliest as the imperious Camma. Of Ellen Terry, with her supreme grace and poetry of motion, Charles Reade (one time lessee of the Old Queen's Theatre, Long Acre, in which Ellen Terry and Henry Irving first met and acted together) described her acting in these words: 'Whether in movement or repose—GRACE PERVADES THE HUSSY'; Ellen Terry wearing her ethereal classical draperies as she only could wear them, and leaving memory damascened with enchanting impressions that absolutely baffle description.

With the advent of *The Cup* Irving broke all records. Never before in the history of the stage had so priceless a jewel been set in so costly a surround—never before in the history of the theatrical world had such a galaxy of talent been called upon to add radiance to so dramatic a masterpiece.

That night, 3 January 1881, Irving climbed the steps to fame higher than he had ever climbed before. What a startling contrast—this flood of wealth, the deafening shouts of approbation, the crowds of distinguished guests, his extravagant home at 15a Grafton Street, Bond Street, and his once modest little suite of rooms in Quebec Street leading into Portman Square where, notwithstanding his humble dwelling, Charles Dickens and so many gifted fortunates gathered round to listen to the youthful actor's clamorous harangues for the renaissance of the English stage—his wild diatribes condemning the outrageous incompetence of the age and its dogged persistency to canonize the commonplace.

But although his friends listened patiently, not one of them really believed that Irving would ever fulfil the task he swore to accomplish—neither did they see in him a ruler with power to command.

"Be careful—be careful," they urged.

"Be careful be damned—to be careful means two steps backwards and I am going forward. I shall rise—I shall not fall—I shall win—I shall not lose." And the frenzied tempestuous words of Henry Irving came true. He did triumph, as no other actor in England ever has done or ever will do again.

And what of Ellen Terry—who will decide—who can decide how much Irving owed to Ellen Terry in the early years of his managerial career? A more ideally enchanting Consort to share the Throne of the Lyceum King it would have been impossible to find.

Clement Scott writes of her:

> 'I wish I could paint with pen, an even vague suggestion of this exquisitely divine personality. Tall, fair, willowy, with hair like spun gold, a faultless complexion, perfect symmetry of movement, and a wonderful deep-toned voice with a tender heart-throb in it that started involuntary tears to coldest eyes. What wonder that artists went mad about her. At the time when I first knew Ellen Terry she inspired fancies of every romantic heroine we most adored in poetry, and when she had done idealizing Tennyson, Browning, William Morris and Rosetti this mystic spirit fled with our illusory imagination to fairyland and became Undine or the idol of Sintram and his companions and the Shadowless Man.'

In these few lines clipped from a letter written by W. G. Wills, the poet-author of so many of the Lyceum successes, he pays affectionate tribute to Ellen Terry's exceptional gifts.

> 'My dear Scott—I will then send you on my book of plays, and you will write and tell me how much I am indebted to the expression of Ellen Terry's reading, and how little my worth would have been without her ideal conception of the characters so divinely played by this enthralling actress. Yours very cordially, W. G. Wills.'

From Ellen Terry herself, I repeat a small extract of a sympathetic little note she wrote to Clement immediately after she had seen his *Daily Telegraph* notice of Margaret in Wills' version of *Faust*.

> 'It is difficult to see the paper, dear Clement, for my eyes are full of tears; but you are wrong, dear friend—quite, quite wrong—I am not a great actress, I am not indeed, I am only a very useful one to Henry. Yours, and yours, and yours affectionately, Ellen Terry.'

Truly an amazingly beautiful partnership. Irving when speaking of Ellen Terry always alluded to her as 'My Partner—or My dear Partner.'

The phenomenal triumph of *The Cup* dimmed for a short space the fascinating figure of Becket. Tennyson had sent his rejected manuscript of *Becket* to Wilson Barrett, then lessee of the old Princess's Theatre, which stood on the site where Waring & Gillow stands now. Barrett had just made an enormous hit with *The Silver King*, a most thrillingly sensational English melodrama by Henry Arthur Jones.

Irving was much relieved when he heard that Barrett had returned *Becket* to its author with a curt message accompanying it: '*Becket* would have to be re-written, and reconstructed. I do not think the author would alter it as it *must* be altered before it could succeed.'

At this precise moment there came another turning-point in Henry Irving's surprising life. America offered him a substantial sum for a short tour, and added a rider to the effect that if it were a question of money any amount would be forthcoming.

Irving chose to accept this amazingly generous proposition as an honour bestowed on his Calling. And with his departure for the States another shadow veiled the image of Becket.

At this juncture, however, Irving decided to be very difficult. He point-blank refused to travel in the orthodox fashion. Why should he have to buy four or six berths in order to get a strip of a cabin to himself—he did not intend to do it. He might perhaps find a boat on which were two or three small suites—but even this did not satisfy him—so he continued to be awkward, and thoroughly unconventional. At last he had a brain-wave. He chartered an entire ship—and for the first, and two or more subsequent tours, the *Mauretania* took him, his company, his scenery, his faithful little Fussie, and all his effects across the Atlantic. And thus, by becoming controller of his own ship,

Henry Irving overcame all discomforts—he started on his journey when he pleased, took as long as he wanted over the voyage and travelled like a king with every luxury he could possibly need.

The ill-fated *Becket* cropped up again while Irving was in America. Tennyson had published his play in book form, and the Martyred Saint—released from his incarceration—could be purchased and perused for about two dollars by anyone requiring to inspect him. Tennyson then wrote many letters to Irving, but none of them received an answer. The poet therefore considered himself very ill-used, and did not hesitate to say so.

Towards the end of the eighties Irving, having mutilated many copies of the printed version of *Becket*, completed as he thought a fairly fine play from the poet's story. He submitted it to Comyns Carr—at odd intervals playwright, theatre manager, reader for Irving, but always a barrister, a merry genial soul. Everybody loved him and his dear wife Alice, who designed many of Ellen Terry's gowns and robes. Comyns Carr's opinion coincided entirely with the actor's. Mr. Carr saw an immense opportunity for Irving as Becket. On the strength of this favourable verdict, Henry Irving invited Tennyson to come and see him.

The play then consisted of a prologue, four acts and about a dozen scenes, just as it did when finally produced.

Irving had begun to read the final act when the Poet Laureate, without uttering a word, rose from his chair, collected his outsize sombrero and strode from the room. Bram Stoker, hovering around in the passage and hearing footsteps, came forward, only to be passed in silence, the poet continuing his way towards the exit through which he disappeared.

Irving, more shocked than angry at Tennyson's abrupt departure, made no further move. He did not even demand a reason for such rudeness. They remained at loggerheads with one another until a tiny slip on the wide stairway at the Athenæum Club brought them together again. They spoke—the breach narrowed—and in the late autumn of 1891 Irving received a play from Tennyson at the moment when he had begun rehearsing his gorgeous presentation of *Henry the Eighth*.

That same year preliminaries were begun with the idea of producing *Becket* in November. The perpetual discussions and disagreements lasted longer than the rehearsals—and precautionary measures were being taken so that *King Lear* could be put on at a very short notice if any emergency required it. With the death of Alfred, Lord Tennyson, in October 1892—

too late for *Becket* to be presented that year as Irving had intended—Shakespeare filled the bill instead.

On 6 February 1893, Irving's fifty-third birthday, the curtain rang up on *Becket* in the presence of an audience unprecedented in distinction—and one of the rarest in Art, Literature, Music, Song, and Science. Never in the whole of his career had any one of Irving's productions been received with such rapture. The two performances in the Henry Irving repertoire that may rightly be pronounced as well nigh faultless are his Louis the Eleventh and Thomas à Becket, both perfect in thoughtful, detailed, and pictorial art.

I quote a paragraph from *The Daily Telegraph* written by Clement Scott of Irving's Becket.

> 'We are inclined to think that Becket is the very greatest of all Henry Irving's stupendous achievements at the Lyceum. Splendid as have been his artistic gifts for the stage, this is, in a measure, his very finest and his best. In the first place—a fact so little understood by the public, and less than ever by the poet with a hunger for the stage—Henry Irving has created a play out of an undramatic poem. He has formed a dramatic substance out of an undramatic cloud.
>
> 'Lord Tennyson's play? For the stage impossible. Look at it now when deftly handled by the craftsman, and behold a play that will last as long as an actor is found who can live in the part of the Chancellor Churchman as Henry Irving does. It is a triumph for an artist to be able in so short a space of time to convey the illumination as it were of a life vowed to duty and consecrated by Faith.
>
> 'The Becket who plays chess with the King—who wears his gorgeous lay robes, who shows his statecraft and ambition—is not the Becket who has become half divine with the sense of his coming martyrdom. Henry Irving has never done anything so subtle, so delicate, or so artistically graduated as this merging of the statesman into the saint.
>
> 'The smile is ever there, so sweet, so captivating, so indicative of character. The smile of the man that won the King's favour is the smile of the martyr ennobled by self-sacrifice and the sense of approaching death. Never during the last thirty odd years has poetry been more faultlessly delivered by an artist. Every line, every sentence, falls with rhythmical measure on delighted ear. It would be difficult to find an elocutionist anywhere who could do more justice to the verse of Alfred, Lord Tennyson than Henry Irving. I have listened to nothing better for many a long day, and then that smile! We have heard of an actress's laugh, or some other memorial link that brings back the past to the present, but it seems to me that in after years, if ever they

come, the sweet smile of Henry Irving as Becket will "haunt me still." Resignation, determination, and the proud spirit of a man chastened by religion were never shown with finer effect. I once thought that Henry Irving could never beat his own record in Louis XI, but he has done so in Becket. As I write I can see his parting with Ophelia in *Hamlet*, his superb individuality in *Vanderdecken*, his exit as Shylock, his exquisite pathos as Dr. Primrose, Vicar of Wakefield, his picturesque devilry as Iago, his combined comedy and tragedy as Louis; but high above them all stands that exquisite preparation for martyrdom in *Becket*. Nothing more beautiful or less artificial has ever been seen on the stage of our time. *Becket* is in every respect a play of which English art can be justly proud.'

As the curtain fell on the final picture of *Becket*—the audience rose *en masse*—they burst into uproarious cheering—they stood up on their seats, they waved and shrieked themselves hoarse. They were literally mad with excitement, and noise seemed to be the only way they could express their approval of the new play.

They clamoured for a speech. Henry Irving, released from the strain and anxiety, knowing that at last his dream had been fulfilled and that others understood and appreciated the wonders of *Becket* as he did, stepped forward to offer his thanks for the overwhelming reception his new production had received, winding up, as he always did, with his usual graceful hand gesture and "We thank you—we thank you one and all, and remain as ever *your very humble servants to command*." The idea came from the Royal Command Performances which, whether at Balmoral, Windsor, Buckingham Palace or any other of Her Majesty's royal residences, were announced on the programmes during Queen Victoria's reign thus: 'HER MAJESTY'S SERVANTS WILL HAVE THE HONOUR OF PERFORMING,' and then followed the name of the play.

The thunders of applause burst forth anew—Irving bowed, the curtain came down, the curtain went up.

Suddenly, with startling shrillness, above the din and tumult, a girl's voice rang out from the gallery with clarion clearness:

"Many happy returns of the day, Mr. Irving."

A wave of silence swept over the whole house. For a second Irving stood motionless—then quick as lightning he flashed a response:

"That is one of the very sweetest greetings I have had to-night—many happy returns of the day, Mr. Irving—thank you—thank you, dear friend—and God bless you," and he waved to the girl in the gallery, who responded : " And God bless you too, Mr. Irving."

The cheers and shouts were renewed—handkerchiefs fluttered more furiously—the whole scene was a spontaneous, unrehearsed and unforgettable tribute to an incomparable actor, and surely such human touches as these add permanence to the impression already imprinted by the glamour and glory of the stage drama.

. . . . . .

Irving was always most charming and generous to me. There are some remembrances so dear that they stand out beyond others, and one in particular I have cause to recollect. It is intimately associated with Henry Irving's picture of Corporal Brewster—a lovely afternoon—and the realization that no matter how valuable the gift—Irving would not even listen to thanks for it.

A charity *matinée* had been organized by me. I had been offered the Prince of Wales's Theatre—then called the Prince's—and W. S. Gilbert had not only given me his *Pygmalion and Galatea* to play free of all responsibilities, but had promised to attend every rehearsal and see us through. He faithfully kept his word.

Tickets not selling very briskly, I bethought me of Henry Irving and the enormous help he had given me in the past. I chose a time when I thought to find him, and being lucky, dived headlong into the reason of my presence, ending up with : " So if you would only just help me once more out of this dilemma—and recite——"

He stopped me abruptly. " I beg your pardon, I don't think I quite understand."

Gracious, what on earth had happened—what had I done ?

" I thought perhaps—you wouldn't mind—saying a few words or giving your name as patron," I stammered.

" Please stop—I cannot either recite for you—or say a few words for you—or give my name to you—here, Bram—Bram, I say." He banged his hand down on one of those little gong bells sitting on the table, then, as Bram made his appearance, Irving changed his voice entirely.

" What are our engagements for Thursday the 29th ? "

" Nothing of importance so far, Chief."

" Well, put this down, *matinée* performance, Prince's Theatre, 29th——"

' WATERLOO ! '

Of course, I should have made liberal allowance for Irving's delicious sense of humour! Had I done so, I could not have doubted for an instant that he would have granted his co-operation.

After that memorable *matinée* with handsome Ben Webster as the Sergeant, and Annie Hughes as old Brewster's grandchild, I went round to the Lyceum in the evening to thank Irving. The Lyceum company invariably dressed at their own theatre and arrived all ready made up to go on to the stage—returning immediately their 'turn' had finished.

When I began to speak—a hurried gesture intimated silence. Irving had very beautiful hands, perfectly proportioned and with fingers tapering off finely at the tips.

"Well, did I please you?" he asked.

"You must know how truly grateful"—I got no further than that.

"That's all I want to know—come over here and look at this." He held a marvellous piece of brocade for me to see—deep geranium pink with threads of yellow gold woven and interwoven into it.

"Is there sufficient to make yourself a cloak? Alice Carr is going to fashion one for my dear partner over there." He pointed to the opposite side of the small corridor to Ellen Terry's dressing-room.

"Heaps—but what a thousand pities to cut it."

"Take it—and when you're wearing it—think of old Brewster and of *Waterloo*. God bless you."

A few frays only still remain of my lovely cloak, but the treasured memory of that day is as clear as crystal and as fresh as a May Day morning.

The following letter, written to me by Henry Irving, confirms a statement he made so often, namely, that he disliked intensely all social gatherings, receptions, at homes, and crowds herded together without any object whatever. He knew our distaste for them, too. He would never be seen at any function of the kind unless business or diplomacy demanded, and, even then he would rush away at the earliest opportunity.

15a, GRAFTON STREET,
BOND STREET, W.

MY DEAR FRIEND—

I wonder was Clement amused or bored last night? As I was leaving I saw the two Clemen(t)'s, just beginning the night or morning.

I was so glad to get away.

After my work I like to sit down and gossip and not stand up and make a fool of myself, and listen to others doing the same. I hope we three shall have a good gossip soon, I should enjoy it immensely.

Believe me,
Ever yours,
HENRY IRVING.

2nd July 1897.

I have been to every Lyceum *première* ever since I can remember, and in all the years of my long life—whether here in England or in any other country—I have heard nothing to compare with the thunders of applause which invariably greeted Henry Irving's first entrance—Henry Irving the first actor to be knighted by his Sovereign for his art's sake alone, and the first actor to have been received at the Court of St. James's.

Recognized as ' The Keeper of the Key ' of the stronghold of Shakespeare and the champion of the poetic, imaginative and classic drama, it has been declared over and over again that Henry Irving accomplished more than any of his gifted predecessors in doing for our stage what State Subventions and ducal grants have done in other countries.

Henry Irving's contemporaries—society at large and the playgoers of his time—cannot deny that he earned and deserved his accolade. But the real, the true, the highest *panache* of praise can only be bestowed on his honoured memory, as it is now—by posterity.

MARGARET CLEMENT SCOTT.

All my life I had been told about and talked to concerning Henry Irving. J. L. Toole, Henry Irving, and my grandfather had been friends as young men, and Irving remained enshrined in his heart, and in my mother's mind, as a great gentleman and a splendid actor.

She, unconventional and imbued with a passion for the stage which I have inherited, took me at some unusually early age to see Irving at the Grand Theatre, Leeds. She always declared that the play was *Sans-Gêne;* I believe that it was Mephistopheles, and still declare that I can remember how the Brocken scene lit up with the entrance of the tall, scarlet figure. How much of that is imagination, how much reality, I cannot say.

I was still very young when Henry Irving came to the town

15A, GRAFTON STREET.
BOND STREET. W.

Dear Friend

I wonder was Clement amused or bored last night?

As I was leaving I saw the two Clement(s)'s just beginning the night or morning.

I was glad to get away.

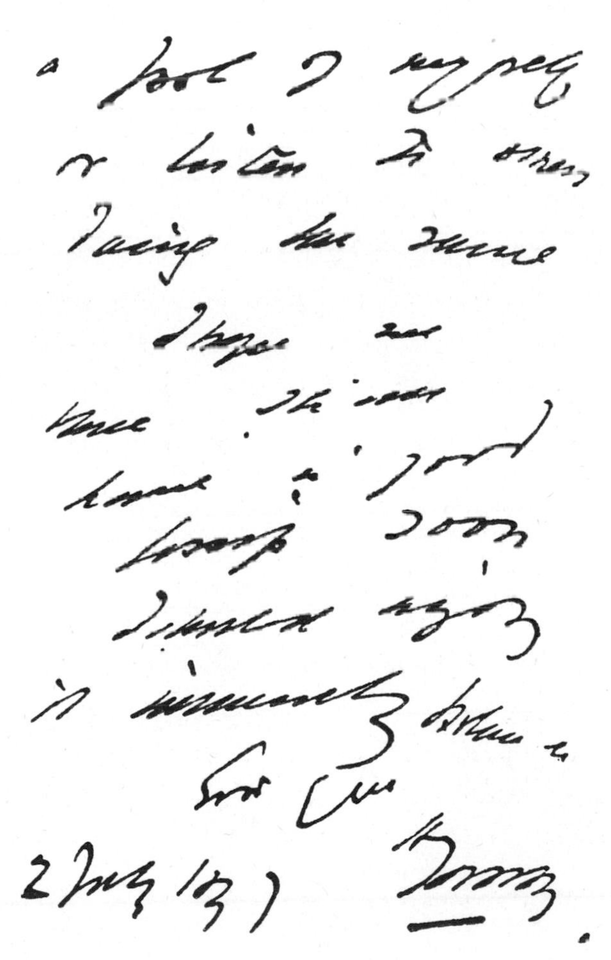

2 July 1937

where I lived, and I went down to the grimy station to watch him descend from his train on a coldish autumn evening. I can visualize him now, raising his hat to the assembled crowd with that courtesy which might be 'stagey', but, in those days, actors did not mind being recognized as—actors. I went home, conscious that I had sufficient money to pay for a seat in the gallery—'augmented prices for the visit of England's greatest actor'—and that the kindly owner of the theatre had promised that he would find a seat for me any other evening I wished.

Monday night came, and with it *Becket*. I was the first person in the gallery queue. I rushed up the stairs of the old Theatre Royal as the early doors opened, and obtained the seat which I had coveted—the middle of the first row. There, with my forehead pressed against the iron bar which prevented the patrons from pitching themselves into the stalls in moments of tense excitement—for it was given to offering melodrama to its audiences, the old Royal—I waited for miracles to happen.

The company, I remember, included Mrs. Cecil Raleigh who played the Queen, and a strikingly pretty, though ineffective actress called Maud Fealey who played Rosamund. I recall nothing of Miss Fealey, Mrs. Raleigh was handsome, and had a certain difficulty with her 'r's.'

'Now am I Henwy's pawawamour and not his wife,' she declared.

And Henry Irving.

I had been told that he was old, that he was mannered, that his voice was unnatural and his diction affected. I saw and heard none of these things. I saw supreme dignity, that kindly tolerance and interest in other men's affairs which should belong to priests and—so seldom does. I heard sheer melody in his voice, measured, sonorous, and beautiful. I doubt if one word escaped me, if my eyes wandered for one second from that fine figure so long as it remained on the stage.

I have never read the play, I never wish to—but even now I recall the intense pathos which permeated the lines about a 'water hen, frozen on her nest,' and the epilogue which followed, when he added that her eggs were still warm.

Are those lines in *Becket?* I don't know. The lines about the water-hen, surely those are there. The lines about the eggs—may or may not be, but for all these years that sense of pathos has remained with me, and that is what Henry Irving conveyed in his acting.

I felt no sensation that this was 'the lead,' he dominated that stage without effort, without insistence on his rights as Becket, he moved gracefully and easily, and—you heard every word, given its proper weight and tone. He was priest, saint, and statesman. He talked with the King, seated at a stone table in a garden or on a terrace, I remember, with the ease and quiet confidence of a diplomat. He was not Henry's spiritual director, he was unquestionably his social and diplomatic equal. The whole thing did not seem to be acting to me—here was Becket, here was the future Saint Thomas of Canterbury, and you never doubted it for one moment.

The Cathedral scene—and I sat tense and almost frightened because I knew what the end must be. The monks were frightened, they scattered, trying to save their own skins. Becket watched them, faintly contemptuous, yet entirely tolerant. He was greater than they, he understood their fear, their inability to remain at their posts. You felt that he was looking back down the ages, recalling the attitude of mind which forbade anger and recrimination, only asking—a little sadly : 'Could ye not watch with me—one hour ?' Standing there, watching the scurrying monks, Becket said : 'I wonder why monks—good men—are such cowards ?' Those were the words, or the meaning or effect of the words I heard. Spoken gravely, with an inflection which was almost speculative, certainly never acrimonious.

And at last those famous lines : 'Into Thy Hands,' which would have given such opportunities for over-elaboration, for mannerism, for—obvious acting. They came simply, as a child might say its nightly prayers, yet ringing through that old and rather dingy theatre, echoing like a clarion call. There was triumph, security, infinite trust in that sound.

He fell, and a stout lady next to me, who might have been some small shopkeeper, hissed : "Gawd, the —'s 'ave murdered 'im ! "

The whole scene was grey in tone, and as he lay there on the steps of the altar, to me, probably to the excited imagination of a very young person, the crumpled figure became absorbed into the grey. With the death of Becket the play ended—drifting away as it were into nothingness.

'But, of course, the play ended, it ends with the murder ! ' Yes, I know, but there was something more than that to it. It ended because Becket was dead, and Becket being dead, he was drawn into the dim grey of the Cathedral.

'Drawn into canvas, and wood and paint, and imitation stained-glass—— ! '

Yes, again, I know all that, but nothing *had* been paint and canvas, any more than I had been watching a man called Henry Irving—I had watched Becket.

I went again. Went for my free seat on Saturday night, which was of course unforgivable of me, only I didn't know then all that I know now. I was given my seat, and went to it, thinking: 'The same miracle can't happen again, it is not possible.'

But the same miracle *did* happen again, and a small, very shabby child sat on a rather uncomfortable chair—because all the stalls were full—and tried to understand 'how it was all done.'

I still ask myself that. Art, knowledge, technique—all those things, and added to them surely—sincerity.

Years afterwards, dining with Leslie Faber and his wife, the talk turned to Irving and his art. Leslie Faber said: "When I am in doubt, when I am not certain as to how this should be said, or that move made, I ask myself, try to hear or to visualize—what would Irving have done?"

Speaking to my mother one day about various dignitaries of the Church, I said: "They're always faintly disappointing, in real life, aren't they?"

"Yes," she replied. "You see, you saw Irving as Becket——"

NAOMI JACOB.

XXXIX

IRVING as KING ARTHUR

Lyceum Theatre, 12th of January, 1895 :—

KING ARTHUR

WRITTEN BY J. COMYNS CARR

King Arthur	MR. IRVING
Sir Lancelot	MR. FORBES ROBERTSON
Sir Mordred	MR. FRANK COOPER
Sir Kay	MR. TYARS
Sir Gawaine	MR. CLARENCE HAGUE
Sir Bedevere	MR. FULLER MELLISH
Sir Agravaine	MR. LACY
Sir Percivale	MR. BUCKLEY
Sir Lavaine	MR. JULIUS KNIGHT
Sir Dagonet	MR. HARVEY
Merlin	MR. SYDNEY VALENTINE
Messenger	MR. BELMORE
Gaoler	MR. TABB
Morgan le Fay	MISS GENEVIÈVE WARD
Elaine	MISS LENA ASHWELL
Clarissant	MISS ANNIE HUGHES
Spirit of the Lake	MISS MAUD MILTON
Guinevere	MISS ELLEN TERRY

PROLOGUE, *Excalibur*. SCENE. *The Magic Mere*. ACT I. *The Holy Grail;* SCENE. *The Great Hall at Camelot*. ACT II. *The Queen's Maying;* SCENE. *The Tower above the River at Camelot*. ACT III. *The Black Barge;* SCENE. *The Tower above the River at Camelot*. ACT IV. *The Passing of Arthur;* SCENE 1. *The Queen's Prison at Camelot;* SCENE 2. *The Great Hall at Camelot.*

I ACTED with Irving three times; twice at the Lyceum and once at Drury Lane in *Dante*. The first time, as Elaine in *King Arthur*, very young, very frightened and awed by the greatness of these famous people, I stood on the edge of the stage afraid. Irving came across from the footlights and thanked me for coming to help in the production, so my shivering anxiety gave place to a happy feeling of being part of a famous company.

No one was allowed on the stage or in the front of the house during rehearsals, and I was desperately anxious to see the play —to watch the great artists rehearse and Irving produce. But no, there were two green-rooms in which those not concerned in the scene waited until called; a green-room for the principals and another for the extra ladies and gentlemen who only walked on. I had only a short scene with Miss Terry in the first Act, but the corpse of Elaine was an important figure in the third Act in which the great scene occurred, the scene in fact which was the play, so I begged to be allowed to be the dead girl so that lying on the bier I might at least be able to listen.

The play was neither Mallory nor Tennyson; I mean that Comyns Carr had not attempted to dramatize either, but had evolved his own conception of the story and the character of King Arthur. This disappointed many and laid him open to even severer criticism. Shorn of its poetic beauty the story is little better than commonplace, the trusting husband, the tempting wife, and the friend whose loyalty is not strong enough to resist. It gave Irving no very great chance. I managed to catch a glimpse of the Prologue, the gloomy lake from whence issued the magic sword Excalibur. Irving was always mystic, and in that wonderful imaginative setting as he listened to Merlin expounding the fate that awaits him he created that atmosphere of awe and expectancy that we all counted on. He had little to do in Act One but play the loving husband and confiding friend, and in Act Two, the exquisite Maying Scene (I caught a glimpse of that too), he did not appear. The lovers and the melodramatic plot of the witch, Morgan LeFay, and her son Mordred, monopolize the action. The great scene was in Act Three when I lay dead on the bier. I was behind those three great personalities: Irving (King Arthur), Forbes-Robertson (Lancelot), and Ellen Terry (Queen Guinevere), and could get my impression of the scene only from the sound, but the thrill of those three unusual and beautiful voices in passionate conflict is still a vibrant memory. How I thrilled with pride when Irving lifted the veil from my face to say:

'Come hither
That thine eyes may gaze on this sweet picture.'

They had taken the letter addressed to the Queen from my dead hand and that draws on the climax:

'Some sin there was though not recorded here,
Some stain that smirched her seeming purity,
Which Lancelot, all too noble, could not urge
Else were it not in nature to refuse
So sweet a gift.'

This leads to Guinevere confessing her guilt—shamelessly, brazenly, while Lancelot suffers in remorseful agony. The

King is dazed, paralysed at first with grief and disillusionment, then in a paroxysm draws his sword and rushes on his friend, but Excalibur drops from his hand. Lancelot goes and Irving has one scene of exquisite pathos with the humiliated Guinevere. It is his one real chance in the play, and exquisitely he took it. But really the part was not worthy of him and I fear the play was not worthy of the Lyceum.

But I really am no critic; I used to feel a great deal more than I ever thought. One night I had been crying and when Irving lifted the veil my face was wet with tears. He stopped me as I was running to my dressing-room to ask if there was anything that he could do to help me. When I said 'No' he patted me on the shoulder and said: "It'll all come all right, my dear, remember we were born crying."

It is always amusing to watch stars 'playing for position' at rehearsals, and I remember Ellen Terry in the early days making a bold entrance ending in the O.P. corner, and every morning Irving gently reminding her that she was to arrive at the prompt corner. She tried it on for several days, pretending she had forgotten, but he forgot nothing, ever, and I needn't say how it ended.

I remember, too, passing through the front of the theatre in the early hours of the morning of the dress rehearsal and seeing old Allen stretched out on the stage in the position of King Arthur's dead body, and Fussy, the beloved terrier, walking slowly and solemnly from the side and climbing on to the chest of the corpse preparing to sleep in comfort, whilst Irving was directing the lighting of the scene. But what I remember best is the intense happiness of being a part of the whole very beautiful production.

One night as the curtain fell on the last act of *Dante*, Irving asked me if I thought that it was a good play. I was dumb. He smiled, a curiously fascinating smile, and said: "Sardou is old, too old; it would take a Dante to write about Dante!"

I feel that it would take an Irving to write about Irving, for genius is a strange indescribable quality and no one can recall his magnetic power, the beauty, sorrow, and wonder which radiated from him in all his many performances without recognizing his genius.

I was too young at first to be able to criticize, too young and too fascinated. I could only absorb knowledge from his great store. Anyway, *Dante* was a poor play and Irving's part was without opportunities. Although I doubled two parts, Pia and Gemma, mother and daughter, there was for me no dramatic moment to create an impression. It was his last production and it was certainly the proudest moment of my career when Irving sent for me to take Ellen Terry's place.

Dante was his last production ; the scenery had been painted in Paris and was, for the scenes in Hell, a revolving panorama. At the scene rehearsal Irving sat in complete silence until the whole canvas had been displayed before him : then he hurled his hat into the distance and remarked as he left the stalls : " They can take it away and burn it. Do they think I am a damned showman ? "

In the last act the Cardinal had a fine death scene. Irving had a great affection for the actor who played the part so he stood absolutely motionless, trying to obliterate himself. But motionless as he was, the audience looked only at him.

During this last season in London he was very far from well and very often really suffering, and when he sat at the wing waiting for his entrance I used to wonder if he could, if he would, make the effort to go through the play. He never failed.

Watching every night I realized the heart-break of this great man whose genius had done so much for the Nation both in England and abroad. He had lost his partner of those many successful years, his mascot, his theatre which had been a shrine to which all lovers of the theatre had flocked for over twenty years, and his library had been sold. Yet then and later when he talked to me at Middlesbrough there was no bitterness, only an unshaken belief in the national importance of the Theatre.

There is now no leader in the Theatre, no outstanding figure, so it is hard to realize that ' the whole of the profession followed him with faith.'

I saw him first in *The Bells*. I had just come from Canada and had seen few plays, so that the experience was overwhelming. Sitting in the gallery I almost screamed aloud, for it was my first glimpse of that power which made the onlooker a part of the character, to suffer as he was suffering, and participate in the agony of his mind.

We students at the Royal Academy of Music went as often as we could to the pit. When, as Charles I, Irving went out to the scaffold he turned to the Queen with that one word ' Remember ! ' I saw a pianist (afterwards famous) wiping the tears from his face with a pink copy of *The Globe*, quite unconscious that the crumpled stiff paper was not a handkerchief.

In *The Merchant of Venice* it was not the return of Shylock to his empty house, or the moments when expecting Jessica he waited forsaken at the gate; it was the startling impression that he made as Antonio said:

> 'Two things provided more, that for this favour
> He presently became a Christian.'

Irving simply looked up and there flashed to us the terrible punishment this meant, the tragic history and the agony of this stubborn race in their resistance to the Christian faith.

There were reasons why *King Lear* was not reckoned amongst his successes. It is difficult for those who have not had actual experience to realize what stupendous powers of physique are called for when acting this 'foolish, fond old man.' Against the wind, the rain, the thunder, it is not easy to convey the emotions of the King, and Irving had a voice of a tenor quality, so that when emotion carried him away he prolonged the consonants and lengthened the syllables to make up for the lack of depth in his voice. Still there was a rare and exquisite vein of poetry, a startlingly concentrated imagination, a mysterious 'otherness' which gripped one's heart. I almost left my stall to follow and help him when, after the brutal treatment of his daughters, he cried: "O fool, I shall go mad," as he went to the 'blasted heath', and still my heart aches as I re-hear him, when after the five times repeated 'Never' the piteous 'Pray you undo this button' followed.

I saw him in *The Dead Heart*, *Becket*, *Don Quixote*, *Charles the First*, *Louis the Eleventh*, and have memories as vivid. I saw most of the great players of my time—Sarah Bernhardt, Mme Duse, Ada Rehan, Mounet-Sully, Coquelin, Lucien Guitry, as well as others not so famous, but none has left equal record in my memory.

Irving always called himself the 'servant of the public' and as the servant of the public there was no subservience but leadership, as a Prime Minister serving and representing the public in its best interests. To him his art was a religion. He knew the vast influence that the Theatre could wield in inspiring the noble qualities in man; and Beauty was the power that stirred his imagination most profoundly. Not sentimentality or self-conscious artificiality but sometimes with grim humour (Louis XI's prayer to the figures in his cap) wonder at the cowardice of men pledged to the religious life—'strange that monks should all be cowards seeing they fear the greatest enemy'—as he awaited death as Becket.

He never made the mistake of being immersed in ugliness, but held a mirror up to it. There is a wide difference between acting a murderer merely as a murderer and showing the misery of the struggle between the immortal wonder of the soul and the disaster of his action.

Before this I had played the Prince of Wales in *Richard the Third* at the Lyceum. Some nights, if the audience liked the little scene I had, they would applaud at the exit; every night it was a joy to fence with Irving as to whether I should get the 'round'. He always tried to stop it, but, if I succeeded, he would congratulate me. When I was shoved on to play Queen Anne at a moment's notice, in a hurried few minutes he explained to me what he wanted. I was nervous but when I came to play the scene it was the tolling of the funeral bell which struck terror in my heart. It was timed so that just as poor weak fascinated Anne was about to give way and fall into Richard's arms, the bell would toll and break the hypnotic spell reminding her and giving her strength to resist him.

He always recognized the power of suggestion and achieved remarkable effects by means of light. For instance, the funeral procession emerged from darkness at the side of the stage, then passed through a slightly more illuminated space to be lost in gloom at the exit. The scene between Richard and Anne was played in a small patch of light.

If he used horses, he never brought them on to the stage. Rosinante had a momentary appearance in *Don Quixote*, but in *The Bells* the horses passed the window at the back of the stage, and only their tails and the sound of the bells showed the audience that they were still there. Beerbohm Tree, great showman as he was, brought horses, ridden by weighty actors, right on to the foot-lights so that the audience trembled for the orchestra.

At His Majesty's, after the murder of Julius Cæsar the senators closed round the body to smear their arms with grease paint; naturally the audience wondered where so much blood had come from. When Irving saw the play every one waited eagerly for his criticism. He only said: "H'm—yes—too much blood!"

With him the Theatre did 'hold a mirror up to nature' creating an illusion of reality. Realism in the modern sense did not exist for him.

As Don Quixote kept his midnight vigil, pacing to and fro by the windmill, the orchestra played a little tune. Irving gave the impression that he was humming it and there was no orchestra concerned. The whole theatre seemed to be impregnated with the atmosphere that he created. When the curtain rose on *The Bells* ' a sense of mystery, the spirit daunted, and said as plain as whisper in the ear "This house is haunted!" '

In all the arts there comes a time when accumulated knowledge, handed down, often unconsciously, comes to a climax, blossoms forth in great beauty, then disappears. The great actors of the end of the nineteenth century were of this order; outstanding not only as personalities, but as inheritors of a subtle tradition.

That kind of acting has gone, for no amateur could have stood on the stage with these giants. We have now in the Theatre charm, elegance, efficiency, intelligence, but Greatness has disappeared. There *were* giants in those days, and the giant who made the deepest and most lasting impression upon England was Henry Irving.

LENA ASHWELL.

XL

IRVING as CORPORAL BREWSTER

Lyceum Theatre, 4th of May, 1895 :—

A STORY OF WATERLOO

WRITTEN BY ARTHUR CONAN DOYLE

Corporal Gregory Brewster	MR. HENRY IRVING
Sergeant Archie McDonald, R.*A.*	MR. FULLER MELLISH
Colonel James Midwinter	MR. HAVILAND
Norah Brewster	MISS ANNIE HUGHES

SCENE : *Brewster's Lodgings.*

WHY does one never see a one-act play now? Is there no room in any managerial programme for the one-act play? There are two or three at least of these which cry for revival—*The Vicarage*, in which Lady Bancroft gave one of her star performances, and there should be at least half a dozen living actresses who would seize the opportunity to play it; *The Man Who Was*, a Kipling story packed with excitement and exploited to its fullest extent by Beerbohm Tree, and above all the *Story of Waterloo*, one of the brightest jewels in Irving's crown.

Conan Doyle had written a one-act piece called *A Straggler of* '15. Irving glanced through it, sent whatever cheque was asked, and for two years the typewritten sheets reposed in his desk. The opportunity for 'presenting' the sketch came when *The Bells* was not thought a long enough bill of fare for a provincial tour, and at Bristol in the autumn of 1894 the re-named *Story of Waterloo* received the unanimous, and vociferous, applause not only of the local audiences, but of a force of London and American critics who had journeyed by special train for the event.

If Irving had too little thought for to-morrow, he certainly, as far as pecuniary considerations were concerned, had far less thought for himself. *Waterloo* was billed for a first performance at the Lyceum in conjunction with an adaptation of *Don Quixote*, and a large public was eagerly expecting to taste its merits.

Then came a message from a Royal lady—the mother of Queen Mary—a dear and devoted friend of the Theatre in general, and of Irving in particular. 'Would Mr. Irving play the *Story of Waterloo* at a special *matinée* in aid of the Newport Market

Industrial Training School?' No thought of taking the edge off the interest in a Lyceum production protruded itself; the answer was an unhesitating 'Yes' and accompanied by a cheque of £20 for a box which was placed at his disposal. There may be some who stand astride the last forty years to say that three happenings on the English stage are fixed in memory: Mrs. Kendal in *The Likeness of the Night*, Forbes-Robertson as Buckingham, and Irving when at the Garrick Theatre he played Corporal Brewster for the first time before a London audience. It was said that Conan Doyle wanted to paint in words and action what Hubert Herkomer would have depicted on canvas; certainly he gave a portrait straight out of Chelsea Hospital. Grey, bent, and hungry for his rations, the old hero of the 3rd Guards still had the fire of battle in his veins, the smell of powder in his nostrils. He cried like a child over his broken pipe, but he stood up straight to attention when the Colonel came into the room. He could remember nothing which had happened that morning, but the tight corner in which the Scots Guards found themselves on the morning of that 18th of June was quite clear in his mind. He dozed like an old, old man in the arm-chair, but when he woke with a start to live again for a moment the great moment of all his days, 'The Third Guards need powder and, by God, they shall have it' rang out with trumpet sound. It was the last effort of a life's battle stoutly fought, and when it died away one knew the 3rd Guards had their full muster in the unseen land.

When the curtain sank there was a silence, intensely significant but almost unbearable in its tension; men who had never before been 'moved by theatrical stuff' were furtively wiping their eyes, women were quite unashamedly 'having a good cry,' a wave of emotion swept the whole house, who by the way had paid pretty smartly for their seats. The stage manager knew his job and kept the drop down until people had a little recovered themselves and were able to give Irving an ovation which admittedly, in volume and sincerity, exceeded anything he had hitherto enjoyed.

In the spring of 1895 there came the award which the recipient insisted was conferred on his 'calling' (he disliked the term 'profession') rather than on himself. Anyhow, the accolade which the Queen bestowed with the words: 'I am very very pleased,' was the first honour conferred by a Sovereign, or a State, on an actor as such; for when Got was accorded the Legion of Honour, it came with the explicit reminder that it was as a professor he had been picked out.

IRVING *as* *CORPORAL BREWSTER* *FROM A DRAWING BY SIR BERNARD PARTRIDGE*

The first congratulations on the knighthood came from Marlborough House; at the suppers on the Lyceum stage Albert Edward was no infrequent guest, and at Sandringham, Irving, in *The Bells* and a scene from *The Merchant*, was the bridge over which Queen Victoria passed from complete aloofness with regard to theatrical doings to renewed and something like keen interest in them.

'Full compliments and 'alf rations, Bill,' murmured a jaded pursuer of De Wet in the weary South African warfare after a congratulatory message had been read out in camp and a short supply of 'bully' and biscuit tendered. Scarcely had the last echo of congratulations, pouring in from every corner of the world, died away when the tide of fortune set in against Sir Henry. Early in 1896 he injured his knee and many months elapsed before he could face the footlights again; the drama about Peter the Great, written by his son, and *The Medicine Man* from the pen of Hichens, were costly failures; his immense stock of scenery was accidentally burnt, and he had to sell his fine library and transfer his interest in the Lyceum Theatre to a company. Lastly, Sardou's *Dante*, produced at Drury Lane, proved wholly unprofitable, and although, both here and in America, Irving rightly remained on the pedestal to which a discriminating public had hoisted him, it was a sick and sorrowful man who undertook in the autumn of 1905 his last provincial tour and to an eager and enthusiastic Bradford audience he recorded his last *adsum*.

It would savour of impertinence for a mere hack playgoer to attempt any appreciation, or criticism, of an artist who seems to grow in stature as he recedes into history. But remembering him—and who could forget him—in something like half a hundred of those representations he so richly offered, remembering him as a man whose heart was as warm as his brain was quick, as a friend who never swerved from his friendships, as a host, or guest, delightful in talk with a charm magnetic for men younger and less distinguished than himself, and with a wit which gave no wound, remembering him under these and under many other lights, one reminds oneself that take him for all in all, one never quite saw his like in this London of ours.

"I remember in the days of my youth," said Mr. Asquith when unveiling the tribute to Beerbohm Tree, "when Mr. Gladstone was at the height of his fame and was often called the 'Idol of the Nation,' that a shrewd observer once said: 'If you were to take a plebiscite as to who was the most popular man in England, he would be easily beaten by Dr. W. G.

Grace,' and I cannot help thinking that he would have found a most formidable competitor in Henry Irving."

GEORGE ARTHUR.

I never met Irving, and saw him on the stage only three times—once in *Faust* at the Lyceum, once in *The Bells* in America, and once at a benefit in *Waterloo*. If I attempted to tell why I missed my opportunities I'm afraid it would develop into a long story about myself. The main reason, perhaps, was that when I was working in the provinces I had no freedom and when I wasn't working I had no money. In those days the young actor used to 'get in on his card' or by writing a polite request to the acting manager of the theatre. Actors are proverbially a good audience, so managers were only too glad to give them any seats that were not likely to be sold. But the Lyceum was always crowded—at least, we believed it was, so we never dreamt of writing there for seats. *Faust* was, I think, the finest spectacular production that London audiences had ever seen. *The Bells* as I saw it in America bore the stamp of age. The scenery was old and worn and Irving was coming near the end of his career. I will leave it to others to describe the magnificence of his acting. *Waterloo* was one of the most perfect studies I have ever seen. While only a few outstanding scenes in the other two plays remain in my memory, I seem to recall every look and every gesture of his Corporal Brewster.

I hope the actors of to-day realize how much the Theatre as an institution owes to Henry Irving. He raised it from what might almost be described as a questionable calling to an honoured profession. He was a great master both as an actor and a producer. Year by year he elevated the Theatre—never degraded it. Irving was the king to whom we all looked for guidance and inspiration. There are fine actors to-day—the standard of acting is probably higher than it was then—but since Irving we have had no great leader. This is probably due in some measure to lack of opportunity. In those days there was not the same perilous competition. It was easier, because less expensive, to establish actor-managership, to hold a theatre and keep together a company, than it is to-day. But we of the present generation can, if we have the will and the courage, uphold the dignity of the Theatre without jeopardizing the interest of the audience. Under great disadvantages Irving succeeded in promoting for the Theatre not only admiration but respect. I hope we are not in danger of losing the position that he made for us. I hope we are not getting loose, and falling into the fatal error of 'playing down' to the audience.

In recent years we have had certain old comedies—old, and bald and vulgar, produced with much relish under the guise of reviving neglected masterpieces. It is difficult for me to believe that those responsible for this display really imagined that they were giving a healthy stimulus to the Theatre of to-day. Irving pulled us out of the mire: we don't want to slide in again. Although almost any mother of a daughter to-day would be able to endure with fortitude the shock of hearing that the young female had 'gone on the stage': and although it would, I think, be difficult to find a father who would not rather see his daughter earning twenty pounds a week in the theatre than lying dead at his feet, or begging for bread in the streets (a complete reversal of the attitude of self-respecting fathers of old), still I think the Stage has lost a dignity that Irving brought to it—and maintained while he lived.

During the last six months I have been a fairly regular attendant at the London theatres, and I have seldom seen a bright and breezy comedy in which 'bloody' and 'lousy' have not been considered valuable props to the dialogue. They are good old English words and were just as accessible to Irving as they are to us, but he would never have stooped to employ them as a mere means of raising an empty laugh. To introduce them for no other reason is bad manners and bad art. Again, it is, I believe, the custom in many well-conducted families to correct a young and disobedient child by an operation of spanking, which is usually accomplished in the privacy of the nursery. The same family would be considerably shocked if the eldest son, having come of age, habitually performed the same operation in the drawing-room upon his young lady friends who had also come of age. But I saw him do it in varying degrees of totality in at least half a dozen plays, and every time he got a laugh. Irving knew that such laughter was not a sign of amusement or a signal of success. I don't wish to talk about the good old days: I merely want to express my belief that the strong position the Theatre holds to-day side by side with the other arts is mainly due to Henry Irving. His tremendous personality, together with his indefatigable labour, gained for him such public admiration and respect that at last, in spite of ancient prejudices, the unprecedented honour of knighthood could no longer be withheld.

George Arliss.

I saw Irving three times—and his *Waterloo* I shall never forget!

But I was too busy, singing eight times a week, and trying to be at my best always, that I never had much time to go to theatres. He was a great actor, the greatest *this* country has produced, nor do I see anyone to-day approaching him.

MARIE TEMPEST.

XLI
IRVING as DON QUIXOTE

Lyceum Theatre, 4th of May, 1895 :—

A CHAPTER FROM DON QUIXOTE

(*An adaptation from Cervantes' Don Quixote*)

WRITTEN BY W. G. WILLS

Master Quixada	MR. IRVING
Sancho Panza	MR. JOHNSON
Father Perez	MR. HAVILAND
Pedro	MR. ARCHER
A Peasant	MR. REYNOLDS
Muleteers	MESSRS. BELMORE AND RIVINGTON
Antonio	MISS DE SILVA
Maria	MISS MILTON
Dulcinea	MRS. LACY
An Old Woman	MRS. INNES
Girls	MISSES FOSTER, K. HARWOOD, AND AILSA CRAIG

SCENE I. *Room in Quixada's House.* SCENE II. *Courtyard of Inn.*

IRVING, I hold, was sometimes mistaken in his choice of plays—or rather, in his choice of material for plays. I dislike general rules ; they are apt to be holed with exceptions as soon as uttered ; but I do believe that a great book never, or hardly ever, affords matter for a great play. Roughly, literature is a thing of meditation ; drama is a thing of action. One of the choicest pleasures in the reading of fine poetry or fine prose is to hang over the line or the sentence that arrests you with its sudden beauty, to savour it slowly, intensely, on the palate, to dwell on the thought, to meditate on the music, to read once more, to linger on the dying fall, unwilling to pass on. In the theatre, when you have done all that, the players are in the middle of the next act, and you have lost a good deal of the plot. Consequently, if you do dramatize a noble book, it means you have to cut all the dream cackle that charms the man reading by the fire, and come to the 'osses of action which hold the man listening and gazing in the pit. And, in spite of a brave attempt by the late Mr. Morrison, the highly gifted dramatic critic of *The*

Morning Post, of all great books *Don Quixote* is the least suited for the theatre. It is a masterpiece of the picaresque—a kind of literature to which *The Pilgrim's Progress* is the most distinguished English contribution—which is, above all, remote from the world of the stage and alien to it. I believe, indeed, that long ago, Miss Grace Hawthorne produced a handsomely costumed dramatic version of *The Pilgrim's Progress* at the vanished Olympic Theatre, but, so far as I remember, the result failed to justify the bold experiment.

And Irving's *Don Quixote* most certainly did not prove an exception to the general rule. It consisted of two scenes extracted from a full-length play which Wills had written, I suppose at Irving's suggestion. There was the scene in the Knight's library, the scene of the watch by the armour in the inn courtyard, and I think another scene, which I have failed to remember. Most of us think of Don Quixote as a dark, sallow, swarthy Spaniard, black-bearded, black-moustached ; but Irving made him fair and red-headed. I do not know what his reasons were ; perhaps he carried his spirit of curious and refined research so far as to hint by means of that red wig that the Knight was of the old Celto-Gothic stock, without any strain of the dark Iberians or of the darker Jews and Moors. If so, I will be bold to say that this was carrying refinement to excess. Antiquarianism and research, unless kept in bounds, are the enemies of the Theatre, where it is above all things necessary to make people see what they think they are going to see. A production which gave us a pursy Hamlet, padded a little less than Falstaff, who puffed and blew after climbing a short flight of stairs, could appeal securely to the best authority in the world, that is to Shakespeare himself ; but we know quite well that it wouldn't do. But all that apart ; there was very little to be said for *Don Quixote* at the Lyceum.

It was while Irving was playing Don Quixote that his knighthood was announced (24 May 1895), and several lines in the play were greeted that night with cheers, lines peculiarly fitted to the occasion : 'Knighthood sits like a halo round my head,' says Don Quixote, and after his attack on the pump there was the dubbing of Quixote as Knight of the Sorrowful Countenance. At the fall of the curtain there was an extraordinary demonstration which he acknowledged with his usual grace as 'an honour conferred through him upon his calling.' That was, in fact, the light in which he always viewed the matter. When the honour had been offered to him by Gladstone in 1883, he said : "Titles for painters, if you like—they paint at home ; for writers—they write at home ; for musicians—they compose at home. But the actor acts in the sight of the audience—he wants a fair field and no favour—he acts among his colleagues, without whom he is powerless ; and to give him any distinction in the playbill which others would not enjoy would be prejudicial to his success and fatal, I believe, to his popularity." However, when the time came it did not prove so ; he honoured the title as it honoured him. It is, perhaps, a question whether it benefited as much as it honoured his calling—whether the recognition of the actor's social dignity was to the advantage of their art.

One word more about *Don Quixote :* A. B. Walkley, who became a recognized authority, was at that time laying the foundation of his career as a dramatic critic by his articles in *The Times*. Of *Don Quixote* he wrote :

> 'For years past Mr. Irving has been entreated on all hands to play Don Quixote. He was so obviously the figure for the part : so obviously the man to give us that blend of dignity and fantasy of which the hero of Cervantes is the great exponent in world literature. Opinions are curiously at variance as to the result. Some people, it seems, think he " guys " the character, errs by excess of farce ; and it may be that—at any rate on the first night, when he felt that the piece, tending to fall flat, must be " lifted " at all costs—he did somewhat over-emphasize the drollery of the part, at the expense of its loftiness, of its romance. Still, to my eye at least, the loftiness, the romance, were there. When the Knight fell on his knees in silent prayer before his armour, I " forgot to remember " that the armour was absurdly ill-fitting, or that it was lying in the horse-trough. I only saw a noble spirit, however distraught, filled with the solemnity of its mission. When he entreated the jeering village wenches to be more modest in their demeanour I ceased to see the wenches, I only saw the chivalrous hidalgo. What does this mean ? Why, of course, that I saw things for the moment with the eye of Don Quixote, not with that of Sancho Panza, which is just the effect one gets out of Cervantes at his best. The complaint raised in some quarters that incidents are introduced for which Cervantes gives no warrant strikes me as the very superfluity of captiousness. To be sure, it is not recorded in the book that Don Quixote used to turn over the pages of *Armadis de Gaul* with his sword, or that he tried to carry a ten-foot lance erect through a seven-foot doorway. But that is mere accident ; these details are in the very spirit of incidents which are recorded in the book and so find ample justification. As to the catchword, " Heaven knows my meaning ; I say no more "—why not ? On the whole Mr. Irving's Don Quixote is as good a thing as we had a right to expect. The real misfortune is that the excerpts

made from the book for stage purposes were not chosen more adroitly with a truer feeling for the poetry and philosophy of the great comic epic.'

And so Irving reached a dignity hitherto unknown by any actor. He had gone through severe struggles in the past to secure any sort of recognition whatever, yet by sheer force of personality and will-power he had beaten down opposition. One does not forget *Punch's* gibe, 'Wherefore are *thou* Romeo?' italicising the *thou* with critical and damnatory intent. And, I think that if you can imagine Irving asking these people: 'Why not?' they would have answered in the manner of Mr. Pickwick, when he objected to Mr. Tupman appearing as a bandit at Mrs. Leo Hunter's Fancy Dress Breakfast: 'Because, sir, you are too old, sir; and if any further ground of objection be wanting, you are too thin, sir.'

Well, I suppose, there was some force in the objection. Irving was forty-four at the time. He was, undoubtedly, a spare man. He was hollow-cheeked. His appearance did not correspond with the common notion of a juvenile lead, with high colours and rounded contours. But, admitting these physical disadvantages, and granting that so far as the outward show went they were disadvantages; I held then and hold still that Hamlet's line might be quoted: 'I have that within which passeth show.' Indeed, there was that within which transformed and transmuted the lean, middle-aged actor into the express image of tragic poetry and burning passion and romance of the glowing south. Never since have I seen in the theatre such a flushing dawn of rose and gold that grew in the sky seen from the window of Juliet's chamber; and in that enchanted and faery light Irving's Romeo was fit to stand and utter enchanted speech. He was the very figure of tragic romance. To the physical defects which were supposed by some to render Irving unsuited to the part of Romeo might be added the matter of his voice. Many stories in which Irving is made to speak, still told by old actors, bear witness to the fact that his natural, or off-stage voice was light, that his diction was precise, staccato, and extremely—sometimes painfully—distinct. Naturally, indeed, there were no deep, ringing, and sonorous tones in that voice of his; he could never hope to emulate the magistral utterance of Sir Johnston Forbes-Robertson. It was rather the voice of genteel comedy than of romantic tragedy. And yet he had the art of turning the reed into a trumpet. Not unjustly, Oscar Wilde, in his sonnet, addresses Irving: 'Thou trumpet set for Shakespeare's lips to blow.' Sometimes he produced his effects by setting the words to a kind of chant. Forty years ago I was writing a book dealing with the art of literature, and somehow this task led me to expound the theory that singing is the natural mode of utterance, while ordinary speaking is artificial. 'You will always find,' I said, 'that where convention has not cast out nature, some kind of "sing-song," some sort of chant is the entirely natural utterance of man in his most fervent, that is, his most natural moments. Listen to half a dozen children—children, you must remember, are all "primitives," and, therefore, natural—playing some game, learning their lesson at school. Their voices are pretty sure to fall into a rude but distinctly measured chant. The Greek drama was intoned, the Koran is intoned, the Welsh preacher of to-day at the impassioned height of eloquence begins to chant, the Persian passion plays are recited in a sing-song. Nay; but think of our great tragic actor. Quite unconsciously, I am sure, Irving elaborated for himself a distinctly musical and measured utterance, so that a skilful musician, provided with scored paper, could have noted his delivery of many passages as if it were music.' And so on, and so on, in support of a thesis which anyone can demonstrate for himself, if he will go to the remoter parts of Wales, the Highlands, or Northumberland, and listen to the talk of the people. But in the point which particularly concerns us, I stand to some extent corrected. For one reason or another, Irving's enunciation of Wolsey's line: 'Farewell, a long farewell to all my greatness,' had particularly impressed me when I heard it, and remains in my memory to this day. I wanted to produce the notation of the line in this article, and consulted a couple of musicians. But they said it would be a very difficult matter, since the sounds indicated were not true notes according to the music of the West, but rather quarter-tones after the manner of Eastern singing.

And then there was another and a more ambitious effort, which also seemed to me a mistake. That was *King Arthur*. So far as costume and scenic apparatus went, it was a beautiful production. The armour was designed by Burne-Jones—and Burne-Jones, having watched a dress rehearsal, went home groaning heavily, a saddened man. I think I know why Burne-Jones groaned.

There is a very ancient Welsh poem called 'Y Beddau'—which means, 'The Graves.' It tells of the places where the Arthurian Knights were buried, giving them their real names, 'Bedwyr,' for example, instead of the Norman-French version,

Bedivere. But it does not attempt to guide us to the grave of the chief of all the Knights. The line which refers to the King's resting-place has been translated : 'The mystery of the world, the grave of Arthur,' but I believe later scholarship prefers to render it : 'Vain is it to seek the grave of Arthur.' There is the keynote of the Arthurian romances ; the note of mystery, enchantment, and the working of spiritual powers behind a veil of illusion. I doubt whether it is possible to translate these things into the language of our modern Theatre. I remember poor Jimmy Welch, who was then appearing in a Celtic play, telling me with the profoundest wrath and disgust that the author had begged him to speak his lines in the manner of an Irish monk of the ninth century. Welch knew it couldn't be done. And the play of *King Arthur* at the Lyceum demonstrated that it couldn't be done ; at all events by Mr. Comyns Carr, the author of the drama. There was an attempt to render the Vision of the Holy Grail. Archer, the famous dramatic critic of *The World*, said it was like a parlour-maid bringing in a *vol-au-vent*. This was rough, but it was not far from the truth. What was done was a presentation of the familiar theme of the deceived husband, the deceiving wife, and the splendid lover, all in the most beautiful fancy dress. And that was why Burne-Jones, a great student and lover of the mysteries of King Arthur and the Holy Grail, groaned as he went home after the dress rehearsal.

Don Quixote, *King Arthur :* these are exceptions ; and in spite of them, the days of Irving at the Lyceum were days mighty and glorious.

ARTHUR MACHEN.

XLII

IRVING as IACHIMO

Lyceum Theatre, 22nd of September, 1896 :—

CYMBELINE

WRITTEN BY WILLIAM SHAKESPEARE

BRITONS

Cymbeline	MR. MACKLIN
Cloten	MR. NORMAN FORBES
Posthumus Leonatus	MR. FRANK COOPER
Belarius	MR. FREDERIC ROBINSON
Guiderius	MR. BEN WEBSTER
Arviragus	MR. GORDON CRAIG
Pisanio	MR. TYARS
Cornelius	MR. LACY
Two British Captains	MR. ARCHER MR. NEEDHAM
Two British Lords	MR. CLARENCE HAGUE MR. BELMORE
Queen	MISS GENEVIÈVE WARD
Helen	MRS. TYARS
Imogen	MISS ELLEN TERRY

ROMANS

Iachimo	HENRY IRVING
Philario	MR. FULLER MELLISH
Caius Lucius	MR. H. COOPER-CLIFFE
A Roman Captain	MR. TABB

ACT I, SCENE 1. *Britain—Garden of Cymbeline's Palace;* SCENE 2. *Rome—Philario's House, The Triclinium.* ACT II, SCENE 1. *Britain—Room in the Palace;* SCENE 2. *Britain—Before the Palace;* SCENE 3. *Britain—Imogen's Bedchamber.* ACT III, SCENE 1. *Britain—Garden of the Palace;* SCENE 2. *Rome—Philario's House, The Atrium;* SCENE 3. *Britain—Room in the Palace.* ACT IV, SCENE 1. *Wales—Before the Cave of Belarius;* SCENE 2. *Wales—Near Milford Haven;* SCENE 3. *Britain—Cymbeline's Palace;* SCENE 4. *Wales—Before the Cave;* SCENE 5. *Wales—Near the Cave;* SCENE 6. *Wales—Before the Cave.* ACT V, SCENE 1. *Britain—Near the Roman Camp;* SCENE 2. *Britain—The Field of Battle;* SCENE 3. *Britain—Another part of the Field;* SCENE 4. *Britain—Cymbeline's Tent.*

IT is a rare thing to find that one is not so old as one feels, and I am surprised to realize that I only saw Henry Irving when

I was still growing up, for his presence has remained in my consciousness. That is, of course, because he treated his personality as a craftsman recognizes his material, and he discovered a series of conventions as a channel through which his mind expressed itself with the greatest freedom and the fewest limitations. The idea of limitation has often been attached to Irving, but solely with reference to the body, and his bodily capability was not wide. His physical conventions were narrow, but only as all true artistic symbolism is limited in order, really, to increase the power of suggestion which in Irving was infinite.

The meaning and aim of primitive art are always unmistakable because of this very restriction of material and implements when suggestion is the object, and Irving had a deep natural wisdom that had to reveal itself chiefly through suggestion; had he developed it otherwise he would have needed conditions both metaphysical and philosophic, which the stage does not easily afford. And it is because of this unerring suggestion that we remember the profound and hieratic personality; it is because of Irving's methods of using that personality that we remember what he suggested, though we might not have agreed with his interpretation. But the crude wisdom was there, the presentation of beauty through the phases of character. Whether Irving chose to represent a state of mind that we agreed with or not, we could not resist the splendour, or the humour, or the doom of what he revealed to us, and that is, I think, why it is impossible to forget his art and his philosophy.

When I saw Irving do Iachimo in *Cymbeline* I had not the technical mind to register the details of his acting, but the colour of the evil that he evoked, the weight of the doom of that evil and the majesty of its descent, seemed almost to point out a new philosophy of the spirit and the world, such was Irving's power. But in the scene of Imogen's bedchamber, which is the obvious climax of acting for interpreters of Iachimo, there was a majesty of ascent and intensification also, and this was due to what I now know was genius in the producer as well as in the actor. But Irving, as a producer, worked that way, his thought extended itself beneath the whole play and provided the one foundation from which he, the actor, could be inspired. Only in Irving's version of *Cymbeline* have I ever been moved by seeing the chest—which is supposed to contain plate, but in which Iachimo is hidden—merely carried across the scene into the room of Imogen, and this was because there hung out of it a piece of red cloth—one could imagine how it had been shut in hurriedly when the chest was locked, and it seemed almost audible, for it was like the introduction of the second theme in the movement of a symphony. And when, in the gloom and tension of the bedchamber scene, the chest opened and we saw that the piece of red cloth was the mantle that Iachimo was wearing, it forced a sudden realization of that crouching, brooding body in the box and it gave a sense of momentum that increased with each phase of the scene. Irving filled that scene with the fumes of evil purpose ; his rhythm constricted all good purpose.

There can be no higher attainment than to give the conviction that an excursion in art is inevitable, and when this happens, as it did in the scene of Imogen's sleep, one feels the joy that lies in all necessary acceptance and also that curious sense of relief which we feel when any situation—in beauty or romance or evil itself—is absolute. The perfect mime will identify himself with his part, and there are a few sublime actors who can identify themselves with the ethical basis of the part, the broad state—beatific or sinister—that is beneath individuality. And here, I think, lay the fault in Irving's conception of Iachimo. He seems to have been so attracted by the effect of the evil which he could encompass in that scene that he viewed the whole play from that position. On considering the play as a whole, I do not find that the character of Iachimo is really evil. The psychological climax in Iachimo cannot be anywhere but in his confession, since this comes as a resolution of the play and at the end of it, and there is no reason to suppose that Shakespeare did not mean Iachimo's confession to be genuine. There could be no true repentance for such fundamental wickedness as Irving made. I believe that the traditional conception of Iachimo is that he is a ' villain,' but we cannot take Shakespeare so lightly as to assume that he brings in the confession of Iachimo merely to round off the play.

We must remember that, in addition to being a supreme judge of character, few people knew the Italian characteristics so well as Shakespeare did. There was every reason for this ; the Renaissance in Italy influenced the whole of Europe. The works of classical authors which we accept now as the foundation for education and thought were awakened in Italy from their slumber throughout the ' dark ages,' the philosophy of the East was first collected and appreciated there, in Italy the art of Greece and Rome emerged in a new birth. That this was apparent to Shakespeare we see in his description of Imogen's bedchamber. The gilding, the carving, the devices would serve for a room in any Italian palace that tourists gape at now, and the unluxurious northern countries had been longing for this geniality.

What Shakespeare felt about the foreign mind is shown in words that he gives to Iachimo in the confession: 'Mine Italian brain 'gan in your duller Britain operate.' It is the alertness, the resource, the inventive quality of the Italian mind that is apparent in Iachimo, and a consideration of the play makes me, at any rate, feel that Iachimo is moved by the spirit of adventure rather than villainy, because adventure would bring out the quickness and lust for new experience that is seething in him. And I feel that he is a spoilt and bored boy, glutted with amours yet longing to be stirred by one, hoping for the ideal of desire in the unknown Imogen and really wakened from his indifference and cynicism when he does behold such beauty, really moved and filled with real desire. The whole situation in the scene of the bedchamber is a conflict between bodily desire that flowers into supreme poetic imagining—which no 'villain' would be capable of—and the desire for mischief and spite and to get the better of the absent husband. As much adultery has been committed in order to spite a priggish husband as has ever been done to ravish some palpitating seductress: and Posthumus, the husband in the play, is a monument of self-complacency and pretentiousness which, in themselves, give sufficient reason for Iachimo's determination to shatter them.

If the character of Iachimo be interpreted as that of an amorous adventurer, cynical about women and ignorant of the high qualities of love, his repentance and his confession come as a perfectly logical event in the play when he perceives that, to him, love has never meant loving, but only indulgence of the body. And in thinking of the body, we have the whole reason for Iachimo's behaviour, for it must be the body in youth. Iachimo has always been presented as an old or middle-aged man—Irving did this—and it is only the absence of maturity that can prevent his villainy from being cold-blooded and disgusting, or his confession from being incredible. When treated from a basis of youth, villainy becomes extravagance, spite becomes humour, evil purpose becomes adventure, and from these there comes into the play a suggestion of the roguishness that is so necessary to it.

Although described as a tragedy in the folio of 1623, *Cymbeline* is really a romance in which the two noticeable sources of inspiration are the fairy-story of Snow-White and the ninth story in the *Decamarone* of Boccaccio. It has often been objected that the sudden changes of scene and place in *Cymbeline* are bewildering—Rome and Milford Haven, the palace, the garden, and the cave, are revolved in a way that does produce a sense of confusion in the spectator, but I feel that Shakespeare did this consciously in order to evade reality and to place the whole proceeding in an environment of romance, in an atmosphere where anything may happen.

Though the making of a fantasia alters the logic of the characters in the play, it does not deprive them of logical treatment. Cloten is not completely a fool, Imogen is one of the highest creations of Shakespeare, and we have seen that it is possible to find in Iachimo a presentation of the conflicts and disorientations that haunt the waning youth of a libertine as well as an extraordinary portrait of a type of character of the Renaissance in Italy which affected men and women through the whole of Europe.

Irving was probably attracted by *Cymbeline* even more for the sake of Imogen than Iachimo, for Ellen Terry was able to pour all her beauty into Imogen and accomplished one of her most memorable works. The name of Irving means a certain thing to us, the name of Ellen Terry means another, but the combination of both—Irving and Ellen Terry—means something different from either. It means communion in the love of beauty, it means a generosity and a consecration that only two very great spirits could strive for and achieve.

One can criticize Irving's interpretations, for only quite colourless work is accepted without question. One could disagree with Irving's view, but it had to be accepted because of his absolute integrity of purpose. And it was a supreme purpose. He seized his object as in an eagle's unswerving grasp, he dazzled in the blue. A simple test that we can apply to a person, or a book, or a creation of art is the question: 'Does it tell me anything I did not know?' Or 'Does it make me think in a new way?' Irving did both; whether his part was superficially congenial or not, he illuminated and, on occasion, he initiated those who saw and heard him into new experiences of the mind and the emotions, into a knowledge of what we may call good or evil, but which, through him, was beauty and truth.

ROBERT FARQUHARSON.

XLIII

IRVING as NAPOLEON

Lyceum Theatre, 10th of April, 1897 :—

MADAME SANS-GÊNE

BY VICTORIEN SARDOU AND EMILE MOREAU
(*Adapted by J. Comyns Carr*)

Napoleon	HENRY IRVING
Lefebvre	MR. FRANK COOPER
Fouché	MR. MACKINTOSH
Comte de Neipperg	MR. BEN WEBSTER
Savary, Duc de Rorigo	MR. F. H. MACKLIN
Despréaux	MR. NORMAN FORBES
Saint-Marsan	MR. H. COOPER CLIFFE
Roustan	MR. TYARS
Jasmin	MR. LACY
Leroy	MR. WM. FARREN, JUNR.
Cop	MR. ARCHER
The Chevalier Corso	MR. CLARENCE HAGUE
Canouville	MR. FULLER MELLISH
De Brigode	MR. BELMORE
Vaboutrain	MR. S. JOHNSON
Jolicœur	MR. JAMES
Rissout	MR. MARION
Vinaigre	MR. REYNOLDS
Jardin	MR. JONES
De Mortemart	MR. PASSMORE
Duroc	MR. TABB
Junot	MR. WIDDICOMBE
De Lauriston	MR. RIVINGTON
Constant	MR. HOWARD
Arnault	MR. INNES
Raynouard	MR. GRAHAME
Fontanes	MR. PORTER
Mathurin	MASTER HAYES
Caroline, Queen of Naples	MISS GERTRUDE KINGSTON
Elisa, Princess of Piombino	MISS JULIA ARTHUR
Madame de Rovigo	MISS MARY RORKE
La Roussotte	MISS MAUD MILTON
Julie	MISS BRENDA GIBSON
Toinon	MISS EDITH CRAIG
Madame de Bulow	MRS. TYARS
Madame de Mortmart	MISS DAYNE
Madame de Talhouet	MISS VYNOR

Madame de Canisy	Miss Crichton
Madame de Brignolles	Miss Yeolande
Madame d'Aldobrandini	Miss Wilomour
A Neighbour	Miss Leslie
Lady-in-waiting	Miss Davis
Catherine (Madame Sans-Gêne)	Miss Ellen Terry

PROLOGUE: *The Laundry of Madame Sans-Gêne, 10th August*, 1792. Act I. *A Salon in the Palace at Compiègne*, 1811. Acts II and III. *The Emperor's Room in the Palace at Compiègne.*

Victorien Sardou was the perfect example of the playwright as opposed to the dramatist. The dramatist, presumably, writes because he has something to say; the playmaker (wright) writes because he must say something. Sardou was the pupil of Eugène Scribe whose construction was relentless as that of the Œdipus; no matter what the story, the method of presenting it was always a lesson in evolutionary logic. As Sardou grew old his fertility of invention waned, and he put the jig-saw together on the principle of the doctor making up a prescription. In this particular play of *Madame Sans-Gêne* one can imagine him reasoning; the public love a historical character—especially the French public—and of all they prefer Napoleon, but they do not want to be harassed by the technical detail of politics, diplomacy, military tactics, or campaigns, so we must find a domestic story. Napoleon sprang from the people, very well then we must search among the *bourgeoisie* for our story. And so old man Sardou turned to his famous cabinet where all the notes of his ideas, cuttings, snippets and oddments, anything and everything he had ever come across that had the germ of drama, was carefully docketed and pigeonholed. He came on the story of the laundress Catherine, who became Duchess of Danzic, and was nicknamed 'Madame Sans-Gêne.' The very thing!

But where was Irving?

In point of fact Irving had nothing to do with it, for the play was written for Madame Réjane. Irving saw her play it at the Gaiety, where she had brought her French Company for a season, and promptly bought it for Ellen Terry. There were those who said that the part would not suit Miss Terry, but in such matters Irving had instinct.

Irving as Napoleon. The idea appeared fantastic; no actor of any period could possibly have been physically more unsuited to any character. He was, in fact, the complete antithesis of *le petit caporal* in every sense, yet no other actor of our time could have brought to it—apart from a miracle of make-up—that quality of greatness that Napoleon must have had. And touching that matter of make-up, it is interesting to recall that the actor who played the part in London with Madame Réjane, Duquesne by name, by a most curious coincidence, was more like Irving in his make-up as Napoleon than Irving as Napoleon was like himself.

Bram Stoker tells the story of the production, how he would have men about him who were big—it was a very six-foot cast—and all the furniture was made taller to dwarf his height. But beyond his over-mastering authority and his always subtle sense of comedy there was nothing he could bring to the play but the dignity he always gave to every part he appeared in, and the perfection of every detail in production.

I remember once playing in a production in which one of the actors, representing Disraeli, had to speak that historic line 'The time will come when you shall hear me!' Had Irving spoken that, he would have convinced you at once that Pitt, Gladstone, and the whole bunch of them would have been as 'tuppence' beside him. But this Napoleon gave him no such opportunity, for *Madame Sans-Gêne* was all Ellen Terry.

It was not until six years later that I got to know the Chief intimately: Gordon Craig said most unjustly that he never gave praise to another actor. I have proof to the contrary in a letter he sent me after seeing my performance of Orlando in Manchester. He engaged me for the juvenile part in *Dante* (another play by Sardou). At the first rehearsal I was in a dither of nerves, but, after my first speech, the Chief came up to me, put his hand on my shoulder, and said: "Take it easy, my boy, take it easy"; and strangely I was never nervous with him again. The early rehearsals were conducted by a French gentleman, an emissary of Sardou's, who was presumed to have at his finger-tips all the master's ideas. Laurence Irving, who had translated the play, was, of course, in attendance, and the Chief sat silent in the stalls—watching. After four days, during which Monsieur Chose had had it all his own way, Irving's voice interrupted the proceedings by calling out: "Laurence! Laurence! What's the French for bloody fool? Tell him he's a bloody fool!" Exit Monsieur Chose, and thenceforth Irving himself directed.

The play was a huge pictorial affair and a special feature of it was a vast panorama which had been painted in Paris. It consisted of a quarter of a mile of canvas which revolved on steel pillars. It cost, I believe, some three thousand pounds. At the first dress rehearsal it stuck. "It'll be all right in a minute, sir," said the master carpenter. " Cut it out," said Irving, and out it was cut. Money meant nothing to him—efficiency everything.

In the last act there was a rather crudely modelled clock. It annoyed Irving. " Get a real one," said he to Loveday. " But, Guv'nor, it will cost a hundred pounds," said Loveday. " I want it," said the Chief.

I think giving up the Lyceum hurt Irving more than anything else in his life. I was leaving Drury Lane one day just as he was coming out. " Where are you going ? " he asked. " The Grafton Galleries," I replied. " Get into the brougham and I'll drive you there," said Irving. As we passed the Lyceum, looking very down at heel, the pillars plastered with old bills, he said : " I suppose they'll make it a boot factory." There was no bitterness in his voice, only sadness.

I remember one night when King Edward VII, Queen Alexandra, the Prince and Princess of Wales (afterwards George V and Queen Mary), in fact the whole succession were in the Royal box. With sardonic humour and the characteristic twinkle in his eye, Irving observed to me : " If someone exploded a stick of dynamite under that box I wonder who would be king ? "

After leaving Drury Lane we took the production of *Dante* to America. On our first night out in the *Minneapolis*, we met a heavy swell off the Cornish coast, and I turned in, not feeling at all good. At about ten o'clock there was a knock at my door. " Who is it ? " I shouted, not too pleased at being disturbed.

" The Guv'nor wants you, sir," said Walter, the Chief's dresser.

In a profane silence I dressed and made my way to the Chief's state-room. I found him sitting at a table littered with letters and telegrams. He looked at me a moment, then he said : " Ha ! You don't look too good." " I don't feel too good," said I. " Sit down, my boy," and he produced a bottle of brandy, glasses, and a long jar, a thing like a glorified galley-pot. He poured out about half a tumbler of brandy, added some water, and said : " Drink that."

I got it down somehow, and then Irving opened the galley-pot in which he kept some peculiarly long and black cigars. " Have a cigar—settle your stomach." I thought differently, but he was right, and we sat there till past three in the morning, and I forgot we were afloat ! I forgot everything but the amazing genius and charm of the man. He talked of the great actors of

IRVING *As* *DANTE*

FROM A DRAWING BY
S. H. SIME

the past, and said he believed that Edmund Kean had greater moments than any actor who ever lived. He admired Salvini as Othello, and he read me bits of *Hamlet* which he illuminated to a degree I should previously have thought incredible. Alas! that I never saw him act it! When I got up to go, he said: "You don't look much like the man who came in just now. Feel better, don't you?" I *never* felt better.

One invaluable piece of advice he gave me: he was discussing my entrance as Nemours in the Third Act of *Louis the Eleventh*. When I first rehearsed the part I entered and at once assailed the cowering King, speaking almost as I appeared. Irving corrected this: "Acting," he said, "is like billiards; always prepare your stroke, observe the exact position, fix it, and then strike; or, to use a different simile: arrest the attention of your public before you launch your thunderbolt or the explosion may cause nothing but confusion."

Dante was a failure in America, and the production which had involved many months of labour and many thousands of pounds was not sold but just dumped there.

"What is *Dante* about?" my brother had asked Irving one night during dinner at the house of Alfred Watson, then dramatic critic of *The Standard*. This was before the original production. "I'm damned if I know," answered the Chief. I don't think anyone ever did know, though when I heard him read it he created such a picture of the man in my mind that I forgot the play—it didn't seem to matter. But in the theatre the greatest acting cannot carry a play if the human interest isn't there. When we had got going at Drury Lane I perpetrated some doggerel that was at once a fairly truthful summary of this play's action and a criticism. I gave it to Mrs. Aria to read. I didn't dare show it to the Chief, but she did, and she told me it amused him vastly.

'After Ugolino's dead
'Cos they wouldn't give him bread;
After Roger's thrust from Christendom the poet;
When you've heard the scream of Nino
And the shouts of Bernadino
And that Gemma's Dante's child and doesn't know it,
And you wonder whether Pia—
It's as well to get it clear—
Was Dante's daughter or his mother or his wife;
And if Malatesta really
Behaved so very queerly
When betwixt the tapestries he thrust his knife.

Then you're taken to St. Clair
And you hear that Gemma's there,
Kept in durance vile by foster-father Nello,
Who after searching attics
Is seized with the rheumatics
And hurried willy-nilly off to Hell-o!
There, with ghostly pantomime
Staged by Virgil, the sublime,
As they toured among the shadows and the spooks.
Dante's harrowed and instructed,
As he's pers'nally conducted,
By this laureated courier from Cook's.
Now we're getting near the end
Of this most amazing blend
When we're introduced to Cardinal Colonna,
Who is playing naughty games
Sending people to the flames,
Enter Dante—tells him straight he is a "gonna."
Come, good people, great and small
And, Sardou, you most of all,
Take heed, for you may find my words unnerving,
Down upon your knees and pray
God forgive this dreadful play.
Sauvé par majesté de Henry Irving.'

On Friday, 17 February 1905, at Bath, Irving unveiled a monument to James Quin, a native of that city and a notable gallant in his day (1693–1766). Quin was the last of that long line of ponderous actors ousted by Garrick. It was a bitter cold journey on the Sunday to Wolverhampton, and I believe the chill he took may have been the direct cause of the Chief's ultimate breakdown.

On the Tuesday night in Bradford—he died on the following Friday—during the performance of *The Merchant of Venice* and just before his first entrance as Shylock, I stood talking to him. He looked very frail as he sat there, and it was painful to note his laboured breathing, but his indomitable spirit shone from his eyes and he was completely captain of his soul. As he rose he said to me: "It is a sad thing, just as one is beginning to know a little about this work of ours, it is time to leave it."

GERALD LAWRENCE.

XLIV

IRVING as PETER THE GREAT

Lyceum Theatre, 1st of January, 1898 :—

PETER THE GREAT

BY LAURENCE IRVING

Peter the Great	HENRY IRVING
Alexis, his Son	MR. ROBERT TABER
Prince Menshikoff	MR. COOPER CLIFFE
Peter Tolstoi	MR. MACKINTOSH
Admiral Apraxin	MR. W. FARREN, JUN.
Prince Dolgorouki	MR. BELMORE
Prince Abraham Lapoukhine	MR. BRYDONE
Prince Zabouroff	MR. ARCHER
Mansouroff	MR. FULLER MELLISH
Alexander Kikine	MR. BEN WEBSTER
Jacob Ignatieff	MR. TYARS
Field-Marshal Count Daun	MR. F. H. MACKLIN
Colonel Bauer	MR. NORMAN FORBES
Major Steinmitz	MR. S. JOHNSON
Two Neapolitan Captains	MR. PASSMORE MR. HOWARD
Carlo	MR. REYNOLDS
Officers	MR. TABB MR. DAVISS
Eudoxia	MISS ROCKMAN
Euphrosine	MISS BARRYMORE
Masha	MISS SHELDON
Catherine	MISS ELLEN TERRY

Boyars, Ecclesiastics, Officers, Officials, Soldiers, Citizens, etc.

ACT I. *Moscow—The Kremlin.* ACT II. *St. Petersburg—Alexis' Room.* ACT III. *Naples—Garden of the Castle of St. Elmo.* ACT IV. *St. Petersburg—Hall of the Senate.* ACT V. *St. Petersburg—Casemate of the Fortress.*

I SAW Irving as Peter the Great on the first night at the Lyceum from the gallery.

We were a little suspicious about it, as we were of any plays by dramatic critics and blood relations. There was a suggestion of favouritism and undue influence which was frowned on by the sturdy independent judgment of the gallery. Laurence Irving's play had been long heralded ; we heard that Ellen Terry had talked 'the old man' into producing it. But it could not have been for her own sake ; she had not much of a part as Catherine.

The play was a depression in five long acts, with murky, mediæval Russia for a grim, and sometimes gruesome, background. It held more psychology than the usual Lyceum play, much more than got across the footlights. The influence of Ibsen was all over the dialogue, but the plot was the old one of conflict between the strong, masterful father and the weak, irresolute son. Robert Taber's performance of the mean-spirited Alexis was great, in the same rank as Irving's brutish Peter the Great. Laurence Irving had got engaged to Ethel Barrymore (so we heard) and she played the light-heeled mistress of the young Prince. The only comedy scene I can remember was where Ellen Terry, after a slanging-match, slapped her face. I remember most vividly William Mackintosh as Count Tolstoi, and I think Suzanne Sheldon, who married Henry Ainley, played a small part well.

Irving's big scene came at the end of the fourth act, when he decides that Alexis must die. His cry: 'Absalom! Oh, Absalom, my son!' brought down the curtain—and 'the house'—in the customary Lyceum style. The abdication of Alexis was an echo of the thunder that we know reverberated round the world in more recent days.

Irving was not up to his usual first-night form, and his speech, one of the shortest I remember, disclosed the reason. He was tremulous with anxiety for the author. He sensed the failure that his play proved to be. If old playgoers need a landmark to place this production they will remember it followed upon the famous interview with Clement Scott (in *Great Thoughts*) in which he said it was hardly possible for a woman who went on the stage to remain pure. And *The Daily Mail* exploited this dictum to the *n*th degree of sensationalism.

There is one first-night in particular which is fixed in my memory by reason of an incident which illustrates Irving's remarkable power over the audience. Has there been any other actor in our time who could 'mesmerize' the whole theatre? It was at the first performance of *Cymbeline* in the autumn of 1896. For some reason I know not, the performance did not open quite smoothly, the actors seemed nervy and the audience became fidgety. As soon as he entered as Iachimo, Irving pulled things together, and 'the house' was with him. Then came the scene in Imogen's bedchamber. A chest which is supposed to contain presents is brought on, and Iachimo, who has wagered with Posthumus upon her fidelity, is concealed in it. Imogen undresses and gets into bed, and when she has fallen asleep Iachimo gets out of the trunk and walks around her bedroom, cataloguing and memorizing so that he may give her husband detailed proof of intimacy. He approaches the bed and, drawing back the coverlet, soliloquises over the sleeping Imogen as he describes a mole, 'cinq-spotted,' on her breast. It is a tensely dramatic scene which the actor must hold firmly. Now it chanced that a ribald saying was current in London's streets at that time, and somewhere at the back of the gallery there came a voice imitating the cockney speech and saying: 'Now we shan't be long!' It was horrible; an outrage. A titter went round the theatre, and it seemed for a moment the whole performance would be ruined. Irving saved it. His wonderful eyes flashed upon the audience with his fierce, piercing look—he seemed to see each one of us—there was at once perfect silence, and when the curtain fell the applause was like the roaring gale, and dashing of heavy seas on a pebbly beach; real Lyceum applause, the like of which is never heard to-day.

Now comes the curious part; my friend (he is known to American playgoers to-day as Henry Herbert) and I clean forgot that incident until we were out of the theatre, walking along the Strand. The great actor that he was, Irving had hypnotized us so that we forgot the interruption which would have disconcerted beyond recovery any of his contemporaries. When I told Gordon Craig about this he, too, confessed he had forgotten, but it came back completely to his memory; for in that production he played one of the juveniles. And how beautiful he was to behold!

The gallery audience at the Lyceum on first nights was unlike any other. The youthful enthusiasts were the minority, for those who had watched Irving from the beginning were always there, constant and loyal and enthusiastic, but always critical. There was the master-bootmaker from Hoxton, the foreman compositor from Marylebone, the Soho dressing-case maker, and such like. We youngsters got to know them and their cronies well, and encouraged their stories of famous Lyceum first-nights which they would repeat on the slightest prompting. They had found Irving, had helped him to climb to the position which they were determined he should maintain without a rival. To them, Beerbohm Tree was of no account, a fashionable actor with a lot of swell friends, and terribly jealous of 'the guv'nor,' they said. One learned many things in the two to three hours' wait, which was quite long enough to secure a seat in the centre of the third or fourth row. Our enthusiasm was not so very extravagant when it came to 'queuing up.'

Irving inspired more affection and esteem than we can realize to-day, even those who criticized his mannerisms admired him for his ungrudging efforts to give his very utmost. They knew he was as loyal a servant of the public as any actor of the day. He was a principal topic in the eighties, and continually discussed. There was Irving mania and Irving phobia lurking in every gathering. Long before I was taken to see him as Shylock I had learned a lot about him, and when I saw, and felt, too, the greatest personality I have known in the Theatre, I heard the Theatre calling me to its service.

There have been better actors, but has there been one whose memory abides? 'Into the night go one and all'; only Henry Irving remains. What particular quality had he that this should be so? I would say it was his sincerity. He loved the Theatre with all his being. Ellen Terry's words: 'His soul was not more surely in his body than in the Theatre. He worked night and day in it, and for it; he thought of nothing else and cared for nothing else.'

Irving raised the Theatre from a level it will, I hope, never again descend to. More than once he declared: 'I am proud of being an actor, and I am proud of my art. It is an art which never dies—whose end and aim is to hold the mirror up to nature, to give flesh and blood to the poets' conception.' When Irving spoke of 'our beloved calling,' you never hesitated to believe him. Who among the profession to-day can utter those three words and carry the same conviction?

The marvel is that he was able to do this; to raise the status of the Actor, to bring dignity to the whole calling, to establish the Stage in its rightful place among the Arts. He did all this not because of birth or connexions, he was of lower middle-class origin, but by sheer hard work. His frequent retort was 'The lucky actor works.' We believed him. In a copy of one of his speeches I have marked his advice to young actors.

> 'They must bring resolute energy and unfaltering labour to their work. . . . Let your ambition be ever precious to you, and next to your good name the jewel of your souls. I care nothing for the actor who is not always anxious to rise to the highest position in his particular walk; but this ideal cannot be cherished by those who are induced to fritter away their time in thoughtless company.'

"Oh! Mahogany and horse-hair! How devastatingly stuffy!" one can almost hear the bright young products of the hundred and one dramatic academies, schools, and studios remark.

ALFRED WAREING.

PETER THE GREAT

Although I saw Henry Irving in three of his great impersonations, my most vivid recollection of that remarkable man is the impression created on the only occasion upon which I saw him face to face, so to speak, without the glare of footlights between us. The occasion was an evening rehearsal of *Peter the Great* on the stage of the Lyceum Theatre. We had been rehearsing the play for about a week but this was the first time the great man had attended; until this evening, rehearsals had been conducted by his son Laurence.

How I was fortunate enough to secure an engagement in a company so distinguished I do not remember. My part was little more than that of a super, and on the morning of that same day I had decided to ask Mr. Bram Stoker to release me from the engagement as I had been offered a good part in the first provincial tour of the play *Monsieur Beaucaire*. I was anxious to join the *Monsieur Beaucaire* company as its leading lady happened to be a young person in whom I was then deeply interested. I may say I have been interested in the lady in question ever since; she has now been my wife for nearly thirty-five years.

When I arrived that morning, ready to put my request before Mr. Stoker, I discovered that Sir Henry was expected to be present at the evening rehearsal. My curiosity to see the great man at close quarters made me decide to postpone the question of my release till after the evening rehearsal.

The whole of the large company had assembled on the stage, and was standing about in groups, when Henry Irving appeared with his son, Laurence, Bram Stoker, Loveday, and others of his staff. For some reason he was in full evening dress, he was probably going on to some reception after the rehearsal. He seemed to me, at that moment, even more remarkable than when I had seen him on the stage. It was as if some Old Testament prophet, Isaiah, say, denuded of his beard, had appeared before us. I almost held my breath in awe. It has often been said that Irving was awkward. On that evening he seemed to me to be not only gentle, in spite of his dignity and austerity, but unusually graceful for an old man in failing health. His eyes were remarkable and suggested mesmeric power; his face seemed to me that of one who had suffered a great deal mentally; suffered almost more, perhaps, than he could endure. There was a combination of frailty and power in the man, as I saw him then. I felt moved, sad; as if I were looking at some noble edifice about to fall. As Henry Irving lived for about three years after that evening rehearsal I do not know why an impression of impending doom should have been created. But it was created.

It is not an impression that I have, since, invented. The impression was so vivid and real to me that I have never forgotten it.

I knew, before that evening, that Henry Irving was the greatest actor I had seen. I know now that he was by far the greatest actor I shall ever see. In a period of our history which produced an unusually large number of great men, in different walks of life, Henry Irving represented, most magnificently, the Theatre.

NORMAN MACOWAN.

XLV

IRVING as DOCTOR TREGENNA

Lyceum Theatre, 31st of May, 1898 :—

THE MEDICINE MAN

WRITTEN BY H. D. TRAILL AND ROBERT HICHENS

WEST END

Dr. Tregenna	HENRY IRVING
Lord Belhurst	MR. NUTCOMBE GOULD
Colonel Anson	MR. FRANK COOPER
Canon Slade-Smith	MR. NORMAN FORBES
Algernon Warrington	MR. BEN WEBSTER
Dr. Rainham	MR. ROBERT TABER
Sir Clement Hope	MR. COOPER CLIFFE
Captain Stopton	MR. EARDLEY HOWARD
Mr. Braybrook	MR. H. PASSMORE
Servant	MR. ALBERT SIMS
Mrs. Culling	MISS ROSE LECLERCQ
Lady Agatha Warrington	MISS MAUDE MILTON
Hon. Alicia Drake	MISS RAY ROCKMAN
Lady Mary Mayne	MISS SUZANNE SHELDON
Dora Bell	MISS VYNOR
Hon. Sylvia Wynford	MISS ELLEN TERRY

EAST END

Bill Burge	MR. MACKINTOSH
Sam Cheeseman	MR. FULLER MELLISH
Carrots	MR. L. BELMORE
Joe Green	MR. T. REYNOLDS
Charley Tagg	MR. ARCHER
Tommy Long	MR. JONES
Mrs. Burge	MISS DOLORES DRUMMOND

Ladies, Gentlemen, Servants, Costermongers, etc.

SYNOPSIS OF SCENERY. ACT I. *The Lecture Hall, East End.* ACT II. *Ballroom at Lord Belhurst's, Mayfair.* ACT III. *The Retreat, Hampstead.* ACT IV. *Garden Fête at The Retreat.* ACT V. *Room at The Retreat.*

MY memories of Irving cover the last twenty-four years of his life, beginning with a revival of *Much Ado about Nothing* at the Lyceum, to which I was taken as a boy in 1882. From that occasion, I have to confess, the abiding memory is not so much of Irving's Benedick as of Ellen Terry's adorable Beatrice. Irving was then going through one of his bad patches from an elocutionary point of view. I understood hardly a word he said; though I do remember the half-Mephistophelian jauntiness with which he went off in the garden scene, saying, "I'll go get her picture." On the other hand I was present at every Lyceum first night from that of *Becket* in 'ninety-three, and was an accredited critic at every one since 'ninety-seven. So I had plenty of opportunity not only of seeing but of studying Irving in nearly all his great parts, and in some to which he gave his own greatness.

So far as a general impression is concerned, I may, perhaps, be forgiven if I quote a little passage from my recently published book, *Dramatic Criticism :*

> 'Of course there was an immense deal of truth in all that has been said about Irving's mannerisms. Sometimes he was quite unintelligible—and the chuckle and the trailing gait were always there. But so was the greatness. The saintly dignity of his Becket, the arch-roguery of his Mephistopheles, the sublimated irony of his Shylock, the ghastly horror of his Mathias, of his Dubosc in *The Lyons Mail* and of his death-scene in Louis XI, and the rich, crusted comedy of his Gregory Brewster in *Waterloo* —all these were products of the stage-nurtured imagination and indomitable will of the man himself. He made one feel the adventure of life by presenting the extremes of villainy and virtue, and idealising both with the power and charm of his personality, itself born of the same imagination and will.
>
> 'From a critical point of view, Irving's art was peculiarly valuable because it was a standing refutation of the very false old adage that "all great acting is a return to nature." Irving's acting was never a return to nature. The imaginative mask was never cast off. His social self was an acted "creation," just like the others. The rarely-revealed man behind was a Somerset boy who became a City clerk and had been a struggling provincial actor playing the policeman in a pantomime when those who were glad to be considered his equals were at the University or being dandled into a learned profession. Irving's "natural" language was the West-country speech, to which he would sometimes recur, but only among his most intimate cronies.
>
> 'At the same time Irving's imagination reached from Becket to Dubosc—he was Becket and he was Dubosc, and Mephistopheles and Gregory Brewster and all the rest, and absolutely sincere in each character. His own private affairs and idiosyncrasies may have been used—as every good actor uses every idea or emotion or atom of nervous energy he can summon up—in the creation of a part. To him nature was just a help or hindrance

to imagination. The attempt to distinguish between " character-parts " and " straight " parts was flouted once and for all at the old Lyceum. Irving was all his characters ; but none of them was he.'

It is significant that Irving so rarely appeared on the stage in modern dress, though he used sometimes to change from Shylock's gabardine during the last act of *The Merchant of Venice* and take his final call in evening dress. This had the queer effect of making Victorian swallow-tails seem like a kind of fancy costume in which the tragic Shylock of half an hour before had deigned to grace the festive Belmont breakfast-party.

Unless I am much mistaken, the only modern play Irving presented and appeared in during his later years was *The Medicine Man*, the not-very-glorious melodrama by H. D. Traill and Robert Hichens, presented at the Lyceum in 1898. According to my old friend, Austin Brereton, ' it was not an acceptable dramatic work for any theatre, and it was entirely out of place at the Lyceum. The ability and attraction of Irving and Miss Terry were powerless to save it from the oblivion to which it was consigned after twenty-two performances.' This was, as a matter of fact, the last season during which Irving acted at the Lyceum under his own management. My own recollection of the play is chiefly concerned with having been present at the dress-rehearsal. I attended this on the invitation of Bram Stoker. With his customary tact, Stoker told me that a notice I had written of Laurence Irving's *Peter the Great* had particularly pleased Irving, and ' the Chief ' had expressed a wish to meet me.

The dress-rehearsal itself was a revelation. A kind of premonition of failure seemed to oppress Irving from the very first scene, in which he had to sit silent and pensive as a distinguished physician listening to the singing of some birds in an aviary which filled a French window at the back of the stage. The actual singing of the birds was—through careful forethought on the part of Harry Loveday—reinforced by some orchestral music, specially composed by Maud Valerie White. Irving sat between aviary and orchestra in a profound reverie.

After a while the orchestral contribution came to its appointed end, and a mild twitter from the aviary was all that broke the hush of expectation. Irving did not begin the expected soliloquy. He just turned to the orchestra and said quietly, but decisively : " Take out thim flutes ! " I can recall distinctly that ' thim ' was the word. Consternation was general. It was explained that the flutes were a vital part of the orchestral display, that they were supposed to suggest the songful atmosphere of morning even in Harley Street, and that Maud Valerie White would be heart-broken and, possibly, angry at their absence. "I don't care," said Irving, unruffled but implacable, "take them out!" And out they went.

The play itself was not, perhaps, deserving of the entire oblivion Austin Brereton suggests. It involved at least two extremely fine performances. One was from Rose Leclercq, as an epigrammatic dowager of the kind popular on the stage at that time. The other was from that able actor, William Mackintosh. He had to play a burglar, named Bill Burge, who came under the spell of the physician and confessed to all sorts of horrible crimes. It was a great chance for Mackintosh, and at the rehearsal he thrilled everybody, giving his speech out to us over the footlights in good forthright style, with Irving listening at the side. On the first night, to my amazement, the speech was quite nullified by Mackintosh having to turn his back upon the audience and make his confession to Irving, up-stage. It was Irving's, not Mackintosh's, face from which we had to gather the emotions stirred by the recountal.

These little sidelights upon the dominance and will of Irving, provided by the rehearsal of a play 'consigned to oblivion,' have always fascinated me. I feel perfectly certain there was no consciousness of arbitrary action either in the extinction of the flutes or in the suppression of William Mackintosh. Irving—so Mackintosh confessed to me afterwards—had quite convinced him that the audience would rather guess the catalogue of crimes from the physician's inscrutable features than be more fully informed from those of the impassioned culprit. It was not vanity with Irving, but faith. It was faith in the old romantic focus upon a single actor, not to be disturbed by extraneous interest or success. It was faith in himself—and without that faith of Irving's we should never have had the gallery of masterpieces of the actor's art that he gave us, from the first entry of Mathias in *The Bells* to Becket's last utterance upon the Bradford stage.

With the commanding will went, as we all know, unfailing courtesy and kindliness and limitless generosity. I remember running across Irving once in a remote village of his beloved Cornwall—I think it was St. Austell. In the village-square another great man—the first General Booth—was holding forth to a little assemblage of villagers. Just round the corner of the lane, whom should I discover listening with a sardonic but appreciative smile upon his face but Irving! I then learned for the first time that he was a great believer in General Booth's work. He sent every week a handsome subscription to the Salvation Army, on the stipulation that no one should know—least of all the General himself!

Perhaps it would be as well to give a suggestion as to what the play was about by a few quotations from my own notice of *The Medicine Man*. This appeared on 5 May 1898, in the now-vanished *Morning Leader*, for which I was then dramatic critic. It filled a column and a half of close print—a length to which not many daily-paper notices run nowadays, though it was short compared with some others of this very play.

> 'Take a little of Svengali, a tincture of Sherlock Holmes, some essence of Dr. Nikola, dilute them in a solution of a few other such beings, bottle them for a while, and when you uncork the flask I should imagine that, like the fisherman's genie of the Arabian Nights, a haunting shape would shadow itself forth something after the figure of Sir Henry Irving as Dr. Tregenna, the "medicine-man" of the title.
>
> 'Dr. Tregenna is, above all, a man of will. That will, with its five acts of victory and one moment of defeat, is the play. Dr. Tregenna is thus uniquely apt for Sir Henry; for it is the sheer force of the Irving will power—the magnetism of the man—that has always covered in his playing those mannerisms which everyone has learned to forgive.
>
> 'There are two subjects of this will—Sylvia Wynford (Miss Ellen Terry)—a fair virgin of "Society," and Bill Burge, a drunken docker (Mr. William Mackintosh). Dr. Tregenna is by profession a brain doctor. He is supposed to cure his patients (or "subjects" as he calls them) by the mere exercise of will—not quite the Svengalian hypnotism, but nearly so. He takes them to his charming asylum in Hampstead, "The Retreat." There apparently—I think the play might be more explicit in these details with great advantage—he does nothing with them beyond aweing them with his personality and getting their minds into complete subjugation to him.
>
> 'In the first two Acts we see the discovery of his first two—shall one say victims—one from London's far East and the other from its near West. He strolls into the lecture-room of a social-work centre in Whitechapel—poor old Toynbee!—and there finds a lecture in course of disturbance through an outburst on the part of drunken Bill, who is beating his wife under the terrified eyes of the impotent Canon—Slade-Smith by name—who is presiding. In a moment Bill is quelled by the magic of Tregenna's silent eye. In three weeks he is undergoing the treatment at Hampstead. . . .
>
> 'In the Second Act we are introduced to a very different sphere.

We see Tregenna seeking his prey at Lord Belhurst's ball in Mayfair. He finds that prey in Lord Belhurst's beautiful daughter Sylvia. There is a secret in Lord Belhurst's life. His wife, we hear, went mad before she died. His daughter is going to be married to a gallant officer, " red-handed from the slaughter of the Afridis "—Col. Anson (Mr. Frank Cooper, of course). Has Sylvia the germs of madness too? Lord Belhurst fears so. He asks Tregenna to find out. Then it is that the play imposes upon Tregenna a diabolical scheme of revenge.

'Tregenna had not always, it appeared, been a heartless hermit, viewing all men and women as a scientific study, and shaking off ridicule as Shylock did that of the " Christian curs." He had loved—and lost. One swift glance at Sylvia had shown him the truth. Her mother had been the woman of his dreams, and Lord Belhurst was the hitherto unknown man who had robbed him of happiness. Tregenna guessed that the reason of Lady Belhurst's madness and of his own self-sought isolation were the same. Revenge is now within his grasp. Five minutes of talk with Sylvia shows that she is as sane as any charming girl might be. But, if he can cure madness by the exercise of will, cannot he also cause it? His revenge shall be to make the daughter as mad as her mother.

'So he induces Sylvia to join Bill Burge at Hampstead. There, learning everything that the mother did in her madness—her little Ophelia-like ways of pulling roses petal by petal and such trifles—Tregenna watches with fiendish delight while Sylvia, under the domination of his will, does the same things. At last he relents. He finds that Lord Belhurst did not know even of his existence when Sylvia's mother was married. Tregenna restores Sylvia and sends her back to her lover. But it is too late. Fate—through its instrument, Bill Burge—is to have a revenge of its own.

'Poor, honest Bill—himself a complete conquest of Tregenna's powers—did not know his conqueror's purposes towards Sylvia. He had suspicions which lashed his sluggish soul to fury. So, just after Sylvia had gone back, Bill murdered Tregenna in his study, throttling him in the calm of a May morning to the dawn-song of the birds.

'Save for this last moment, the drama of the play is wholly in the mind of Tregenna. It cannot express itself in action, and does not altogether in words. There are other evidences of the lack of an experienced dramatist in the authorship of *The Medicine Man.* But one can now and then forget the play's failings in the sombre, inhuman figure that Sir Henry Irving makes of Tregenna, stalking through drawing-rooms and treating people with a stark rudeness that would not have been tolerated even from Dr. Johnson in a more submissive age. Sir Henry, by the way, wears all the suits of the day, from morning to night—

serge reefer, velvet jacket, grey frock, immaculate swallow-tail. Otherwise he makes no attempt to appear as other men are. The marvellous face is, all through, framed in the rough-lying hair just over the collar that we know so well.'

Such was the story of *The Medicine Man* as told by myself on the morning after its production. Of course the simple truth about it—which one naturally refrained from emphasizing at the time—was a consciousness on Irving's part of the enormous success that Beerbohm Tree had just enjoyed as Svengali in *Trilby*. One saw clearly enough Irving's desire to restore the waning fortunes of the Lyceum with something on the same lines. No one could have played such a part better than Irving ; but the two ' literary ' dramatists had not sufficient mastery of their newly assumed art to give him a chance.

It is saddening to me to think that of the London daily-paper critics who attended that first night no other survives. But a weekly critic—and a supremely distinguished one—is still as full of wit and wisdom and intellectual vigour as ever he was. This is what Bernard Shaw wrote about *The Medicine Man* in *The Saturday Review* :

> ' There was infinite comedy in the first night of the play at the Lyceum. It lasted from eight to past eleven and contained just matter enough for a half-hour pantomimic sketch by Mr. Martinetti. Sir Henry Irving was perfectly delighted with his part and would evidently have gone on impressing and mesmerising his devoted company for three hours longer.
>
> ' Miss Ellen Terry, on the other hand, was quite aware of the appalling gratuitousness of his satisfaction. To save the situation she put forth all her enchantments, and so beglamoured the play act by act that she forced the audience to accept Sylvia as a witching and pathetically lovely creation of high literary drama. . . .
>
> ' Mr. Hichens will retrieve *The Medicine Man* easily enough, for he has by no means mistaken his vocation in writing for the stage, though he had better avoid collaboration with the chartered dulness of academic history and the solemn frivolity of academic literature. It would take ten years of hard descriptive reporting for *The Star* or *Daily Mail* to teach Mr. Traill to observe life and to write seriously. The first tinker he meets will tell him a better ghost-story than the vague figment, despicable to his own common sense, which he has thought good enough to make a theme for the most exacting of all the forms of literary art.'

S. R. Littlewood.

XLVI
IRVING as MAXIMILIEN ROBESPIERRE

Lyceum Theatre, 15th of April, 1899:—

ROBESPIERRE

By Victorien Sardou

(*Rendered into English by Laurence Irving*)

Maximilien Robespierre	Henry Irving
Clarisse de Maluçon	Miss Ellen Terry
Olivier	Mr. Kyrle Bellew
Augustin Robespierre	Mr. F. D. Davies
Benjamin Vaughan	Mr. H. Cooper Cliffe
Lebas	Mr. Fuller Mellish
Buonarotto	Mr. Leonard Calvert
Couton	Mr. Locke
St. Just	Mr. Tamworth
Old Duplay	Mr. Brown
Simon Duplay	Mr. S. Johnson
Maurice Duplay	Mr. F. Hayes
Didier	Mr. C. H. Kenney
Gerard	Mr. W. Graham
Billaud	Mr. Louis Calvert
Jagol	Mr. Hatch
Amar	Mr. Sharp
Voulland	Mr. Barton
Rulh	Mr. F. M. Paget
Vadier	Mr. James Craig
Thuriot	Mr. Lionel Belmore
Tallien	Mr. Laurence Irving
Fouché	Mr. C. Dodsworth
Lecointre	Mr. Ferguson
Legendre	Mr. Morris
Héron	Mr. F. Tyars
Count Harday de Hauteville	Mr. James Booth
De Bussey	Mr. Charles Garry
The Recorder of the Revolutionary Tribunal	Mr. Gilbert Yorke
Haly	Mr. R. P. Tabb
Another Jailor	Mr. W. Marion
Collas	Mr. J. Archer
Barassi	Mr. T. Reynolds
Urbain	Mr. Eric Blind
A Workman	Mr. Jennings
Maréchal de Mouchy	Mr. Ellis
De Broghie	Mr. Lomnitz

De Kersaint	Mr. Eardley Howard
De Pons	Mr. Frank Lacy
D'Armaillé	Mr. Alec Weatherley
Provost D'Arlincourt	Mr. Sinclair
Cottant	Mr. Charles Vane
Dorsun	Mr. Parsons
Charles Leguay	Mr. Percy Nash
The elder Leguay	Mr. Frith
Gournay	Mr. Young
Lavergne	Mr. L. J. S. Wood
Mauclerc	Mr. Herbert Innes
Sourdeval	Mr. H. G. Lane
Maleyssie	Mr. Ernest Martin
The young De Maillé	Miss May Holland
Marie-Thérèse	Miss Winifred Fraser
Madame Duplay	Miss Crosse
Madame Lebas	Miss Suzanne Sheldon
Cornélie	Miss Georgie Esmond
Victoire	Miss Ida Yeoland
Madame de Narbonne	Miss Maud Milton
Madame de Lavergne	Miss Edith Craig
Mademoiselle de Bethisy	Miss Cecilia Radclyffe
The Maréchale de Mouchy	Miss Maud Anstey
Madame Maleyssie	Miss Nellie Huntley
Charlotte Maleyssie	Miss Winifred Kean
Claire Maleyssie	Miss Martia Leonard
Madame d'Avaux	Miss E. F. Davis
Madame de Choiseul	Miss Gertrude Claridge
Mademoiselle Lacroix	Miss Emily Archer
Madame Héré	Miss Mellon
Madame de Narbonnes's little girl	Miss Tarvin
Shade of Marie Antoinette	Miss Rosita Tennyson

Members of the Convention, of the Committees; Ushers of the Convention; Gendarmes of the Convention; National Guards; Police Agents; Jailors; Townspeople, etc., etc.

Act I, Scene. *A Nook in the Forest of Montmorency.* Act II, Scene 1. *The Courtyard of the Prison of Porte-Libre;* Scene 2. *The Place de la Révolution (now de la Concorde).* Act III, Scene. *The Sitting-room in Duplay's House.* Act IV, Scene 1. *A Room in the Rue du Martroy;* Scene 2. *A Hall in the Prison of the Conciergerie.* Act V, Scene 1. *A Room in the Committee of Public Safety;* Scene 2. *The Hall of the National Convention.* Period of the Play—*July* 1794.

In 1794 Maximilien Robespierre was thirty-six, stood five feet two, was mean in appearance; his career was the apotheosis of the second-rate.

In 1899 Henry Irving was sixty-one, over six feet, and was the most interesting and magnetic personality of the post-Disraeli period.

So it will be seen that, judged by modern standards, he was the last person suitable for the part. Broadly speaking, Irving had two moods in his acting: the horrifying and the saintly. In the former category came Richard III, Dubosc, Louis XI, Mathias; in the second Becket, Charles I, Shylock, and even Wolsey. He could thrill and he could touch. And since it would be very difficult to make Robespierre at all saintly or touching he went into the horrifying category, emerging as a cross between Macbeth and Dr. Primrose—a thoroughly crafty but inaccurate presentment.

It must be admitted that the play gave him few chances to do much else than shiver and shake, whine and stagger about the stage. It told of an early love, an illegitimate son who had grown up (so that Robespierre must have begotten him at the age of fifteen) and the situation was: shall the father send his newly discovered son (in whom he can have had no interest at all) to the guillotine? If memory serves me, he saved the youth, a thing Robespierre would never have done.

But the piece was workmanlike as a medium for Irving. It gave him scenes with ghosts, tumbrils, etc., and was as good as any of the old plays as a vehicle for an actor. And it was so magnificently set on the stage that it gave me a thrill for romantic acting that I still possess.

At that period Sir Henry was infirm, but he could still hold an audience with his lightest word, or with a lift of one of those dark, triangular eyebrows. If a very young reader wants an idea of how his acting came over let him imagine George Arliss with all the emotional intensity of Chaliapine. Half-way between the two will be found Robespierre in 1899.

Irving was his own best performance. A mediocre actor can hide himself in the identity of the part, a great actor hides the part in himself. The character of Robespierre became filtered, as it were, through Irving's extraordinary personality. If some younger student of the stage were to ask me: Was Irving a tragedian or a comedian or a character actor? I should have to say that he was a character actor first, last, and all the time. Now a character actor is one who is neither powerful enough for tragedy, nor funny enough to be a comedian. But none the less, character acting can reach great heights. The character actor is unwise if he tries for tragic laurels. This was the mistake Irving made a number of times. In striving for impressiveness through passion he attained only melodramatic success.

Robespierre was a splendid piece of melodrama and thoroughly exciting. On to this Irving grafted what might be called an essay on Robespierre. It was taken from unsympathetic history, which we have now more or less rejected, and showed him as a bloody-minded, cold-hearted, mincing, pernickety old man. Never did we see the little buttoned-up formalist who shrank from blood, but the result was an effective and creative piece of acting.

Robespierre, as he entered to dreamy music over a small bridge in a wood scene, appeared tall, a little bent; his face was very sallow, and his eyes were hidden behind green spectacles. His collar seemed so high as to give him an appearance of shrinking into it; his hair was powdered and in one roll tied with a bow at the back; his legs were thin and spindly, and he walked with a long stride; his gait was a little like a daddy-long-legs. Later, he was shown in his famous blue coat, nankeen breeches, and silver buckles. He read papers short-sightedly, holding them close to his eyes; he chatted sometimes with his spectacles pushed up on his forehead. The striped waistcoat was there, too, and the large cravat which gave the impression that the man's head had already fallen and been stuck on again. Evidently the character had been studied with scrupulous care—but from an unhistorical angle. I have since seen Robespierre very effectively acted as he really must have been in real life by Vladimir Sokoloff in a German production.

But in commissioning the piece from Sardou I fancy Sir Henry had taken his idea of the character from Carlyle's 'sea-green incorruptible'—given it a twist of Dickensian quaintness, and asked for scenes with blood, terror, remorse, sardonic humour—all that had 'gone over' well in other *rôles*. But it was a portrait of any murderer, Crippen, or Neil Cream in the late eighteenth century, vivid, adroit. I can see him now at the foot of the rostrum in the Convention polishing his spectacles and shivering with fear as he is counted out.

Irving's sense of period was unimpeachable. His dress and manners were always exactly of the age and character he portrayed. The rather snuffy atmosphere of the late eighteenth century sat upon him perfectly. You would have said that he could never act any other period if you had not also seen him as Becket or Charles I.

I always found Irving's mannerisms charming, and I could never understand the objection to them. He pulled faces, minced his words, was slow, sometimes spoke with his teeth shut, pounded with his foot on the stage, and drew out the vowels in the words, so that a speech like:

> '. . . My mother kneels,
> As if Olympus to a molehill should
> In supplication nod. . . .'
>
> (*Coriolanus.*)

came out like this:

> '. . . Me mother kn-e-els,
> As if Oly-y-mpus to a mo-o-o-lehill-l-l should
> In supplica-a-tion nud. . . .'

If the young student reads that over aloud slowly, with the teeth a little closed, he *may* get a caricature of how Irving's late acting sounded.

Robespierre was not in verse, but in rhetorical, stilted prose. But stilted prose full of feeling as this was gave tremendous chances for graceful, stylish acting such as Henry Irving always gave his audiences. He was stagy. But you have to be a very good actor to impress audiences with stagy acting as Irving did. To me all his faults appeared as added delights. Beside him all other actors of his time, and most of them since, appeared commonplace.

In the scene where the ghosts of all the people he had guillotined appeared to haunt him he was slow and he ranted. The gallery loved it. Galleries always like the worst. But, all the same, even though I was a schoolboy at the time, I recall being made uncomfortable. It was shame-making. He had no physical power then, and little vocal strength. Soon after, he crocked up and his part was undertaken by his son, Laurence. It was in the quiet passages that he was most compelling as Robespierre, as he was always, to my mind, in all his parts. Tremendous physical force was not his in 1899, and I doubt if it ever was. His *magnetic* force was always what told. His Coriolanus fell down on the physical side, and his Shylock was clever rather than legitimate—so clever and compelling that no actor since his time—not even Mr. Gielgud—can see Shylock any other way. To tackle Macbeth or Othello an inspired ox is better. Craft and imagination will not do.

It is sometimes stupidly said by the young that Irving's acting was never in the picture. *It always was.* The picture was constructed round it. And what pictures! How much of Robespierre was Irving as an actor, and how much Irving as a director or *régisseur* (I discard the word 'producer' because it means nothing) who can say? The production helped the actor, the actor the production. Irving exploited his weaknesses so cleverly that they became part of his strength. His productions stay in my mind even now as the best I have seen. Tempo and rhythm were as perfect as a performance of the ninth symphony of Beethoven by Toscanini. The very dust on the stage acted and was significant. Atmosphere was produced, period, dramatic effect, by means and genius far beyond any known to the young men in sandals and grey flannel trousers who 'produce' to-day. Each set of scenery was right for what had to take place in it, and each set kept the unity of the production together, although it was in contrast to the one before. During the progress of Scene One, the audience could never guess what Scene Two would look like, with the result that the eyes of the spectators were constantly refreshed. Quiet scenes were contrasted with tumultuous scenes.

In those days drama was always accompanied by music, and Irving was especially careful that this incidental music should give the right note and atmosphere of the play, and I am sorry the theatres have abandoned this practice. The films do not disdain this old-fashioned convention. They are too wise.

One scene is indelibly impressed on my mind: a scene where Ellen Terry begs Robespierre to intercede for their grown-up son whose head is to fall. I can picture them now, peering through the *jalousies* as the death carts go by. I see Ellen Terry on the floor, kissing Irving's hands, with tears streaming down her face, and the 'Old Man' wiping his forehead, peering through the slats of the blind. I can hear the rumble of the tumbrils and the shrieks and boos of the mob. How well all such stage effects were done at the Lyceum! There were no 'faint murmurs' like 'noises off' we get to-day. These effects must have taken days to get right. These mob shouts really did freeze the blood, not only of schoolboys, but of grown-ups too. In every device of direction Irving was a master.

I did not know then that the entrancing person I saw was old, ill, and unhappy. I was intoxicated with glamour. Even to-day I can see the pale face, the thin hands and black brows that were so gloriously mobile, and hear the quavering tones that were so expressive. But I was too young to know that what I beheld was another Glastonbury Abbey—the tragic ruin of a great masterpiece.

The reader who is unfamiliar with the story of our last great actor may be asking at this point why Sir Henry was ill, and unhappy. It seems an odd thing that a man who, for so many years, had made his living and a great deal of money out of the acting of tragedies should, all the while and unconsciously, have been the protagonist in a private one. Yet so it was. And a tragedy almost perfect in form.

On the evening of 19 December 1896, Sir Henry Irving at the height of his fame had revived *Richard the Third* with all the usual success. In an account of this performance written by Mr. Bernard Shaw we read that on the first night: 'He seemed . . . not to be answering his helm satisfactorily . . . out of temper with his own nervous condition.' At all events, on reaching his home in Grafton Street, he slipped on the stairs and broke a bone in his knee. *Cymbeline* was revived without him and Ellen Terry and played to bad business. *Olivia* followed, with Ellen Terry and Herman Vezin, and only played for nineteen performances. The season of 1896–97 resulted in a loss of £10,000. While on tour in 1897 his beloved dog, Fussie, while in pursuit of a sandwich in the coat pocket of one of the stage staff, fell down a trap in the stage and was killed instantly. To anyone as fond of old friends in general, and dogs in particular, this loss was far from being the least painful that Irving suffered in those darkening days. In her memoirs, Ellen Terry describes how Irving ate his supper that night with the dog's body curled up near him, and talking to it as if it were still alive. She says: 'After the dog's death Henry was really alone.'

1898 was a bad year for Irving. *Peter the Great* and *The Medicine Man* proved disasters. Then his scenery was destroyed by fire, leaving him with only those sets which happened to be in the theatre at the time. Again he fell ill. While walking with Lord Rosebery he got his feet wet, contracted pleurisy, and for some time lay at death's door. This illness weakened his chest, and, in consequence, his diction, though as careful as ever, was robbed of power. Also, in this unlucky year, the Lyceum became a limited liability company on terms very disadvantageous to Irving. So that when *Robespierre* was produced the great actor was suffering in fortune, mind, and body. A story is told how Irving, on the first night, received two ovations on his first entrance, a false and a genuine one. Robespierre's was preceded by one of his spies, wearing a red coat who reconnoitred stealthily. The coat however was familiar to Lyceum audiences. It was one Irving himself wore in *The Lyons Mail*. Consequently, as the actor entered with his back to the audience, he was mistaken for his chief and received a tremendous reception. Afterwards, when Robespierre himself appeared, the applause lasted for five minutes, so glad were the spectators to see their beloved actor recovered and at work once more.

But the end was in sight. Never, after that fatal saunter in the wet grass with Rosebery, did 'the Chief's' health and strength return. His heart, physically speaking, was never strong again, though in a metaphorical sense it can never be said to have weakened by a jot beneath the 'bludgeonings of chance.' To his last days, we are told, his favourite word was one that describes his whole glorious career—'Triumphant.'

JAMES DALE.

XLVII

IRVING as CORIOLANUS

Lyceum Theatre, 15th of April, 1901 :—

CORIOLANUS

WRITTEN BY WILLIAM SHAKESPEARE

ROMANS

Caius Marcius Coriolanus	HENRY IRVING
Titus Lartius	MR. LUGG
Cominius	MR. TYARS
Menenius Agrippa	MR. J. H. BARNES
Sicinius Velutus	MR. JAMES HEARN
Junius Brutus	MR. LAURENCE IRVING
Young Marcius	MISS QUEENIE TARVIN
A Senator	MR. TABB
A Herald	MR. NASH
An Ædile	MR. MARK PATON
A Soldier	MR. FISHER
1st Citizen	MR. C. DODSWORTH
2nd Citizen	MR. CLIFFORD BOWN
3rd Citizen	MR. KENNEY
4th Citizen	MR. REYNOLDS
Volumnia	MISS ELLEN TERRY
Virgilia	MISS MABEL HACKNEY
Valeria	MISS MAUD MILTON
Gentlewoman	MISS EDITH THOMPSON

VOLSCIANS

Tullus Aufidius	MR. W. E. ASHCROFT
Lieutenant to Aufidius	MR. MARSDEN
Volscian Lord	MR. BULLER
Sentinel	MR. L. BELMORE
1st Servingman	MR. J. ARCHER
2nd Servingman	MR. ABLETT
A Citizen of Antium	MR. LAMBERT

ACT I, SCENE 1. *Rome—The Forum ;* SCENE 2. *A Room in Marcius's House ;* SCENE 3. *Near Camp of Cominius ;* SCENE 4. *Rome—A Street ;* SCENE 5. *A Street—The Forum ;* SCENE 6. *A Street ;* SCENE 7. *The Capitol.* ACT II, SCENE 1. *Rome—The Forum ;* SCENE 2. *A Street ;* SCENE 3. *Room in Coriolanus's House ;* SCENE 4. *The Forum.* ACT III, SCENE 1. *Antium—Before Aufidius's House ;* SCENE 2. *Rome—The Forum ;* SCENE 3. *A Camp near Rome ;* SCENE 4. *Rome—The Forum ;* SCENE 5. *Antium —A Public Place.*

TWENTY-TWO years before Sir Henry Irving produced *Coriolanus*—that is to say on 25 July 1879—he announced that during the next season he hoped to present this play at the Lyceum, but at the close of that season, his only reference to it was that Mr. Alma-Tadema had completed 'his magnificent series of studies' for it. At the close of yet another season, 1881, he announced that *Romeo and Juliet* would be his next 'Shakespearean venture' to be 'followed in due course' by *Coriolanus*.

This promise was not redeemed for twenty years, and when his final decision to revive the play was made public, many of his friends and admirers doubted his wisdom in presenting it, at a time when, struggling against illness and misfortune, he would in all probability lack the energy to portray such a strenuous part.

A review of the stage history of the play—which is a short one—will partly explain his friends' misgivings as to his policy.

Coriolanus was first printed in the folio of 1623, but when written and where first played we can only conjecture. From internal evidence of style and metre it would appear to belong to Shakespeare's later years, probably about 1608–1610, and from the references to the part in the Funeral Elegy on the death of Richard Burbage, who died 13 March 1619, we gather that it was one of that actor's creations, and therefore the Globe as the place of production.

The first recorded production of Shakespeare's text was at Drury Lane, in 1820, all previous representations being either impudent mutilations by Nahum Tate and John Dennis, or an amalgam of Shakespeare's with another tragedy of *Coriolanus*, written by James Thomson, the poet of *The Seasons*. Thomson went for his fable, not to Plutarch, but to Dionysius Halicarnassensis and Livy, both of whom call the mother of Coriolanus, Veturia, and the wife, Volumnia. The scene takes place wholly in the Volscian Camp, and his plan differs materially from Shakespeare's, except in the Fifth Act. His Coriolanus, too, was a much more amiable character, 'with every virtue of civil life adorned.'

Six months after Thomson's death, it was produced at Covent Garden, on 13 January 1749, by James Quin, for the benefit of the poet's family, and ran for ten nights.

Although generally considered unsuitable for the stage, being too declamatory, with very little action, Thomas Sheridan thought otherwise, and from it and Shakespeare's play, compiled his *Coriolanus, or, The Roman Matron*, announced as by Thomson and Shakespeare! It was played at Covent Garden, on 10 December 1754, with Sheridan himself as Coriolanus, and enjoyed a few years' popularity. 'In this alteration,' wrote a critic in *The European Magazine*, 'the best parts of Shakespeare and Thomson are retained and compose a more pleasing drama than that of either author separately.'

In Roman parts John Kemble excelled all his predecessors, especially in Coriolanus. Indeed, no actor has ever been so identified with a classical part. Yet he did not trust to Shakespeare alone, but made use of Sheridan's compilation, when preparing his acting version. His first three Acts were judiciously altered from Shakespeare, with omissions only, but in the Fourth and Fifth Acts many lines and speeches from Thomson were retained, the final scene between Coriolanus and Aufidius being mainly his. These additions not only escaped censure, but appear to have been welcomed, in his historic revival, at Drury Lane, 7 February, 1789.

With Kemble it was a case of the actor fitting the part and the part fitting the actor, and his appearance, proud bearing, and the haughty tone of his voice, combined to make his performance a unique one. His first entrance was most effective, if a little theatrical. When he stalked on, a most imposing figure, his built-up sandals adding two inches to his stature, wearing a long red cloak, with which he made much play, the mob fell back as though they had run against a mad bull, and he looked, in the eyes of the audience, as if he had the power to beat forty of them. For nearly thirty years it remained his most popular part, and in it he gave his farewell performance, at Covent Garden 23 June 1817, when it was admitted that he had never acted so superbly.

When, on 29 November 1819, at the same theatre, Macready made a successful attempt to rival Kemble as Coriolanus, that success was evidently partly due to his having been influenced by the older actor's reading, for *The Morning Herald* wrote that he 'approached Kemble in the magic power of imposing an illusive image of physical grandeur upon the sense of the beholder, merely by some slight change of attitude or action.' That is the last record of the Shakespeare-Thomson *Coriolanus* on the London Stage, for it was replaced by the original text, at Drury Lane, two months later, 24 January 1820, with Edmund Kean as Coriolanus.

Macready first played the text at Drury Lane 27 May 1831,

but it was not until 12 May 1838, under his own management of Covent Garden, that he gave to the stage his scholarly production of *Coriolanus*, which added to his fame as producer and actor. A most heroic figure, it became one of his best Shakespearean parts, which he frequently played during terms of management there and at Drury Lane.

During these years his rivals in the part were John Vandenhoff and Charles Dillon, and after his retirement in 1851, his two lieutenants, James R. Anderson and Samuel Phelps, carried on his tradition. All these actors gave what the critics called 'powerful impersonations,' and at the time of the Lyceum revival a few old playgoers retained memories of Phelps's vigorous acting, and shook their heads when it was announced, and the 'old-time tragedians' ridiculed the idea of Irving attempting the character.

I was fairly well acquainted with this stage history of the play, and had a good knowledge of the text, but I had never seen it acted, and so I went to the Lyceum with an open mind. And as I have never seen it played since, I give my impressions of that performance without being influenced by the opinions of others who saw the play later.

It was during the second week of the run that I saw *Coriolanus*, and it was indeed a revival worth waiting for. It was Irving's last Shakespearean revival at the Lyceum. After thirty-seven years it is difficult to remember all the details, but some were so vividly impressed on my mind that I have never forgotten them.

It is one of the longer Shakespearean plays, so I knew it would have to be considerably compressed. I thought the 'cuts' were generally very judicious, and also the omission of the fighting scenes before Corioli, such scenes being difficult to represent on the stage with conviction.

The production was the finest I had seen at the Lyceum. The scenery, some of the best work of Hawes Craven and Joseph Harker, from the designs of Sir Alma-Tadema, was of rare beauty, using that word in the sense that Keats uses it, in his 'Ode on a Grecian Urn,' 'beauty is truth, truth beauty,' for the archæological accuracy of the mounting was a great feature of this revival.

One scene I can still visualize, remarkable for its simple grandeur—'The Capitol.' Against grey stone walls, with little ornamentation, tier upon tier of seats filled the whole back of the scene, on which were seated the white-robed, grey-bearded senators, whose interest in the proceedings was intense. When at the close of the scene, wishing him good speed, they exclaimed with one voice: 'To Coriolanus come all joy and honour,' one felt it was no ordinary crowd just speaking in unison, but that there was individuality in it, as if each senator was speaking for himself. Indeed, throughout the play, the crowd is a sort of moving background, quite as important as the chorus of a Greek tragedy. And although an extremely well-balanced company gave Irving capital support, the crowd—excelling any formerly seen at the Lyceum—gave him much more. And it is to this turbulent rabble, seething with discontent, and with enmity in their hearts towards him, that Coriolanus first enters. Irving's entrance, unlike Kemble's spectacular one, was almost unobtrusive, but once there, how he filled the stage! Before that scene was over, it was evident that his was Shakespeare's Coriolanus—the proudest man the poet ever drew.

And his conception of this proud man, so obsessed with the sense of his own superiority that he can brook no interference even from his friends, and possessed with such excessive contempt for the plebeians that he can scarcely give utterance to it, was masterly. Instead of hectoring the mob he stabbed it again and again with his quiet contempt and scorn, but he never descended to sneer. This contempt he extended later to the Tribunes, and his scornful retort to Sicinius (Act III, Scene 2) I especially remember, perhaps because it is a familiar quotation:

> '*Shall* remain!
> Hear you this Triton of the Minnows? Mark you
> His absolute *shall*.'

The following scene, in his own house, in which his mother and friends counsel moderation when he goes to face the incensed people, was a perfect specimen of Irving's art, acted with playful, if at times grim humour, culminating with the last lines—into which he put such meaning—as he leaves for the Forum:

> CORIOLANUS: The word is *mildly*. Pray you let us go:
> Let them accuse me by invention, I
> Will answer in mine honour.
> MENENIUS: Ay, but mildly.
> CORIOLANUS: Well, *mildly* be it then. *Mildly*.

Yet, arrived at the Forum, he throws all discretion to the winds, and in spite of the promptings of Menenius and Cominius, instead of trying to appease the citizens, he insults them with such arrogance that they drive him from the city.

With what concentrated scorn, yet with dignity and self-possession, he replied to their sentence of banishment:

> 'You common cry of curs! whose breath I hate
> As reek o' the rotten fens, whose loves I prize
> As the dead carcases of unburied men
> That do corrupt my air, *I banish you;*
> And here remain with your uncertainty!'

What a contrast to Edmund Kean, who, we are told, spoke these lines with 'all the virulence of execration and rage of impotent despair, as if he had to strain every nerve and faculty of soul to shake off the contamination of their hated power over him.' That scene closed the Second Act.

The Third and last Act opened in Antium, before Aufidius's house. Rather a drastic 'cut,' but theatrically effective for our next view of Coriolanus was as the solitary exile waiting outside the house, uncertain of his reception. Within the house, Aufidius was struck with the stranger's dignified appearance:

> 'Thou hast a grim appearance, and the face
> Bears a command in't, though thy tackle's torn,
> Thou show'st a noble vessel. What thy name?'

It was the soldier who answered him, incisively recounting his wrongs, and while admitting the wrongs he had inflicted on them, offered to repair them by leading them against his own countrymen. But Irving never lost his dignity nor became a suppliant; it seemed as if he conferred a favour.

Irving gave us another phase of the character in his meeting with Menenius—a little suspected one, of gentleness. He was firm in his refusal to discuss matters with him, but tempered his refusal with kindly remembrance of their former friendship.

> 'Therefore, be gone
> Mine ears against your suits are stronger than
> Your gates against my force. Yet, for I loved thee,
> Take this along; I writ it for thy sake
> [*Gives a letter*
> And would have sent it. Another word, Menenius,
> I will not hear thee speak.'

The great scene of supplication with Volumnia and Virgilia was ineffective. Up to this point Miss Terry's Volumnia had been quite good and interesting, if scarcely the Roman matron, but in this scene she was overweighed. Irving was very happy in his delivery of the opening speeches, but in Volumnia's final pleading, one of the greatest and most moving speeches in all Shakespeare, Miss Terry was unconvincing, and this evidently reacted upon Irving, whose last two speeches were also rather ineffective.

But Volumnia had succeeded in her mission. His pride and inflexible purpose to humble Rome, or to use his own words, 'Rome's mechanics,' were borne down by her supplications—the son had yielded to the mother—and he returned to Antium to face the enmity and jealousy of Aufidius. There was resignation in Irving's Coriolanus, as, facing the conspirators, after calmly stating his case, he realized that he had sealed his doom. With every inducement for railing—indeed the text would warrant it—

> 'Pardon me, lords, 'tis the first time that ever
> I was forced to *scold!*'

he answered the taunts and insults of Aufidius with quiet disdain, even in the lines:

> 'Measureless liar, thou hast made my heart
> Too great for what contains it.'

Then, with flashing eyes, and defiance in his voice and whole bearing, he reminded them of their former humiliation:

> 'If you have writ your annals true, 'tis there,
> That, like an eagle in a dove-cote, I
> Fluttered your Volscians in Corioli,
> Alone I did it. Boy!'

And so he met his death at the hands of the conspirators, not only because he had made peace with Rome and withdrawn the Volscian army, but as a result of the treachery of Aufidius, so that when the curtain fell on the words 'He shall have a noble memory,' much sympathy was felt for the victim of it.

And still identifying Irving with the part, one mused what might have been his fate under happier circumstances. He had virtues, but by the overweening sense of his own superiority he forfeited his place in the history of the great sons of Rome.

FREDERICK HARKER.

XLVIII

IRVING as DANTE

Theatre Royal, Drury Lane, 30th of April, 1903 :—

DANTE

WRITTEN BY MM. VICTORIEN SARDOU AND EMILE MOREAU
(*Rendered into English by Laurence Irving*)

Dante	HENRY IRVING
Cardinal Colonna	MR. WILLIAM MOLLISON
Nello Della Pietra	MR. NORMAN MCKINNEL
Bernardino	MR. GERALD LAWRENCE
Giotto	MR. H. B. STANFORD
Casella	MR. JAMES HEARN
Forese	MR. VINCENT STERNROYD
Bellacqua	MR. G. ENGLETHORPE
Malatesta	MR. JERROLD ROBERTSHAW
Corso	MR. CHARLES DODSWORTH
Ostasio	MR. FRANK TYARS
Ruggieri	MR. WILLIAM LUGG
The Grand Inquisitor	MR. WILLIAM FARREN, JUNR.
Paolo	MR. L. RACE DUNROBIN
Ugolino	MR. MARK PATON
Lippo	MR. JOHN ARCHER
Conrad	MR. W. L. ABLETT
Enzio	MR. F. D. DAVIES
Fadrico	MR. H. PORTER
Merchant	MR. R. P. TABB
Merchant	MR. H. GASTON
Townsman	MR. T. REYNOLDS
Townsman	MR. A. FISHER
A Servant	MR. J. IRELAND
Pia dei Tolomei / *Gemma*	MISS LENA ASHWELL
Abbess	MISS WALLIS
Francesca	MISS LILIAN ELDÉE
Helen of Swabia	MISS LAURA BURT
Sandra	MISS ADA MELLON
Picarda	MISS E. BURNAND
Tessa	MISS HILDA AUSTIN
Marozia	MISS MAB PAUL
Cilia	MISS ADA POTTER
Lucrezia	MISS E. LOCKETT
Julia	MISS MARY FOSTER
Fidelia	MISS DOROTHY ROWE
Maria	MISS MAY HOLLAND
Nun	MISS EMMELINE CARDER

Nun	Miss E. F. Davis
Custodian	Miss Grace Hampton
A Townswoman	Miss Mabel Rees

SPIRITS

The Spirit of Beatrice	Miss Nora Lancaster
Virgil	Mr. Walter Reynolds
Cain	Mr. F. Murray
Charon	Mr. Leslie Palmer
Cardinal Boccasini	Mr. M. Faydene
Cardinal Orsini	Mr. J. Middleton
Jacques Molay	Mr. W. J. Yeldham

PROLOGUE. *The Tower of Hunger, Pisa.* Act I, Scene 1. *The Springtide Fête, Florence ;* Scene 2. *Malatesta's House.* Act II, Scene 1. *The Death of Pia ;* Scene 2. *The Convent of San Pietro.* Act III, Scene 1. *The Campo Santo, Florence ;* Scene 2. *The Door of Hell ;* Scene 3. *The Barque of Charon ;* Scene 4. *The Fiery Graves ;* Scene 5. *The Circle of Ice ;* Scene 6. *The Bridge of Rocks ;* Scene 7. *The Valley of Asphodels.* Act IV. *The Papal Palace, Avignon* (1303–1314).

It may confidently be asserted that the average Drury Lane playgoer is not a Dantist. . . . It is necessary to insist upon this point, for the simple reason that the *Dante* which Sir Henry Irving produced last night at Drury Lane has been produced, naturally, for the Drury Lane playgoer. It is directly addressed to him ; it takes into account his little fraction of knowledge and his very big fraction of ignorance ; if the average Drury Lane playgoer believes in it, likes it, and is impressed by it, why, then it has achieved his object. It is necessary, we say, to insist upon this point because for Dantists, for people who know and love their *Divina Commedia*, the Drury Lane *Dante* will not do at all. When they are asked, as they are, to swallow the story of an amour—an adulterous amour—between Dante and Pia dei Tolomei, they will at once remark that, where much is uncertain, one thing is quite certain and that is that Dante had not even a bowing acquaintance with this lady. And for the evidence they will say : see Canto V of the *Purgatorio*. Further, they will point out that the house of the Malatesta was not at Florence ; that the love story of Bernadino, brother of Francesca da Rimini, and Gemma, daughter of Dante by Pia dei Tolomei, is all nonsense ; that it was not Cardinal Colonna who reigned in Avignon ; that the several ' circles ' in the Inferno and Purgatory Scenes of the Third Act are all mixed up, like Sancho Panza's cabbages and baskets ; and so forth, and so forth. They will say all this and more. Probably they will invent an additional ' circle ' in Hell,

IRVING *AS* *DANTE*

FROM A DRAWING BY
CHARLES A. BUCHEL

for the especial benefit of MM. Sardou and Moreau, who have laid sacrilegious hands upon one of the greatest poems in literature. The people for whom this *Dante* is intended are, first and foremost, the playgoers—there are legions of them—who have fallen under the spell of Sir Henry Irving's magic personality. Whatever he chooses to play is, they feel, good enough for them. So long as he figures in the foreground of the scene, giving them the postures and the diction and the picturesque presence which they know, they are quite content. There remain in the people—men and brethren, even these, as weak as flesh, if not weaker, who cling to the old-fashioned prejudice that a play should be a play; that it should have strong, continuous and cumulative dramatic interest. These people, we conjecture, will leave Drury Lane not quite so contented as the others. . . .

M. Sardou was not bound to choose this particular subject. Having chosen it, he had two courses open to him. (1) Either he should have handled the poet's life, or so much as anyone knows of it, or (2) he should have let life and text go, and have invented a brand-new drama of his own. As a matter of fact, he has tried to blend both methods. He has strung little Dantean episodes, more or less authentic, on a cock-and-bull story of his own invention. The result is a ramshackle, confusing, rather irritating *malino*.

As for Sir Henry, it is, of course, obvious that if ever man was born to look Dante to the life he is that man. The moment he emerges from the porch of the church at Pisa you recognize the fresco profile. And he wanders through the play—for really he is only a wanderer—with just the right air and accent of ascetic severity and melancholy aloofness. He seems not to be of common clay—for that matter Sir Henry Irving (even if he be playing Jingle or Macaire) never does. And yet Sardou would have us believe him to be of the commonest clay; he is the lover of Pia dei Tolomei, a married lady, and the father of her child Gemma. No sooner have we learned this than we are interrupted by a hollow groan from a tower window in the left, at which a gaunt form appears, crying for bread. It is of course Count Ugolino. When Dante, horror-stricken, pleads for the starving man's release the terrible Archbishop Ruggieri throws the keys of the tower into the river. Dante, enraged, dashes down the Archbishop's crozier and is forthwith excommunicated, but he does not quit the scene until he has replied with what may be called a counter-curse.

Act I opens with a glow of colour and sunshine—the springtide fête at Florence. A young painter is at his easel; who could it be but Giotto? A cloaked figure crosses the stage scowling; it is Malatesta, who has moved house from Rimini to Florence. . . . And that fair-haired girl? Miss Lena Ashwell, representing Gemma, Dante's daughter grown up. And that cowled Monk? Dante himself, the exile returned, in disguise. After an affecting interview between father and daughter (in which Sir Henry reached an unusual pitch of simple tenderness) a woman's shriek is heard from Malatesta's house. The scene rapidly changes to the interior, and we see Malatesta wiping his bloody sword, and the dead bodies of the lovers half-hidden behind a curtain. In the confusion Pia's husband carries off Gemma, pursued by Dante, and the spectator's mind begins to get as confused as the turmoil of the scene.

In Act II we see Miss Ashwell, who was Gemma a moment ago, turned to Pia once more. As Pia, she dies in the foul air of the marshes, and immediately reappears as Gemma in the Convent of San Pietro. Enter Dante and Bernadino leading a rescue party. Dante, hiding with Gemma behind the arras, nearly suffers the fate of Polonius. The sword of one of the soldiery, probing the arras, has pierced his side, and he is left for dead on the floor.

But in Act III he is alive again, mourning over the tomb of Beatrice in the Campo Santo at Florence. His old love appears to him in a vision, and bids him, if he would find Gemma again, visit the Nether World. So said, so done. Virgil promptly appears and conducts Dante to the Door of Hell, past the Fiery Graves, through the Circle of Ice (interview with Ugolino), on towards the Bridge of Rocks (interview with Pia) and finally to the Valley of Asphodels. These interviews result in the information that Gemma has fled with Bernadino to Avignon. Needless to say that all the Infernal and Purgatorial 'Circles' are triumphs of scenic weirdness.

Finally, Act IV. Dante arrives at Avignon, where the man who ought to be a Pope but is only a Cardinal Legate has just condemned Gemma and Bernadino to the stake. But Dante tells him that his own hour has come—and tells him so in one of the finest declamations of the play. At the stroke of six down falls the Cardinal Legate a dead man. Gemma and Bernadino are saved.

Was this rather puerile story worth inventing? Could not some real poet have contrived a worthier scenic arrangement of the Dante legend which might still have exhibited Sir Henry

Irving in every side of his remarkable personality. But, in its absence, there is the Drury Lane *Dante* of MM. Sardou and Moreau, rendered into English by Mr. Laurence Irving—to take or to leave. We know what the Dantists will do—but the others? Well, the others applauded the whole affair last night with a positive frenzy of enthusiasm.

A. B. Walkley.

In *The Times*, 1 May 1903, and reprinted here, by permission, from *Drama and Life* (Methuen).

There are qualities in men and women, inherited or acquired, which often rival their finest work: generosity, practical kindness, an unshakable sense of honour. All these qualities I found in Henry Irving. On three occasions when he was going to America to act during the winter season I had his theatre, the Lyceum, then the classic and first theatre in London. It would be hard to find a man more considerate or fairer to deal with. He also showed thoughtfulness and generosity in leaving a good staff of stage hands and a number of useful properties.

Before he left for America he came to see me. I was much impressed by his face; it wore the serious regard of a thinker, a scholar; but when he smiled the grave look vanished and it was like the sun emerging from an austere sky—a smile radiant as unlooked for. He told me he felt that I was making a mistake in opening my first season in England with *Ingomar* (a very charming old play translated from the German); he thought it old-fashioned and feared that the London public would laugh at it. He suggested that I should do better to take all his *Romeo and Juliet* scenery and start with Juliet.

I told him that it would be a far greater mistake to make my *début* before the London public in the *rôle* which their idolized Ellen Terry had acted during the long and recent run of that play at the Lyceum; I preferred to risk it and begin with *Ingomar*. But he was still unconvinced. Then, smiling, he said: "Here is a piece of advice which you would do well to follow. Always remember that a half-crown and a goose at Christmas, given to the right people, will make your life in London a bed of roses." Even at that first interview I felt we had become friends.

Ingomar was given and everyone—from the royal box to the pit—seemed to delight in it. Irving was the first to wire hearty congratulations, adding that he was glad that I had not followed his suggestion. There is something fine in a man who makes no excuse for having given the wrong advice. His telegram came from Liverpool, where he and his company were about to embark for their first season in America.

For me his greatest performances were in *Louis the Eleventh*, *Charles the First*, *The Lyons Mail*, *The Bells*, and *The Corsican Brothers*. He was also unforgettable in a short play called *A Story of Waterloo*. Unfortunately, I never saw him either in *Hamlet* or *Becket*. No one in the world could have looked Dante as Irving did. He *was* the poet himself. His acting also fitted his appearance and brought one back to Florence and those glorious days of art when Giotto built the tower and all the art was impeccably beautiful. His movement and voice seemed made for the character. It was after that performance that he told me he would be sure to die a poor man, though when I saw the play the house was crowded. Little did I think it was the last time I should see him and acting so superbly. It was his last new production in London though not the last part he played, which was Tennyson's *Becket*. *Dante* was not successful either in London or in America.

In the Lyceum of those days there was a large room furnished with armour, a long table and many comfortable chairs; close to it was a good kitchen. It was known as the Beefsteak Club and was built on the site of the old club of that name which in its heyday boasted of such members as Garrick, Hogarth, Doctor Johnson, Goldsmith, and Sir Joshua Reynolds. There all the great artists and literary men were wont to assemble, and here it was that Irving gave his celebrated suppers. At one of these Irving pointed out to me a large, pleasant, boyish-looking man at the table and said: "That is young Harmsworth. He edits a paper called *Answers*. I prophesy a fine career for him." Irving was right: young Harmsworth afterwards became Lord Northcliffe. Toole was at that supper too; it was the last time I saw him. As we were leaving Ellen Terry said to me: "There is no use speaking to him, he won't know you; he does not recognize me." As we were going down the rickety old stairs he patted my head, but I could sense from his eyes that he did not know me. I believe I am right in saying it was down those stairs that Irving fell and broke his leg, an accident that brought his production of *Richard the Third* to a premature end and involved him in serious financial loss. He revived the play later, when it proved one of his most triumphant successes.

A box at his theatre was always at my disposal. One night I took Lord Lytton (father of the present earl), Lady Lytton, and their daughters to see *Faust*—a play written by Wills. Lord Lytton was a gifted linguist and knew the great literature of many foreign countries as well as he did his own, and was known to be an outstanding literary critic. He was particularly fond of Goethe's *Faust*. He thought Wills's *Faust* a poor play and grew restless during the performance. When it was over we went on the stage to see Irving, and on his asking Lytton what he thought of the play he received a frank answer. Lytton said that he considered the scene in which Mephistopheles boasted of his powers particularly bad. " A being possessed of such powers would never stoop to boast of them. Why, my boy Victor could have written a better scene ! " " You see," said Irving, smiling, " Wills did not write that scene, it was I who wrote it." Consternation spread over Lytton's face; he confessed to me afterwards that the interview had given him a bad night.

Ellen Terry told me a story of Irving and William Terriss, his dashing leading man. Irving, being punctual himself, demanded punctuality from his actors; Terriss was not infrequently late at rehearsals. On being rebuked for this he was always ready with an excuse. Once he ascribed his lateness to his watch; on another occasion to the cat having kittened in his only pair of trousers. Finally, he arrived one morning half an hour late and Irving, his patience exhausted, told him that they would have to part company. Terriss looked very sad and replied: " Governor, you'll be sorry you have spoken to me like that when I tell you that I was up all night nursing my poor mother. She died this morning." The warm-hearted Irving was all sympathy and apologized for having spoken to him harshly. Not long after the play had begun Terriss was airing his eye at the peep-hole in the curtain when Irving passed. " Governor," said Terriss, " please look at that sweet lady on the gangway in the first row of the dress-circle . . . my mother ! " Irving's sense of humour restrained him from saying anything. He just smiled ! The story is characteristic of both men and was told to me as true.

One evening at a very distinguished gathering a friend both of Disraeli and Irving told me that there was a marked resemblance between the two men: that not only in certain mannerisms but in turn of mind they distinctly reminded him of each other.

Irving was nearly always correct in the costumes he chose for his productions, though happily he allowed himself a certain amount of licence when it was a question of achieving a picturesque effect. He told me that he once wanted red-heeled shoes in one of his historical plays. A learned man questioned him about it, asking what authority he had for such a feature in the costume of the period in question. Irving replied that his authority was an ancient manuscript in the British Museum —knowing his questioner would never trouble to look it up. In Tennyson's *Becket* he wore the picturesque black and white habit of the Dominicans. This was an anachronism, for Becket was martyred in 1170, the year in which St. Dominic was born. Irving was right in exercising this licence, for the habit he wore was both becoming and effective. No one noticed the anachronism.

To me his character, culture, and personality were even greater than his great acting.

Irving's death was a shock and sorrow to multitudes of playgoers. Our old friend, Canon Weldon—then living in the cloisters of Westminster Abbey—invited us to dine and sleep there the day before the funeral. We accepted his invitation with gratitude. Our host, knowing my predilection for seeing great cathedrals in solitude by night, suggested our visiting the Abbey at a late hour. A man who had helped to prepare Irving's last resting-place met us with a lantern as we entered 'that wilderness of tombs.' Here and there this meagre, solitary light fell upon the ghostly figures and effigies 'of those who in life kingdoms could not satisfy. Shapes, forms, artifices devised to catch the casual notice of passers and save from forgetfulness for a few short years a name which once aspired to occupy ages of the world's thought and admiration.' We passed into St. Faith's Chapel, where, on a catafalque flanked by six tall candles, lay the mortal remains of Irving, the coffin covered by a pall made of small lustrous leaves, which looked like an Arthurian armour. So many times had one seen Irving surrounded by enthusiastic crowds, brilliant lights, that it seemed hardly possible that it was he who lay, his last night upon earth, in the silence and dusky light of St. Faith's Chapel. We knelt in prayer beside the coffin. On leaving the bier-side our guide with the lantern led us to the resting-place they had prepared which lay next to the tomb of David Garrick. Part of the wall between the two graves had broken away and we were thus enabled to see the coffin of Garrick. Time had dealt kindly with it.

Our footsteps, as we passed through the empty aisles, awoke unearthly echoes. The door clanged to; and the Abbey bell struck midnight.

MARY ANDERSON-NAVARRO.

XLIX

IRVING AS STAGE MANAGER

In January 1903 died Miss Roma Guillon Le Thière, Marion de Lorme in *Richelieu* and Lady Ashton. Irving tore the announcement from *The Morning Post* of the 9th inst., and sent it to Austin Brereton: 'In July 1869, she produced at the Haymarket a comedy written by herself, entitled *All for Money*. The cast included Miss Amy Sedgwick, Sir Henry Irving and Mrs. Stephens.' Irving underlined '*produced*' and added: 'No, she did *not*, she wrote a comedy; Miss Amy Sedgwick produced it and forgot to pay actors' salaries the last week. *I* was one of 'em.'

The producer then was the manager; the word had no use in its modern sense. The *metteur en scène* was simply stage-manager, who knew his Theatre from float to horizon cloth; who could not only act any part in the play but tell his actors how it should be done—even show them; a far more important accomplishment.

The Autocrat of the modern Theatre is of another sort; he has theories on rhythm in lighting, colour in movement and dimension in speech, which quite often he finds difficult to communicate. This has been known to cloud the meaning of the play. But he consoles himself that if the play fails the fault must be with the cast—or possibly the author; if it succeeds the glory is certainly his.

The stage-manager was not starred—or is it 'featured'?—he lived in the theatre and worked, keeping a repertory of a dozen or twenty plays ready for production.

We hear of the Producer sitting with his cast round him day after day for a year creating the atmosphere of a new play, which suggests a congregation of Buddhas solemnly contemplating their navels.

The Theatre is changed but I doubt the moderns could teach the old stage-manager anything about atmosphere.

Irving was a stage-manager.

Irving possessed in the highest degree the gift of the superlative stage-manager, the gift of co-ordinating, single-handed, all the various entities that make a stage production; the actors, the scenery, the costumes, the lighting, the music, the effects.

He had been stage-manager at the Queen's and the St. James's before he joined Mr. Bateman at the Lyceum. What he may not have learned in a long experience of standard plays with their conventional, formalized business, intuition taught him.

This was abundantly proved when he became manager. He was impatient to impress; he did not wait till curtain-rise to imbue his public with the spirit of the play, he caught them in the vestibule, even before they entered it, for the three flaming torches above the portico of the old Lyceum symbolized the spirit within; they were more arresting than the lights to-day in Piccadilly Circus; electric light is static, even though it wink; those flaming torches were alive.

And within the spirit gripped you; it had enveloped you before you took your seat; gas-lit candles in their wine-coloured shades glowed softly on the myrtle-green and cream and purple with its gilt mouldings and frescoes and medallions by Bartolozzi: the green baize in a diffused bluish mist; the music that did not start but insinuated itself upon you till the baize melted and you were in the picture, beholding, yet part of it. Let it be the battlements of Elsinore—the Witches' heath—Doctor Primrose's orchard—Mathias' inn—or the river at Hampton Palace, you were in it and of it before the action of the play began.

I speak, of course, of Irving's Lyceum; such effect would be impossible in the music-hall Mr. Barrasford built into its shell when the old theatre was gutted.[1] Of that theatre only the portico remains. As you enter you are rudely reminded of what once was by a bust, a crude travesty of his noble features, that seems to have been set up by a jeering, if not malignant hand, to recall past glories and decry them. It is better so. What he created is dead—beyond resuscitation.

In that different world the Theatre was loved as an institution, it was a centre of art and gathered a dignity which, alas! is gone for ever, thanks in great part to the impertinent familiarity of the gossip-writer and the inquisition of the press photographer.

We are in the old theatre; the curtain is risen and we are attent—in Alsace—in the Burgomaster's inn. All is calm; the men drink and drone, the woman knits, the fire glows comfort, though without is a heavy snowfall and a rustling wind, all is calm—Is it? there is—*something*, something swirling in the gale, sinister, foreboding—we lean forward, concentrated, rapt—suddenly a *crash!* We sit tense. The gale has blown in a

[1] The Lyceum rebuilt as a music-hall was opened under the management of Thomas Barrasford on the 31 December 1904.

window and smashed a tray of glass that stood before it—nothing: —but the sense of foreboding persists—tension is strained to the utmost—a sudden gust, a swirl of snow and He stands in the doorway—' 'z I! '—and thereafter tension never relaxes. Our eyes riveted upon him, we devour his every movement; he unlaces his boot; someone lets fall the word 'mesmerist'; his fingers stiffen, his eyes speak apprehension—fear. Gordon Craig was mistaken; there are no bells yet, not till he is seated at the table with Walter and Hans, his profile towards us, his wine-glass at his right hand; as he turns to lift it we see his face full, and at that moment comes the whisper: 'Polish Jew'; *that* is what wakens the jangling in his brain and we hear the echo of those ghostly bells which have haunted him for years and are to knell him to his death.

And so in every play was each effect as carefully prepared.

Comparisons were made between Irving's settings and Tree's. There was no comparison. Tree put on some striking scenes; Irving never. His were not striking, they were inevitably *right*. If squalor was required we had it—grandeur, dignity, they were there, but never obtrusively, never challenging attention. Irving gave richness, Tree was gaudy. Both were accused of smothering Shakespeare. It was not so; Irving decorated Shakespeare as a priest his altar; Tree as a trader his shop window.

Note the different attitude to costume; Irving would have nothing white, it was too crude, every shirt, cuff and kerchief, every scrap of lace was tea-tinted. The clothes were lived in. Don Pedro, Don John, Claudio and Benedick, returned from the war, each commander with his staff and colour, bore evidence of campaigning; richly apparelled as the period and their station demanded but worn, slashed and cobbled; their boots had known service.

The troopers come at the double to the King's tent at Newark, road-stained, grimed, bespattered, with jingling spurs and clatter of accoutrements. The halt in a cloud of dust, is electric.

In *Joseph and his Brethren* Tree marched Egyptian soldiers across the desert *in gilt armour!*

In *The Belle's Stratagem* powder was worn and the manner that goes with it; bearing and gait matched the red-heeled shoe. That meticulous care is no longer practised. An historical drama or period comedy is a happy excuse for fancy dress as worn at the Chelsea Arts Ball. If *The School for Scandal* or *The Rivals* is revived, appropriate costume is discarded, it requires too much study and practice of deportment, which indeed takes years to acquire. Now that Fred Terry has passed there is none to set the example, unless it be Eric Maxon or H. O. Nicholson. So they change the period to Directoire whose decadent manner has a certain affinity with the slouch of to-day.

If armour is borne all is burnished—no dent, no tarnish, no rust, even after battle; no tattered standard, no bandaged limb. Not long since there was an imposing spectacle in the period of Queen Anne. How did they carry their hats?—wear their stockings?—and their swords?—and draw them? Obviously the Producer could answer none of these questions. It was ludicrous—and disgraceful.

Did you see the crowd dissolve when Claudius cried: "More lights!" Did you note the shudder that quivered as Louis fondled the peasant Marthe? Did you hear the mob in the *grève* below when they first perceived Dubosc? That was stage-management.

Did it strike you that the country dancers in *Robert Macaire* were country-folk and no other?—that the students and grisettes who danced in *The Dead Heart* were that and no better? Tree's ballet on the Cyprus landing-stage had migrated from the *Folies-Bergères*—apparently.

They said Irving had no ear for music. "Cut that and alter that," he told Hamilton Clark, who grumbled to Ellen Terry: "The Guv'nor doesn't know a thing about it, but he's right." The same with Sullivan. Irving listened to his score for *Macbeth*, walked up and down humming, gesticulating, indicating what he meant to do and what he wanted. Sullivan said: "You're right, Irving, much better than mine, much better," and altered it there and then.

Irving would have no electric light, it glares; his six rows of argand burners in the float glowed softly and gave depth; electric flattens. He performed miracles with gas and calcium lights: the sunset on the quicksands in *Ravenswood*, the dawn in *Romeo and Juliet*, the mystic lake and apparition of Excalibur; they have never been rivalled—even in Oscar Asche's *Mameena*.

We have seen nothing in design or lighting since his time that he did not anticipate—except the novelty of making the picture sprawl outside its frame.

Effects were always perfect. Nothing is less like the sound of breaking glass on the stage than—breaking glass. It never convinces. That and the slamming door are the property man's nightmare. The real thing won't do and as the acoustics in each theatre vary so must the device that convinces, but rarely does it. At the Lyceum it did.

If you heard the thunderstorm in *Faust* you won't have forgotten it—at first you thought it outside the theatre, didn't you?

You *felt* that glide of the royal barge on the river at Hampton Palace; you *felt* the ripple and lap of the water.

The visions in *The Corsican Brothers*, *The Bells*—do you remember the mesmerist's hands?—compelling, ghostly hands, attached to no arms or body—the apparition of Vanderdecken? —of Banquo's ghost?—the aura of Hamlet's father? The crowd-effects—the brawl in *Romeo and Juliet*—the hacking open of the door in Dubosc's attic—the whole process of the attack on the Bastille—the ceremony of Hero's Wedding—the ritual in the Temple of Artemis—the flock of frightened monks before the irruption of knights in the cathedral—Lesurques passing outside the cabaret with Lambert and Guernard as Dubosc lounged in chewing his straw—Ravenswood's black cock's feather on the quicksands of sunset-lit Kelpie's Flow. All were flawless in their verisimilitude.

How did he stage-manage his actors? With infinite and untiring patience, tolerant of all but incompetence. A stage-manager is not a schoolmaster; he expects technical ability in his cast, yet some quite effective actors have none, and to such Irving was merciless. He engaged the best; he paid the most liberal terms; he had a right to expect perfectly equipped players.

Gordon Craig says he danced through his parts, the implication being that the company were a *corps de ballet*, regimented. I prefer a different analogy; for him the play was a *concerto*, and he the soloist. Each movement has its rhythm; a false note, a late attack, a miscalculated rest disrupts the whole. We know the actor who can't—or won't—respond to the beat, who reads with false accent—perversely stresses the wrong word, he jars the whole. He may make his effect but he is an incomplete artist.

In a review of a well-graced actor's reminiscences the writer reproached him that he told much of what he had done, little of how he did it. But could he? Technique cannot be explained: it cannot be taught or copied, it must be evolved in relation to personality; for each individual an individual technique. Three steps to the chair; the right hand shifts it; sit, the left hand falling on its arm; raise the head, the brows knit, the eyes fixed *there*, on that point, as the left elbow finds the spot where the hand was and the hand travels to the chin. Then speak. All carefully planned, the timing accurate to a pulse-beat. Yet to say you do it tells nothing, *how* you do it is all, and that 'how' is peculiar to *you*. I don't say all acting must be done so, but all actors should be able so to do. There are some quite capable who cannot, but they are not the best.

I have met three opponents in stage fights, knowing in each case that my life was in my defence. That is not acting; it's incompetence. The reason the duels at the Lyceum were always convincing was not only that the sword-play was perfect but that the fencers *acted*.

It has been objected against Irving that he was unfair to his fellow-actors, that he bullied at rehearsal, cut their parts and strove to break the spirit of any likely to rival him. Even Gordon Craig seems to support this for he writes: 'If anyone had shown inspiration in Irving's company he would have promptly been sacked.' Certainly for those of us who saw him and his company in play after play this was not apparent; rather did he inspire many whom we knew as 'sound' actors to rise above their mediocrity, and under his direction the best bettered themselves. Haviland's Fool in *King Lear*, Terriss' Mercutio, Forbes-Robertson's Buckingham, Fernandez' Leonato were all touched with divine fire. Others had opportunities they *might* have used. In *King Arthur* he gave the play to Forbes-Robertson, as he did *The Medicine Man* to William Mackintosh. The accusation won't hold. It is not easy to answer it calmly. But as ever his detractors strive to show him as small as themselves. And Ellen Terry?—that devastating, incalculable, unstable woman, to whom he gave poise, direction, control. The perfect Olivia; the ideal Beatrice, yet never the same without his Benedick; Ophelia, sad, demented wraith; an aureole of yellow hair, enquiring nose, mouth like a gashed pomegranate; but Juliet lacked tragic force, a sensuous girl, exquisite in her lighter moods but incapable of emotional depth. How came it that she disappointed as Imogen, Shakespeare's most perfect woman? There was no flaw; the skill, the grace, the charm, were at their ripest. There perhaps is the answer; we had waited overlong, the fruit was too mature.

The critics in the main were fair to Irving—after the public had acclaimed him. A personality so masterful is certain to provoke antipathies. It is strange how every journalist is considered capable of dramatic criticism; such utter ignorance of history and technique of the art as most of them parade would immediately disqualify their verdict on a musical composition or painting. In his pungent essay on the subject, Boucicault said: 'A dramatic critic should be thoroughly acquainted with the principles and craft of dramatic composition, the art of acting, a student of dramatic literature and an experienced spectator of performances. If he has not this storage in his mind he is no more than one of the audience perverted by a little knowledge. In a dramatic performance there is a perfect fusion of the author and the actor. It is a nice appreciation only that can detect whether the merit of the author or the craft of the actor creates the effect or how much applause is due to the one or the other. Again it requires a fine perception to follow a scene and find through the misconception of the actor what the author really meant.' Though with regard to the last sentence I would ask, how many actors have been damned for perfect playing of unsympathetic parts misconceived by the critic?

But here, possibly, Mr. Shaw thought to have found his justification for condemning Irving's Shylock: 'There was no question of a bad Shylock or a good Shylock he was simply not Shylock at all—he played in flat contradiction of the lines and positively acted Shakespeare off the stage.' Such an artist in words as Mr. Shaw knows well how effectively they may be used in contradiction of a sense that is merely obvious. I cannot recall the *minutiæ* of Irving's reading, but very vividly I recall the total effect which was consistent and convincing. Mr. Shaw, arrogating to himself insight to Shakespeare's mind, expresses merely the opinion of Mr. Shaw. It is bold but not convincing. However Shylock be played he cannot escape the sympathy of the public.

As for acting Shakespeare off any stage of which he is given possession—well, we know Mr. Shaw for a master of paradox, second only to G. K. Chesterton.

Mr. Shaw gibed at Irving as illiterate, not only in the Press, but private correspondence, afterwards, in gross taste, made public.

> 'There are four depths of illiteracy,' he wrote, 'each deeper than the one before.
>
> I. The illiteracy of H—— I——.
>
> II. The illiteracy of those illiterate enough not to know he was illiterate.'

The other points do not concern us.

The implication being that, as an illiterate, Irving was incapable of appreciating the graces of contemporary dramatic literature.

'My own art,' wrote Mr. Shaw, referring to the Lyceum, 'the art of literature, is left shabby and ashamed amid the triumph of the painter and the actor.'

The actor. Exactly.

Irving had refused a play by Mr. Shaw and Irving was right.

Irving, the manager, had to find plays with parts suitable to his leading actor, the mainstay of his theatre. Plays may attract but the great actor always draws given that he has parts worthy of him, parts of a certain stature; classic, historic, mythical, legendary, figures of dignity. If Irving rejected any such play no doubt it has since made the fortune of some other manager and the reputation of some star. I haven't heard of it.

'Mr. Shaw is no dramatist,' said A. B. Walkley.

'A critic, not a creator at all,' wrote Max Beerbohm, 'a brilliant dialectician, a master of paradox, but a play is a different matter.'

A monologue is not a play, entertaining though it be, and in the cast of Mr. Shaw's plays there is only—Mr. Shaw.

Granville Barker did well, as John Tanner, to make-up as Mr. Shaw; logically all the other characters should also have made up as Mr. Shaw—and this does not apply only to *Man and Superman*.

Irving had no mind to make up as Mr. Shaw.

Mr. Shaw's attack is weakened for us who know his animus against Irving. James Agate has recorded his words in *Ego III*. 'The reason,' said Mr. Shaw, 'that Irving when he first appeared in Dublin was hissed for three weeks was that Barry Sullivan had taught Dublin what to look for in an actor, and Irving was nothing like it. He had no voice, and, when you looked closely at him, *no face*.' (The italics are mine).

It will be remembered that Irving was greeted with cat-calls and hisses on his first appearance as Cassio in Dublin *before he was allowed to speak*.[1] This kind of misstatement hardly supports Mr. Shaw's case against Irving. He is at liberty of course to prefer the art of his compatriot, but unhappily London would have nothing of Barry Sullivan, it voted him a 'mouther' and old-fashioned. He may not have had the pronounced mannerisms of Phelps—the overworked eyebrows, the shrugging shoulders and the heaving chest: or of Phelps' master, Macready, whose walk as well as speech was so punctuated by pauses, that on his entrance one had time to admire the shape of his nose before one saw an ear—but he was an exemplar of that school, now happily extinct. Irving had corrected their ponderosities as Kean had corrected Kemble's and Garrick Quin's.

[1] See account of Irving's appearance at the Gaiety Theatre, Dublin, in 1860, page 49.

So Barry Sullivan retired to the provinces—permanently; and when Bancroft gave, at the Garrick Club, a supper, to which all the leading figures of the stage were invited, to bid Irving Godspeed on his first visit to America, Barry Sullivan excused himself, for, as he said: "he could not bring himself to acknowledge the justice of the position which Irving had undoubtedly attained."

Undoubtedly. A position which made his burial in Westminster Abbey inevitable—and Mr. Shaw claims the credit for that. He wanted it, he said, 'for the benefit of the profession.' Such magnanimity! He had dissuaded Lady Irving from publishing statements which would have made that ceremony impossible. Yet if, as Mr. Agate's report implies, it was hate or greed or both that prompted Lady Irving's spleen, it had been better left to stultify itself by advertisement. But again, if there was a deeper implication, which Mr. Shaw's story of Lady Irving's vindictiveness conveys, any suggestion of moral irregularity was nullified in advance by Another Lady whose concern for morality even Mr. Shaw will not question. As She bestowed the accolade upon Irving She added graciously: "It gives me very great pleasure, Sir."

Charles Lamb, writing of the Caledonian, said that 'the twilight of dubiety never falls upon him.' It could never have fallen upon that dour Scot, William Archer—least of all in the theatre. He was another who was quite sure—of many things; of the greatness of Ibsen, for example, in face of determined opposition and much opprobrium, and in that his judgment was vindicated. But this champion of the new cult, as then it was, had a foible: he professed to despise melodrama and its exponents. Vituperation is a mild word for what the vials of his indignation poured upon them—as though Ibsen never descended to melodrama, if it be descent! It is a form that demands most consummate skill in stagecraft.

Archer's conception of the ideal Theatre would limit it to pure comedy, which is simply the exposition of character, and stark tragedy, the struggle of man against destiny. If the playgoer could not find his relaxation in these he must be a cretin.

Entertainment? Amusement? Ignoble and degraded cravings! This positive Scot did not appraise the English temperament, or if he did he sought to 'reform it altogether,' so Irving must be squelched. *The Bells*, *The Lyons Mail*, *The Corsican Brothers*, *Louis the Eleventh*—balderdash! But his bias carried him further. *The Fashionable Tragedian* had shown that his animosity extended to the man personally, whom his nonconformity decided was a pernicious influence. Having shot his youthful bolt when its victim was still struggling and defenceless, it seems possible that dubiety did shadow him. When it became certain that the shaft had missed its aim and its object stood not only unscathed but established, the mode of attack became more guarded, more subtle; scratchings and pin-pricks in place of the withering fire of contempt and the bombardment of abuse. Many were deceived and cried: 'Our critic has recanted!' He never recanted and Irving sank into old age and lamentable fortune, victim to the last of a malignity which had pursued him for twenty-eight years.

But Irving's spirit avenged him; it haunted his enemy with ghosts of Iago and Mephistopheles so that he writhed in nightmare and dreamed a play and on his wakening the High Priest of Ibsen laboured and brought it forth and lo, it was a *melodrama!* Nightmare indeed! The departed spirit, like magnanimous Jove, had descended upon him in a shower of gold; the play brought Archer a small fortune. But the obsession had been so potent that the pivot of its plot was the Irvingesque character of the Raja of Rookh.[1]

The Press, as it affects the box-office, naturally concerns the manager, but as actor, Irving was little affected by critics. None could be more severe on his efforts than himself and for their revilings—his severe religious upbringing in the home of the Penberthys and the punishment he had taken in Dublin had bred a stoic.

Wasn't it Tree who said: 'I've bought a play from every one of the critics, I ought to have a good press'?

An admirable passage in Somerset Maugham's *Summing Up* advises those who lack fertility of invention and natural aptitude for creation to avoid the art of literature. He might offer similar advice with equal wisdom to those contemplating a career on the stage. Industry and charm are invaluable qualities in any calling but they will never make an actor, for the actor must both invent and create. If he cannot discern in his part something more than the obvious he will never rise above mediocrity. Irving always found implications that no other actor could perceive—that is genius. An Oxford Don may make a tolerable Brutus but he will be an intolerable Cassius, for Brutus may be recited, Cassius must be acted—though Mr. Ivor Brown considers it a part for a 'ham' actor, which in my day

[1] It was stated that William Archer admitted that the plot of *The Green Goddess* was revealed to him in a dream.

meant ' hamachoor '—incompetent, but I believe the word has a different (American) sense to-day.

When Somerset Maugham affirmed some months ago that we had no great dramatist and no great actor, Mr. Sydney Carroll attempted to answer him but could make no case; his best was to quote a long list of competent, and in some cases brilliant, people but he dared not claim greatness for any one of them. As for the dramatists, Mr. Maugham is undoubtedly right. We have had nothing like a great play since his own *Sheppy*, which asked for those gifts of imagination in its performance that the stage lost with Irving. We talk of him as intellectual and that he was, but to make the complete actor imagination is essential, intellect will never do it. It was by his imagination that Irving triumphed.

The failure of *Dante* and, in a lesser degree, of *Robespierre* proves if proof is wanted—that the towering figure alone will not make for success; it needs a columnal idea to support it. Yet plays of ideas in which the persons are mere mouthpieces appeal only to a limited public. These are truisms but must be insisted upon when reviewing the causes of Irving's downfall. The unfortunate *Peter the Great*, followed by the still more disastrous *The Medicine Man*, shook the very foundations of his position. Then that frame of ' whipcord and steel,' as Bram Stoker has it, succumbed to pneumonia and pleurisy, and though men of sixty may recover from pneumonia they do not recover from such disaster as fell upon Irving on 18 February in that ill-omened twentieth year of his management (1898) when all the scenery of forty-four productions went up in flames. That loss was irreparable. There would have been no need for *Robespierre* and *Dante*, nor for *Coriolanus*, for among those forty were a score that would have revived successfully. The result was bankruptcy. The uprooting of his home in Grafton Street was a fell stroke; the sale of his books and treasures was worse. It did not affect his art, maybe it gave it a finer edge, added poignancy to the martyrdom of Becket, the misery of Mathias, the isolation of Shylock. But the manager was broken; the theatre-man was ousted from supreme control and in his place —a corporation!—a syndicate!

A syndicate has no beneficence, it exists for one purpose and it is futile to suppose that a management whose eyes are fixed on the box-office will prosper; a flash in the pan is not prosperity, there must be concentrated artistic endeavour. Irving had proved that the sure means of winning the money-goal. The manager should be an artist, not an accountant. Nor can the

Theatre afford the luxury of directors, for profit must remain in the treasury to finance future enterprise and assure the actors continuity of work—not for their bread and butter, but for the betterment of their art—not filched from the till to foster extraneous ventures. When to such practices are added suppuration by speculative renters and the tyranny of trade unionism, art succumbs, for it is the stage only that can be bled to meet these charges; the office will demand first claim on profits —which it will tell you are absorbed by the Entertainment Tax.

Irving held the lease of the Lyceum, and at the same time that the London County Council was subsidizing his opposite neighbour, the Gaiety, to the extent of ten thousand pounds it was demanding that he should lay out a similar sum on repairs at the Lyceum. The syndicate was inevitable.

There was no Entertainment Tax in 1898 but other disintegrating forces were at work: inflation of salaries heralded the victory of commercialism; a law to prevent children, even those born in it, following the profession from their earliest days, and so purging them of the acting spirit, without discriminating between gutter-snipes who sought to shine as the Six Little Sunbeams and the embryo Edmund Keans, Madge Kendals, and Ellen Terrys; agitators inculcating the virus of trade unionism among the staff; the influx of a social class who had hitherto despised the actors' calling but revised their judgment in view of the dignity conferred on it by Irving's knighthood. He had resisted it for twelve years,[1] in the interest of his art, remembering his own humble origin and that art is not born in Universities.

So acting technique gives place to a slouching deportment and effete manners, the impersonators of Hamlet, Shylock, and Othello merely behave—as themselves. In place of small groups of enthusiasts studying as Irving did with Henry Thomas at Sussex Hall, and the efforts of true amateurs like Charles Dickens and his family in private theatricals, which *were* private, we have societies by the thousand hiring theatres to air their vanity and sponging up all the patronage for weeks before and after to the ruin of the legitimate actor and the result that the provincial Theatre, at least, is practically dead.

It has been leeched to death. Everyone in the theatre is paid too highly, including the actors. Fifty years ago there was none, from leading man to scene-shifter, but was there because he loved it. All made some sacrifice, for the financial reward was inconsiderable. The Theatre cannot thrive if every super,

[1] Irving had been urged by Gladstone to accept knighthood in 1883.

every member of the orchestra, every property man must have a wage to keep a wife and rear a family: these should be part-time jobs, as they were in Irving's day: two shillings a night—sixpence more than other managements paid—was merely tobacco-and-beer money. The orchestra had more, of course, and I am not concerned with Opera, but all were small tradesmen and their assistants, clerks and artisans, who loved the Theatre as well as the actors loved it; but now, perhaps, there is little there to love.

F. B. Chatterton, the manager of Drury Lane, declared: 'Shakespeare spells ruin!' Irving proved the contrary. Yet it will always be true when Shakespeare is no more than adequately acted. So in order to make Shakespeare pay the plays must be 'produced' with Russian—or Turkish—or Bessarabian trappings; with chromium plating, or a colour scheme of rose-pink and pea-green, by Reinhardt or Komisarjevski, or one of their disciples; or advertised with a cant of educational values, supplemented by the semi-pathetic, serio-comic appeal of a personality like the late Lilian Bayliss; or served *al fresco*, when a visit becomes a kind of picnic, a camping-out adventure and a gamble with the weather; or 'dressed modern,' a queer —and economical—eccentricity that on occasion achieves a success of curiosity; or that bewildering affectation, 'Shakespeare in curtains,' a poverty-stricken device, which leaves all to imagination—sometimes even the acting. But none of these, however remunerative, proves the drawing power of Shakespeare; it proves only that there are still cranks in the world—and snobs.

All these, by the way, get remission from the Entertainment Tax on the plea that they are educative.

Only when greatly acted and fittingly set is Shakespeare truly represented, but as setting fit for Shakespeare has now become an economic impossibility and there is no great actor in sight the prospect of a Shakespearean revival is remote.

Mr. Geoffrey Whitworth, Secretary of the British Drama League, an organization of a hundred thousand amateurs—or is it a quarter of a million?—who is also secretary to the National Theatre, a company which owns a building site in the Cromwell Road, clamours for the abolition of the Entertainment Tax—and more; he maintains that the Theatre should enjoy State subsidy and quotes Irving on the subject, conveniently ignoring an important point in Irving's argument: '*Quid pro quo* is a maxim which holds good of State aid, and a time might come when an unscrupulous use might be made of the power of subsidy.' Besides, as there are still worthy people who regard the Theatre as the gateway to perdition it would be manifest injustice to penalize them to gratify the vanity of Mr. Whitworth's hundred thousand or quarter of a million.

Yet if Mr. Whitworth could substantiate his claim that the furtherance of artistic ideals was indeed the goal, much might be said for it, but suspicion is strong that a commercial element lurks in the background, in which case it might be in the interest of art, and ultimately of the calling, to treble the Entertainment Tax.

I am sure Chatterton would not have liked the Entertainment Tax, but Irving would have recognized the justice of it. He would have said: 'Our calling has lost its quality, actors are content to sacrifice their supreme possession, individuality, and form a trade union. We have allowed our art to become an industry; like other industries we must bear our share of the burden.' But if Stratford, the Old Vic, Regent's Park, and Westminster are immune, the Lyceum would also have had a case for remission, for it was truly a National Theatre.

What is a National Theatre? It is not bricks and mortar—nor reinforced concrete. It is a company of players well used to playing together (essential) the classics and masterpieces of a nation's dramatic literature, versed in the original business of the plays and handing it on from generation to generation. Such a theatre will be certain to owe its existence to the genius and enthusiasm of one man: no Council nor Committee could inspire it, a Board of Directors would stifle it. Who can be loyal to the ideals of a Board of Directors—except on Friday night?

Irving's detractors persist even though more than the third of a century has passed since we laid him to rest. It is less than three years since I read in a theatrical journal a peculiarly virulent attack upon his art, written in most arrogant terms by a young gentleman—he is a Producer, by the way—who when Irving was playing his last week's engagement at Bradford was probably still at his prep. school. His conclusion was that to-day Irving would not be tolerated. It is deplorable that one 'drest in a little brief authority' should so pontificate as to demonstrate his judgment as lamentable as his ignorance.

To a group of enquiring youngsters Tom Heslewood gave the answer quite conclusively: "If Irving were living to-day," he said, "he would adapt himself to modern conditions, or, which is more probable, modern conditions would adapt themselves to him."

But even so I would accept the verdict of none who saw Irving *for the first time* after his sixtieth year. The crushing misfortunes of 1898 were more than enough to wreck any man and, though his will was indomitable and for seven more years he fought on, his enemies as vituperative as ever, something more than the old vigour was missing; all the dignity was there, the technique supreme as ever, but a certain weariness had crept in; there was no longer joy in the work.

He had worked in the theatre, almost without intermission, for forty-two years, he had played six hundred and sixty-seven parts. No other leading actor had ever approached that record —which prompts a thought: we know that David Garrick came to London (1737) at the age of twenty-one and started business as a wine merchant. Four years later, with less than six months' professional experience, he acted Richard III at Goodman's Fields Theatre and at once drew the town; his success was acclaimed as 'uncontested and epoch-making.' Is it really conceivable that this raw amateur with no technical experience, who in all his career played only ninety-three parts, can have been as great as tradition reports? Did he spring, like Athene, 'full-armèd from the brain of Jove'? His mannerisms of pronunciation and gesture were so extravagant[1] that they would have moved Irving's worst detractors to praise him by contrast for his naturalness, could they have swallowed prejudice. And what would they have said to Garrick's adaptations of Shakespeare? I suspect that Garrick owed more than tradition allows to his personal affability—to his parlour tricks, to those charades in drawing-rooms, impromptu impersonations and after-dinner speeches. He had the 'gift of the gab' *in excelsis*. His most flattering 'press,' and the best known, emanated from 'Partridge.' His ascendancy would appear to have been accepted all too easily. He left a fortune of £100,000, but he was not only manager of Drury Lane, he was a wine merchant. His demise 'eclipsed the *gaiety* of nations.' Quite so.

Of a very different stamp was Edmund Kean, who had bought experience dearly through a long and painful apprenticeship. Kean had great moments—as Othello—as Richard III—as Shylock—as Sir Giles Overreach. Was it, one wonders,

[1] Garrick said *Iserel* for Israel, *metron* for matron, *Horetio* for Horatio; yet none of these is worse than John Philip Kemble's affectation of *varetshu* for virtue, and *sarevant* for servant, both carefully articulated in three syllables. Garrick also cultivated a sort of stutter, and Samuel Foote infuriated him by mimicking his dying scene as Lothario thus: 'Adorns my tale and che-che-che-che-cheers my dy-dy-dy-dy-dying heart.'

perhaps the same great moment? Did he characterize?—interpret? Hazlitt found his Richard 'deficient in that regal jollity and reeling triumph of success,' whereas his Iago he judged 'an excellent good fellow and lively bottle companion.' He adds: 'The light which illumines the character (Iago) should rather resemble the flashes of lightning in the murky sky which make the darkness more terrible,' which is exactly what Irving gave us—*pace*, Mr. Shaw!

But Iago, after all, is nothing—unless Othello is missing. If Othello be really *there* who notices Iago, except as 'support'? And Othello was Kean's top-notch. But listen to Hazlitt again. "Though powerful the whole effect is thrown away in a wrong direction. He wants imagination, that faculty that contemplates events and broods over feelings with a certain calmness and grandeur. He is often in the highest key of passion, too uniformly on the verge of extravagance, too constantly on the rack. This does very well in certain characters but it is not so in the lofty-minded and generous Moor."

'Kean,' said Palgrave Simpson, was 'a stuttering spasmotic mannerist.' He had a voice 'raucous and husky,' but as a singer, a sweet baritone, witness, Tom Tugg in *The Waterman;* a nimble harlequin, animal impersonator and pantomimist; graceful in repose, but with a strut that carried him across the stage in three strides. His sole excellence was in that sudden gust of passion.

Garrick, by the way, stood five feet three inches, Kean five feet four inches, a small matter but significant; the bantam is seldom modest.

Charles Cartwright had the most remarkable voice I ever heard, it reminded you of iron filings rusting in nitric acid; it grated, it bit. He was a fine actor and he used that voice to wonderful effect. But I saw him once attempt Dan'l Peggotty! Cartwright had been at the Lyceum in his young days and I believe was one of Irving's doubles in *The Corsican Brothers*.

Irving's voice was capable of the same effects; he had a method—yes, a trick, if you will—tricks of technique are tools of the actor's craft—of jerking out a phrase in menace like the sudden shooting of a bolt in an iron socket; he used it as Dubosc—as Richard III—as Iago—as Mephistopheles; it had also flexibility and could command the depths of pathos. I need not give examples. His diction has been the subject of endless argument—talk of the Somerset accent, though it was more like to have been Cornish, some have included it with his mannerisms as a detriment he could not control. How mistaken. Is it to be supposed that he unconsciously said: 'I shall be *ritz!*'—'Mer-ci-ful *Got!*'—'ta-ake th' rup from m' *thrut!*' Imagine yourself choking with the noose squeezing your wind-pipe and judge whether a clear articulation is nearer truth than those sounds. Picture the ghost-like apparition of your enemy in the moonlight while you are gloating in the thought that he is helpless at your mercy. If in your terror you don't clip your syllables I'll say you have no nerves. As to 'ritz,' the value of its erosive vibration needs no explanation —or defence. My point is that these 'tricks' were deliberately employed and justified their use. James Agate writes of his 'natural deficiencies' and his 'wilful faults.' It is true that he had no orotund voice; we could spare that for clarity of diction and variety of tone. Orotundity makes for monotony. And the walk—no doubt was one of the 'wilful faults.' That it was wilful I am positive, and it gave us effects of preparation—of emphasis—of definitude beyond estimation: that sudden halt in a rapid advance, whether the climax were to be an embrace or merely a handshake; it was like the bolt shot back before it falls to its socket.

No syllable that fell from him was ever lost to my ears, nor was I ever conscious of aught but grace in his eloquent gesture and strength in his mobile features. Whoever could hear him say, as Romeo, 'Then I defy you, stars!' and rest unmoved had no sense of pity nor tragic beauty.

Did you notice how he said, 'over—there'? First his eyes travelled to the point he wished to indicate, then his index emphasized it and the word clinched it.

Did you see him look at you—the audience? Once, perhaps, in the evening. 'I was a Dauphin once!'—'I won't have her!'—both these thoughts he shared with none on the stage, a confidence between him and you. You never 'caught the eye' of Charles I or Becket.

The sole 'mannerism' I detect that may be half unconscious is the stamp of the foot on occasion when some actor by a slur or a false emphasis misses a beat which must be made up or the *tempo* is ruined—or perhaps the audience fails to take a cue—some audiences are numps—I don't mean for applause, that would be unwelcome interruption, but that mental response which the actor delights in or despairs of.

His eyes God gave with the soul that shone through them, together with that nice discretion as to their best use. The miracle was that such goodness could counterfeit maleficence —could so terrify.

To the variety of his humour I cannot hope to do justice. Contrast those two scamps, Jeremy Diddler and Robert Macaire; how little they have in common. It was not for nothing that Irving had been the constant guest of Charles Mathews at Pelham Place. Imitate him? No, but he had absorbed the insouciance of that mercurial spirit who knew rest only as an affliction, and mirrored it as Jeremy unbuttoned your coat and threw back the lapels, but he hadn't the predatory eye of Macaire; and the smile was frank, not wry. Benedick's humour was dry, wit crackled from it; Richard's oily and sensual; Mephistopheles' menacing; Louis' terrible. The infinite pathos of Charles' smile; the kindly tolerance of the good Vicar's. The reproach of Lesurques' silence—the foreboding of Iago's!

It was said that in his private relations he sometimes used a cruel humour. Meeting Tree, the proud proprietor of the new-opened His Majesty's Theatre (trumpeted in the Press for months), beaming self-satisfaction, avid of gratulation, Irving chirped: "Hullo, Tree! Doing anything?" Unhappily Tree's sense of other peoples' humour was weak.

But Irving's large humanity could never stoop to injure; ruthless he could be, never ungenerous.

Some highly acclaimed actors do their work perfunctorily; you feel their heart is not in it even as you admire their facility. Some give sparingly, seeming to advise you that they could do better if it pleased them. Some work so strenuously as to defeat their end. With Irving there was no apparent effort, in fact you forgot he was acting at all; he wasn't: he was living in another body with another mind; he had projected his spirit into another soul of his own creating, and though the technique did not vary, those who knew him well knew when the projection was most absolute, and on those nights one felt the joy in the exercise of his art. Though intellectual, his work never failed to move the emotions; the vibrations of his personality, instinct with imagination, touched even the prosaic passage with poetry, his technical accomplishment was so masterly that the artist almost wept for joy in its utter perfection—this no critic who did not answer Boucicault's standard could perceive, nor could the public suspect.

There was a handling of papers and a flinging of Wolsey's train to waiting pages that brought a lump to one's throat for the sheer beauty of its perfect proportion, its precision, its finality.

He had the nicest sense of adjustment, an unerring instinct for co-ordinating his effects to a complete inevitability; he scorned emotional insincerity, he was incapable of artistic anarchism; his best effects were urgent, rapid, though never hurried, always male, sometimes inelegant though he had also sinuous grace, yet ever avoided monotony. And some he irritated because he would not finish the curve of movement or speech but would break it by a halt and dive off at a tangent. He would have made mincemeat of Racine's Alexandrines.

He was always Irving, yes; but it was a different facet of Irving that he showed you in each character and Irving had as many facets as a cut diamond and they flashed blindingly as the light of his genius played on them.

At the Centenary Memorial Performance at the Lyceum (23 May 1938) six actors attempted six of his best known parts. It was well they were six. No six could have been more unlike each other, yet no more unlike than he was unlike himself in each of the six characters. Not one of the six faintly suggested him in any one of the parts nor made any one of the parts seem a possible vehicle for a great performance, though in his hands all six were as great as unlike. It was a foolish experiment and served only to show the weakness of the plays and prove how dependent is the modern actor on his author. He made the plays not they him. Fleet Street is not remarkable because Doctor Johnson walked there, but it was when he did.

Able critics maintain that creative genius in interpretation is a contradiction in terms, but those who have seen other actors in a *rôle* that Irving sustained have learned that a great actor does with his material as the great painter, sculptor, musician, he transcends it. He raised *The Dead Heart* to the level of a classic. *The Bells* in his hands became an astounding psychological investigation. Yet he knew that success in such plays did not make for immortality. The actor's name that is not associated with the classic drama of his country will not live. So he gave us a Hamlet that has not been approached for fifty years; an Iago that was unapproachable; a Richard that excelled; a Shylock that established a tradition. They flung 'character actor' at him in depreciation, as though every several part were not a character. It is the reproach of the tragic actor that he rarely characterizes; he declaims Macbeth and Brutus, Othello, Coriolanus, and Hamlet, all in the same person. Irving spared us that and gave us instead a series of surprises in exposing the inner being of each character he presented. He not only read, he interpreted. Even in those parts where physical limitations made perfect interpretive characterization impossible, such as Othello, Macbeth, Lear, were such flashes of illumination that to discover inadequacy seemed mere perversity. This was particularly true of Macbeth which grew in conviction with every fresh acquaintance. His magic was due not only to the dominance of his personality, his compelling glance, his tranquillity, his charm—he was a quiet man—but to that astonishing creative faculty that discovered to us enchantment at the heart of every subject that engaged him and made it seem integral and inevitable.

What was the secret of this magic? Where and how did he derive the inspiration that moved thousands, stirring them to the very depths of their being by what was called his magnetism? Poets are born. And she who bore him, the austere Mary Behenna, that gentle religionist, who wept at the thought of his casting his lot with the depraved denizens of a wicked calling, as she feared it, may have breathed the ardent spirit of her Baptist faith into her child and sent him forth, clean of heart, to face conditions far coarser than any we can now imagine. Some such explanation there must be, for of all truths one is clear—that he faced life and the many trials that awaited him, both before and after the days of his great triumph, with a simplicity, a steadfastness, and a fortitude otherwise quite inexplicable.

No man had more, nor more venomous enemies than Irving, and they pursue him even after death with 'envy, hatred, and all uncharitableness.' So bitter is their gall that they would revive him to revile his features, his gait, his utterance; they exhume him to spew their scurrilous ink upon his corpse and pursue his ghost even in their posthumous publications.

One fact remains; his individuality, whether as actor or man, stamped itself upon his time and conferred upon the art he served a dignity it had so far never known, and which fell from it with his death. An individuality which was a force that made not only better actors, but spread an influence which led many lives outside the Theatre to a higher purpose. He touched the common things of life with spirituality making them beautiful, and to the spiritual he gave rationality and intimacy so that we embraced it without self-consciousness.

His detractors are answered every 13th of October by the love that brings red roses to his resting-place at Shakespeare's feet in Poet's Corner. Maybe it is this faithfulness that fans the smouldering embers of their hate; when this malice has burned out and they also have found rest—and forgiveness—may the red roses—lingering fragrance in the quiet temple—still bear witness that love outlasts traducement and that nobility of purpose and high endeavour still find enshrinement in the hearts of men.

H. A. SAINTSBURY.

INDEX

A

B

C

D

J

K

U

V

W